MW00451424

Choctaw Crime and Punishment, 1884–1907

Also by Devon Abbott Mihesuah

Cultivating the Rosebuds (Urbana, 1993)
American Indians (Atlanta, 1996)
(ed.) *Natives and Academics* (Lincoln, 1998)
(ed.) *Repatriation Reader* (Lincoln, 2000)
The Roads of My Relations (Tucson, 2000)
(ed.) *First to Fight* (Lincoln, 2002)
Indigenous American Women (Lincoln, 2003)
The Lightning Shrikes (Guilford, 2004)
(ed., with Angela Cavender Wilson) *Indigenizing the Academy*
    (Lincoln, 2004)
Recovering Our Ancestors' Gardens (Lincoln, 2005)
So You Want to Write About American Indians? (Lincoln, 2005)

CHOCTAW CRIME AND PUNISHMENT, 1884–1907

Devon Abbott Mihesuah

UNIVERSITY OF OKLAHOMA PRESS : NORMAN

This book is published with the generous assistance of the Wallace C. Thompson Endowment Fund, University of Oklahoma.

Library of Congress Cataloging-in-Publication Data

Mihesuah, Devon A. (Devon Abbott), 1957–

    Choctaw crime and punishment, 1884–1907 / Devon Abbott Mihesuah.
      p.   cm.
    Includes bibliographical references and index.
    ISBN 978-0-8061-4052-0 (hardcover) ISBN 978-0-8061-9034-1 (paper)
    1. Choctaw Indians—Oklahoma—Politics and government. 2. Choctaw
Indians—Oklahoma—History. 3. Wilson, Charles, d. 1884. 4. Lewis, Silan,
d. 1894. I. Title.
    E99.C8M54 2009
    976.6'00497387—dc22

                                    2009007270

The paper in this book meets the guidelines for permanence and durability of the Committee on Production Guidelines for Book Longevity of the Council on Library Resources, Inc. ∞

Ayupachi Fiena tok: Charles Wilson amafo chito atok
. . . ill ikyimmi ikbʋnno.

To my great-great-grandfather Charles Wilson.
And to those who resisted.

CONTENTS

ILLUSTRATIONS

Acknowledgments

Thanks to Bob Blackburn, Josh Clough, Carolyn Couch, Jennifer Silvers, William Welge, Chad Williams, and Terry Zinn at the Oklahoma Historical Society; Stacy Leeds, Marion Dyer, Dennis Kunnell, Joyce A. McCray Pearson, and Tony Brown at the University of Kansas; Alexandra Shadid, Kristina L. Southwell, and Eileashia Lackey at the Western History Collections, University of Oklahoma; Jerry Akins, Fort Smith National Historic Site Archives; Ed Meyer, living history volunteer, Fort Smith National Historic Site; Chuck Raney, corresponding secretary of the Fort Smith Historical Society; D. Aaron Holt at the National Archives, Southwest Region, in Fort Worth, Texas; Mary Frances Morrow at the National Archives and Records Administration in Washington, D.C.; Renna Tuten at the Richard B. Russell Library for Political Research and Studies at the University of Georgia; Louise Wiles at the Pittsburg County Genealogical and Historical Society; Mary Johnson and Janet Frankovic at the Five Civilized Tribes Museum in Muskogee, Oklahoma; J. Myles Felihkatubbe, Vicki Prough, and Vonna Shults of the Choctaw Nation of Oklahoma; Brenda Samuels, Norris Samuels, and Mike Stewart at the University of Oklahoma for their assistance with the often challenging translations; Angela Walton-Raji, great-great-great-granddaughter of Jackson Crow; my mother Olyve Hallmark Abbott for her genealogical advice; my aunt Betty Watson and cousin Jo Ellen Gilmore Gamble for family stories; and the library staff at Baker

University in Baldwin City, Kansas, for the use of their microfilm machine copier. I also thank the University of Kansas for research support. And as usual, thank you to my husband Josh and my children Toshaway and Ariana for their love and encouragement.

Revised excerpts of the essay "Choosing America's Heroes and Villains: Lessons Learned from the Execution of Silan Lewis," *American Indian Quarterly*, Volume 29, Number 1/2 (2005): 239–62, appear throughout chapters 4, 5, and 6. Used with permission of the University of Nebraska Press. Copyright © 2004 by the University of Nebraska Press.

A longer version of the essay "Unfinished Choctaw Justice: The Murder of Charles Wilson and the Execution of Jackson Crow," *Chronicles of Oklahoma* 86, no. 3 (2008): 290–315, appears in chapter 1.

Choctaw Crime and
Punishment, 1884–1907

Choctaw Nation, 1884.

Introduction

Presiding over the rolling hills of LeFlore County in far eastern Oklahoma is the cedar-covered Sugar Loaf Mountain, known to Choctaw (*Chata anumpa*) speakers as *Nvnih Chufvk*. From Sugar Loaf's peak one can see the Winding Stair Mountain to the south and Cavanal Hill and the foothills of the Kiamichis to the west. Nvnih Chufvk also overlooks Vaughn Cemetery, resting place for citizens of the old Choctaw Nation county of Sugar Loaf and the more recently deceased residents of modern-day LeFlore County, Oklahoma.

On August 7, 1884, residents of Sugar Loaf County gathered at the cemetery to bury my great-great-grandfather, full-blood Choctaw Charles Wilson. His second wife, Martha, their young children (by his Chickasaw wife, Lizzie), local Masons, and other citizens of the Choctaw Nation stood in the sweltering August heat as friends lowered Wilson's casket into the ground. Wilson's death was indeed a tragedy. He had consistently served Sugar Loaf County: he had been elected judge, sheriff, county treasurer, and court clerk and had been appointed tribal lighthorseman and U.S. deputy marshal for Fort Smith, Arkansas. The 1884 elections for Choctaw chief, as well as for Sugar Loaf County sheriff, ranger, judge, and representative to the House, had taken place the day before, and many Choctaws had high hopes that the forty-year-old Wilson, a member of the Nationalist Party, would be elected the Sugar Loaf County representative.

Charles Wilson had been brutally murdered. The first report stated that he had been shot nine times and beaten in the head until it was "crushed" and that his unknown assailants had fled the area. But as time revealed, Wilson had not been the victim of random violence at the hands of the outlaws who roamed Indian Territory after the Civil War. Rather, he was the victim of a planned crime by men he knew well—politically prominent Choctaws and members of the rival Progressive Party. One of those Choctaws, Robert Benton, served as a member of the Choctaw House of Representatives, was the brother of the county judge, and ran as Wilson's rival for Sugar Loaf County representative. As the events unfolded over the next four years, all the Choctaws who took part in the crime were set free by jurymen who also belonged to the Progressive Party, while Jackson Crow, the lone black man who played a role in the killing, paid the ultimate price for his part in the murder.

Ten years and three months after Wilson's burial, Choctaw Silan Lewis and his wife, Sally, arrived at Wilburton, Indian Territory, a town named after Will Burton, one of the contractors who built the Choctaw, Oklahoma, and Gulf Railroad (later renamed the Rock Island Railroad) in the 1890s. Situated amid lush, green, tree-covered hills and about forty miles from Nvnih Chufvk, Wilburton was once the location of coal mines and is the closest town to Robber's Cave, now a state park that features a complex system of tunnels and underground halls that housed the booty of Indian Territory outlaws. Some say that when the harvest moon is bright, you can hear the music of Fiddlin' Jim, a man smitten with Belle Starr and who had been killed at the entrance of the cave by a jealous suitor.

Silan Lewis worked a farm west of Pine Mountain, near present-day Blanco in Pittsburg County. A lean, dark man with hands calloused from farming, Lewis wore his hair short, dressed like a white man, and spoke some English. Like Charles Wilson, Lewis was a Nationalist who believed that the Choctaws should maintain control over their governance system and retain tribal sovereignty and land as promised by treaties with the federal government.

The principled Lewis had been respected enough by his tribesmen to be elected sergeant of arms of the Choctaw Senate in

1880. He was then appointed sheriff of Gaines County by Chief Smallwood in 1891 and was the Nationalists' candidate for that position a year later. Lewis willingly served his tribe, and many people liked him; but, in a reversal of his normal behavior, Lewis emulated the men who killed Charles Wilson and set out to rid the Nation of those Choctaws with differing political views. After the disputed tribal election of 1892—in which several Progressives were elected, including Chief Wilson Jones, Lewis and forty other disgruntled Choctaws conducted a killing spree through Moshulatubbee District. And they succeeded. Lewis and his fellow Nationalists killed five Progressives and would have killed more if they had not been betrayed.

Because of his deep-seated beliefs and intense frustration over the rapid influx of white settlers into the Choctaw Nation and the even more rapid loss of tribal culture, Lewis took out his anger in an uncharacteristic way. And it was because of his crime that Lewis and his wife traveled to Wilburton in November 1894. They were not going there for a social visit; they had arrived for his execution.

To make Lewis's story more compelling, Lewis's executioner was Lyman Pusley, a Progressive Choctaw who himself had been tried, convicted, and sentenced to death for murder. But as was characteristic of the wealthy and politically powerful Choctaws showing favoritism to each other during these decades, not only was Pusley exonerated of murder, but he was even appointed deputy sheriff. What may be more galling is that over thirty-five years after the staunchly Progressive Pusley shot Lewis the Nationalist, the former claimed that he not only had kept Lewis chained to his bed prior to his execution, but that he and Lewis were friends, thus creating the oft-used mythology of Lewis, the romantic condemned warrior, asking that his "friend" Pusley be the one to shoot him through the heart.

In the 1892 election, citizens of the Choctaw Nation were more entrenched in their political parties than they had been in 1884. By 1892, citizens supported either the Choctaw Progressive or Nationalist parties. The Progressives, also known as the "Eagles," were mostly affluent citizens (or at least aspired to be) who were amenable to allotment and statehood. Supporters of the Nationalist Party—also called "Standpatters" or the more uncomplimentary "Buzzards" and "Snakeheads" (although the latter term was not used until after the turn of the century to designate those Choctaws who opposed allotment)—steadfastly stood devoted to the terms of the 1830 Treaty of Dancing Rabbit Creek, which assured the Choctaws the management of their own affairs and the keeping of their lands in common.[1]

Wilson and Lewis were not the only Choctaws to resist the inevitable severalty and tribal dissolution. In 1896, twelve years after Wilson's murder, a contingency of at least two thousand Choctaws led by Nationalist Jacob Jackson made plans to move to Mexico so they could live as a sovereign nation without having to answer to the U.S. government and without the constant intrusion of whites onto their lands. In 1905, Progressive Chief Green McCurtain expressed concerns about a Nationalist Choctaw minister named W. F. Tobly who had become leader of a group known as the Choctaw Snakes. Tobly and his men stood adamantly against allotment and had the reputation of being potentially ruthless toward anyone who supported McCurtain and the impending allotment process. The charges were unfounded, however, just as they were against the Muscogee Snakes led by Chitto Harjo (Crazy Snake) and Ned Christie, an anti-allotment Cherokee Keetoowah accused of murder.

Yet another Choctaw, Nationalist Daniel Bell, also known as Crazy Snake, had been elected chief by a group of separatist Choctaws, who, disgruntled with the pro-allotment Progressive tribal government, established their own Choctaw government. Creators of this "new" Choctaw Nation, which operated outside the tribe's legal authority, planned to take control of the government from Chief Gilbert Dukes so that the Choctaws could live by their "traditions and customs" and "once more . . . meet about the council fires[.] There will be game to kill, we will have heaps of cattle and ponies and something else to eat besides sofka and corn pone."[2] Like Bell and Tobly, not every Choctaw was interested in white ways. Many rejected the missionaries' overtures, preferred the company of other Choctaws, spoke their tribal language, and

practiced their tribal ceremonies. These Choctaws and their descendents were as willing to fight and die for their culture and
tribal sovereignty as other Choctaws were willing to do the same to
protect their material assets. The efforts of the Nationalist Choctaws often met the disapproval of affluent, acculturated Choctaws,
such as one who commented in the late 1880s about the "condition
of the fullbloods," stating that the "fullblood Indian is almost on a
standstill. . . . [he] is too careless. . . . The man is a slave to the
animal part of his nature."[3] It was in large measure the clash of
values among the Choctaws that led to defamatory name-calling
and an impressive number of assaults and murders.

Events in the Choctaw Nation in the late nineteenth century were
complex, volatile, and ultimately troubling to those who prefer tribal
histories without vignettes of intratribal factionalism. But that is the
reality of history. Many of the mixed-blood and full-blood Choctaws
were politically and economically savvy, and they knew how to
function in the white man's world. Impending severalty and statehood combined with the disparity between the wealth of some
Choctaws and the poverty of others led to suspicion and resentment.
Because the tribe was composed of individuals with knowledge
of the old ways and of the new, including rationales as to why
Choctaws should keep or lose traditions, Choctaw citizens made
individual choices as to how they wanted to live. And they often
used violence to express themselves.

This book is not just about angry Indians fighting among themselves. Because of the influx of whites, which first began in their
homeland in the Southeast before the removals of the 1830s and
continued in Indian Territory until Oklahoma statehood, the Choctaw Nation struggled to find ways to defend itself against those
people who would use every legal means and loophole, including
marriage, to acquire what they wanted from the tribe: land, resources,
and wealth. Those whites who managed to gain a foothold on the
tribal lands, including illegal intruders, stayed.

Opportunistic whites and dramatic sociocultural changes were
difficult enough for the tribe to manage, and the challenges they posed
became exacerbated by an extremely high crime rate. Thousands

of offenses were committed in Indian Territory after the Civil War. Most of the crimes were committed by non-Indian deviants, but as the years went by many Choctaws also broke laws. The behavior of many unprincipled white intruders who coveted Choctaw land and resources and of many Choctaws who were frustrated, dysfunctional, intoxicated, or looking to find wealth at the expense of other Choctaws, resulted in a dangerous population. Individuals sought to find ways to survive in a hostile environment, even if that meant to steal and to act out frustrations by abusing others. The tribe felt hard-pressed indeed to find ways to cope with almost daily murder, rape, theft, and assault. Crimes committed by Choctaws against Choctaws in the Nation were handled in the tribal courts, while those noncitizens (and some Choctaws accused of crimes) were sent to the federal court at Fort Smith or to one of the other federal courts established to assist in the overwhelming caseload. The Choctaw county courts handled hundreds of cases per year, requiring the services of judges, jurymen, clerks, and guards. At the same time, the Choctaw Nation remained on guard against the possibility of the United States interfering with Choctaw tribal laws and cases.

Although the Nationalists and Progressives butted heads on many issues, they were both concerned with defending the Nation. They grappled with challenging questions: How could the Choctaw Nation resist intruders and dictate tribal membership? What were effective ways of preventing abuse of tribal resources, stemming the accelerating crime rate, and controlling the influx of railroads, coal companies, and cattlemen? The Choctaw Nation struggled to protect its government, land base, school system, and treaty rights. Life for Indians in nineteenth-century Indian Territory was challenging, to say the least, and it did not help matters that crime, punishment, and politics collided in cases involving murder, money, land, and tribal citizenship.

This book, therefore, explores the experiences of Choctaws who resisted one another's values and policies. It also addresses the tribe's resistance to intrusions onto their lands, to the taking of their resources, to crime perpetrated by outsiders and wayward Choctaw citizens, and to the policies of the federal government. During the time period explored here, crime, politics, and social values were inexorably intertwined. I readily admit that this is not the definitive book on Choctaw history in the decades prior to statehood, and I realize that the sheer number of personalities and value systems involved, combined with the complexity of the federal and tribal laws and the extreme stress and anguish felt by the Choctaws and their supporters, offers the possibilities of countless personal stories and exploration of many more political, social, and economic events.

I chose to highlight the cases of Charles Wilson and Silan Lewis because events surrounding their lives illustrate the intensity of the problems faced by the Choctaws in the late nineteenth century. Since removal to Indian Territory in the 1830s, the tribe continually passed laws, bills, and acts to develop and streamline its system of governance in an effort to arrest, try, and convict criminals; protect itself from the effects of the thousands of intruders that poured onto its land; and defend itself from the paternalistic policies of the U.S. government. Even with the many laws that seem clear in their intent, often it was just as apparent that the collision of the social values and the political adherences of those judges, jurymen, defendants, witnesses, and chiefs determined the outcome of the trials. Numerous times political affiliation, level of wealth, and connections with the chief determined one's fate.

This book is also partially a personal project. As a citizen of the Choctaw Nation I am concerned with tribal survival, empower-ment, history, and current issues, but I am particularly interested in Charles Wilson because he was my forebear. Dozens of my other ancestors were born, married, received allotments, and were buried in the areas described in this book. Family stories abound about Wilson. At the forefront of the Wilson mythology is the theme of Wilson as a victim of murder at the hands of a Choctaw "gang" led by a black man. But this version never set right with me. While family stories often provide a great deal of information, they can also be as full of holes as a bullet-ridden jacket. Still, the story of Wilson has been with me for so long that it served as the basis for my novel, *Roads of My Relations*. As I did for others in the novel, I changed Charles Wilson's name to Matthias Lamb and his daughter's to Tish (in the novel she is portrayed as a skilled horsewoman because my grandmother claimed she watched her mother ride her large black horse almost everyday) but kept many of the facts of the case intact because it is a good story.

On a personal level I needed answers about his death. After discovering the details of Wilson's murder and understanding that others who were part of the killing went unpunished, I would be less than honest by not admitting that I want some restitution, even if it is only bringing the story to light. That only one of Wilson's killers was punished is a travesty, but it also makes me wonder if anything—socially, culturally, politically—would have been different if Wilson had lived to become the Sugar Loaf County representative. His rival, Benton, the man who witnesses agree pulled the trigger first, held a very hard pro-allotment, pro-acculturation stance and during a critical period in Choctaw-white relations voted to allow more railroads and whites to enter the Nation. In the years following Wilson's death, Benton and another man who reportedly contributed to Wilson's murder, Peter Conser, found themselves in power positions and remained supporters of the Progressives' agenda.

I also have always been intrigued with Silan Lewis and have often thought about why he returned for execution instead of leaving Indian Territory. Both Lewis and Wilson emerge as figures in the Choctaw record as either someone who was brutally killed (Wilson) and another who was ready to kill (Lewis). The lives of these two men also support the mythology of other stories: Wilson as the victim of a "murderous Negro" and a fallen U.S. marshal (always a popular topic), and Lewis as the jealous Indian bent on destroying those who did not support his candidacy for Gaines County sheriff or as the romantic savage who adheres to "tradition" and honorably returns for his execution.

Though aspects of the Wilson and Lewis cases remain somewhat mysterious, both have several other interesting similarities. In both cases, the political strife within the Nation made some men so angry that they killed their political rivals. To say that the animosity the political parties held for each other was venomous does not adequately describe the situation. For years Nationalists and the Progressives accused one another of corruption and dishonesty, and threats flew back and forth.

This political fighting extended to the courts as well. The cases that followed Wilson's murder and Lewis's arrest were handled with varying degrees of ineptitude and unquestionable prejudice. A look at the jurors in all the trials—some of whom were criminals themselves—reveals why certain men were found guilty and others not. Indeed, political standing accounted for many decisions and actions—including crimes—in these decades. Repeatedly, one can find cases of murderers and rapists being freed because of their families' stature in the Nation. Being wealthy or friends with the tribal chief, a tribal council member, or an affluent intermarried white man could take one far, including being acquitted of murder.

The social surroundings of the times of both the Wilson and Lewis cases were extremely violent. Throughout the 1880s and 1890s, across Indian Territory and among all the tribes, cases of murder, rape, theft, larceny, and whiskey peddling numbered in the hundreds (many crimes were not reported so there actually could have been thousands of transgressions). Most of those crimes were committed by the white intruders who swarmed across Indian Territory, but as time went by the Choctaws also started behaving badly.

The actions and behaviors of the Choctaws who appeared to have accepted Christianity and white cultural values without question demonstrate the pervasiveness of colonization. Many people believe that the "aftershocks" of contact were limited to the first century after contact because during that time millions of deaths from disease occurred and much tribal land was lost. But many indigenous scholars argue that effects of colonization have continued to the present day. All Natives who know their histories and who are active in their tribal cultures are aware that traditional tribal ways of life are still disrupted in a myriad of ways.

The Choctaw Nation may have managed to regain its sovereignty to a certain extent, and there are many Choctaws who speak their language and who maintain the old stories and some ceremonies; but, generally speaking, the tribe has not maintained traditional cultural continuity, which is why there are thousands of Choctaw tribal members today who possess a spectrum of worldviews, value systems, blood quanta, and appearances. Because of intermarriage and the subsequent dominance of nonindigenous spouses, combined with the missionaries forcing their opinions on the tribal culture, over time the Choctaws understandably became fearful of extermination. Many consequently adopted the ways of the colonizer. Many Choctaw children were (and are) raised in environments where Choctaw traditions either were not mentioned or were held up as secondary to the mores of white (mainstream) society. Therefore, Choctaw readers will have varied opinions about the individuals discussed here.

Many of the same individuals who were associated with the Wilson case were also part of the Lewis case. Robert Benton, the man who witnesses agree killed my ancestor, Charles Wilson, served as the captain of the militia that guarded Silan Lewis prior to his execution. Some of the men involved in the Wilson case in 1886 sat on the juries for the Nationalist trials in the 1890s. The man who recorded the Lewis murder trial officiated at the marriage of my great-grandparents who lived in Red Oak until the 1930s. Sadly, their daughter—my grandmother—was one of those Choctaws who sold her allotment for a pittance, and now my widowed mother retains only the mineral rights to that land. My great-grandfather, William Elliot Abbott (whose son married Wilson's granddaughter) delivered two of Silan Lewis's wife's babies. Charles Wilson's sister Mary married Dave Pickens, the son of Chickasaw Chief Edmund Pickens, first chief of the Chickasaw District of the Choctaw Nation in 1841 and later the second controlling chief financial official and treasurer.[4] And in a strange twist of familial relations, Dave Pickens's sister Rachel was the first wife of the Progressive Choctaw Wilson N. Jones, the man supported by Progressives such as Robert Benton and Peter Conser, but who Nationalist Silan Lewis hated so much that he tried to kill.

Finally, the cases of Wilson and Lewis set the stage for discussions of cause and effect of other events that occurred in the 1880s and 1890s, such as differences of opinions between political parties over how to best tangle with the federal government so their treaty rights would be honored, distributions of wealth among tribal members, the handling of cases in the Choctaw and federal courts, curious judgments, rules regarding juries and presiding judges, and advantages to having political connections. Studying these people and notable events in Choctaw history also provides an opportunity to consider research methodologies and strategies to use when presented with a dearth of data.

While many of the stories can be reconstructed, there is not enough information to create accurate dialogues or interior monologues (which is one reason why I also write fiction). Although I remain intensely curious about all of these men I write about, and no doubt I always will wonder what motivated them, angered them, and gave them peace of mind, I cannot pretend to know what they were really thinking. No amount of staring at the only photograph of Silan Lewis gave me a rush of insight into his thoughts, although the catalysts for his motivations seem fairly obvious. Therefore, because the vast majority of the sources used to create this book are primary, this history is created from my interpretations and any errors are mine.

PROLOGUE

By the time of Charles Wilson's death in 1884, the Choctaw Nation in Indian Territory was not inhabited only by Choctaws. The populace consisted of approximately eighteen thousand full- and mixed-bloods ("Choctaws by blood"), intermarried whites, and freedmen. In addition, throughout the Union Agency, which included the Choctaws, Cherokees, Chickasaws, Muscogees, and Seminoles, were scattered another thirty thousand white traders, railroad employees, government workers, farm laborers, visitors and "pleasure-seekers," claimants to citizenship who were denied the status but stayed anyway, and men and women who were simply intruders. The populace lived in homes ranging from shanties, wagons, and tents, to large plantation-style houses surrounded by hundreds of acres of fenced range and farmland, and every sort of structure in between.[1] These farmers, traders, miners, loggers, ranchers, businessmen, merchants, whiskey runners, criminals, missionaries, cattle rustlers, horse thieves, Indians of other tribes, Christians of various denominations, and interlopers all interacted with one another, sometimes furiously. And so did the wealthy and poor mixed-blood, full-blood, traditionalist, Nationalist, and Progressive Choctaws.

The demographics of the Choctaw Nation had changed over the decades, and so had Choctaw culture. Subtle and obvious cultural transformations were evident by the 1820s when many of the

Choctaws had adopted many traits and values of the Euroamericans. Like some Cherokees, Chickasaws, and Muscogees, a portion of the Choctaw tribe had become convinced by missionaries to speak English exclusively, to answer to English names, to abandon traditional religious ceremonies including certain burial practices, to desist using the services of the *alikchi* (Choctaw physicians), and the *hattak fullish nipi foni* (bonepickers) who removed flesh from the deceased after they had decayed for months on a scaffold. Many Choctaws cut their long hair, stopped the customs of head flattening and heavy tattooing, and ceased the traditional social, animal, and war dances. The concept of a tribal mentality—that is, group cohesion as opposed to individualism—rapidly diminished among many families. A large portion of the tribe lost track of which *iska*, or clan, they belonged to, and, like some Natives of other tribes during the same time period, internalized colonization to the point that they viewed anyone who practiced cultural traditions and who was not a Christian as "uncivilized."

Not only had the social and value system been modified and transferred to Indian Territory when Choctaws were forced west in the 1830s, the traditional Choctaw system of governance and punishment also had transformed to imitate the U.S. form of administration.

In 1826, the Choctaws replaced their traditional laws with the first of seven written constitutions (adopted between 1826 and 1860) that were similar to the U.S. Constitution, with a Bill of Rights and three branches of government: legislative, judicial, and executive. The Nation was divided into three districts—Moshulatubbee (First), Apukshunnubbee (Second), and Pushmataha (Third)—each with a district chief; one of those chiefs was elected to serve as the chief executive. A fourth district, the Chickasaw District, was added later. The Choctaw General Council, comprising the Choctaw Senate and House of Representatives, was responsible for creating and passing laws and was supreme over the executive and judicial branches. These constitutions were amended and enhanced through the years, but their basic form remained the same.[2]

To deal with crime and to protect itself from legal maneuverings, the tribe instituted a multifaceted system of justice. The highest court in the Nation was the Supreme Court, consisting of three judges, one from each of the three districts. The judges had to be at least thirty years of age and were elected to four-year terms by a joint vote of both houses of the General Council. One of the judges served as chief justice, and only two men were needed to create a quorum. The Supreme Court had only appellate jurisdiction and met twice a year (April and October) at the capitol in Tuskahoma. The Supreme Court could issue writs, judge on laws and declare them unconstitutional, and also give opinions when requested to do so by the chief.[3]

Each district had a district court, also known as circuit courts, that were overseen by an elected judge and had original jurisdiction over criminal cases, including felonies, as well as civil cases such as contract disputes and controversies dealing with monies over fifty dollars. The district courts controlled county courts and issued writs and process. Indictments were handed down by a grand jury. The indictment might be justified because of testimony of one of the jurymen and each juryman was expected to inform the district attorney of law violations. One man was selected to keep minutes of their meetings, which were held when the jury agreed upon a time. Some men were apparently "career jurymen," those individuals who served in case after case, while other citizens may have served only once or twice.[4]

The lowest court, the county court, convened on the first Monday of each month. This court reviewed criminal cases and could refer them to a higher court, although the General Council had the authority to hold and determine suits in the courts. The county courts also could issue writs and process and "bind any person to keep the peace." The county courts also were responsible for cases "necessary to the internal improvements and local concerns of their respective counties," such as recording the discovery of minerals, marriage licenses, and sale of improvements. Many of the cases listed in the county court records also appear in greater detail in the district court records. County judges were elected for a period of two years. The county judges oversaw courts of probate and decided matters related to estates, and they appointed clerks of their choice who often also served as county treasurer. All judges in the Nation (supreme, district, and county courts) were compensated for their work.[5]

This system of governance was much different than the traditional manner of conducting Choctaw social and political business. There is some debate over how the precontact Choctaws organized their society and maintained order, but historians generally agree that they divided themselves into two clan groups called phratries, or *iksas* (although the term "iksa" can also refer to other subdivisions and, later, to Christian sects), which were further divided into more localized iksas and a kin system of related individuals who had common matrilineal (female) descent that defined a person's social, political, religious and economic roles. A person's clan was determined by her mother; hence, women possessed much political and social power, in addition to a network of female relatives that guaranteed support and companionship. Family iksas were the primary enforcer of tribal process and law, such as resolving arguments and punishing those transgressors against tribal laws. The tribe as a whole functioned when individuals, through the authority of their iksas, voluntarily followed tribal customs without force. They were compelled not because of written laws (there were none) but because of the consequences of ostracism and ridicule. Everyone reportedly understood that there were consequences for bad behavior. Murder, for example, was punishable by blood revenge; that is, the family of the victim was allowed to dispense with the murderer, or if he was not available, another male member of the family would suffice. As per custom, the guilty person did not attempt to escape. To do so would not only dishonor him, but another member of the family could be substituted and killed.[6]

Before removal to Indian Territory, Choctaws lived in numerous small towns across what is today Mississippi, western Alabama, and eastern Arkansas, and they were clustered into four groups: the *Okla Hannali* (People of Six Towns), who wore tattoos around their mouths, lived to the southeast; the *Okla Falaya* (Long People), who lived to the west; the *Okla Tannap* (People of the Opposite Side), also known as *Ahepat okla* or *Haiyip atoklolo*, who lived to the east; and the *Okla Chito* (the Big People), who lived in the central area and by the time of contact had probably melded into the others. Each of these towns within the districts had its own town chief who answered to the district chief. In addition, each town had a variety of officers, including the *Tichou mingo* (chief's speaker) who organized events such as ceremonies. In times of war, warriors were led by their war chief and his assistants, the *Taskaminkochi*. There also were individuals with distinction, such as the Beloved Men who had distinguished themselves in war. The head district chief and a few assistant chiefs essentially acted as a Council. The three district chiefs consulted together on matters that affected the entire Nation, such as war, peace, trade, or negotiations with other tribes or white intruders. The district chiefs also appointed men to their councils. No one person dictated terms. When all the district chiefs and their councils needed to meet together, runners brought a bundle of sticks to them. With each day that passed a stick was discarded from the bundle so the chief would know when he was to appear at the meeting. Although only the chiefs and their councils were allowed into the meeting, the Choctaw populace was invited to hear speeches and to participate in the feasts and other activities that accompanied the meeting.[7]

After several years in Indian Territory, the Choctaw government created the "Skullyville Constitution" in 1857, which replaced the district chiefs with one "governor" or chief.[8] Almost immediately afterward a group of conservative Choctaws who preferred the traditional method of governance countered that constitution with their own, the "Doaksville Constitution" (drafted at Doaksville), replete with their own officers. The conflict between the two groups threatened to develop into violence until a compromise constitution was agreed upon in 1860. One Choctaw recalled, "the Chiefs refused to give up the old set up. The other crowd refused the old way. So that started trouble."[9]

The revised Doaksville Constitution of 1860, then, was a compromise document that was primarily a copy of the U.S. form of governance with a central authority figure. This constitution included an executive branch with an elected principal chief, three district chiefs who could serve a maximum of two consecutive terms, and an elected national secretary, treasurer, auditor, and attorney, each of whom served two-year terms. The legislative branch included a bicameral General Council composed of the Senate, with four senators from each of the three districts, and the House of Representatives, with 18 to 20 elected representatives. The judicial branch consisted of a Supreme Court and county courts. Although numerous amendments were passed over the decades, the basic laws remained intact until 1907.

Many whites were eager to settle in the tribal nations after the Civil War. A major temptation for white men was the stipulation in the Treaty of 1866 that allowed anyone who married a Choctaw to be deemed a citizen of the Nation giving non-Choctaw men access to the resources they wanted.[10] Chickasaws living in the Choctaw Nation also were answerable to the Choctaw laws because of their dual citizenship outlined in the treaty of separation.[11] And so were citizens of the Cherokee, Creek, and Seminole nations by virtue of the North Fork Village compact of 1859. Choctaw and Chickasaw criminals were extradited between the tribes by terms of the Treaty of 1855, but the federal government dictated that Choctaws were required to turn over criminals to state and federal authorities, who did not have to reciprocate.[12]

Because marrying a Choctaw woman often was a white man's key to success, a law was passed in 1836 that stated any white man who married a Choctaw woman could not "dispose" of her property without her permission. Nor could he divorce her without "just provocation." If he did, he would have to pay a fine decreed by the court and would lose his tribal citizenship.[13] Another law stated that any man who "runs off" with a woman was to take her to the nearest captain, have the marriage ceremony performed, and would be advised by the said captain not to physically abuse her or "[cut] off her hair."[14] In 1849, an act dictated that any white man living with a Choctaw woman had to marry her, otherwise he would have to leave the Nation. The General Council also attempted to monitor behavior by adding that no white man "under a bad character" would be allowed to marry a Choctaw woman "under any circumstances whatever."[15] Clearly, this law was not instituted only to protect women. The council passed the law to make sure the Nation did not become overrun with criminals and opportunists.

In the post–Civil War years the numbers of whites moving into the Choctaw Nation continued to grow. Hundreds of whites leased Indian land to farm or ranch, while others built sawmills and explored for coal. And they did not stop coming. More white men and Choctaw women married, and mixed-bloods married other mixed-bloods and whites, resulting in more mixed-blood children. Although there remained populations of full-bloods, they were rapidly becoming a minority in their own land.

Many of the whites who had infiltrated the Choctaw Nation were earnest and simply trying to survive; but, as Indian Agent John W. Lane observed, many other white trespassers possessed "little regard for the moral law" and were "illiterate, roving, ragged, and profligate." They were not particularly ambitious, either, living in wagons, tents, huts, and cabins and, according to Lane, "totally indifferent to the education of their children."[16] The mischievous behaviors of some of these people apparently influenced some tribal citizens.

Residents of Sugar Loaf County, where Charles Wilson had served as sheriff, county clerk, and treasurer, consisted of 738 Indians, primarily full-bloods, and some of them employed white workers to assist them on their farms.[17] Although Sugar Loaf County had not yet been overrun with non-Indians, political infighting and frustrations among Choctaws were expressed in a variety of bad behaviors throughout the Choctaw Nation. In August of 1884, the infighting escalated, culminating in the murder of my great-great-grandfather, Charles Wilson.

CHAPTER 1

THE MURDER OF CHARLES WILSON AND THE EXECUTION OF JACKSON CROW

Now, since the fears and the loyalties of that period have faded, people generally concede that the tribal courts were ruled more by influence than law.

—From J. J. Robbs, "The Murder of Charles Wilson, A Choctaw"

In the 1890s, newspapers advertised the Kully Chaha township as a "Mountain Resort," a veritable "perfect paradise to the invalid and overworked." Kully Chaha means "high spring" in Choctaw, and it emerged as a favorite spot in the heat of the summer. Berries, grapes, and nuts grew in abundance. Horses, cattle, and hogs roamed the area along with turkeys, white-tailed deer, and quail. Fish filled the rivers and streams, favorites being catfish and sun perch. Kully Chaha featured a post office, established in 1881 along with J. U. Morrow's drug store, blacksmith "shop," and another store belonging to Joe Barnes. The Moshulatubbee Masonic Lodge Building stood a mile east of town.[1] Because of the many cliffs and boulders, Nvnih Chufvk is difficult to climb on foot. Even today there is no foot trail, and its steep sides are nearly impossible to traverse, either on horseback or with four-wheel drive.

Early in the sweltering morning of August 7, 1884, Sugar Loaf County resident Fleema Chubbee made his way down the rutted Fort Towson road at the base of Nvnih Chufvk, the wagon wheels squealing in protest at the rough road.[2] The day before he had worked since dawn as election judge for the Sugar Loaf County election and had not started home until dark. Now he sat on the hard seat of the wagon, heading north, when he spotted a bloodied body sprawled in the road. Drawing closer, he realized that the gravely injured man was someone he knew well—full-blood Choctaw Charles B. Wilson, county treasurer and court clerk, and a former lighthorseman, sheriff, and judge. Wilson also had served as a U.S. deputy marshal since 1872, was a member of the Moshulatubbee Masonic Lodge, and owned a mercantile store in Kully Chaha.[3] Fleema Chubbee discovered that Wilson had been shot numerous times, had bled profusely, and had stopped breathing. Although Fleema Chubbee found a thready pulse in Wilson's wrist, the mortally wounded man would not live much longer. To make matters worse, wild *shukha* (hogs) had gathered and appeared eager to investigate. Luckily, a white man passing by agreed to protect Wilson while Fleema Chubbee rode off to find assistance.[4]

While Fleema Chubbee hurried his team to the nearest house, another Choctaw, C. C. Mathies, was sitting under his oak trees when young King Sullivan ran into his yard to breathlessly tell him that he had witnessed a shooting and that the victim lay in Towson Road several miles away. Mathies immediately set out to see for himself and along the way met several other Choctaws who had also heard the news. But Wilson had died by the time Mathies reached him. Choctaws Abel Harris and Adam Morris had also arrived and together they conducted a cursory examination of Wilson's wounds. They ascertained that Wilson had been shot at least twice in the chest—once in the back under the left shoulder and near his spine, and "once in the pants." One of the chest wounds resulted in bone and flesh being torn away and "drug out of his body." Wilson's head injury looked especially terrible; the back of his bloody and fractured skull looked as though "something like heavy iron or wood [had] done it. . . . The scalp was all broken into jelly back there." The men wrapped Wilson's body in a blanket and loaded him into a wagon to take him home, where they stripped him of his blue three-piece suit. The damage to his body immediately became apparent; one shot fired into his back appeared to have exited his thigh, another went through his other thigh, and yet another entered his back and exited an arm. Each entry wound was marked by red swelling and black powder marks. The wounds appeared so awful that a few men became queasy and left the room.[5]

Some speculated that Wilson had been waylaid by one of the many outlaws roaming Indian Territory. That seemed a reasonable assumption because Wilson was the county treasurer, and some believed that he always carried money with him. But citizens who knew Wilson had other suspicions because his political beliefs were not in line with the status quo of the county.

Charles Wilson was born in 1844, ten years after his parents endured the forced removal from Mississippi. Family testimonies reveal that several immediate family members perished on the trek west; ironically, Charles's father Lewis (a headman of the Okla Hannali District) had signed the 1830 removal treaty. When the family arrived in Indian Territory, they settled in Atoka County in Pushmataha District, and after the Civil War, Charles moved to Sugar Loaf County. Because he could speak and write in both Choctaw (Chahta anumpa) and English, Wilson was a desirable choice for tribal offices. By the 1860s the citizenry deemed Wilson trustworthy and competent enough to elect him sheriff several times, and in the 1880s they elected him county clerk and later county judge. At the time of his death he worked double duty as county clerk and treasurer. He established the trading store of Wilson and Ryan and became a master of the local Masonic Lodge, along with other Choctaws such as Nationalist leader Jacob Jackson.[6] Wilson's sister Mary married David Pickens, the son of a Chickasaw chief, Edmund Pickens (Ochantubby). Ironically, Wilson N. Jones, a Progressive who would later play a major role in Choctaw politics, married David's sister (and Chief Pickens's daughter), Rachel.[7] Wilson, however, was a Nationalist. Rachel Pickens Jones died in 1855, and had she lived the family gatherings would have been interesting indeed.

Many stories have been told about Wilson, one being that while he served as sheriff in the 1870s, Judge Charles Benton ordered him to arrest livestock thieves. Wilson caught twenty-two men led by

Dixon Booth; all were found guilty, and eleven were executed.[8] A more fanciful tale is that while a lighthorseman Wilson single-handedly killed a gang of cattle rustlers by making them "all kneel down" and shooting them "one at a time."[9] In 1880, Col. John Q. Tufts, the U.S. agent for the Union Agency of Muskogee, Indian Territory, organized a unit of Indian police comprising lighthorsemen of the Five Tribes (Choctaws, Creeks, Chickasaws, Seminoles, and Cherokees). Sometimes those men were recruited to serve as deputy marshals. Because Wilson had served as a lighthorseman and much of his mercantile business came from the men who worked at Fort Smith, he seemed a logical choice for U.S. deputy marshal.[10]

Exciting tales of "legendary" lighthorsemen are not unusual. The men have been revered as hard-riding tamers of the land. Many men have claimed to have been lighthorsemen but were not; and many storytellers identify lighthorsemen who were actually either sheriffs or U.S. marshals. Some claim that the lighthorsemen were the only forms of law enforcement in the Choctaw Nation prior to Oklahoma statehood in 1907, when in actuality the lighthorsemen were the dominant law enforcement agency among the Choctaws only from 1834 to 1861. After that time, sheriffs and their deputies wielded much more power and authority.

The tribe's lighthorsemen had been established prior to removal, when the wealthiest Choctaw families included the Folsoms, LeFlores, and Pitchlynns. At the time, some Choctaws advocated acquiring white ways of law enforcement. One of those advocates was John Pitchlynn, the son of British trader Isaac Pitchlynn. He married a mixed-blood woman, Sophia Folsum, and together they built a trading post, owned and used black slaves, and created a cattle dynasty. A powerful voice in the tribe, Pitchlynn favored the creation of schools, churches, and new means of legal governance, including using lighthorsemen for law enforcement. In 1824, Greenwood LeFlore and David Folsom organized the Choctaw Lighthorse, and Peter Pitchlynn, son of John Pitchlynn and former student at Nashville University, served as the first head of the company.[11] Although the lighthorsemen were originally put under the control of the mixed-bloods, by 1826, that control was transferred to the command of the district chiefs, a move that satisfied the chiefs because it left some tradition in Choctaw law enforcement.

The concept of organizing lighthorsemen—that is, horse-riding law men—to enforce laws was not a new idea in Indian Territory. The Cherokees were the first tribe to institute the concept. In 1808, they passed an act creating "regulators" who were supposed to primarily protect the widows and orphans and stop horse thievery and general robbery; they had the authority to kill any alleged guilty party who resisted their arrest. In the Cherokee Nation, each district was assigned six lighthorsemen.[12] That the Choctaws also decided to establish their own lighthorsemen was a huge departure from their traditional form of law enforcement, as was the centralized form of government they adopted. In general terms, the problem of liquor importation and white intrusion, in addition to the desire of the wealthy mixed-bloods to protect their assets, caused the tribe to rethink its strategies of imposing good societal behavior and establish a corps of lighthorsemen.

The lighthorsemen continued to enforce Choctaw laws but they were not all powerful.[13] Those convicted of murder might be shot by a lighthorseman, but only at the behest of a judge. Lighthorsemen could make the decision to lash someone they deemed guilty of a crime. But there is no written law allowing them judgment to execute someone unless that alleged criminal resisted arrest or if they tried to kill or injure a lighthorseman. For example, in 1839, judges for the Choctaw Supreme Court and the lower courts were authorized to order the lighthorsemen to bring criminals to court, and anyone refusing arrest was liable to be shot. Just prior to the Civil War, the problem of murders became serious enough that the Choctaw General Council decided to pass an act authorizing district chiefs to offer rewards to the general Choctaw population for the apprehension and/or killing of "out lawed murderers and other criminals who may escape beyond the reach of justice."[14] In 1840, a law was passed stating that those suspected of committing murder were to be apprehended by the lighthorsemen and held until they could be tried in court. Three years later the judges in each district were authorized by the Constitution to order the lighthorsemen to bring forth alleged criminals or witnesses to a crime and to collect monies from the losing party in a non-murder trial to pay the witnesses and jurymen.[15]

Lighthorsemen rode their own horses and used their own weapons. Little mention is made in the records of what the lighthorsemen ate or where they slept, but they probably traveled like hunters. One account mentions that "the light horsemen carried no excess equipment such as militiamen carry; a horse, saddle, rifle and revolver were the regular equipment, while a few hands full of parched corn and some jerked beef in their pockets or saddle bags, was the ration this army subsisted on while they moved swiftly from place to place."[16] One problem they faced while riding through the Nation for days or weeks at a time was that they often did not come into contact with residents who might feed them.

The Choctaws were skilled agriculturalists who grew a variety of crops, notably corn, squashes, and potatoes. Traditionally, there were several ways to prepare corn, or *ta^nchi*, by smoking and drying the kernels to preserve them; use of hickory wood deterred insects. In cold months, the stored corn was rehydrated and cooked with meat. Hunters carried a bag of either cracked corn (that required strong teeth to eat) and/or some ground corn to mix with water. They might have eaten cracked corn softened with milk and honey (if they had access to those things) as a cold meal. Hunters also carried potatoes, or *ahi*, that were thinly sliced and dried over a hickory fire, similar to a potato chip without the grease. The lighthorsemen also shot game, caught fish, and in the more populated areas could simply ask to be fed.[17]

There is no record as to what the early Choctaw lighthorsemen looked like, but there is one commentary about the Cherokee lighthorsemen from Englishman John Payne who observed a regiment in 1840. He wrote that the men were "armed and wild looking horsemen," and the leader was a "tall and reckless looking man, with red leggings and a shabby green blanket coat."[18] No doubt that riding through the countryside for days without benefit of a bath or laundry might make one look "wild-looking"; but as for clothing, there is no record as to what the men were required to wear. Photographs taken decades later of Choctaw and Seminole lighthorsemen reveal that they wore what white lawmen did: button-down shirts, vests, jackets, long pants (often with the hem rolled up), boots, hats, and a bandana.

Even though most lighthorsemen did their duties, not every one thought the lighthorsemen did their jobs well, especially if the lighthorseman arrested a family member. Apparently, some Choctaws believed that the lighthorsemen often would "spot" a target, shoot the person dead, and then later claim self-defense. Peter Pitchlynn discussed in an 1860 letter to his father the murders of an intermarried white man named H. C. Flack, Flack's son, and a full-blood Choctaw named Wall Folsom. A lighthorseman, Feletah, had asked the assistance of James Gibson, David Harkins, Clay Harkins, Loring Harkins, and Turner Turnbill to accost and destroy the Flacks' liquor. In the process, Flack, his son, and Folsom were killed. "The lighthorsemen are in the bushes," Pitchlynn wrote. And he expected that once word of the "murders" got out there would be even more bloodshed. Pitchlynn claimed in his letter that Col. Sampson Folsom, a former Civil War officer, said that the "damn Lighthorsemen" needed to be exterminated.[19]

Although a few of the lighthorsemen's missions went awry, others were effective, which is why the Choctaw administration depended on them. But many lighthorsemen became weary. They had their hands full with more than just alcohol abuse, election organizations, and various crimes. The men were assigned to sell stray cattle and horses found by Choctaw ranchers in the Nation to the highest bidder and the profits were split between the individual who found the strays and the Choctaw Nation's public fund.[20] In addition, one Choctaw lighthorseman from each district was required to serve as sergeant-at-arms at the General Council meetings;[21] one lighthorsemen was to be appointed at each of the Nation's schools;[22] and lighthorsemen also were to remove any home or other settlement located within a half mile of a salt work.[23] They had to remain vigilant because they also were required to remove anyone who settled within 440 yards of an established settler without the latter's consent.[24]

Despite their work, lighthorsemen needed assistance. By the 1860s, the lighthorsemen did not provide enough manpower to address

Choctaw Lawmen: (left to right standing) unknown person and Peter Conser; (seated) Ellis Austin and Stanley Benton. Courtesy Research Division of the Oklahoma Historical Society.

the growing number of crimes being committed in the Choctaw Nation. In October 1860, the principal chief was authorized to commission sheriffs who had been elected by the residents of their counties. Trying to separate the various law enforcement categories appears daunting; listed in the Choctaw Nation district records are the positions of judge, high sheriff, sheriff, deputy sheriff, special deputy sheriff, ranger, national lighthorseman, county lighthorseman, lighthorse captain, and private militia. None of these positions were held by women. Unlike the appointment of the lighthorsemen, the indoctrination of the sheriffs and deputies was complex, and the tribal council clearly put a great deal of thought into making sure the men were kept in strict control. Each sheriff could appoint and fire deputies,[25] and because of the number of crimes committed throughout the Choctaw Nation, the sheriffs were not always picky about who they chose to deputize. One citizen recalls that "us boys were always being deputized to go" after the various outlaws who roamed the nation.[26] Another man who served as a lighthorseman for a year pointed out an obvious drawback to being a law enforcement officer in a society in which crime was a daily occurrence: "When a man had to help arrest his friends, he seemed to lose face."[27] This may partially account for the rapid turnover of lighthorsemen, sheriffs, and deputies.

Whereas previously the lighthorsemen were the only ones who could seize and destroy liquor, by 1860 sheriffs and constables also could destroy liquor without warrant.[28] The problem of liquor running through the tribe was serious indeed and it was not only the citizens and intruders who abused it. Peter Pitchlynn commented in an 1860 letter to his father that the liquor law was a "dead letter in this country," that anybody who wanted to "drink with impunity" could, and that included the lighthorsemen and officers who he claimed also got drunk "whenever they feel like it." It was Pitchlynn's opinion that "our nation is going to the dogs."[29]

Familial connections, such as those made by the Pitchlynns, often dominated Choctaw politics. Prominent residents of Sugar Loaf County in the 1880s included members of the Progressive Benton family. Robert Benton, a full-blood, had been a ranger, county and circuit clerk, and probate and county judge in the 1870s, and he became a vocal member of the Choctaw House of Representatives in the 1880s. In 1881, he cast a "yea" vote for granting the right of way of the St. Louis and San Francisco Railway through the Choctaw Nation, a move heartily opposed by Nationalists.[30] Robert's brother Charles H. Benton served as Sugar Loaf County judge throughout the 1870s and 1880s, and as sheriff, Charles Wilson had been answerable to him.[31]

That Robert Benton voted for the railroad is significant because the establishment of the railroads had serious social, economic, and political impacts on the tribe.[32] The United States' 1866 treaty with the Chickasaws and Choctaws stated that the tribes would grant a right of way through their lands, from north to south and from east to west. Railroads were a powerful force in Indian Territory, as were the many businesses that sprung up alongside them. The railroads allowed easier access to the tribe's resources, and the Choctaws knew it. The tribe was, in fact, involved in more than a dozen pieces of legislation regarding railroads between 1869 and 1884.[33] For example, the tribes were allowed to buy stock in the railroad company, and they could pay for that stock with land on either side of the rails in six-mile sections. Choctaw public money could be used to invest in the railroads but the tribe was justifiably concerned that it would have to tax its citizens and workers to support the government. Worse, the tribe would be giving the money to the hated speculators. The Missouri, Kansas, and Texas Railroad was built during 1871–72 and extended through Indian Territory, while the Atlantic and Pacific ranged from the northeastern corner of Indian Territory to Vinita and extended to Sapulpa by 1889. In 1887, the St. Louis and San Francisco Railway was created from Fort Smith to Paris, Texas, and extended to Coffeyville, Kansas (as the Kansas and Arkansas Valley) from 1888 to 1889. Around the same time, the Choctaw Coal and Railway was built from South McAlester to Wister. With so many rail lines crossing the Nation, another serious concern emerged about the increasing white population.[34] Many Choctaws were displeased with the railroads not only for what they represented and the advantage they gave intruders, but also because of the destruction they caused to the environment and to their livestock.

In the summer of 1884, the Choctaw Nation prepared to elect its new chief, either the Progressive Edmund McCurtain of the powerful, wealthy McCurtain family, or the Nationalist Joseph P. Folsom. McCurtain's father Cornelius had been chief of the Mosholatubbee District, and his brother Jackson was president of the Senate and was elected chief in 1880 and 1882. Edmund McCurtain held several political positions in the Choctaw Nation including judge of San Bois County(also known as Sans Bois County), trustee of schools, representative to the National Council, and superintendent of education. In 1883, McCurtain, along with Green McCurtain, Edmund Burgevin, Napoleon B. Ainsworth, and Ellis Austin, received approval from the Tribal Council to form the Poteau Slack Water Navigation Company, a joint stock company that invested in improving the Poteau River so that steamers and flatboats could more easily navigate. They also were given permission to charge a toll for using the river, and the tribe would receive a percent on the yearly net earnings.[35]

McCurtain's opponent, Joseph P. Folsom, was a Nationalist and a member of the council who opposed the St. Louis and San Francisco Railway charter and also stood in staunch opposition to allotment. Although he lost the 1884 election to McCurtain, Folsom retained his determination to fight the Dawes Commission later. Ten years later he would write and propose a bill to the General Council stating that anyone who would "betray said land and Choctaw country into the hands of a foreign power," could be punished by jail time, a fine or even death.[36]

The candidates had much potential to create some dynamic platforms with the numerous, perpetual issues burning throughout the Choctaw Nation. Crimes such as murder, whiskey running, and thefts, as well as the presence of intruders and the crumbling of Choctaw traditions continued to divide the tribe. The building of railroads, discovery of coal, desire for wealth, and pressure and influences put on the tribe by intermarried whites, missionaries, and the U.S. government resulted in the creation of dozens of laws addressing

*Principal Chief Edmund
McCurtain (1884–1886).*
Courtesy Research Division of
the Oklahoma Historical Society.

crime and punishment, taxation, and royalties. Another crisis was
the continuation of the violence that raged during the Civil War,
when the county courts basically stopped functioning and outlaws
were seemingly everywhere, stealing horses, cattle, and anything
else they could find, and killing and raping without fear of arrest.
The morale of the Choctaws waned as they witnessed the hard work
and diligence of the lighthorsemen but also the many intruders and
some of their own tribespeople blatantly disregarding the laws.[37]
Choctaw citizens understandably sought leadership to protect their
families, land, culture, sovereignty, and monetary wealth.

Election day fell on the sixth of August. Sugar Loaf County voters
considered the merits of the candidates for chief as well as the candidates for Sugar Loaf sheriff, judge, ranger, and representative to the
General Council. Pre-election debates proved especially exciting
because both Wilson and Robert Benton had decided to run for the
coveted position of representative.[38]

In a debate held the night before the election, the political arguments raged as the men "got tighter" from drinking. Personal verbal attacks from Wilson and from his Nationalist followers reportedly humiliated and angered Benton and his contingency. Indeed, this could not be construed as a polite gathering; both Wilson and Benton openly threatened to kill each other.[39] Wilson and Benton had been acquainted for years and had ample things to say to one another. Not only did they represent rival political parties, Wilson had successfully sued Benton two months before in a case involving guardianship of an abandoned property.[40]

Early on the morning of election day, officials set up the voting tables and poll books to document the voters' choices. Throughout the day, by horseback and wagon, male voters trickled onto the courthouse lawn. Some men who had debated late into the previous night had camped out on the lawn, and witnesses recall that more than a few of them remained intoxicated. Numerous citizens saw Wilson and his nephew Edmond Pickens on the grounds throughout the day.[41] The poll book was supposed to have been secured for tabulation after the election, but because numerous individuals, including Nationalists Wilson and Pickens, are not listed as voters, it remains questionable as to whether the books were tampered with.[42]

After the discovery of Wilson's body the next morning, Lowman Jack, Fleema Chubbee, Adam Morris, and Josh Hickman followed horse tracks leading away from Wilson's body and eventually traced them through the "thickety place" close to Robert Benton's property.[43] In addition, several unidentified people cautiously came forward to tell authorities what they knew about the killing. Considering who witnesses say they saw kill Wilson, the parents of young King Sullivan were justifiably afraid for his life and they insisted their child be guarded in the jail house.[44]

Word of Wilson's death spread quickly. The first newspaper accounts stated that Wilson had died "accidentally." The following report changed that more accurately to "murder" because his head was "crushed" and "nine buckshots" were found in his body. Because of the heat and humidity Wilson's twenty-five-year-old second wife Martha quickly arranged for his burial in the still-used Vaughn

Second grave stone of Charles B. Wilson. The first had almost completely deteriorated. Author's photograph.

Cemetery at the base of Nvnih Chufvk. The gregarious Wilson had a penchant for social drinking and in his capacity as county officer and businessman had cultivated many friends in the Choctaw Nation and at Fort Smith. His first Chickasaw wife and sister Mary Pickens had extended Chickasaw families and friends who also became acquainted with Wilson. As angry mourners stood in the August heat watching Wilson's casket being lowered into the ground, they wanted those men rumored to have killed Wilson punished.[45] That proved to be much easier said than done.

Based on witness testimonies, Choctaw authorities soon felt they possessed enough evidence to arrest ten tribesman: John Allen, Robert Benton, Peter Conser, Charles Fisher, Jim Franklin, Joe Jackson, Ned McCalis, Cornelius McCurtain, Dixon Perry, and John Slaughter.[46] These men were not outlaws roaming the countryside looking for someone to rob; all were Choctaw citizens who knew and lived fairly close to one another. McCurtain, Conser, and Fisher were deputy sheriffs, while the others are listed in tribal documents as regular voters, witnesses, jurors, and farmers. Despite the satisfaction some felt over the arrests, the situation remained traumatic for the Wilson family and friends because Charles's seven-year-old son, Willis G., died of unknown causes less than a month after the murder of his father.[47]

Jackson Crow, a freedman farmer who "made good crops" also had ridden with the accused group, but he was not initially arrested because Choctaw courts only heard cases in which the parties involved in a crime were Choctaws. Rumor positioned Crow as the son of a Creek father and a "negress," although some Choctaws believed him to be a black man and former slave, possessing no Indian blood.[48] His Indian blood, or lack of it, however, remained beside the point.

Freedmen like Crow were granted all the rights and privileges of citizenship, except the privilege of receiving the tribe's annuity payments, when the Choctaws passed the Freedmen Bill on May 21, 1883. Those who did not desire to become citizens and those who did not register under the Freedman Bill were considered intruders and subject to forced removal from tribal lands.[49] Regardless of Crow's bloodline, he had not registered as a Choctaw freedman and therefore was not considered to be a citizen of the Choctaw Nation. On August 12, 1884, a warrant for Crow's arrest was issued by Stephen Wheeler, the commissioner of the U.S. District Court in Van Buren, Arkansas, charging him with murder. Crow would be tried at Fort Smith in Judge Isaac Parker's court, not in the Choctaw courts.[50]

Considering the number of cases in which noncitizens living in Indian Territory were accused of serious crimes, the federal government was aware that something needed to be done. In 1851, the U.S. Congress authorized the federal court for the Western District of Arkansas in Van Buren jurisdiction over the western counties in Arkansas and all of Indian Territory.[51] In 1871, William Story was appointed as the district judge, but after corruption charges Story resigned in 1874. His replacement Isaac Parker was born in 1838 in

Belmont County, Ohio. Parker had served as a city attorney in St. Joseph, Missouri, circuit attorney, circuit judge, and U.S. Representative from Missouri's seventh congressional district from 1871 to 1875. During his tenure as judge, he tried an impressive 13,490 cases, with 344 of those being capital crimes.[52]

Parker's reputation as the "hanging judge" was earned because he did indeed sentence 160 convicted criminals (four of them female) to die by hanging (although only seventy-nine actually died on the gallows), but the image of Parker as an eager executioner is not so well founded. He dealt with some of the most vicious individuals to haunt Indian Territory. Parker was well aware of the lawlessness of the territory, and he also knew that white intruders were the main source of the problems. Parker estimated in 1885 that "seven-eights" of his "business" came from Indian Territory. Despite the large number of cases he saw that dealt with tribal matters, Parker admitted that he had never been to Indian Territory, had never sat in on any tribal court proceedings, and had no knowledge of how the tribal courts functioned.[53] That knowledge, however, was not necessary for him to severely punish murderers and rapists, and to a lesser extent horse thieves, whiskey runners, and timber poachers. Nevertheless, Parker barely put a dent in the violence that pervaded the tribal nations.[54]

The ever-growing white population was stressful enough, but the violence proved worse. Criminal activity and violence in Indian Territory had become so overwhelming by 1866 that Chief Allen Wright remarked that "every species of lawlessness, violence, robbery and theft" had spread through the Choctaw Nation.[55] In 1867, he commented that the number of murders had not subsided probably because of the volume of transient criminals passing through the tribal nations. Out of serious concern he then proclaimed that those noncitizens who wanted to live in the Choctaw Nation had to acquire permits to stay. The strategy proved effective for only a few years, because by 1869 many of the county officers had resigned before their tenures were completed, leaving many parts of the nation without law enforcement and no ability to punish intruders.[56]

Isaac Parker. Judge at Fort Smith from 1875 to 1896. Among the men he sentenced to hang was Jackson Crow, one of the men who murdered Charles Wilson in 1884. Courtesy Western History Collections, University of Oklahoma.

Jackson Crow had already met Judge Parker before Charles Wilson's murder. In 1882 he served as witness for the defense of Edward Folsom, a Choctaw man executed for the murder of William Massingill. In 1883, Charles Wilson, then a U.S. deputy marshal, and T. A. "Bert" Brown took Crow to Fort Smith to stand trial for the murder of one Uriah Henderson. Witnesses recounted that Crow admitted killing Henderson and had even shown Wilson the grave. But Henderson's body was never found, and ultimately Crow gave bail and agreed to return to the court when there was "sufficient time to hear and decide upon the charge against him." Crow then hurried back to the Choctaw Nation and nothing more was done about the murder of Henderson because the Wilson killing overshadowed that case.[57] Of note is that during the two months that Wilson and Brown kept Crow in custody, Wilson and Crow conversed in Choctaw quite a bit and at one point Crow informed Wilson that on his escape or

Some U.S. deputy marshals who worked out of Fort Smith. Courtesy Western History Collections, University of Oklahoma.

release he would kill Wilson and Brown. Deputy Brown recalled that Wilson laughed as he translated what Crow had said, and that Wilson did not take the threat seriously.[58]

Jackson Crow had been raised in an unstable and dangerous society, and, not surprising, he proved himself skilled with firearms. He knew the Kiamichi Mountains well, and after Wilson's death he easily avoided capture. In the meantime, of the ten men originally arrested, four were formally charged by the Choctaw court with the murder: Allen, Benton, Conser, and Perry. Crow is named on the docket despite the U.S. government wanting to try him at Fort Smith. Because Crow had gone into hiding for over a year, another arrest warrant was issued on November 20, 1885.[59]

Although formally charged with murder, Robert Benton still got what he wanted. The voting results for the sheriff and representative races remain missing, so it cannot be ascertained who actually won the election; but with his adversary Wilson dispatched, Benton became the Sugar Loaf County representative to the Tribal Council.

Regardless, in October of 1884, just two months after the murder of Wilson, Robert Benton was recorded as a member of the Choctaw House of Representatives from Sugar Loaf County. He was even appointed to draft the rules and regulations that governed that legislative body.[60]

Why was the accused murderer Benton allowed to be present at the General Council meetings? According to the Choctaw Constitution, "Representatives shall, in all cases except by treason, felony, or breach of the peace, be privileged from arrest during the session of the general council, and in going to and returning from the same."[61] That Benton, a man who had been charged with murder, was allowed to attend the council meetings illustrates the courtesy extended to those in league with the political entity in power. Sometimes, powerful political figures or simply good friends of the current Choctaw leadership got more attention than those of the opposite political party. As an example, McCurtain, the principal chief in 1881, supported the tribal council's bill making an appropriation of a reward of one thousand dollars for the arrest and delivery of William Hughes, the man accused of murdering Joseph Lanier, the Progressive Sheriff of Skullyville County, in 1881.[62] There would be no such bounty offered in the case of the murdered Nationalist Wilson.

Another curious aspect of this case is that Wilson is not listed as a voter in the poll book, even though a number of witnesses saw him at the election on August 6. Also missing from the list of voters are the men who claimed to have seen him at the courthouse, his friends who assisted in recovering his body, as well as other residents of Sugar Loaf County who voted in previous elections. But, all the arrested Progressive men are listed as voters. The pages listing the election results for sheriff, representative, county judge, and ranger also are gone.[63] There is no concrete explanation for the missing names and pages, but it is curious that the election judges were Fleema Chubbee (spelled "Felemachubbee" in the poll book), who served as the guardian of Edward Benton, a close relative of Robert and Charles Benton, and Nail Perry, a man whose mother had owned Crow and who later served as a witness for Crow's defense at the Fort Smith trial. In the 1884 election, the "election judges" in every precinct just happened to have voted for the winner of their precincts and the majority of them were Progressives.[64]

There is no mechanism to prove that pages were purposely removed or that voting lists were altered, but there is no way to disprove it, either. It was not until 1890 that the tribe specified a somewhat secure method for recording and tallying votes, and even then it was not theft proof. In the 1830s the candidates and their supporters were separated into lines by lighthorsemen and the appointed judges counted the number of supporters in each line. The judges then submitted their tallies to the district clerks who passed the tallies on to the district chiefs.[65] Apparently, the judges were required only to "do justice according to law" and make certain that no one voted after the polling closed.[66]

By the 1860s, the tribe realized that standing in line behind one's choice was not an accurate way to count votes, so in October 1860 an act was passed authorizing the county judges to appoint three "discreet" election judges in each precinct who would create two poll books for the district and county judges and two for the principal chief and national officers. The election judges made a public proclamation about the date and time of the election, then provided ink, paper, and pens. The judges selected two election clerks whose responsibilities included writing election tickets for each voter, collecting the tickets before writing down the names of voters, and marking the voters' favored candidate next to their names and under the appropriate columns. After the voting was completed the clerks tallied the columns and give "certificates of election" to those with the highest number of votes. The clerks then certified and sealed the poll books and returned them to the national secretary to be stored in the Nation's "archives." Interestingly, a perusal of the poll books shows that in many instances the election clerks were supporters of the candidates who won in their precincts. In the 1884 election, for example, in every precinct, the election judges just happened to have voted for the winners in each of their precincts. Although the Choctaw Nation created laws that were supposed to punish anyone who was found guilty of tampering with votes, influencing voters, allowing unqualified men to vote, or any number of other possible transgressions, the opportunity for vote tampering was undeniable.[67] Piecing together who was victorious for the offices other than chief in the Sugar Loaf election of 1884 has to be done by perusing court and Senate documents to discover who is listed in those positions.

Eighty-eight men are listed as voters that day in Sugar Loaf County; for chief, the Progressive McCurtain won eighty-three votes to Folsom's five, perhaps indicating that despite the Nationalists' claim of winning the debate on the night before the election, the Progressive voters were in the majority in that part of Sugar Loaf County. Numerous Nationalist names are missing from that list, however. If all the residents had voted, then perhaps the outcome would have been a bit different. In the end, McCurtain was elected chief, defeating J. P. Folsom 1,578 votes to 1,044.[68]

Like other Choctaw murder cases, there are no testimonies available. The only item available for scrutiny is the court docket (almost illegible in faint pencil), which is brief with no elaboration, along with the Fort Smith court case file.[69] After the jury listened to the evidence and debated the case, they declared the men not guilty ("Hvttvck anuhtukle choli ish pia toh ohoni tuk v. Bob Benton, Peter Consor, Dixon Perry, John Allen aiena kvt inidiyable keyv acbilel itibia a haffoshke.") and the four were released on May 13, 1886.[70]

Why did the jury come to this decision? John Slaughter, a man initially arrested, watched Benton shoot Wilson, but he was afraid to state in Choctaw court what he witnessed. He swore twice to the Choctaw grand jury that he did not witness the murder, but on the third time he revealed the details.[71] According to Slaughter (who reiterated his testimony at the Fort Smith trial), when Benton and Wilson met on the road the day after the election, a sarcastic exchanged occurred, with Benton saying, "Good morning Charley." Wilson replied, "Good morning Bob." Benton then asked (even though he knew the answer), "What office do you hold?" Wilson answered, "I am Deputy Marshall." Benton asked Wilson for his "papers," but Wilson did not have any.[72] Benton requested Wilson's pistol and Wilson refused to give it to him. Benton felt along Wilson's side for the gun, then Wilson told him it was on his other side. Benton took the gun and asked, "What have you got a grudge against me for?" before quickly shooting Wilson three times. Benton then began hitting Wilson in the head with the pistol butt. Wilson fell to his knees and managed to take a hold of the pistol while still in Benton's hand so that Benton could not pull the trigger. Crow then stepped forward and shot Wilson in the back. Benton snatched the pistol out of Fisher's hands and shot Wilson again. After Wilson had been dispatched, Fisher asked for Wilson's pistol and Benton gave it to him. Benton mounted his horse, turned to the group and said, "You all keep this to yourselves; if anyone tells this he will be served the same way."[73]

According to Choctaw law, no one was allowed to carry a weapon in the Choctaw Nation except sheriffs, deputies, lighthorsemen, and the militia. Choctaw police were authorized to take pistols from offenders and to levy a fine against them. But Wilson was a U.S. deputy marshal, everyone knew it, and the law did not apply to him; but, he apparently did not carry papers stating that he served in that capacity. Benton and some of the other men carried pistols and rifles, thus implying that they were either deputies, or else deputies Conser, McCurtain, and Fisher had asked Agent Tufts or a Choctaw judge if they could summon other citizens to assist them in the arrest.[74]

Benton, however, is not listed as serving as a deputy that year. Further, Robert Isham held the position of sheriff of Sugar Loaf County in 1884 and it seems odd that he did not take part in the confrontation if Wilson carrying a weapon was perceived as a serious transgression.[75] The question remains as to why Wilson, a U.S. marshal, prominent tribal officer, and former lighthorseman with no criminal background would be deemed worthy of such attention other than the reality that he and Benton were political rivals who intensely disliked each other? Clearly, the Progressives held a beef against Wilson, and Benton took the lead in the confrontation. Benton's declaration of the pistol law apparently was his and his companions ruse in the plan to eliminate a political threat, and the jury found it a convenient rationale to declare them not guilty of murder.

That Slaughter initially refused to testify is not surprising, because those accused of the murder were prominent Choctaw citizens. The comparatively poor Slaughter—who was not politically influential—took to heart Benton's threat. Although Slaughter finally told what he knew, he also had already sworn twice that he did not know anything. Consequently, the court arrested him for perjury.[76] Yet the Choctaw grand jury that heard Slaughter's version of events declared the men not guilty anyway.

The other Progressive witnesses who were arrested for the murder, namely Charles Fisher, Jim Franklin, Joe Jackson, Ned McCalis, and Cornelius McCurtain, were not about to testify against their friends and political allies. Joseph Jackson, for example, was such a devout Bentonite that he later stated that he did not even know what position Benton was running for, but voted for him anyway.[77] The main reason for the verdict was that the jury consisted of an array of Progressives. The jury members—Jimpson Thompson, Jackson Sam, Edmund Pusley, James King, Dave Moshumeutubbe, William Hawkins, John Pulcher, William King, Lyman Bohanan, Hiram King, William Nahe, and Jack Roe—were prominent politicians, county officers, and wealthy landowners who knew each other and had solid histories of voting for Progressive candidates.[78]

For examples, Lyman Bohanan, Hiram King, James King, John Pulcher, and Edmund Pusley voted in precincts in which McCurtain won over Folsom.[79] It is unknown how Jimpson Thompson voted in 1884, but in 1892 he voted in the Okchanak Chito precinct that overwhelmingly voted for Jones over Jackson (141 to 1).[80] The affluent Bohanon leased out much of his land to coal mining entrepreneurs.[81] James King and Hiram King also voted for the Progressive Thompson McKinney for National Secretary in the 1879 election (McKinney was later elected chief), and James King's name appears in a poll book for an unknown district in which Jones received the majority of votes over Jackson in the 1892 election for chief.[82] James King himself was found guilty of violating the pistol law in 1883, but obviously that had no impact on jury selection.[83] Hiram King attended the Choctaw Academy, and a decade after Wilson's death can be found in the court records as violating the permit law, but he died before the case was tried.[84] James King had been sheriff of San Bois County in 1874, violated the pistol law in 1883, then a few months after the Wilson murder attended the 1884 General Council meeting at Tuskahoma as member of the Senate with fellow Progressives Robert Benton and future chief Wilson Jones.[85] In less than a decade, Benton had become an influential enough Choctaw to be elected captain of the militia. Jurymen Dave Moshumeutubbe and John Pulcher knew Robert Benton well enough to be appointed as two private militiamen in 1893 after the explosive uprising following the election of Progressive Wilson N. Jones as principal chief over the Nationalist Jacob Jackson.[86]

John Pulcher and Edmund Pusley were related. Captain George Pusley's daughter, Phoebe, married a Pulcher who settled in the vicinity of present "Pulcher" in Pittsburg County, and started a farm about the time of the Civil War. Their son, juryman John Pulcher, served as a deputy sheriff, as sheriff, and later as county judge of Gaines County.[87] In 1884, the quarter-blood Pulcher voted for the Progressive McCurtain for principal chief.[88]

Slaughter may have been arrested for perjury, but note that in the court ledger book, two pages after it is noted that Benton and the others were released, there is another entry that states Slaughter and "Felemontubbee" were to be paid the rather large amount of five hundred dollars by the court for "appearing day to day and court to court until discharged."[89] Both men were in the Choctaw court room during the 1886 trial, and there is no notation as to their specific duties, perhaps implying that the men were firmly in the control of the Progressives. Nevertheless, because the prominent Choctaws were not punished for Wilson's murder, the blame had to fall on someone. This meant the only person left to face the charges was Jackson Crow.

While his colleagues accused of murder awaited trial in the Choctaw Nation, Crow hid in the Poteau (Kiamichi) Mountains. Deputy T. A. "Bert" Brown spent thirty-two frustrating days searching for Crow after Wilson's death and never saw him. Then in December 1885, Marshal Charles Barnhill of Krebs received an arrest warrant to apprehend Crow, and soon afterward Barnhill, Deputy Marshal Algie Hall, and their posse of eleven full-bloods spent nine days tracking Crow before chasing him to his log home. Crow refused to come outside so the posse waited in the freezing weather for several days until January 2, when Barnhill's feet became frostbitten. In pain and losing patience, Barnhill set fire to the building. Crow, fearing for the lives of his wife Kitty and his children, surrendered. After Crow's arrest, the posse doused the fire in order to save the house. Meanwhile, Crow admitted to Barnhill that he rode with Benton because Benton was supposed to arrest Wilson for violating the pistol law. According to Crow, Benton tried to take Wilson's pistol, but the latter refused and after the two men struggled Benton shot him. Then Peter Conser shot Wilson in the back. Crow's statement to Barnhill was the extent of his confession, because at the Fort Smith trial Crow claimed he could not speak English.[90]

Hall slept handcuffed to Crow the first night and then again at the home of John McClure, a white intermarried citizen the second night. Barnhill, his deputies, and prisoner Crow then commenced the cold and uncomfortable trek to Fort Smith, Arkansas. Along the way Barnhill lost a few toes to frostbite. The distance from Poteau Mountain to Parker's court is approximately thirty miles, a comparatively shorter distance than what many other alleged criminals traveled to get to Fort Smith. Some transgressors who were arrested farther west and south reportedly had to ride a month in a deputy sheriff's wagon or on horseback with their hands tied.[91] Barnhill did not travel alone with Crow; their posse was provided for them by law, as were the cooks. Deputy marshals had a tough job escorting prisoners over difficult terrain, especially if they had to deal with more than one prisoner; someone had to always be vigilant while the prisoners were transported in a wagon and slept guarded in a tent. Nevertheless, many lawmen were killed or injured while escorting prisoners.[92]

At Fort Smith, Crow faced squalid prison conditions for almost a year until his trial began. As observed by Anna L. Dawes, the daughter of allotment proponent Henry Dawes, the crowded, stifling, and smelly cells that were situated under the courtroom were prime examples of "mediaeval barbarity." Prime opportunities for conflicts arose daily, as the cellar housed everyone from full-blooded Indians to white men to black men and mixed-bloods of all types with a range of personalities. Some men were indeed cold-hearted murderers, while others were imprisoned because of a misunderstanding or comparatively minor transgression. Those bitter men convicted of a murder and sentenced to be hung were allowed to mingle with those who had not yet been tried and who may have been innocent. There is no way to determine how many impressionable men were negatively influenced by the vicious stories told by the "wild and ungovernable men around them."[93]

The ceiling was only seven feet high, and each cell had four small windows and one doorway. No sunlight and few breezes reached the prisoners because a large veranda stretched the length of the building. During the summer the flagstone floors were wetted down, resulting in "rising steam and dampness." The men slept on wooden cots that doubled as chairs during the day, and prisoners were given "slop pots" with which to wash their faces. They were allowed to more completely wash only occasionally in a communal water barrel. Their toilet consisted of an open urinal tub that sat in the old fireplaces with the flues serving as ventilation. Since there was no running water inmates were required to "honey dip" the pots with buckets and empty them in an outside pit. Dawes aptly describes the place as "horrible with all horrors—a veritable hell on earth." She places the blame for the conditions on the U.S. government and not the city of Fort Smith, because in 1884 a U.S. marshal had sent a report to the Department of Justice detailing the serious problems with the jail cells and nothing was done.[94]

Arkansas attorney William M. Cravens, who had served in Judge Parker's courtroom, told the Committee on Indian Affairs in 1885 that the site of the Fort Smith courtroom was an "abominable place," mainly because the prisoners were kept directly below the courtroom, where during afternoon sessions "there is a very bad odor." He even claimed that he thought it was "an amusement" to Judge Parker to hold court in such a place. Parker sarcastically told the committee's chairman that he "forgets that I served in the House of Representatives, and it is much better here than there."[95] Actually, Parker did not like the Fort Smith jail accommodations. He claimed that there had been fewer problems with "sickness and disease" in

the ten years that he had served, but he did not approve that criminals were confined together regardless of the seriousness of their
crimes. Parker seemed especially concerned about younger men
coming into contact with those hardened criminals who might teach
them inappropriate behaviors.[96] Jackson Crow did indeed encounter
a variety of personalities during the long year he languished in the
prison before his trial began.

Crow found representation from the experienced trial lawyer
William M. Mellette of the Fort Smith firm of Barnes and Mellette;[97]
but no available list of jurymen for Crow's case exists. Judge Parker
did reveal that jurors were selected without prejudice to their political
affiliation, race, or previous servitude. He asserted that he had never
seen "a better class of jurymen" as he had at Fort Smith and the
black and white men served together as jurors "without rancor."[98]

Numerous witnesses took the stand to tell similar stories about
Wilson's murder. Most agreed that on August 5, the male citizens
of Sugar Loaf County met at the county courthouse near Summer-
field to eat watermelon, drink whiskey, and debate. Wilson and his
nephew Edmund Pickens had ridden twenty miles to the courthouse
from Wilson's home, spending the night under a tree by the side of
the road. Along the way Wilson reminded Pickens of the rumor
that Robert Benton and Jackson Crow planned to kill him (Wilson).
After arriving at the courthouse Wilson tied his mule at the gate and
Pickens watched him confront Benton. The men spoke in Choctaw
about the gossip that Benton planned to dispatch him. Benton loudly
denied that accusation. Benton and Wilson parted company then
resumed their arguing that evening.[99]

The next morning, August 6, as Pickens prepared to leave the
courthouse to find paper and ink for the election judges, Benton
intercepted Pickens to assure him that he held no animosity toward
his uncle. After voting, Wilson and Pickens rode to friend Simon
Tachubbee's to eat dinner and then started toward Wilson's home.
They had not traveled half a mile when nine of Benton's cronies overtook them. After informing the two men that carrying weapons was
violation of Choctaw law, Wilson and Pickens were arrested and
escorted back to the courthouse where Benton waited. Pickens agreed

to give up his pistol. Wilson carried a rifle and pistol, and after he and Benton quarreled about Wilson's right to carry weapons, Wilson relinquished the rifle, but not his pistol. Perhaps weary of bickering, the argument ceased when all agreed to take up the issue a week later. After departing the court grounds, Wilson told Pickens that he planned to stay at the Goodnight's boarding house instead of riding all the way to his home, so Pickens bade his uncle farewell for the last time then went on to Wilson's home. What happened during the night is a mystery, because Mary Goodnight states that she had dinner waiting for Wilson but that he never showed up. Other witnesses, however, report that Wilson once again faced his adversaries the next morning.[100]

Choctaw Joe Jackson stated in court that the morning after the election, the ten men originally arrested had ridden together down Towson Road. Crow informed Joe Jackson that Wilson was to be killed, so the unnerved Jackson left the group with the intention of heading home. He had gone but a short distance when he heard a loud "whoop" behind him, so he turned and went back. Out of sight, he heard Benton ask Wilson what office he held, followed by a bit of conversation, then several gunshots. A few moments later, Benton and the other men caught up with Jackson and told him not to tell what happened. Jackson did not witness the shooting, but correctly guessed that Wilson had been shot, so he went home. Out of curiosity he returned to the scene a short time later where he saw a bloodied Wilson on the ground surrounded by another group of concerned men.[101]

The Fort Smith jury heard all they needed to in order to find Crow guilty of murder on February 8, 1887. Damning testimonies left no question that Crow assisted in Wilson's murder; but Crow's attorneys nevertheless had a few more things to say, and they motioned for a new trial. First, the defense argued that Crow was a freedman and should be tried in Choctaw court. They claimed that Charles Benton, the forty-two-year-old probate judge of Sugar Loaf County and brother of Robert, claimed to have registered Crow and his sister as citizens of the Choctaw Nation in July 1885. Benton claimed that he did the registering because Crow had no horse at that time and could not travel to San Bois County. Thomas D. Ainsworth, the chief commissioner of the Freedman's Registration, and Cooper Conser, a relative of Peter (all of whom were Progressives), substantiated the claim that Benton registered Crow. That claim was discounted at the trial, however, because if Crow had indeed been registered, it took place after the murder. Of note, however, is that there is no Crow surname on the freedman rolls.[102]

The defense also argued that not all the witnesses to the murder had testified. On July 30, 1887, several men, including Peter Conser, Henry Jefferson, Elum McCurtain, Charley Benton, and Thompson Cooper were called to Fort Smith. They never arrived. Perhaps they were leery of the many bandits that roamed the area or did not wish to brave the poorly maintained roads and bridges that led to Fort Smith.[103] One man who hauled freight back and forth from Indian Territory to Fort Smith stated that he often saw dead men lying by the side of the road on his route. Government Agent John W. Lane commented in the late 1880s that the Choctaw Nation's roads were in bad condition because "Indians never devote any labor to the highways." Indeed, Choctaws would use a road until it became impassable, and instead of repairing it would choose another route. There were few bridges crossing over waterways, which often meant that travelers would have to take much time finding ways to pass. Another reason may have been that in the late nineteenth century, witnesses were paid only fifty cents per day for their services and were not reimbursed for food, hotel, or any other travel expense.[104]

One trip to Fort Smith for witnesses was arduous enough, but sometimes they were required to make more than one journey. Traversing the uneven roads, dealing with the wear and tear on wagons and horses, losing monies after being away from crops, and facing the possibility of being robbed (or worse) by the numerous criminals prowling the tribal nations were strong deterrents for witnesses and victims who had to attend trial to give testimony. But the witnesses for Crow's defense could have traveled together for safety in numbers, so most likely they refused to testify because they felt loyalty to Benton, whose political power and wealth continued to grow. Certainly, the family of the child who witnessed the crime had no intention of making the journey alone. The defense also maintained that Slaughter had sworn twice in Choctaw court that he knew nothing about the killing of Wilson but that he finally admitted to a Choctaw jury at Fort Smith that Benton had shot Wilson.[105] The objective, of course, was to allow Crow the same opportunity for exoneration in Choctaw court as Benton, Conser, Perry, and Allen. After all, the inconsistencies of the tribal courts were well known, as expressed by U.S. Indian Agent Robert L. Owen, who commented in his 1886 report that "the Indian courts as a rule are not well conducted."[106]

On one hand, one might think that Crow was the "fall guy" in this case because he was black. After all, the Choctaws had a history of trying to alienate blacks from tribal life. Reflecting the Choctaws' adherence to the South's value system, in the 1830s the lighthorsemen had the job of punishing "negro slaves" who acquired property. According to Choctaw law, "negroes" were not allowed to have any property or arms (unless he was a "good honest slave" with a "written pass from his master or mistress"), and any individual who violated the law could be "driven out of company to behave himself" or receive ten lashes dispensed by the lighthorsemen if he should commit the transgression a second time.[107] Moreover, the captain of the lighthorsemen was responsible for executing a bill of sale for the purchaser of runaway negroes,[108] and, on October 15, 1846, the tribe declared that no slave could be emancipated without petition of the owner to the General Council. If the former slave ever returned to the Choctaw Nation he or she could be arrested by the lighthorsemen and offered for public sale.[109]

The tribe was not keen on intruders settling on their lands, regardless of their color. Article VII, section 11 of the Constitution of the Choctaw Nation, revised in 1842 and reiterated in 1852, stated that "from and after this adoption of this Constitution, no free negro, or any part negro, unconnected with the Choctaw or Chickasaw blood, shall be permitted to come and settle in the Choctaw Nation." The Constitution also forbade the tribe from adopting a "negro" or descendant of one into the tribe.[110]

The quality of life of a black man or woman in the Choctaw Nation varied. After the Civil War the Freedmen's Bureau became aware of "deadly persecution" toward blacks within the Nation. Some blacks were still enslaved by their "savage masters," who had become "more cruel in their treatment." Some Choctaws beat or shot their former slaves to death.[111]

Blacks and Choctaws intermingled, although it is not clear if they formally married. According to Progressive Choctaw Napoleon Ainsworth in 1885, he did not know of any Choctaw who had married a "darkey." Yet the *Branding Iron*, a newspaper published at Atoka, reported in 1884 that any "Negro" who married a Choctaw would not be granted tribal citizenship, inferring that they did marry.[112] Regardless, the freedmen were not allowed to attend schools alongside Choctaws, and they were not allowed to hold tribal office. Many Choctaws were of the hope that the United States would take the blacks out of their Nation, which was, according to Ainsworth, why the tribe took so long to decide what to do with them after the 1866 treaty.[113] Another opinion came from G. W. Harkins, a Choctaw lawyer and intermarried Chickasaw citizen. He believed that the "half-breeds and intelligent full-bloods" were fearful that the freedmen would join with the dissatisfied full-bloods and would then somehow "control the country" if the freedmen were adopted.[114]

Ten years after the Civil War ended the Choctaw Senate had proposed a bill enabling the chief to form a commission to confer with the Chickasaws about the 1866 treaty. Section 2 of the bill stated that the 1866 treaty "has died by its own limitations" and that not a single condition outlined in Article 3 of that treaty was binding. Further, the freedmen "have no title or interest in the land and moneys of the Choctaw and Chickasaw Nation, and if they were to receive either, then "such lands and moneys must be given to them as a matter of charity in expressed terms."[115]

Testimonies given by freedmen in 1884 reveal their fear that they would never receive equality within the Choctaw Nation. A common refrain about the freedmen after the Civil War was that even though they were legally no longer slaves, they had no money and no place to go. So, without other options many of them stayed with their former masters. Several men interviewed by the Committee on Indian Affairs expressed concern that they would not receive more than forty acres. They also wanted access to political office, to be able to marry Choctaw women, and to receive an education. Freedman Charles Fields stated that despite the reality that "the Indians raised me from a boy . . . I always got along with the Indians; we were always friends, except in one thing. I have no education. . . . They don't give us equal rights, and that scares me."[116] While it may be true that many Choctaws and freedmen were "friends," or at least collegial, not all Choctaws felt compassion toward blacks. "A very small portion of the Choctaw people are in favor of educating them," stated Choctaw Lem Reynolds in 1885. "We think they should be located in the western part of the country. The idea is to get them out of the country west of 98." Yet, in response to the question, "Is there a great deal of prejudice against the negro here?" Reynolds said, "No, sir."[117] Of course, a good many of the Choctaws he referred to were actually either intermarried whites, or mixed-blood Choctaw and white with a vested interest in keeping the freedmen from gaining any power or property in the Choctaw Nation.

Some Choctaws were not amenable to giving the freedmen much of anything, nor were they desirous of intermingling with them. A Choctaw woman who reminisced in 1910 about her school days at Tuskahoma commented about seeing the dark-skinned girls: "I have never been so scared in my life. I shake when I think about it. There were so many fullblood girls blacker than anybody you ever seen. . . . I don't believe they were all just Indian, they were mixed with this other race. . . . I cried and I cried and I cried because I was up there with them black kids. I just don't like the looks of [those] people. . . . That bunch of little old black kids I tell you just looked like flies flying around."[118] Another well-to-do Choctaw found it hard not to have blacks working for her after the war. In 1917, her comment says much about how she viewed the subservient role of blacks. While she was capable of cooking, washing and milking, she preferred not to: "Let me say right here, I never have got used to it. I feel better today to call a negro to wait on me."[119]

Even if no Choctaws were prejudiced against blacks, it would have done Jackson Crow little good. Despite the defense's objections and demands, Judge Parker upheld Crow's death sentence. President

Grover Cleveland declined to pardon Crow, who instead of acting like he did not understand the telegram allegedly said in clear English, "That's all right."[120] Fort Smith guards then relegated Crow to his unpleasant dungeon until his execution on April 27, 1888.

After a restless night of praying and some singing, the morose and reportedly scared Crow, along with two other convicted men who committed murder in the Choctaw Nation—Owens D. Hill, a black man who murdered his wife, and George Moss, a white man who killed another man—walked the short distance to the platform that stood in the southeast corner of the large courtyard. Hill wore a strange card pinned to his chest that bore the letters M, S, and B made from the hairs of his mother, sister, and brother. Clergymen Rev. R. C. Tylor and Rev. S. M. Fisher prayed with them, then the three men climbed the thirteen steps to the platform that stood six feet high. Below was a trench, three feet wide and three feet deep dug for those taller condemned individuals. The heavy hanging beam was twelve feet above the ground. After placing the nooses around their necks and black hoods over their heads, the trap was sprung by hangman George Maledon. As was common after hangings, because the prisoner's neck might have broken but the heart still beat, the three men hung by their necks for thirty minutes until surely dead. Around one o'clock in the afternoon the men's bodies were lowered. Crow and Moss were placed in coffins and then buried in Oak Cemetery. Hill's body was given to his sister.[121]

Despite Crow's execution, what remains troubling to Wilson's family even today is that Robert Benton had a clear motive to kill Wilson, but none of the eight men riding with Benton and Crow made any effort to stop the premeditated murder. The accomplices carried on as active participants in Choctaw politics and lived long, prosperous lives.

Robert Benton's role as murderer had no effect on his career. In the next twenty years his name appears consistently in the Choctaw political records. In 1885, the year after Wilson's murder, Benton became district attorney of Mosholatubbee District. Five years later the Eastern Precinct elected him senator.[122] He also acquired money and bought several home sites in the Choctaw Nation.[123] He served

Gallows at Fort Smith. Author's photograph.

as captain of the militia for Moshulatubbee District, at least in 1893, and then again in 1901.[124] In May of 1900 he was sworn in as district attorney pro tempore.[125]

Peter Conser, another of the released men, was a thirty-two-year-old half-blood in 1884 who farmed twenty-four acres. Conser also became wealthy later in life; by the 1890s he owned 660 acres and had established a blacksmith shop, gristmill, sawmill, and general store. He also was deputy sheriff and had been a candidate for sergeant-at-arms in the House of Representatives.[126] According to one biographer, "Uncle Peter" was "associated with the following Indians in tribal affairs [who] exerted a powerful influence: Ed, Jack and Green McCurtain, Alfred Wade, Gilbert Dukes, Jefferson Gardner, Thomas McKinney, and Ben Smallwood, all tribal chiefs and Wesley Anderson." In addition, Conser also was "associated" with prominent Judge N. J. Holson, who in 1892 would be targeted for death by the traditionalist Nationalists. It is unknown what "powerful influence" means other than the author's desire to elevate Conser's stature, but what is certain is that with the exception of Smallwood, all of Conser's colleagues were wealthy Progressives.

He established the Conser Post Office and built a store that operated until 1920.[127] Conser reportedly "entertained chiefs, senators, and other political greats from all over the Choctaw Nation" in his home outside Heavener, and after his death, his family donated the now famous Conser Home to the State of Oklahoma.[128] Oklahomans now celebrate him as the only lighthorsemen in Choctaw history to be "prominent," "a great Choctaw," and "no tough got tough enough to dare Peter."[129] Conser served as a lighthorseman for two months in 1887, for five months in 1892, and for six months in 1893. Intermittently he served as deputy sheriff of Sugar Loaf County in 1884, 1887, and 1888, and was sheriff in 1894. Although most of the men who were appointed to the post of lighthorseman served for less than one month (and some for just a few days), there were numerous, less affluent Choctaw men with no property to donate to Oklahoma who served longer than Conser.[130]Among the others who were exonerated for Wilson's murder, Charles Fisher became Garfield County superintendent in 1894;[131] Joe Jackson accepted the appointment of

Peter Conser. Conser was accused of being one of Charles Wilson's murderers, but was freed along with other Progressives. He later would become active in Choctaw politics and served as a lighthorseman. Courtesy Research Division of the Oklahoma Historical Society.

special deputy of Skullyville in 1903; and Fleema Chubbee received a commission as deputy sheriff of Sugar Loaf County in 1887.[132] Spring Hill Precinct citizens deemed John Slaughter trustworthy enough to serve as election judge for the 1894 election.[133]

Jackson Crow's reputation is completely different from the Choctaws who were exonerated. In his *Hell on the Border*, W. G. Harmon includes the *Fort Smith Elevator*'s article about Crow's execution almost word-per-word:

> On the morning of August 7, 1884, the dead body of Charles Wilson, a prominent citizen of the Choctaw Nation, was found in the road. The find created a great sensation, as Wilson was well known. . . . With the exception of [Jackson] Crow, all [the culprits] were Indians and could only be tried in Choctaw courts.[134]

Harmon, however, omits the last sentence in the original *Elevator* article, which reads: "The only regret expressed in this case is that some of his companions in the Wilson murder were not made to suffer with him."[135] Indeed, in most accounts, Crow is the man saddled with the reputation as the instigator of the murder, as if everyone else involved was innocent. Crow also is labeled as a "renegade," a "most desperate and very bad man,"[136] and "a bad citizen, mean, unruly, dangerous, and reckless" with "many other crimes" attributed to him.[137] Perhaps one Choctaw adequately summarized the guilt of the parties involved by stating that it was widely known that Crow could be counted on to support powerful Choctaw citizens in their "murderous designs" and that "the more prominent Indians used him as a means of disposing of an enemy."[138]

Wilson's family lived on. His son Archie (known to the elders in my family as Uncle Archie) later sported long braids and attended Jones Academy.[139] His daughter Ida became a skilled horsewoman; my grandmother Eula watched her mother ride her large black horse every day up and down the roads around their Red Oak allotment. Eula married Thomas Abbott Jr., the "middleweight [boxing] champion of the Southwest," in 1913–14. Abbott also served as chief of police of McAlester, Oklahoma, from 1933 to 1940 and coached the football team at Sacred Heart. His father, Thomas Sr., lived in the Choctaw Nation and worked as a physician for the mining towns around what is today McAlester, including modern day White Chimney, Scipio, Indianola, Canadian, and Krebs. Abbott was elected as the first mayor of McAlester and drew the blueprints of the town of North McAlester, which was incorporated in 1907.[140]

In retrospect, one wonders if anything—social, culturally, politically—would have been different if Wilson had lived to become the Sugar Loaf County representative. His rival Benton, the man with a motive to kill and who witnesses agree pulled the trigger first, held a very hard pro-allotment, pro-development stance. During a critical period in Choctaw/white relations, Benton voted to allow more railroads to enter the Nation. But as history tells us, many Nationalist Choctaws, like Silan Lewis, Willis Tobly, Daniel Bell, and Jacob Jackson,

Tom and Eula Abbott, the author's grandparents, ca. 1920. Eula was the grand-daughter of Charles Wilson, and Tom Abbott was the boxing champion of the Southwest (1913–1914), served as the chief of police of McAlester (1933–1940), and was the son of William Elliott Abbott, the physician who worked the Choctaw Nation's mining towns. Author's photograph.

as well as men from other tribes, such as Cherokees Ned Christie and Red Bird Smith and the Muscogee Chitto Harjo, also fought against the tide of white encroachment onto their lands and failed.

Despite the laws and treaties that attempted to spell out who was and was not considered a citizen and who had jurisdiction over the various people living in the Choctaw Nation, the matter of tribal citizenship is complicated. The U.S. Congress enacted the precursor to the Indian Major Crimes Act as the ninth section of the Indian Appropriations Act of March 3, 1885, which allowed U.S. courts jurisdiction over the Indians accused of the crimes of murder, manslaughter, rape, assault with intent to kill, arson, burglary, and larceny. In his 1885 annual report, the commissioner of Indian Affairs described the legislation as a "step in the right direction" and once again expressed the notion that "Indians should eventually become subject to and enjoy the protection of all laws in the same manner and to the same extent as other persons."[141] On March 1, 1889, Congress approved an act moving the western and southern parts of the Choctaw Nation from Fort Smith's jurisdiction and instead placing them under the jurisdiction of the federal court for the Eastern District of Texas in the city of Paris. That act also provided for a federal court at Muskogee. The latter had jurisdiction over cases "not punishable by death or imprisonment with hard labor," including larceny and assaults, and over civil suits involving more than one hundred dollars.[142]

Indian Agent Leo Bennett deemed the addition of the court in Muskogee a success, and that combatants in civil disputes no longer had to "shoot it out" to deal with their differences. And he meant that literally. Bennett was witness to enough violence that he commented, "In human society there exists a horde of incarnate canine appetites, restlessly seeking to slip the leash of law, that they may be unrestricted [to] indulge in vice and crime."[143] It sometimes seemed that almost everyone behaved badly. As one pioneer boldly described his lifestyle in the Nation, "As I grew older I did some horse thieving and cattle rustling along with my farming."[144] It should not be surprising, then, that as of September 21, 1889, five hundred suits had been filed at Muskogee. The judge, Hon. James M. Shackelford, was in Bennett's opinion, "a terror to the evil-doer" and the court as a whole "has proved a blessing to the country."[145]

Bennett essentially pleaded to have the Muskogee court enlarged, arguing that the increasing number of outlaws engaged in murder, robbery, whiskey running, gambling, and prostitution were ruining Indian Territory. Wrote Bennett, "Their influence is corrupting, their touch is pollution and their influence is demoralizing." Worse, their children were "nurtured in crime and do not know the right from the wrong." He also asserted that the court's jurisdiction should extend to civil cases over twenty dollars and cases involving divorce, child custody, and alimony.[146]

Bennett sang the court's praises, but the tribe was not happy with the creation of a federal court in Indian Territory. According to the Choctaw General Council and Chief Smallwood, the establishment of such a court demonstrated to the tribe that the federal government "hesitates not to exceed its legitimate authority and jurisdiction, and continues its encroachments on the Choctaw rights." Nor did the council think much of the persons involved in the cases. As far as the Choctaws were concerned, they believed that the federal court had "congregated around it a class of persons whose sole object is to manufacture litigation and multiply its causes." The council members did not deny the large numbers of serious crimes being committed in their Nation and in Indian Territory, but it maintained that the people associated with the courts knew nothing about Choctaw law or customs and probably were determined to extend their laws over all of Indian Territory.[147] Their fears were indeed justified.

Although Benton and other Choctaws were exonerated for the murder of Charles Wilson, it is interesting that in 1889 Agent Leo Bennett reiterated the sentiments of the former Agent Owen about the mediocre conduct of the Choctaw courts by arguing that no Indian should be disallowed from being afforded the same legal protection as white men. He was concerned that Indians were being denied the "peace, comfort, security, and perfect liberty" that was available to white men and that an Indian man was not "regarded as a man with a man's rights and privileges and a man's duties and responsibilities." He believed that the Indian agency system was "antiquated" and "detrimental to the higher development of man."[148]

It is not clear if he was speaking of those who were victims of crimes or those who were accused of them.

Even though the tribe demonstrated that it was capable of dealing with many crimes, the reality was that juries were often clearly prejudiced against the defendants even before hearing testimony. This was especially apparent in cases revolving around political infighting, such as the murder of Charles Wilson, the misdeeds of the wealthy Pusley family, the crimes of Chief Wilson N. Jones's son Willie, and the murders that occurred after the election of 1892 and that are discussed in the following chapters.

To be sure, the Choctaw judicial system was inconsistent in quality, fairness, and record keeping. But the Choctaws also had to contend with the issue of encroachment by the federal government into their jurisdiction. Although the lighthorsemen were given the authorization to arrest those who had allegedly committed crimes, events did not always run smoothly. In 1883, the fifty-one-year-old Thompson Nowahaya from Kiamitia County served as captain of the national lighthorsemen, and John Bohanan was a deputy sheriff of Kiamitia County.[149] Together they attempted to arrest Alexander Shield, a white citizen of the United States who violated the pistol law by carrying one. In the process, Shield was killed and Nowahaya and Bohanan were arrested and taken to the U.S. court at Fort Smith to be tried for murder. The tribe approved the sum of five hundred dollars to pay attorneys Clayton and Cravens to defend the two Choctaw law enforcement officers.[150]

The trial of Jackson Crow and the subsequent refusal of Judge Parker and President Cleveland to overturn the case because of the claims that Crow was a registered freedman illustrates the confusion over who was and was not a citizen of the tribe. It also presented an opportunity for the federal government to intercede in tribal and federal court business. In Jackson Crow's situation, the government did not intervene. But it did in the case of Eli Lucas, a Choctaw accused of killing a black man in the Choctaw Nation ten years later.

The circumstances surrounding Lucas's case were similar to the those in the trial of Jackson Crow. In the Crow's case, his attorneys and some of his colleagues argued that Crow was a registered freedman and therefore should have been tried in a Choctaw court. Regarding Choctaw Eli Lucas, the victim in the case was deemed a black man, not a registered freedman, yet the federal government had other ideas about that. What is also interesting is that no place in the testimony in the case of Jackson Crow is Crow referred to in offensive terms. In comparison, the language used in the trial of Eli Lucas almost a decade later is shocking in how casually the attorneys and witnesses use derogatory terms.

Prior to the Crow and Lucas cases, the Supreme Court had already made a ruling on the question of tribal citizenship in the case of *United States v. Rogers* (1846). In this case, Rogers, a white man married to a Cherokee woman, killed another white man also married to a Cherokee. Rogers claimed that he was immune from prosecution in a federal court because he was a citizen of the Cherokee Nation, but the court declared him a white man by race and he could not use political affiliation to change that.[151] Two years after Crow's execution, Congress passed the Act of February 6, 1889, in which section six granted the "writ of error" to the Supreme Court in all criminal cases tried in a U.S. court in which there was a death sentence. Two more years later, the Act of March 3, 1891, was passed in which section five allowed the Supreme Court to review a case when there was a conviction for a capital crime.[152] The government acted on this law in the case of Lucas.

In the fall of 1894, the Choctaw Eli Lucas was convicted of the murder of Levy Kemp, a black man (the court file refers to him in a variety of ways: "darkey," "nigger," "colored"). Prior to this crime, Lucas had violated the pistol law and committed assault and battery.[153] Lucas also had been taken to Fort Smith to stand trial in December 1894 for stealing a horse worth thirty dollars from a white man, N. C. Naylor. The court file states that he was given the option of being released on seven hundred dollars bail on the order that he return in February 1895 for trial or he would have to stay in jail; but this was a moot point since he was on trial for murder at the same time.[154] That same year, Eli divorced his wife Sisces for unknown reasons, although the court records show that he, the plaintiff, was the aggrieved party.[155] Lucas was a Progressive; in the 1892 election he voted in the Okchanak Chito Precinct of San Bois County, where voters overwhelmingly voted for Wilson N. Jones for chief over Jacob Jackson, 141 to 1.[156]

According to witness testimonies, Lucas had told his friends that he had deliberately followed Kemp from a ball game and killed him, with his rationale being that Kemp grew annoying to a "nigger woman," Hannah Sokay, with whom Kemp was staying. Lucas also told another witness that Kemp was "crazy," which was another reason he killed him. After hearing Lucas tell his story, some of the witnesses then looked for the body and found Kemp's dismembered skeleton, the arms missing and the skull laying a few feet from the rest of the bones because animals had found it after he had been shot. What is not revealed in the court records, but is stated in a newspaper, is that Lucas's attorney claimed that Lucas told this story as a joke, that it was not supposed to be taken seriously except that he wanted his friends to think that he was capable of killing. The attorney also asserted that despite the firing that had gone on in the area where Kemp's body was found, Lucas did not do the shooting. Rather, Kemp could have been shot by any number of other people.[157] Because Kemp was not a registered Freedman among the Choctaws, Lucas was tried at Fort Smith.[158]

The jury found Lucas guilty on June 11, 1895, and his attorneys filed an appeal on June 27. Isaac Parker disregarded the appeal and on July 9 of that year sentenced Lucas to be executed on October 1. Barnes and Rutherford, Lucas's attorneys, made a lengthy appeal, but what ultimately caught the attention of the Supreme Court was the issue of Kemp's status in the Choctaw Nation. Attorneys for Lucas charged that the Fort Smith judge erred by telling the jury that "in the first place, you are required to find that Kemp, the man killed, or the unknown man, if you believe that his name has not been established, was a negro and not an Indian. That means that he was a citizen of the United States. That means that the court has jurisdiction of the case under the law."

Further, the attorneys stated that the court erred in not telling the jury that if there was any testimony "tending to establish the fact that there were parties, citizens of the Choctaw Nation by the name of Kemp, that this was a circumstance tending to show that the man called Kemp was a citizen of the Choctaw Nation."

The attorneys also argued that the court should have made it clear to the jury that the government should have proved beyond a reasonable doubt that Kemp was not a citizen of the Choctaw Nation. The idea behind that, of course, was if Kemp was Choctaw, or a freedman citizen by Choctaw law, then the case would have been heard in Choctaw courts, not at Fort Smith.

The Supreme Court heard the appeal. In *Lucas v. United States* (1896), the court conceded that Judge Isaac Parker was correct in his assertion that Kemp had not been "adopted" into the tribe (and indeed, his name does not appear on any roll of freedmen). But the problem arose because "the allegation concerning Kemp's citizenship was not restricted to his being a negro, but added the averment, 'not an Indian.'" Further, the court stated that the government bore the burden of truth to prove that Kemp was not a citizen, not simply to presume that he was not. The court also stated that the judge erred in allowing the testimony of John LeFlore, who testified that he had heard Kemp state prior to his death that he had come from Little Rock, because that was a declaration against his interest.[159]

The court reiterated a variety of cases pertaining to jurisdiction over tribes, such as *Ex Parte Mayfield* (May 25, 1891), in which the court did not appear to deny laws and treaties that defined tribal, state, and federal jurisdiction, notably the Western District of Arkansas, the District of Kansas, and the Eastern District of Texas. The court cited Section 2145, Revised Statute, of the Act of March 1, 1889, which stated that "the general laws of the United States as to the punishment of crimes committed within the sole and exclusive jurisdiction of the United States, except the District of Columbia, shall extend to the Indian country," and section 2146, which provided that "the preceding section shall not be construed to extend to crimes committed by one Indian against the person or property of another Indian."[160] Additionally, the court had recently decided the case of *Alberty v. United States* (1896), in which it cited the Act of May 2, 1890, which provided for "a temporary government for the territory of Oklahoma," and stated that "the judicial tribunals of the Indian Nations shall retain exclusive jurisdiction in all civil and criminal cases arising in the country in which members of the Nation by nativity or by adoption shall be the only parties." The court interpreted that to mean:

> The parties to a crime, as well as parties to a civil controversy; and as, under the present condition of the laws pertaining to the Choctaw tribe, negroes who have been adopted into the tribe are within the jurisdiction of its judicial tribunals, it follows that the averment in the indictment in the present case that Levy Kemp, the murdered man, was a negro, and not an Indian, was the averment of a jurisdictional act, which it was necessary for the prosecution to sustain by competent evidence. Such averment implied that there were negroes who were, and those who were not, Indians, in a jurisdictional sense.[161]

Although it was clearly stated in the Lucas trial that Kemp was a "Negro," the court took issue with how the question of his citizenship was handled by Judge Parker. "As the accused was a Choctaw Indian, as the killing took place in the Indian Territory, and as Kemp was alleged and conceded to be a negro, the question arises, what was the legal presumption as to the latter's citizenship?" the Court asked. "Is it to be presumed that he was a citizen of the United States, or that he was a member and citizen of the Choctaw tribe?"

In what appears to be a case of the Supreme Court looking for anything it could possibly find to interfere with the case, the court ruled that Judge Parker was incorrect in his statements to the jury regarding Kemp's citizenship: "The view of the trial judge, therefore, seems to have been that a finding of the fact that the deceased was a negro established the jurisdiction of the court," they wrote, "by reason of a presumption that a negro, though found within the Indian Territory, was not a member of the tribe." The court argued that if there was to be any presumption, it should have been that "a negro found within the Indian Territory, associating with the Indians, is a member of the tribe, by adoption."

The court also cited the case of *United States v. Rogers*, in which Rogers, a white adopted citizen of the Choctaws, committed the crime of murder but was tried in federal court because there were no statutes that extended Indian control over the adopted citizens.[162] In the case of Eli Lucas, the Supreme Court argued that even if there was proof of Kemp not being a citizen of the tribe, Parker still erred by presuming Kemp was not a citizen and saying so to the jury.

Parker's decision on Eli Lucas was reversed in 1896, and according to Parker's biographer Michael J. Broadhead, the overturning of that conviction infuriated him. But this was not the first or last time the Supreme Court responded to appeals in such cases. Between 1891 and 1897, of the forty-four death penalty cases appealed from Fort Smith, the Supreme Court found reversible errors in thirty of them, and for the most part focused on Parker's instructions to the juries, just like in the Eli Lucas trial. In the appeal trials, sixteen of the thirty defendants were either acquitted or discharged; fourteen were once again found guilty of their crimes.[163]

Despite Jackson Crow's attempts for a retrial, the Supreme Court did not grant him one and President Cleveland refused to interfere with the proceedings. But the Supreme Court did interfere in plenty of other cases involving white and black men. As the time grew closer to when the government would make final plans for allotment of tribal lands, it appears that U.S. politicians felt increasingly empowered to intrude more into the jurisdiction of court cases dealing with Indians despite laws that spelled out who had authority.

The tribe continued to face the dilemma of how to deal with intruders accused of, and victims of, crimes. According to the 1866 treaty, those who intermarried with Choctaws acquired all the rights and privileges of a citizen: the right to vote, to hold office, to sue and be sued, to be tried for offenses, and to be punished if found guilty. A problematic case arose when a Choctaw by blood, Stephen Belvin, was charged with killing A. E. Powell, a white man and Choctaw citizen by intermarriage. Belvin was arrested and held for hearing at the circuit court of the third district. But he also was arrested and held for trial at the U.S. District Court at Paris, Texas, even though his being held was against the Article 38 of the 1866 treaty, which read, "Every white person who, having married a Choctaw or Chickasaw, resides in the said Choctaw or Chickasaw Nations, or who has been adopted by the legislative authorities, is to be deemed a member of said Nation and shall be subject to the laws of the Choctaw and Chickasaw Nations according to his domicile, and to prosecution and trial before their tribunals, and to punishment according to their laws in all respects, as though he was a native Choctaw or Chickasaw."[164]

A flurry of cases arose in the late 1880s in which the federal government overstretched its limits. Captain Joe Everidge, Turner Everidge, and Martin Everidge were charged with killing a white man Luther, a citizen by intermarriage, and were held at Paris under bond. Still another incident occurred when Sam Harris, a freedman, killed another freedman, Sam Brown from Towson County. Harris was then taken to Paris for trial instead of staying within tribal boundaries where he should have been tried.[165]

In August 1890, the Choctaws were once again indignant about the McAlester federal court that had been established in May. Chief Edmund McCurtain sent a letter to Agent Leo Bennett complaining about the option allowing Indians to take their oath of citizenship to the United States. It was McCurtain's belief that the only ones doing so were those who had committed a crime and wanted to escape being tried in Choctaw courts. And, he claimed to know some people who had done just that. McCurtain also took issue with the "collection law." He told Bennett that whites could make any claim against an Indian and take him to court and the Indian must pay, but when a white man owed an Indian money, then nothing could be collected from the white man unless he was worth at least five hundred dollars. McCurtain pointed out that many of the white intruders came to the Choctaw Nation without any money and when they ended up owing money to an Indian, it was never collected.[166]

In the decades to come, Choctaws remained troubled with citizenship discrepancies, the encroachment of federal jurisdiction in their business, and myriad other issues. The tribe adequately dealt with many of its legal problems pertaining to crime; but, as illustrated in the case of Charles Wilson, justice was not completely served. As the next chapters discuss, justice may have been done for one Silan Lewis, but not for others also accused of the same serious crime. And, improprieties within the Choctaw administration also went unpunished. Indeed, in nineteenth-century Choctaw society, cultural adherence and wealth determined who was in power, and power and fairness in the courtroom were not always synonymous. This was true not only for the Choctaw court system, but also with how the United States chose to deal with the tribe.

CHAPTER 2

NATIONALISTS AND PROGRESSIVES

These differences in political beliefs caused some pretty hard feelings among the Indians.

—Wesley McCoy

During the 1880s, life continued to be difficult for indigenous people across the United States. Tribes had been relegated to reservations and suffered the physical consequences of poor food, inadequate shelter and health care, in addition to the mental anguish of having lost their loved ones and their land. While whites celebrated the surrenders of Sitting Bull in 1881 and Geronimo in 1886, the Sioux and Apache tribes grieved. During this decade the already decimated bison herds were almost slaughtered into extinction by buffalo hunters; even though the Plains tribes had not been assigned to reservations, their hunting culture had changed forever. Farther away, the Northwest Coast tribes were disallowed from performing the Potlatch Ceremony. In 1887, Congress passed the General Allotment Act, resulting in the loss of millions of acres of tribal land. Two years later, two million acres of tribal land were purchased from Indian Territory tribes in order to facilitate the great Land Run. Choctaws were indeed worried.

Choctaw citizens read the various Indian Territory newspapers and discussed among themselves the fates of other tribes. Choctaws were cognizant of the power of the U.S. government to destroy them, but to their detriment, Choctaw factionalism solidified because the Choctaw political parties could not always agree on how to handle the many issues facing them, including allotment, white intrusion, crime, loss of culture, freedmen citizenship, per capita payments, railroads, coal mining, and the potential loss of control of their tribal government. In addition, the tribe was hampered by the dissatisfaction the conservative Choctaws felt toward the wealth of many of their fellow tribesmen and especially toward the opportunistic whites who used every means to extract as much as possible from their status as intermarried citizens.

To protect tribal interests and to keep the government out of their affairs, Choctaws often tried to make it appear to the federal government that there was no animosity among the citizenry. Because the Progressives were the most educated and verbally aggressive of the two political parties they did most of the talking to the U.S. officials. This seemed to please the government representatives. For example, at no time during the Committee on Indian Affairs interviews in 1884 did the committee members ask if the men speaking were representative of all Choctaws. One Choctaw, Sampson Cole, could not have been more obvious in what he was trying to accomplish when interviewed by the committee members. In response to every question about the state of affairs in the Choctaw Nation, his replies were constructed to give the impression of a subservient tribe willing to obey the United States:

Q: Do you know how the Choctaws feel towards the people of the States?
A: I know of no ill feelings towards the Government of the United States.
Q: Do the people of the Choctaw Nation want to make their Nation as much like the United States as they can?
A: They are striving towards a higher advancement all the time.[1]

In another example, in his 1884 interview with the committee, Progressive Napoleon B. Ainsworth claimed that although there were indeed Progressive and "non-Progressive" parties within the Nation, he gave the impression that all tribal members had a "friendly feeling" toward the railroads and toward the United States, when in reality the railroads were a sore point of contention within the Choctaw Nation. He also asserted that the Progressives were in the majority and increasing, and that the full-bloods were "as progressive as any of them."[2] Full-blood Robert Benton and some of his fellow tribesmen in Sugar Loaf County, for instance, were Progressives. But the reality was that the Nationalist faction was largely made up of full-bloods, and many of them had little interest in becoming imitation white men.

Ainsworth was correct, however, in stating that all Choctaws believed that the United States would not, in the future, honor its agreements with the tribe and that white people in general would "be unjust to everybody else." Therefore, he deemed it prudent to limit their rights in the Nation. He also expressed his concern about the tribes' "friends" in Congress after a Mr. Morgan of the committee commented, "I don't think there is a man in Congress of the United States who believes they have the power to do this [take your land]." Ainsworth responded, "I would agree with you on the Senate, but not on the House."[3]

Ainsworth, along with full-blood sheriff Sampson Cole and former judge E. F. Krebs, also expressed the sentiment of many of the Progressives in the mid-1880s. They stated their belief that the Choctaws were well on their way to becoming successful large-scale farmers and businessmen; but in the tribe's defense, they also conceded that they were not yet prepared to compete with the United States.[4] On May 26, 1885, many Choctaws told the committee that they desired the acculturation of their tribe, and they knew that the way to accomplish this goal was to focus on their children. The tribe had passed a law requiring that all children between the ages of seven and eighteen attend school, and if parents did not send their children they were required to pay a fine of ten cents for each day they missed. This was not a realistic goal, however; many Choctaws lived far from schools, so the law was not always enforced.[5] Cole thought Choctaw businesses might be able to compete with the rest of the country but was quick to add that it would not be for another "few generations, when our schools have had their full effect." He did not necessarily look forward to that time, but he also conceded that he was aware of the "history of the weaker party to a treaty."[6]

Ainsworth and Cole were not completely truthful in their statements to the committee. Cole claimed that crime and divorce rates had decreased, when in reality both had increased in several districts. He also stated there were no objections among the Choctaws to "any parties coming here" and "taking off coal"; but many Choctaws objected to the numbers of noncitizens building entire communities around coal mines. When it came to the freedmen, Cole stated that any "licentiousness" occurring in the Nation was on the part of "the whites and the blacks, not from the Choctaw women." He also claimed that the Choctaw men "do not go after the colored women." Cole further claimed that he arrested very few men for violating the liquor law. To the contrary, many lighthorsemen, sheriffs, and deputies made dozens of arrests each week for "whiskey having." The primary cause of violence throughout Indian Territory could in large measure be attributed to the overwhelming influx of whiskey into tribal lands. Louis C. Tennant testified the same day about the effects intoxication had on the Choctaws. He asserted that Choctaws did not have the "passionate love" for whiskey that the whites had but that they suffered the same effects from imbibing. In regard to the political divisiveness, Cole made the understatement that in regard to those protesting the election of certain chiefs, "It is contested sometimes very strong."[7]

Although Choctaws possessed differing ideas about the accumulation of wealth, retention of Choctaw culture, and how to deal with outsiders, members of both political parties wanted to maintain their identities and status as Choctaws. Tennant, for one, made it clear that all the Five Tribes were determined to keep their specific governments and sovereignty and "not . . . be together, one people."[8] The Choctaw Progressives hoped to create the impression of a harmonious Choctaw Nation in an effort to keep their Nation separate from the Cherokees, Creeks, and Seminoles.

While the men who testified before the committee calmly commented on the concerns that Choctaws had regarding the federal government's plans to allot their lands and phase out their government, the Nationalists were not as ready to pander or gently converse. James Culberson, a Choctaw clerk who transcribed dozens of court cases in the 1880s and 1890s (including the Nationalist trials that are discussed in subsequent chapters) stated, "The Nationalists did not simply react. For generations, these families had told stories of the removal, attempts at land grabbing, promises not kept by the government, greed of the white intruders and the disruption of their culture." He knew of many Choctaws who believed that the full-bloods should "have the majority representation in the tribe, not the wealthy mixed bloods."[9] The Nationalists planned to make clear their intense frustrations not only with the federal government's plans for severalty, but also with the way the Progressives had chosen to deal with the tribe's problems.

As previously mentioned, one of the most influential families in Choctaw politics was the McCurtain family, the most notable of which was Jackson F. McCurtain, a Progressive elected chief in 1880. His younger brother Edmund succeeded him as chief. In 1886, yet another Progressive, Thompson McKinney, with strong support from the McCurtain family was elected chief. McKinney prevailed over Nationalist Benjamin F. Smallwood, a mixed-heritage Nationalist with a lifetime of experience in Choctaw politics and business.

Benjamin was the son of William Smallwood, a mixed-blood (his father Elijah was an Englishman born in South Carolina and his mother a Choctaw woman), and Mary LeFlore, a French-Choctaw mixed-blood and the sister of Thomas LeFlore. William and Mary Smallwood arrived in Indian Territory during the removal and settled in Kiamichi County to farm. William served as a member of the Choctaw General Council in 1863, and Benjamin attended school at Shawneetown and the Spencer Academy.[10] After finishing school, Benjamin assisted his father on the family farm and by 1847 struck out on his own as a farmer and rancher. That year he also served as a ranger in Kiamichi County. Like many ranchers, Benjamin also operated a mercantile business, accepting cattle for merchandise, and it was not long before he became one of the wealthiest men in the Choctaw Nation. In 1849, he married Annie Burney, a Chickasaw; after her death during the Civil War, he married Abbie James. Although barely out of his teens, Smallwood also acted as speaker of the Choctaw House of Representatives on four occasions. Before

Principal Chief Thompson McKinney (1886–1888). The Progressive McKinney was elected because of the strong support he received from the McCurtain family. Courtesy Research Division of the Oklahoma Historical Society.

entering politics more seriously, he served as captain in the Second Choctaw Regiment in the Confederate Army. In 1881, he opposed the granting of a right-of-way to the Frisco Railway (while Robert Benton, T. D. Ainsworth, Joseph Everidge, and other Progressives favored it). During his time as a Choctaw politician from 1847 to 1890, Smallwood also traveled to Washington, D.C., as a delegate.[11]

Smallwood lost the election to Thompson McKinney in 1886, but he defeated Wilson N. Jones in 1888. Jones was the youngest son of a mixed-heritage father, Captain Nathaniel Jones, born around 1827 in Mississippi in the Greenwood LeFlore District. The elder Jones was known as a Pearl River half-blood (his mother was of the mixed Choctaw and French Battiest family) and a member of the Okla Falaya clan. Nathaniel served on the Choctaw General Council

Principal Chief B. F. Smallwood (1888–1890). The Nationalist Smallwood experienced a difficult time as chief since the House and Senate at that time were almost entirely Progressives. Courtesy Research Division of the Oklahoma Historical Society.

and as an annuity captain who was responsible for the distribution of annuity payments to the tribe. After surviving the removal in 1833, the family settled on the Little River.[12]

Jones's first wife, Rachel Pickens, was daughter of the Chickasaw chief Edmund Pickens, and Rachel's brother married the sister of Charles Wilson. After Rachel died in childbirth, Jones, always aware of the rewards of an opportunistic union, married Luisa LeFlore, the granddaughter of District Chief Thomas LeFlore, in 1855. Wilson Jones started out as a farmer. Although he was not formally educated, he did have a knack for business. A Jones family legend is that Wilson was so poor when he lived in the eastern part of the Choctaw Nation that relatives looked down on him because he could not afford to properly salt his bread. His poverty did not last long, however, because after moving to Blue County he earned enough money as a farmer to establish a mercantile store three miles west of present-day Cade, Oklahoma. He accepted cattle in exchange for his goods, a strategy that allowed him to prosper so dramatically that his role in the cattle business became one of the catalysts for the rise of violence in Indian Territory.[13]

Jones's cattle business continued to thrive, and in 1867 he acquired a partner, James Myers. In four years the two obtained over one thousand head of cattle, which Myers drove to Fort Scott, Kansas. Myers took the money and ran, however, and was never heard from again. Despite being left with debt Jones remained undaunted, and shortly after the completion of the Missouri, Kansas, and Texas Railroad (MK&T), his mercantile business boomed. He moved to Shawnee Creek and diversified his business. He became the financial sponsor for B. J. Hampton and L. A. Morris's business at Caddo, but that endeavor failed. The business was in Jones's name, and he alone was left indebted to the St. Louis wholesale creditors. He lost in the resulting Supreme Court case, *Jones v. Baer, et al.*, the first case to be filed in the first federal court in Indian Territory.[14]

Jones remained determined to succeed in business, and by 1890 he managed to become one of the wealthiest men—Indian or white—in all of Indian Territory. His store, cotton gin, and apple orchard prospered, and his decision to invest in various coal ventures along the railway also proved fruitful. He built a "palatial" and "lavishly furnished" home near Shawnee Creek with fourteen rooms (one being large enough to use as a courtroom), each furnished with a fireplace. In addition to his business ventures, he also served as a school trustee in 1884 and national treasurer in 1887. He later built another sizeable home in Sherman, Texas.[15] Jones's only son William, or "Willie," was born in 1860 and educated in schools at Booneville, Bolivar, and Springfield, Missouri. The reportedly likeable Willie also was a temperamental alcoholic whose actions reflect the way crimes were handled in the Pushmataha (Third) District.

In the early 1880s, the modest cattle rancher and intermarried Choctaw Alex Powell opened a trading store. As the business grew, so did his herd. Powell ran a cord that was attached to a bell from

Principal Chief Wilson N. Jones (1890–1894) and his grandson Nat. The Progressive Jones was one of the wealthiest men in Indian Territory. Silan Lewis and other Nationalists were willing to kill Progressives to keep Jones and the Progressives from power. Jones escaped the tragedy of allotment by moving his large estate to Texas. His grandson Nat leapt to his death from the top of a sixteen-story Oklahoma City building in 1916. Courtesy Research Division of the Oklahoma Historical Society.

the porch of his store to his bedroom so those coming late to do business pulled the rope and Powell heard the bell. One night after he went outside to see who had rung the bell someone stepped from behind a bois d'arc tree and shot him twice. Before he died, Powell identified the shooters as Willie Jones and Steve Belvin. For years afterward, when Chief Jones rode by the site of the shooting he would stay far on the other side of the road and would refuse to look at the store.[16] One day, while that case simmered, Willie Jones and Madison Bouton conversed as they walked along the Main Street of Caddo. Bouton was a white man who had married Christina Folsom, the daughter of Israel Folsom, and stood as the rival cattleman for the open range in the area where the elder Jones ranched. According to witnesses, Jones suddenly drew his pistol, shot Bouton, and then mounted his horse and hurried home.[17] That his father, Wilson N. Jones, was the district chief at the time may account for why the case never came to trial.

Willie Jones did face a jury trial for the murder of Powell in February 1887. What makes the case significant is that the man assigned to oversee the jury was Jones's good friend, Chris Bench, who had conveniently been commissioned a deputy sheriff.[18] Also that month, the other accused murderer, Belvin, had been commissioned a deputy sheriff of Jackson County under Progressive Josh H. Crowder. The jury declared Willie Jones not guilty, but ironically, Bench would later play a role in Jones's death.[19]

There is no mention in the court record of Belvin standing trial for the crime, and he would later become sheriff of Jackson County after Crowder.[20] However, in another incident, Belvin attempted to shoot L. A. Morris, a clerk who worked in the Hancock Store in Caddo and the same man who left Wilson N. Jones high and dry after their Caddo business failed in 1882. This act apparently went unpunished as well.[21] In November 1887, Willie violated the pistol law and paid a five-dollar fine. That same year he was found guilty of adultery.[22]

Also in 1887, Willie Jones married Emelia McCauley. They produced one son, Wilson Nathan. Not one to settle into a calm life, in 1888 father Willie and his friends Tuck and Chris Bench and Jackson County Sheriff Josh Crowder, went drinking near Garrett's Bluff on the Red River. After emptying their whiskey bottles, they crossed the river into Texas to buy more. When they returned the men became angry with one another for some reason, and Tuck Bench shot and killed Willie Jones. Frightened for his life, Tuck Bench then left Indian Territory for Northern Arkansas and did not return until Wilson N. Jones died in 1901. After the elder Jones discovered his son had been killed, he had a steel-paneled jail built on the grounds of the Boggy Creek courthouse with the intention of imprisoning his son's killers in it, but they were never jailed there.[23] One Choctaw later commented that Jones would not have been so angry over the incident if the killer had brought the body home instead of leaving his son where he fell.[24]

Because Sheriff Crowder reportedly did not try to stop Tuck Bench from killing Willie Jones, he and Chris Bench went into hiding for a week after the killing. The Bench brothers and Crowder were indicted for the murder of Willie Jones, and thus a feud began between the Crowder and Jones factions. Belvin and the Bench brothers were brought before the court on February 3, 1890, but when their case was called, they pleaded "not ready." The trial was then set for February 5, 1890. They came before the court twice again, and both times the judge postponed the case. The Benches and Belvin attended the trial each day, but for unknown reasons the case never came to trial. Sheriff Crowder, however, never bothered to show up for the trial. He repeatedly forfeited his bonds but easily secured more, because there was no law in the Choctaw system that allowed for a collection on a bond. His case simply continued to be postponed from term to term until the issue faded away.[25] Years later, Josh Crowder met his fate when he and a friend were shot and killed by a few black men while trapping near Shawneetown on the Red River. According to one version Crowder had attempted to "leave the country" while out on bond, and as he boated down the Red River, the black men killed him, rolled his body into a wagon sheet, and threw him into the water. They took his watch, gun, money, and boat.[26] The killers were later tried and convicted in the federal court at Atoka and sentenced to life in prison.[27]

In the fall of 1888 Jones decided to run for Choctaw chief on the Progressive Party ticket, and he made it clear that he advocated education and adopting the ways of white society:

> Those of us who are old, and who knew the Choctaws when they were an uneducated people, when they had no written form of government, when the council was held around the campfire and might [govern] the actions of the assembled warriors, such of us can but be impressed with the changed and improved conditions of the our people. The wandering bands have now become one solid nation; the camp fires have been superceded by the legislative hall; the hunting grounds know the buffalo no more, and in their place has come, to stay, the farm.[28]

Like many Indians in Indian Territory, Jones desired to live like a white man, yet at the same time preserve his identity as a Choctaw. (Also note that because of the decimation of the bison on the plains, he mentions bison, even though Choctaws were not buffalo hunters to any notable extent. The Choctaws were mainly agriculturalists.) He also behaved like a consummate politician. To outsiders, he crusaded hard for the rights of his tribespeople and spoke about his love for the tribe: "I love the Choctaw people. I love our Nation and her government." Jones also was a master of doublespeak. He talked indignantly of the "covetous eye of the land grabber." But while the poorer Choctaws lived in small houses, sometimes referred to as "shanties," made of logs without plastering to keep out cold wind and often having little or no furniture or "comforts," Jones built a large and comfortable home and had more fenced land than any other Native in all of Indian Territory.[29] Jones meant that whites were the land grabbers, but although Choctaw law prohibited the fencing of more than one thousand acres by any one person, Jones had seventeen thousand fenced acres and five thousand head of cattle in the area between Caddo and Boggy River. About 550 of those acres were used for crops. According to one pioneer, if your fence was even one foot beyond that length, the lighthorsemen could sever the fencing.[30] Because of his power position, however, Jones never faced the inconvenience of a cut fence.

The tribe fretted for decades about the noncitizens who used their land for farming and cattle, so in 1870 the General Council passed a law prohibiting any citizen from leasing their lands for grazing. Those caught leasing land to whites paid the fine of 150 dollars, half of which went to the informant. Ten years later, the council passed another law prohibiting noncitizens from starting cattle business in the Choctaw Nation without a permit; and even then, they could not own more than ten animals.[31] Despite the law, in 1885 Chief Edmund McCurtain expressed concern that the Choctaw Nation could be inundated with the cattle of noncitizens. In response, an act was passed in 1887, over the veto of Chief Thompson McKinney, that forbade any noncitizen from raising citizens' cattle on shares.[32]

Jones lost the 1888 election for chief to Smallwood, but Smallwood's tenure would be troubled and volatile. Jones's followers were furious, and they wanted Smallwood to know it. Because the Progressives "threatened a political disturbance" during his oath of office, Smallwood was sworn in at the Roebuck Hotel in Tuskahoma rather than at the capitol, where the Progressives (who sat in the majority in both the House and Senate) were in session. Unfortunately, during Smallwood's tenure the political divisions of the Nation were so great that he did not accomplish much. The council, for example, consistently ignored Smallwood's recommendations for more schools; yet, after Wilson N. Jones later became chief, he reiterated the same recommendations. They were carried out with no credit given to Smallwood.[33]

Smallwood continued to espouse his conservative views, notably that he believed the Choctaw Nation should govern its own affairs without interference from the U.S. government:

> The law authorizing an appeal to the United States authority in cases where the matter of citizenship in the Choctaw Nation has been passed upon by the authorities of this Nation, should receive your attention. As it now stands it appears that any action by this Nation is useless because it determines nothing, but allows the claimant to set aside the findings arrived at and appeal the case to another tribunal. The action of the Choctaw Nation should be declared a finality in the matter. Interference with this right to determine the question of citizenship for our people cannot be safely conceded to any other authority.[34]

Smallwood certainly acted upon this belief after a payment due the tribe from the Leased District (land between the 100th and 98th meridians for the Plains tribes' use) arrived as per the treaty of June 22, 1855. By the terms of the treaty, the Choctaws received a paltry $600,000 and the Chickasaws $200,000 to lease seven million acres between 98 and 100 degrees west longitude. In addition, the tribes ceded their lands west of 100 degrees longitude.[35] By terms of the subsequent treaty of April 28, 1866, the Choctaws received an additional $300,000 for ceding all the formally leased land to the United

States. The stipulation was that within two years each freedman would receive 40 acres and full citizenship (except annuities) or one hundred dollars if they elected to leave the Nation. If the Choctaws did not admit the freedmen, they would not receive the money because it would instead be used to pay the 8,200 Choctaw and Chickasaw freedmen whether they decided to leave (and receive one hundred dollars) or stay (and receive their acreage, worth approximately $328,000); either way, the amount would be more than $300,000. Since most of them stayed in the Nation, they received allotments collectively worth $1,282,000. Ultimately, in 1930 it was deemed by the Court of Claims that the $300,000 was not for the cession of land, but only for the granting of land and citizenship to freedmen. According to the Court of Claims, "In the final analysis, the Choctaws and Chickasaws received nothing for the leased district lands, because the value of the lands finally allotted to the former slaves exceeded the $300,000."[36]

The complex Leased District issue remained a point of contention among the Choctaws. Smallwood illustrated why it was a sore point when he authorized distribution of the Leased District monies without a Net Proceeds Commission audit. That included him, of course, and he received $5,500. The fairness of the payment is questionable, but it does illustrate why the Choctaw politicians of both parties took such an intense interest in the matter of distribution payments.[37]

Unfortunately for Smallwood and the rest of the Choctaws, U.S. Indian Agent Robert L. Owen reported in 1888 to the commissioner of Indian Affairs his observation that all the tribes in his jurisdiction suffered from lack of social and political structure. "The Indians have apparently no power of organization," he wrote, and instead of possessing "centripetal motion and cohesion under dangers alleged," they demonstrated "only centrifugal motion." His assertions stemmed in large part from watching the intense political fighting between the Choctaws and Chickasaws and among themselves, in addition to the intratribal disagreements among the Delawares and the Cherokees.[38] This kind of negative commentary from outsiders continued throughout the decade until the Choctaws' lands were finally allotted.

Understandably, Smallwood did not feel eager about running for another term, but he did anyway. In 1890, he lost to Progressive Wilson N. Jones whose enthusiastic Progressive followers were determined to take control of the Choctaw government. Jones won by only about two hundred votes, however, which exemplifies how the tribe (or the men, at least) was divided between the Nationalist and Progressive parties. Smallwood did, however, win a place as one of two Nationalist representatives from Atoka County with William Harrison; other winners included Mitchell Harrison as treasurer, William Wilson as auditor, A. Telle as national secretary, and C. S. Vinson as national attorney.[39]

Both the Progressives and Nationalists expressed concern about allotment. Wilson Jones stated in 1890 that "as an individual citizen and as Principal Chief I am opposed to sectionizing our country."[40] But he stood against allotment for different reasons than the full-bloods. As Agent Bennett assessed it, the full-bloods were no longer blind followers of the "half breeds" and the intermarried whites—the men who "lay out for themselves large farms in the richest bottoms, graze the free grass of the country, reap revenues from the coal interests, and keep their hands upon the national purse strings." He compared the disparity of wealth to the full-bloods receiving skim milk while the wealthy mixed-bloods and whites skimmed the rich cream for themselves.[41] Indeed, the federal government wanted to proceed with severalty, and one of the rationales it used was that the full-bloods needed protection from the greedy mixed-bloods. Giving them their own land and not allowing it to be sold to unscrupulous buyers who would pay less than the worth of the land would provide that security.

Choctaw citizens held tribal land in common and were allowed to work a parcel as long they did not cross onto another's land. Some, however, appropriated more land than they could possibly farm. Some lived in large, rambling homes, while the poorer full-bloods lived by a stream or river sometimes next to other full-bloods on the same socioeconomic level. They hunted, fished, and farmed just enough to feed their families, and many of them did not take part in political activities.[42] The full-bloods were not necessarily jealous of the others' success in gathering wealth, but they did take issue with their greed and opportunism.

The old arguments between tribal members over allotment, sovereignty, lease payment monies, and white intruders came rushing forth in 1892, but with a greater intensity than before. Many of the Progressives were educated mixed-bloods who supported the reelection of the current Chief Wilson N. Jones. His Nationalist opponent was the college-educated Jacob Jackson, who represented, for the most part, uneducated, traditional full-bloods who were not willing to stay quiet about their concerns.

Both Jackson and Jones opposed the termination of tribal sovereignty, but for very different reasons. Jones appeared mostly concerned about the loss of economic advantages, including his own—most notably his large estate that would be broken up by allotment. Jackson focused more on the loss of cultural survival, self-determination, and the pride of the full-bloods and mixed-blood traditionalists. Other major points of contention between the two groups included the per capita payment of at least one hundred dollars to every Choctaw from the Leased District; the sale of liquor in the Nation and who benefited from the proceeds; the socioeconomic position of the freedmen in the Nation; the retention of missionaries as teachers in the school system; the introduction of new, potentially diseased cattle into the Nation; and the unequal balance of wealth and power within the tribe.

The flow of whites into the Choctaw Nation continued unabated. A prominent Choctaw leader during the early National period was Pushmataha, who had predicted problems and remained adamantly against allowing any intermarried white man a position of power in the Choctaw system of governance.[43] And he had good reason. At least by the mid-eighteenth century, white men had entered the Nation in large numbers and established trading posts and plantations, and many became major players in Choctaw politics and culture. Like they did in other tribal nations, white men married Choctaw women and produced mixed-bloods who eventually became prominent community leaders. These mixed-bloods were often educated in white schools and became exposed to Christianity, learned patriarchal thought subsuming females, and became impressed with the American system of governance. By the beginning of the nineteenth century, white encroachment on Choctaw lands caused much consternation among the wealthy mixed-bloods. Their accumulated wealth needed protection, and one way to accomplish that was to create a more desirable internal (tribal) system of law and order.

After removal in the 1830s, the Choctaws allowed whites to live in their Nation, but only if they had written permission from the tribal chief or the U.S. agent; any Indian who was not Choctaw had to obtain permission from the National Council. White merchants paid an annual tax of "one fourth percent" of the amount of their capital on each year's purchase, and the monies went toward suppressing whiskey running. Ironically, many of the white men made their living doing just that.[44] Dealing with whiskey, violence, railroads, and potential U.S. government interference proved stressful enough, but there also seemed good reason for concern about the white men who prospered from marrying Choctaw women. Once they realized how to become citizens, many of these men quickly took advantage of their situation. They acquired not only land but also wealth from ranching, farming, coal mining, and selling a variety of goods.

One Choctaw observed in the late 1880s that the white women who came to the Choctaw Nation and married the full-blood Choctaw men were often as undesirable as the white men. He thought that the full-bloods "might have benefited themselves very much if the women had possessed morals and intelligence, but they have been imposed upon by the most degraded types, and none but a race of desperate half-breeds is the result." He acknowledged that some of the intruders were decent people, but that others were "ignorant and indolent" and caused many of the Choctaws to "give way to their baser passions," which, he said, "irritates me every time I think of it."[45] Choctaw Progressive Robert J. Wood, who testified in 1885 before the Committee on Indian Affairs, expressed the feeling of many of his fellow tribesmen on this issue:

Q: How do your people like the idea of white men coming into your
   country?
A: Some of our people like it and some of them do not.
Q: Some good men marry into the tribe?
A: Yes, sir. They marry into the tribe and become good citizens, but
   there are some who don't marry, don't rent land and do nothing.
Q: Do some of these bad white men marry girls in your country?
A: Yes, sir.[46]

The continued influx of whites who married Choctaw women
created havoc. One white pioneer, William Ervin, commented, "When
I was a boy there were few white girls in this country. A fellow had
to marry an Indian or not at all." But he didn't necessarily bring his
heart into it. According to Ervin, if a white man wanted to marry a
Choctaw woman he had to find ten men who would vouch for his
good character, and the prospective groom also had to pay one
hundred dollars. Ervin had no intention of paying. "I said I would
not pay a hundred dollars to marry any woman, so I just went to
Antlers, got my license, and we went down to Goodland and got
Parson Gibbons to marry us." What many Choctaws found unaccept-
able was the reason why these white men married the Choctaw
women. For example, Ervin and his wife Nellie had divorced, but
with statehood came the opportunity for him to acquire land as an
intermarried citizen. "When we found that we were going to have
statehood," said Ervin, "lots of folks tried to get me to re-marry Nellie
under Choctaw law." One can only guess as to how enjoyable these
unions were. In Ervin's family, one brother married a full-blood
woman, separated from her, married another Choctaw woman and
they too, separated. Another brother married a full-blood, then separated, remarried, and separated again before marrying a white woman.
A third brother also married a full-blood; when she died he married
a mixed-blood.[47] This is not say the unions between opportunistic
whites and Choctaws always were the fault of the whites; the
Choctaws also had to agree to marry.

Another white man who profited from the laws that allowed
white men to become citizens of the Nation after marrying Choctaw

women was "D. Morgan," who married as soon as he arrived in the Choctaw Nation. After the marriage he immediately bought livestock and prospered by raising and selling cattle. He somehow acquired 3,800 acres of land eight miles east of Durant, with 1,500 of that land deemed rich farm land. Even allotment did not slow his determination to acquire wealth. He claimed to have received two hundred acres in the allotment process while other family members got one thousand acres. In his memoirs he states that he "had 1200 acres of rich farm land," which apparently means he had risen to the status of white patriarch over his Choctaw family. With profits from his ranching he attained "considerable interests" in Durant; in addition to donating to the local church and school, he helped build the First National Bank, which he served for twenty-six years, first as vice president and then director. Morgan then was part of the construction of the Durant Cotton Oil Company and a stockholder in the same. Like other wealthy intermarried white men, Morgan became "an intimate friend" of Chief Wilson N. Jones.[48]

Another impressively wealthy white man in the Choctaw Nation was Colonel J. J. McAlester, a former Confederate officer who had lived for a time with a man named Weldon. The latter surveyed the Choctaw lands for coal and apprised McAlester of his findings. McAlester learned his lessons well. Clearly determined to make a fortune, McAlester married a Chickasaw woman, Rebecca Burney (sister of Chickasaw governor Ben Burney), in August 1872, and that union gave him rights to settle in the Nation. After starting a variety of ventures, McAlester's discovery of coal around 1886 launched him into the highest economic class in Indian Territory.[49] Other men also profited from the discovery of coal. Because some Choctaws felt amenable to leasing the coal fields to outsiders in exchange for royalties on each ton mined, coal companies imported workers into the Choctaw Nation. The number of miners working in camps at Alderson, Krebs, Lehigh, Hartshorne, and McAlester— to name a few—steadily increased to approximately eight thousand in 1901. The Choctaws possessed a strong aversion to entering the coal mines, which is one reason why vast majority of coal miners in the Nation were non-Native.[50]

Miners often required medical attention and that meant untrained "physicians" flocked to the camps. The tribe as a whole had long since stopped using the services of the alickchis and most of the non-Choctaws would not have used one anyway, although some Choctaws certainly preferred to consult a traditional doctor. The problem of untrained men claiming to be physicians had become such a serious issue that in 1884 the General Council passed a law dictating that three citizens of the Choctaw Nation—who also were graduates of a reputable medical school—would serve as the examining board to test applicants who desired to serve as physicians in the Nation. Applicants would either present their certificate of formal training or would take an "exam" to ascertain their knowledge.[51] My great-grandfather, Thomas Elliott Abbott, for example, attended medical school at Paducah, Kentucky, for one year, then learned more medical care from two German doctors. After passing the tribal medical test, "Dr. Abbott" served as physician for the Bolen-Dornell, Dan Edwards, McEvers, and Galveston coal companies. He answered as many calls from Choctaw citizens as he could, accepting produce and chickens as payments for his services and reportedly "became acquainted with every pig trail within 30 miles of McAlester in any direction." He was so determined to get to needy patients that he often risked his life. On one occasion he spurred his horse into the Little Wild Horse Creek (also known as Cole Creek) and the horse was swept from underneath him and drowned. Abbott managed to salvage his instruments and then walked the eight miles to the patient's home where he delivered a baby. With Oklahoma statehood came more stringent regulations regarding physician qualifications. Abbott then retired from "medicine" and instead managed Hotel Eller, which served the railroad and stage coach passengers. He certainly made a name for himself, because citizens elected him the first mayor of McAlester.[52]

J. J. McAlester continued to prosper. He opened a general store, and after the construction of the railroad was complete, his store and coal business soared. Around 1885, the cities of South McAlester and North McAlester formed. In just a few ledger books featuring sales from 1891 to 1894, J. J. McAlester bought dozens of houses, herds of cattle, partial or entire coal claims or interests in the claims,

Dr. William Elliot Abbott, the author's great-grandfather and a physician who served the Choctaw mining towns and delivered two of Sally Beam's babies after Silan Lewis died and she married Choctaw George Beams. Abbott served as the first mayor of McAlester, and his son, Thomas, married Eula Self, granddaughter of Charles Wilson. Author's photograph.

and became the "guardian" of numerous minors. McAlester took advantage of being a sheriff's surety by watching the latter's activities and quickly bidding on all property the sheriff may have legally taken. Either his wife (known only as "Mrs. J.J. McAlester" in the ledgers) fell into the same buying mode as he did, or he used her name to buy properties.[53]

McAlester did not forgive trespassers on "his" Choctaw land. He wrote numerous letters to men who had either inadvertently or intentionally settled on any of his many properties. He made Richard Kincade and the Community of the Methodist Episcopal Church aware in 1891 that they trespassed on his claim and had no right to do so.[54] That year McAlester also wrote a straightforward letter to a James Townsend:

You are hereby notified that you are in possession of one certain stone house known as the Old Hall Stone House which is my property. I have paid for the said property. You are notified that you are occupying my ground unjustifiably and without my consult. And you have taken possession of my log stable and crib, and fence rails and have never paid any rent for the use of any of them, nor any compensation whatever for any of them. . . . I demand immediate possession of my said property.[55]

By 1898 McAlester had established himself as one of the wealthiest men in Indian Territory, and even the newspapers were concerned at his wealth and power. "J.J. McAlester seems to think that the poor white man in the territory is being, has been and will be, badly treated," wrote editors of the *Indian Citizen*. "McAlester is a specimen of this bad treatment and has grown rich under its fostering care. . . . The fullblood Indian is the one who needs to be protected." The *Washington Post* described him as "big and florid faced," with at least half a million dollars in mines, farms, cattle, and ranches.[56]

Jones's "good friend," the aforementioned D. Morgan, for example, was typical of many white pioneers who liked to point out their wealth by stating that "I have been unusually successful in most all my undertakings." Perhaps that is true, but also like many wealthy men who took advantage of the tribe, he also rationalized that "I have been a leader in every movement for civic improvement as well as a leader in every moral and religious issue that has developed through the years." He also illustrates the irony of the violence of Indian Territory. Like many others, Morgan railed against Indian Territory violence and the "rank animosity" that existed, but he also liked to boast that he knew the "noted bad men of their day," specifically Jim Therber, Tandy Fulsom, and Lon Gardner.[57]

Another white man who strongly supported Wilson Jones was Mattie Lou Ray Harris, who became Jones's manager around 1904 and later served as marshal of Caddo and deputy U.S. marshal. Harris described Jones as a "high class aristocratic man and the soul of honor." Harris was another man who had accumulated enough money living on the Choctaw lands that he was able to buy and sell cattle for his living after resigning from law enforcement.[58]

Jones indeed had made friends with McAlester, Morgan, and other elitist white men, but Jones also was an intelligent man and cognizant of the problems his Nation faced. He often mentioned issues of special appropriations and "race antagonism" in the tribe's dealing with intermarried whites, white intruders, and freedmen.[59] How he dealt with those issues, however, caused serious problems.

Jones carried on an incongruous relationship with the whites. On one hand, he never hesitated to criticize the white men, but on the other, he also had no problem befriending those who benefited him. Jones was not the only Choctaw leader who seemed a bit confused about the status of whites, and he appeared slow to comprehend the repercussions of allowing them the advantages of citizenship. Those Choctaws in power positions through the years had allowed white men who married Choctaw women to become virtual Choctaws, yet they complained about the power the white men had. The General Council granted permission for them to build toll roads and bridges, yet they would complain about how much money the entrepreneurs accrued. The council passed laws allowing intermarried white men to take as much land as they could farm but became angry over how much land whites managed to acquire. It appears that many of these leaders made decisions without foresight for the Seventh Generation—that is, the concept that the current generation should make plans to benefit the tribe seven generations into the future. This idea usually pertains to ecological aspects of tribal decision making but also can refer to decisions made about other crucial matters, such as the tribal land base, citizenship, and economic development.

The 1892 election became essentially a showdown between the tribal factions. Wilson N. Jones's opponent that year was the Nationalist Jacob Battiest Jackson. Jackson was a member of the Six Towns Indians (originally known as the Bay Indians from southern Mississippi) who moved west with his family in 1850. He lost his father Holbatubbee during the journey, and his mother passed away in 1864. Jackson attended Fort Coffee Academy and in 1862 enlisted in the Confederate Army. Jackson was then appointed sheriff of Skullyville County and elected to the same office the next year but resigned

Jacob Jackson, the Nationalist leader who never won the chief position, but attracted thousands of followers. Silan Lewis and other Nationalists were tried and sentenced to death after violently protesting the 1892 election in which Wilson N. Jones defeated Jackson by a miniscule margin. Stringently opposed to allotment and statehood, Jackson proposed that a faction of the Choctaws move to Mexico. Courtesy Research Division of the Oklahoma Historical Society.

in 1867 to attend school in Little Rock. Afterward, he attended King's College in Bristol, Tennessee, for a year; then the Choctaw General Council financed his education at Roanoke College in Salem, Virginia. On his return he built a home two miles west of Double Springs, later known as Shady Point.[60]

In 1874, Jackson opened a law practice in Skullyville and eventually was elected senator and national secretary. In the meantime he married Levicy Westley. A champion of education, Jackson can be credited with instigating the creation of the orphan schools and Spencer Academy.[61] Despite his education in white schools and success at what one could call non-Indian endeavors, Jackson continually found favor with conservative voters who became more vocal about their opposition to the number of white intruders who had illegally settled on their lands, to those who had intermarried with Choctaw women, to those who made large amounts of money from their use of Choctaw resources, to the intrusion of the railroads, and to those who profited from selling liquor.

Jackson firmly believed that Choctaws had the right to retain their lands in common and not have them broken up by allotment. He never backed down from that stance. For years Jackson reportedly never believed it really was the intention of the federal government to allot tribal lands and instead planned to use the provisions of the 1866 treaty to keep a consistent threat over the tribes in case of another Civil War. Jackson finally comprehended the whites' desire for tribal territory and he strengthened his resolve to save Choctaw lands.[62] Jackson's stance resonated with the conservatives, and he acquired hundreds of followers, mainly full-bloods. County Clerk James Culberson, who witnessed dozens of court cases and became familiar with the personalities and politics of the times commented, "The full bloods thought the mixed bloods were not Indian enough to love land like full bloods."[63]

Jackson argued against statehood because he feared white intruders would convert Choctaw hunting lands to farms. Rights would be taken away from Choctaws, they would pay heavy taxes, and a class system according to color would designate dark-skinned Choctaws as servants. On the other hand, Progressives expected intrusion, but they believed the Choctaws might profit by renting out their lands to white farmers. The roads could be paved, and the children could freely intermarry with whites without prejudice in order to enjoy the same privileges as the white people.[64]

Progressives and Nationalists were blunt in their assessments of each other. Inside a volume of Choctaw records is an undated note, a hand-written commentary written by an anonymous Nationalist who makes a comparison between those he perceived as disreputable Choctaw politicians and the notorious Cherokee outlaw group, the "Cook Gang":

> The action of the Cook gang in the Cherokee Nation is simply a verification of the old but trite maxim, "Chickens will come home to roost."

The Cooks, as I have been told, are Cherokees and doubtless the legislative custom is the same there as it is here, that is—"The fat cows eat up the lean ones." If so, the Cooks have been reared under a clandestine robbery carried on the Councils of their Nation for fifty-odd years. They likely have become so accustomed to see legislation benefit only a few to the detriment of the many that highway robbery may appear to them only [a] pleasant pastime and possibly they wonder why the Nation is exercising itself to its utmost to secure their arrest when they rob only non-citizens when the law-makers go scott-free although they have manipulated through councils many laws the benefits of which can inu-re [sic] only to the rich and affluent.[65]

As another individual commented years later, the more "wily" Choctaw politicians made sure to side with the Progressives so they might become recipients of what the powerful men of the tribe could offer them. Nationalists, however, "placed the continuation of tribal existence above all other issues" and met with continued and organized opposition from the Progressives.[66] As opposed to the "Non-Progressives" (as some people referred to the Nationalists), who were rightly concerned about what the federal government might have in store for the Choctaw Nation, the Progressives painted a rosy future for the tribe as long as the tribal citizens "would follow blindly into the modes and customs of the white men."[67] The two newspapers of the day also took sides, with the Atoka-published *Indian Citizen* supporting Jackson and the *Choctaw Herald*, published in Tishomingo, behind Jones. A review of both papers in the 1890s reveals how passionately both sides believed in their candidates. Not only were the editors of the papers direct in their opinions about the candidates, so were Nationalist and Progressive citizens who attacked each other with accusations of impropriety, lying, and corruption.

The Leased District money and its distribution to Choctaw citizens and to intermarried white men remained a major dispute between the two political factions. Specifically, the tribe argued over who should manage the money because whoever controlled the purse strings also had a hand in deciding who got paid. In 1891, Congress appropriated almost three million dollars to the Choctaws and Chickasaws in return for almost 2,300,000 acres of the Leased District that Congress had given to the Arapahoes and Cheyennes. President Benjamin Harrison was not amenable to the bill because he viewed it as the United States paying for lands it already owned. Harrison asserted that Choctaws were being "bilked" by their agents and attorneys but also said that it was preferable to the consequences of defeating the entire bill.[68] The Net Proceeds claim issue became more complicated as evidenced by the commentary written by a frustrated Wilson Jones after he visited Washington, D.C., as a Choctaw delegate in 1891 to try and secure the amount due the tribe:

> We called upon the Secretary of the Interior. The President was absent. The Secretary of the Interior said that he would have all things ready for the inspection of the President on his return. When the President returned the Secretary of the Interior went away and the President said that the matter was of such an intricate Nature and so difficult to be understood properly he could do nothing until the return of the Secretary of the Interior and advised us to return home and when in the routine of business he reached the matter he would notify us. . . . So we returned and waited the Call but up to the present time we have received no Call.[69]

Nationalists and Progressives remained worried about the passage of the 1866 treaty, which, in regard to payments, stated, "And pursuant to an act of Congress approved May 28, 1830, the United States do hereby forever secure and guarantee the lands embraced within the said limits, to the members of the Choctaw and Chickasaw tribes, their heirs and successors, to be held in common; so that each and every member of either tribe shall have an equal, undivided interest in the whole."[70] Because the political rivals were concerned about who would and would not get a share of the recently released monies, the old questions flared of who really was allowed to live within the Nation and who was considered a citizen of the tribe. Article 7 of the 1866 treaty stated that "all persons, with their property, who are not by birth, adoption, or otherwise citizens or members of either the

Choctaw or Chickasaw tribe, and all persons, not being citizens or members of either tribe, found within their limits, shall be considered intruders, and be removed from, and kept out of the same, by the United States agent."[71] The key to this list of intruders however, were the "exceptions," which according to the treaty included those individuals employed by the government (and their families), those traveling through or trading in the Nation (with proper licensing), and those given special permission to establish residence within the Choctaws' territory.

In accepting his party's nomination as a candidate for chief, Nationalist Jacob Jackson told the Choctaw citizens what they wanted to hear: that they could expect "fair play in every department of our government, in the courts, in the council and chief's office. . . . Our officers should be chosen of our very best men [. . .] who can and will do their duty and who will not disgrace their position of trust by continuous drunkenness as we have seen among our friends of the opposite party in high places at the general council." But, he also reiterated what his supporters talked about continually: "The National Party is opposed to the unwise legislation of April 1891, discriminating in the per capita bill against our citizens, the intermarried whites, because the treaty right of the intermarried white is clear."[72] The Nationalists stood against class legislation; that is, they wanted to include the intermarried whites in the distribution of per capita payments. One Choctaw explained that he felt sympathy for the whites because non-Indians had large families, while Indians have few or no children, and under this act the white children could draw more money.[73]

That the Nationalists—usually full-blooded, Choctaw-speaking, and passionate about traditions—were so fervent about paying the intermarried whites, many of whom were merely opportunists, is somewhat confounding. While Nationalists said they supported the intermarried whites receiving their share of the Net Proceeds funds, they were essentially saying they supported tribal sovereignty; that is, the Choctaw tribe as a sovereign Nation would honor the agreement with the United States to consider intermarried whites as citizens of the Nation.

In this respect, the Nationalists might be similar to those Cherokees who supported the inclusion of freedmen as tribal citizens because they were made so by an 1866 treaty.[74] But, by supporting the intermarried whites, those same Nationalists also would have to support those men they so vehemently disliked: the white men who only married Choctaw women to gain a foothold on the Choctaw Nation's resources. Many did not like the white men at all but believed that honoring their tribe's treaty agreement was more important. This is not to say the Cherokee freedmen were opportunistic. But, the Cherokees' vote to remove the freedmen as tribal citizens perhaps illustrates the enmity and confusion some Indians felt—and perhaps always will—about allowing non-Indians into the tribe.

The Progressives, however, did not favor allowing the intermarried whites to receive per capita payments from the Leased District. They often criticized whites for their problems even though the Progressive leaders were mixed-bloods, some being less than one-sixteenth Choctaw blood. But those Progressives who criticized the whites, like Wilson N. Jones, also had many white friends; Jones reportedly profited from relationships with the wealthy intermarried citizens. Indeed, in 1885, Napoleon B. Ainsworth, a prominent Progressive who regularly served in the Choctaw political system, blithely commented to the Committee on Indian Affairs that "I would say there was no prejudice" against a full-blood Choctaw woman marrying a white man.[75] The Progressives also were staunchly against the freedmen receiving any per capita payments. In fact, Jones did not want to pay anyone their share, but rather preferred to put the per capita monies into the treasury for the day when the tribe faced "severe trials or a famine."[76] The white men who supported the Nationalists often used peculiar strategies in their attempts to get their messages across about Progressives. One letter writer, "Naholo Sopokane" ("old white man"), believed that the Progressives were fearful that if the Nationalists won the election those with a higher percentage of Choctaw blood would get more of the Leased District money. The whites, he claimed, were opposed to the Progressives politically, but were their friends financially. Besides the business ventures, that claim did not make sense: the Nationalists were supportive of the intermarried whites receiving their share of the Leased District monies, but the Progressives were not. He wrote that "they [the Progressives] suffer from a 'peculiar epidemic,' ancient in origin, known among the Hebrews, Babalonians [sic], Egyptians, Greeks and Romans and is known among the English speakers as 'Ichforwriting.'" This, the writer continued, can affect the victims' brains "injuriously, causing the brain to expand to the point of bursting if pressure is not alleviated by scribbling written fantasies, imaginings and startling legends wherewith to regale the public ear and create public opinion." This letter writer also expressed his amusement at how some Progressives denied their white blood.[77]

The continued importation, selling, and drinking of whiskey also remained a significant point of contention. After the 1830s removals, the General Council authorized lighthorsemen to sell the possessions of any person who could not pay the fine for bringing whiskey into the Nation. Some whiskey runners and drinkers were adept at hiding their products, so the council saw fit to pass another law authorizing lighthorsemen to search any suspicious person's house or dwelling, wagon, boat, packhorse, bag, or saddle bags for "intoxicating liquors" and then destroy it.[78] Choctaw law required lighthorsemen to visit the neighborhoods within their districts at least twice a year to pronounce what essentially amounted to useless speeches about abstinence.[79] Ultimately, this fight over the influx of whiskey into the Nation proved endless and futile.

Fighting the whiskey traffic proved dangerous, so lighthorsemen did not always act alone. In 1848, they were authorized to enlist the aid of Choctaw citizens when they needed help apprehending a Choctaw accused of a major crime or if they needed help destroying whiskey. If that citizen agreed, he could earn one dollar. If the citizen refused he could be fined five dollars; two dollars and fifty cents could be divided between the lighthorsemen and the district attorney.[80]

In the 1880s a law was passed providing for three militia companies (A, B, and C) of fifty men each. These regulars served the orders of the chief and assisted the sheriffs in doing "things necessary for the preservation of good order," such as executing court sentences, arresting and guarding prisoners, putting down riots, and "spilling whiskey."[81] The liquor issue continued as a grave problem in the Nation, in part because citizens drank in secret. One pioneer recalls that drinking "bouts" took place in the woods, away from homes, where men would drink as much whiskey as they could, then would send runners to Fort Smith for more. Men knew that they would become intoxicated to the point of passing out, so beforehand they lit bonfires so they would have a warm place next to where they hit the ground. Women, it was noted, stayed out of this particular activity.[82]

Choctaws discovered whiskey available for sale on the Texas side, resulting in increased importation of liquor into the Choctaw Nation. One could float across the convergence of the Red and Kiamichi rivers on a ferry, so lighthorsemen strategically placed themselves along the banks in order to capture the whiskey runners. The more intrepid whiskey runners acquired the fastest horses they could find, then waited until the ferry almost reached the bank. They then kicked their horses into a sprint so they would hit the bank at full speed and hopefully outrun the lighthorsemen. The chances of eluding the lighthorsemen were reportedly fifty-fifty.[83]

Agent Bennett reported that in July 1889, at least five thousand gallons of liquor had been destroyed throughout Indian Territory. Ninety percent of the cases heard at Fort Smith—including murders, assaults, and robberies—had direct connections to the use of whiskey. Bennett estimated that at least one person died per day from the results of liquor consumption, and he considered whiskey running the "most pernicious of all evils."[84] The next year, Bennett stated that the percentage of cases stemming from liquor use hovered at ninety five percent.[85] A favorite spirit, particularly among miners, was "Choc Beer" a drink made from barley, hops, and a dose of alcohol as the base, although recipe variations included oats, corn, malt, sugar, and yeast. Fishberries (also called Indian berries or Oriental berries) was the chancy ingredient. The berries are indigenous to East India and contain picrotoxin, a highly poisonous constituent, which is why they can be used externally in very small amounts to kill head lice. Because fishberries also are used to slightly stun fish to make them easy to catch and a specific concoction can ease nausea, someone evidently thought its inclusion as an ingredient in Choc Beer might provide a desirable physical effect on the drinker. And it certainly did. Miners in particular liked it because they claimed it was a "tonic" and a healthier alternative to the available water that they claimed was polluted.[86]

Bennett expressed his frustrations about the importation and selling of liquor throughout his tenure as Indian agent for the Union Agency. Those who wanted to sell and buy it always seemed to find a way to avoid getting caught, and he admitted that despite the attentiveness of the Indian police, the consumption of whiskey, wine, and Choc Beer continued. In fact, in 1891, Judge Bryant of the federal court for the Eastern District of Texas in Paris, in contradiction to Choctaw law, ruled that it was not illegal to ship malt liquor to Indian Territory. In reaction to this good news, beer saloons were established in the southern and western sections of the Choctaw Nation. Indian Agent Bennett, however, cited Choctaw law and ordered the saloons to be closed and the liquor seized. The U.S. marshal for Indian Territory refused to accept the beer, and worse, when tribal officers took beer from white men in Lehigh and Coalgate, they reacted by filing lawsuits in the newly established federal court in Muskogee. Judge Isaac C. Parker compounded the problem by ruling that although according to Choctaw law beer was illegal, that law did not apply to U.S. citizens living in the Territory.[87]

In 1890, Bennett answered a letter from O. W. Case, the assistant superintendent of the Pacific Express Company, in which Case had asked what authority the Indian police had to search his train cars for liquor. Bennett answered that section 2130 of the U.S. government's Revised Statutes reads that no ardent spirits were allowed to be transported into Indian Territory, and anyone who sold liquor to Indians would be punished by imprisonment and/or fine. Section 2140 also stated that Indian police were authorized to search for and destroy beer, wine, and whiskey found in boats, wagons, sleds, and so on. He went on in considerable detail about the laws and jurisdictions of the Indian police, including a statement that Indian police who damaged a package by using "unnecessary violence" in searching it would be responsible for damages to that property.[88] Case was amenable to Bennett's explanation, and after Indian police

were allowed to inspect the train cars the amount of liquor transported in those trains slowed dramatically. But the Missouri, Kansas,
and Texas Railroad never allowed any inspections, which resulted
in a continuous flow of liquor into the Nation.[89]

The various rulings on who could buy and sell liquor, combined
with the tribe's desperate attempts to stem the amount of whiskey
and Choc Beer in the Nation, caused serious confusion and animosity.
The Nationalists accused the Progressives of allowing their white
friends to sell whiskey and beer in their saloons so all of them could
profit. And they certainly did because consumption continued among
the farmers, miners, merchants, and politicians throughout the Choctaw Nation. It is no wonder that the beer controversy exploded into
one of the most volatile issues before and after the 1892 election.

One individual, who called himself "Big Indian," typified the
sentiments of the other Nationalists about Choc Beer by asking,
"Where does our Choctaw County Judge get his authority by law
to issue confectionery license to non-citizens for the purpose of
running saloons in the Choctaw nation, to sell beer and other drinks
which is against our laws?"[90] The Nationalists also argued that the
Progressive leaders ignored the concerns of the Choctaw citizens
over the amount of liquor being sold in the Nation by noncitizens.
The responses they usually got was the "rationalization" that the
"whisky runners" possessed a U.S. license to sell liquor. Many writers
to the *Indian Citizen* argued that the Choctaw leaders were being
bribed to ignore their law and that "any citizen that has two ideas
above a pet coon knows that our officers have no right to destroy
the property of any non-citizen, in the way of spilling their beer,
but we do know that our officers have the right and power to stop
drinks of any kind from being sold in the Choctaw Nation."[91] One
writer referred to the "the lager beer council" of Tobucksy Council,
which consisted of corrupted Choctaws and noncitizens who strate-
gized to allow the white men to vote for Jones in the 1892 election.
Another suggested that Jones wanted to license saloons and use the
revenue to finance a tribal railroad that would bring Choctaws an
annual annuity.[92]

Indian Agent Dew M. Wisdom referred to the whiskey problem
as "a fruitful source of evil, disorder and crime," and that part of

the difficulty in dealing with the selling of Choc Beer was that women did much of the selling. According to Wisdom, women "are more troublesome to deal with and punish than a man."[93] Even if some women sold whiskey, men were the ones drinking it. After the nominees for the Gaines County Convention were announced in January 1892, the *Indian Citizen* admonished that "we want sensible and honest officials, so candidates will do well to keep sober during the canvass."[94]

Nationalists thought the Progressives were corrupt and even argued that many of the uneducated and poor Choctaws believed that if they did not vote for Jones, they might "live no longer."[95] Many Nationalists refused to roll over to that threat, like writer "Big Injun" who stated in a letter to the *Citizen*, "The Government license that they talk so much about does not protect them from the local laws and this is as plain as a Billy Goat on a rock fence. Now what are our officers going to do? They have either got to say that they are taking pie or throw up the sponge! . . . We want this business stopped."[96]

In June 1892, the Progressive Party passed a resolution stating that "we fully endorse and sustain the zeal and energy manifested by our Principal Chief in his efforts to suppress the sale of beer and malt liquor in the Choctaw Nation." Nationalists believed that resolution to be "a tissue of falsehoods, builded [*sic*] on a colossal lie. What has Wilson Jones done to suppress beer? Not a single thing." Writers also expounded on the "corrupt [Jones] administration" and the "false statements made by the Jones administration"; they contended that the administration's behaviors and statements were "indefensible" and would lead to "demoralization and revolution."[97]

What to do about the freedmen also remained a dilemma. Nationalists asserted that the Progressives had a "deep hatred for the Negro race," yet befriended them in case they could vote in the 1892 election. The proposed bill of October 1891 would have allowed them to vote, but it was repealed. It did indeed appear as if the Progressives "only pretended to befriend the colored citizens in order to use him." The freedman E. D. Colbert expounded on this "fair weather friendship" in a letter to the *Citizen*, in which he states that the freedmen "can be used at the polls as tools to select Indian officers . . . and when it comes for one to be shot or whipped at the post he is a fullblood citizen, but when it comes to share a part of any monies he is not known as a citizen."[98]

One writer to the *Citizen* named "National" wrote an interesting commentary called "The Wailing of the Pole Cats" in which he differentiates between three types of "cats" (Nationalists, Progressives, and freedmen). The "short stripe pole cat" (the Nationalist) is the "sweet smeller" who opposes progression. The "broad stripe pole cat" (the Progressive) mixes with other cats and destroys the family purity, that is, racial purity; this cat is also known as the "grand king." The "coal black pole cat" (the freedman) is hard to handle and to keep satisfied after being easily enticed by "dangling silver dollars" and endless barbeques and feasts at the "grand king's castle." With regard to the "coal black pole cat," "National" wrote, "You can rub him down 'til the election is over, and then if he is inclined to hump his feline back as his disappointment let the kittens go 'til we need them again."[99]

The Progressives also proposed that the Choctaw schools no longer be run by missionaries. Nationalists were not necessarily in favor of converting the entire Nation to Christianity, but they did argue that the missionaries were infinitely more desirable than those they believed would take their place: "boodle hunting political office seekers" and "evil doers." By contrast, the missionaries were "sober," "pious," and representatives of the being that would protect them from evil: God.[100]

Yet another difficulty stemmed from the numbers of white men establishing themselves in the Choctaw Nation as merchants. In an attempt to control the number of merchants in the Nation, the "permit law" was reiterated in the 1866 treaty with the Choctaws and Chickasaws. In the mid-1870s, that permit law was again revised, making it more difficult for traders to be licensed. Not only were traders required to obtain written permission from the chief, but they also had to secure the signatures of twenty citizens of the Nation (in 1876 this was reduced to five citizens) and disclose specifics about where the business was located and details of the projected capital and earnings. The merchants had to secure a one-thousand-dollar bond to guarantee their payment of the annual tax. The permit could be renewed annually, but only after the chief received an endorsement for the merchant from the revenue collector. Those mechanics, artisans, and merchants could also receive permits for twenty-five dollars a year. Noncitizen laborers also had to pay a tax, although the General Council periodically changed the amount of the payments.[101]

By the 1880s, enough deception had occurred by those required to pay taxes that the tribe felt compelled to pass a bill that would force those persons, companies, corporations, licensed traders, and those under royalty contracts who made "false statements of royalty or taxes" to lose their permit and in some instances to be removed from the Choctaw Nation.[102] Amos Tecumseh got a first-hand look at the effectiveness of the permit laws while serving as collector of permit fees from noncitizens and a head tax on all stock owned by noncitizens under the tenure of Chief McCurtain (1880–84). He met with much resistance to the tax from both noncitizens and citizens, who told Tecumseh that they objected to the permit tax because it drove away the men who leased land from them. While the tribe gained money from the taxes, the Choctaws who leased the land stood to lose. Noncitizens objected because they asserted that the Choctaw citizens had promised them that they would pay the tax if and when it was enforced.[103]

One white man who felt entitled to whatever he wanted from the tribe admitted that he decided to let the "Indian police" bluff him and not pay the money for the permit to farm on Choctaw lands. Every time the Choctaws came to collect the permit money, the white man took out his Winchester and said he refused to pay. They finally stopped asking him. He asserted that several white men were whipped for not paying their permits, but he attributed that punishment to them acting "timid" instead of being "bold" and refusing to pay.[104]

A variety of other inevitable issues arose in the months before the 1892 election. Many Nationalists worried that Spanish long-horned cattle entering the Nation carried disease and were infecting their cattle.[105] Another Nationalist felt indignant that Skullyville County Judge John Taylor had lived with a white woman for five or six years, knowing that as a privileged Progressive he would not be punished for illegal cohabitation.[106] Jones and his council also made some interesting legislation that angered the Nationalists. Apparently, the chief had no problem with excusing the bad behavior of his supporters. In April of 1891, he approved a resolution that would pardon one Willie Anderson of Jackson County, even though Anderson had, while drunk, fired a bullet into a Pullman car in Atoka. The rationale was that "he has always been a good citizen, and we believe truly that he will never again err in such a manner."[107]

Also controversial were the effects of the railroads, which continued to cross the Choctaw Nation. The St. Louis and San Francisco Railway, for example, started out from Fort Smith, Arkansas, to Paris, Texas, and ran across grazing land, which resulted in the deaths of numerous Choctaw cattle and horses; plus, Choctaw timber supplies were being depleted to make railroad ties. According to County Clerk James Culberson, who listened to many court cases, some of those full-bloods were angry at not only the intermarried whites and Progressives such as Robert Benton, J. W. Everidge, J. D. Dukes, and T. D. Ainsworth, but also at some Chickasaws, because they believed them responsible for approving the construction of the railroads.[108]

In the spring of 1892, rumors flew across the Choctaw Nation that the Nationalists were plotting to murder key Progressives. The Nationalists denied vehemently the accusations, and some of them refuted the charges in the *Indian Citizen*. "A Dark Skin; National Man," made his opinions clear: "We are going to vote with our mouths, we can't elect anyone with guns and 6-shooters. We are going to elect our officers all on the dead square. All you pie men that have got so much money to spree on if you would only quit drinking so much and got the snakes out of your boots, why you wouldn't always be imagining that someone wanted to kill you."[109]

For sure, Nationalists continued to hurl accusations of impropriety against the Progressives, but the Progressives did the same thing. Newspapers ran aggressive letters—usually from anonymous letter writers—that were taken to heart by members of both sides. Rumors of murder plots abounded, and the Nationalists remained convinced of a plot hatched by the Progressives to kill them. Some claimed to have an affidavit signed by turncoat Nationalists stating that the Nationalists Jonathan Dwight, Maurice Cass, Silas James, Matthew

Henry, Sol Folsom, Jones Thompson, William Bond, William Kinches, and Willamson Hunt were going to murder Progressives Green McCurtain, Lewis Lucas, Jerry Folsom, and Simon Johnson. Three prominent Nationalists—C. E. Nelson, Victor E. Locke, and J. G. Farr—accused the Progressives of creating the story for political purposes and claimed that one of the so-called Nationalists, Maurice Cass, was actually a Jones supporter. Once again, the Nationalists reiterated their concern that Jones was roughly riding over the Constitution, laws, and rights. They claimed that Jones had no business going to San Bois County to scrutinize this alleged and unclear assassination plot because the chief of the Nation had no legal power to investigate any criminal or civil cases.[110]

In 1890, Chief McCurtain continued the Choctaw tradition of presenting a false picture of the state of the Choctaw Nation to the federal government. He had embellished the condition of the political situation in the Choctaw Nation by stating that the tribe was "prosperous and happy" and that even though it had gone through an "exciting political struggle," there were "no hard feelings" between the political parties.[111] To refer to the 1890 election for principal chief as merely "exciting" demonstrated his penchant for propaganda. The enmity between the Progressives and Nationalists was so hostile that it compelled the new chief, Progressive Wilson N. Jones, to comment that that campaign was "the bitterest and most hotly contested campaign I have ever known in our Nation."[112]

To make matters worse, within the next two years the hatred between the Nationalists and the Progressives would erupt into exactly what McCurtain claimed was not happening: disturbances, hard feelings, violence, and murder. But to be fair, McCurtain, like other Choctaws who were well aware of serious tribal factionalism, was shrewd enough to understand what it might mean to his people if the federal officials perceived that the tribe could not peacefully manage its affairs.

A curious dichotomy had been at work in the Nation for decades. While many Choctaws complained about the greedy whites, they were also taking as much land as they could for themselves. Many were concerned about federal policies that were clearly intended to benefit non-Indians, yet at the same time those Choctaws in political power often manipulated the court system for their benefit. Many Choctaws resented that the U.S. government removed them from their homelands—a removal that resulted in the mass death of many of their family and friends, in addition to the continued destruction of their culture by missionaries and white intruders—yet a good many Choctaws married whites and became Christians. The Nationalists organized themselves to protest against allotment, white intruders, the railroads, and financial mismanagement, yet Progressive Choctaws tried to present a harmonious image to the U.S. government. It is no wonder that the election of 1892 also turned into a violent confrontation among those Choctaws and their white allies who so fervently disagreed with each other.

CHAPTER 3

THE ELECTION OF 1892 AND THE LAST LEAGUE OF THE CHOCTAWS

So we are going to elect Jacob Jackson or break a fiddle string.

—An anonymous Nationalist, 1892

On August 3, 1892, the male citizens of the Choctaw Nation cast their votes for chief; the two candidates were the Progressive Wilson N. Jones and the Nationalist Jacob Jackson. The Choctaw men also voted for county sheriff, representative, ranger, and judge. Because of past improprieties in the voting process, the tribe again changed its voting procedure, adding more layers of security in an attempt to prevent tampering with the poll books. But the new rules were not always effective.

According to the new laws, after voting was complete the sheriff or one of his deputies took the poll books from their district and delivered them to the county judge, who in turn gave the messenger a receipt for the books along with a note stating their condition (soiled, mutilated, etc). The judge then put the poll books into a "secure box" that could only be opened with a key by the national secretary. If the judge became ill or otherwise unable to deliver the poll books to the national secretary, then the latter traveled to the judge to gather the poll books in person. The national secretary passed the box to the Speaker of the House of Representatives and also received receipts. If the

Table 1
Election Results for Choctaw Chief, 1892

	Wilson N. Jones	Jacob Jackson
Apukshunnubbee District		
Wade County		
High Hill Precinct	6	30
Pushmataha District		
Atoka County		
Atoka Precinct	71	78
Black Jack Grove Precinct	9	51
Little Boggy Precinct	0	15
Red Oak Precinct	10	5
Round Lake Precinct	5	50
Sulphur Spring Precinct	3	40
Blue County		
Boggy Depot Precinct	9	33
Caddo Precinct	129	49
Durant Precinct	22	18
Jones Precinct	12	22
Jacks Fork County		
Antlers Precinct	3	50
Chickasaw Precinct	9	33
Nanih Hikia Precinct	6	16
Sardis Precinct	111	11
Many Springs Precinct	N/A	N/A
Unknown Precinct		
Jackson County		
Itakshish Precinct	20	2
Pigeon Roost Precinct	39	65
Fiale Hills	66	5
Kiamichi County		
Good Land Precinct	132	94
Good Water Precinct	8	20
Saw Mill Precinct	5	18
Sugar Creek Precinct	24	4
Moshulatubbee District		
San Bois County		
Little San Bois Precinct	6	100
Okchanak Chito	141	1

Table 1 (*continued*)
Election Results for Choctaw Chief, 1892

	Wilson N. Jones	Jacob Jackson
Skullyville County		
Brazil Precinct	59	47
Cache Precinct	10	20
Double Springs Precinct	9	9
Greenwood Precinct	1	12
Skullyville Precinct	53	23
Sugar Loaf County		
Blackfork Precinct	71	10
Easton Precinct	13	27
Long Creek	28	28
Spring Hill	22	7
Tobucksy County		
Folsom Precinct	8	7
High Hill Precinct	0	28
McAlester Precinct	42	49
Savanna Precinct	N/A	N/A
South Canadian Precinct	29	4
Unknown Precinct (probably Gaines County)	49	20

Results compiled from the 1892 precinct poll books in CTN 64.

speaker became incapacitated, he appointed another national official to act in his place.[1]

Despite the tribe's attempts at safekeeping the voting results, the process remained lengthy and there were plenty of opportunities to intercept the precinct poll books and manipulate the outcomes. Indeed, after the 1892 election, both Nationalists and Progressives intercepted some of the precinct poll books. Nationalists rationalized their actions by stating that Jones's supporters made up the majority of the General Council and asserted that the prejudiced council was planning to find a way for Jones to appear to be the winner regardless of the vote tally.[2]

In the extant poll books for the 1892 election, only ten of the seventeen counties in the Choctaw Nation are represented, along with merely a small part of what is probably Gaines County. Results are

Table 2
Indian Citizen Tally of Election Results for Choctaw Chief, 1892

County	Jackson	Jones	Total
Towson	147	12	159
Atoka	240	131	371
Tobucksy	168	88	256
Blue	132	191	323
Red River	138	121	259
Eagle	65	99	164
Skullyville	111	132	243
San Bois	101	146	257
Bok Tuklo	57	23	80
Cedar	86	18	104
Wade	45	100	145
Nashoba	67	130	197
Sugar Loaf	72	134	203*
Gaines	79	77	156
Jacks Fork	72	125	197
Kiamitia	136	169	305
Jackson	72	125	197
Total	1,833	1,799	3,622

*Incorrect tally.
Source: *Indian Citizen*, September 1, 1892. This tally was done at the National Party meeting at Atoka.

missing from the counties of Bok Tuklo, Cedar, Eagle, Nashoba, Red River, and Towson.[3]

One of the two precincts in which Jones did not win any votes was Little Boggy in Atoka County. Not surprising, at least five of the Nationalist men who would participate in the upcoming Progressive killings lived in that area. High Hill Precinct is notable in that it is the only precinct in which the polls records show who each man voted for.[4]

The *Indian Citizen*, however, shows a different tally from what is in the poll books. According to the *Citizen*, Jackson defeated Jones by a vote of 1,833 to 1,799. The newspaper had access to representative precincts in all of the counties, but this does not mean that all the precincts in all the counties were available to the paper.

Editorialists argued back and forth about the loss or gain of a few votes every time they were recounted by those who had a vested interest in the outcome. According to the Progressive vote counters, Jones won by a mere eight votes, a small enough margin that the Nationalists believed the votes had been manipulated. This infuriated the Nationalists, who remounted their accusations of Progressive vote tampering. The *Indian Citizen* persistently challenged the *Choctaw Herald* to explain how it was that Wilson Jones could declare himself the official winner. To further rationalize their argument that the Progressives were dishonest about the election, the *Citizen* reiterated the Nationalists' concern that the Progressives were attempting to lay the blame for every problem in the Choctaw Nation on either them or the intermarried white men. The *Citizen* noted that those Progressives who accused the intermarried whites of being the instigators of the tribe's problems were often those with only one-sixteenth or less Choctaw blood.[5] The voice of the Progressives, the *Choctaw Herald*, continued to claim that Wilson N. Jones had more votes, specifically reporting that Jones won in crucial Gaines County by 23 votes. But the *Citizen* argued that Jackson prevailed in that county with 79 votes to Jones's 77 votes. The *Herald* also calculated that Jackson won Towson County by 111 votes, while the *Citizen* claimed Jackson won by 185.[6] Both sides claimed that the other had "doctored" the results and had allowed noncitizens to vote. Clearly, a fair count would be difficult to come by.[7] That the voting results of the key precincts and districts were appropriated is quite possible since of the seventeen districts, only ten have results available to scrutinize. Interestingly, although the voters are listed in the poll books, how each person voted is not available as they usually are in earlier elections. For most precincts, what scholars are left with for the election of 1892 are the names of the voters and the tally results on separate pages. In most of the poll books, the names of the candidates appear alongside simplistic marks, that is, one vertical mark to signify one vote, four vertical marks and a diagonal one through them to signify five, and so on.[8]

Throughout September and October, editors of the *Indian Citizen* continued to rant at the *Choctaw Herald* for declaring Jones the winner and at the unknown persons who allegedly took a poll book that the *Citizen* claimed would have clearly shown Jackson was the winner of the election. "The tally of the votes delivered to the speaker of the house showed a majority for Jones of eight votes," the newspaper's editors wrote. "One poll book of Toboxy [sic] County which gave Jackson a majority of 40 votes was missing. Eight from forty leaves 32 majority votes for Jackson, which is what we have claimed for him all the time. Five precincts were thrown out in which there was only one vote for Jones and all the balance for Jackson. What do honest people think of such proceedings as this?" The *Citizen* accused Dick Naile, a deputy from Tobucksy County, as the culprit who carried the Tobucksy poll book and lost it. The *Citizen* questioned if the election judge or the deputy bore the responsibility of taking the poll book to the Supreme Court judge. The paper also asked for the receipt in order to clear Naile's name, otherwise, as the editors contradicted themselves, the blame should fall upon the Supreme Court judge J. G. Garland.[9]

Another point of contention between the parties was that among the missing poll books is the one from Gaines County in which the popular and well-known Nationalists Silan Lewis, Simeon Wade, William Anderson, and James Parker were listed as candidates for county sheriff, ranger, judge, and representative, respectively. There is no way to ascertain how many votes the men received, but other records indicate that the Progressive nominees—John Perry for sheriff, Billy Bee for ranger, Simon Nelson for judge, and Jackson James for representative—were the winners, either by honest vote or by tampering.[10]

The Nationalists were fed up. On the night of September 11, 1892, approximately fifty men including William Anderson, Daniel Bond (also seen in the records as Bon), Prymus Brown (a Chickasaw freedman also known as Thomas Brown), Joshua Calvin, Lewis Carney, Robert Carter, Kingsberry Harkins, Dan Jefferson, Sam Jefferson, Silan Lewis, Eli Lomas, Charles McCoy, Thomas McGee, Robert Miller, Johnson Parker, Houston Perry, Price Tallipoose, William Taylor, Simeon Wade, James Walker, and Moses Williams met along Gaines Creek to strategize how to kill those they blamed for the tribe's problems and the further destruction of their way of life.[11] Despite previous denials that they planned to kill anyone, the Nationalists held a long-standing hatred for many of the Progressive Choctaws. In retrospect, it is likely that some Nationalists harbored for years the idea of assassinating key Progressives. The election of Jones and the other Progressives in Gaines County, plus the questionable defeat of Lewis, Wade, Anderson, and Parker caused them to finally act.

One of the Nationalist leaders and candidate for Gaines County sheriff in 1892 was Silan Lewis, a full-blood Choctaw between fifty-four and sixty-four years old.[12] Lewis had been active in politics since the 1870s, and in 1880 he received the largest number of votes (eight votes out of twenty-eight, with the other twenty votes distributed among six other candidates) in the Senate to become the sergeant-at-arms. In that capacity he was authorized to ensure order among the participants and onlookers. That Lewis was voted to such a position might infer that he had law-enforcement experience, but he is not mentioned in any other document as being a sheriff or deputy sheriff prior to 1880.[13] In 1882, the Progressive Silas James defeated him for the sergeant-at-arms position. In 1884, the year that McCurtain defeated Folsom in the election for principal chief, Charles Wilson was murdered, and Robert Benton became the Sugar Loaf County representative; Lewis did not make an attempt to run for office.[14]

In 1891, Silan Lewis was appointed as a juror in a "violation of stock law" case and documents refer to him, along with the other jurors, as one of the "good and lawful citizens of Mosholatubbee District."[15] Indeed, Lewis had been deemed a respectable man. So much so that even though Chief Smallwood had been defeated in the August 1890 election by Wilson N. Jones, one of Smallwood's last actions was to commission Silan Lewis the sheriff of Tobucksy County on October 7, 1890, as a replacement for the deceased Josh S. Naile.[16]

Sheriff Lewis quickly selected George Beams as his special deputy sheriff and was required to "act in my [Lewis's] place and stead in his duties as defined by law for his position." Lewis also quickly appointed Ben F. Grubbs and Edward Williams as special deputies along with Albert Folsom and D. J. Byington as regular deputy sheriffs.[17] Ironically, in 1896 George Beams later would indeed act in Lewis's stead when he married Lewis's widow.

Although Wilson N. Jones stated in 1890 that "towards my opponents I shall harbor no ill will or prejudice," Lewis did not stay in his position as sheriff for long.[18] After all, Jones had just been elected chief and he gave every indication of being a man who knew exactly who his friends and enemies were. If Jones did not know personally his allies and foes, then the many Progressives who supported him certainly did. In his first message as chief of the Choctaws, Jones made his plans for his opponents clear when he said, "No officer under me must be surprised of an investigation[. If] I find him incompetent or derelict in his duties he is removed."[19]

Jones believed that he had the law on his side when he made that statement. Problem was, he did not follow it. In 1887, the General Council passed a bill stating that any national or district officer who committed a misdemeanor while in office could be removed. Before that could happen, however, "full specification" of the charge along with "at least two respectable witnesses" had to come before a judge to be sworn. If the principal chief deemed the charges of such a nature that might "endanger the public good," then the accused officer appeared before the chief and showed cause as to why he should not be removed. The chief forwarded to the national secretary the charges, specifications, and evidence against the transgressor, then all that information came before the Speaker of the House of Representatives. If the House of Representatives believed the person should be removed from office, then it sent an article of impeachment to the House for trial.[20]

There is no documentation detailing what Lewis did to make Jones deem him "incompetent" other than that Lewis did not support him for chief. Nor did Lewis participate in any hearing. Despite Jones clearly stating in his 1890 address that "I shall expect you as law makers to set an example in honesty, in patriotism and in industry, for all officers whose duties shall be to enforce the laws by you enacted," Jones simply removed Lewis as Sheriff and replaced him on November 22 with his Progressive supporter William Johnson.[21] Johnson immediately stacked his special and regular deputy positions with eleven men within the first month and another nine the next year.[22] Johnson's sureties were the two wealthy white men, R. B.

Coleman and J. J. McAlester, the latter of whom found his stride in the 1890s as one of the most powerful men in Indian Territory.[23] This would not be the last time Jones attempted to remove an officer without justification.

But Silan Lewis was well liked among the Nationalists, so he became a leader of the plot to kill Progressives. Simeon Wade, a thirty-seven-year-old full-blood who had been the Nationalists' choice for Gaines County Ranger, stood next in command. Not much is known about the other men who rode with Lewis and Wade other than that none had much, if any formal education.[24] The oldest was probably Charles McCoy, at fifty-one, with James Walker the youngest at age twenty. Only some of the names have been located through the Choctaw circuit court and Supreme Court dockets and in interviews in the *Indian and Pioneer Histories*. A few are shown to have voted in various Choctaw elections, and fewer still appear on the Choctaw Dawes Rolls, which are the lists of individuals who were accepted by the Dawes Commission between the years of 1898 and 1914 as members of the Choctaw tribe; six names have not been located, not even on the early census records of the Choctaw districts.[25] This is not surprising, however, because many full-bloods often avoided people and events not in line with their ways of thinking.

Further insight into Lewis comes from court clerk James Culberson. Apparently, Lewis's family and their friends had "always been active in talking against" the Choctaw government and had been part of past political infighting. Not only had they been active, but according to Culberson, they "kept the grievances of former ties alive by agitation and much wild talk."[26]

After the election, Nationalists knew that the time had come to act. The group agreed that Lewis and Wade would lead two groups of men on a series of assassinations throughout the nearby Choctaw counties. They targeted officials of the First Judicial District of the Nation including the Moshulatubbee district judge, Noel J. Holson, and his brother, County Judge S. F. Holson, in addition to certain intermarried white men who fenced in large pasturelands and wealthy mixed- and full-bloods who had leased their lands to non-Choctaws. They also wanted to kill the Progressive mixed-blood Gilbert Wesley

Dukes, a wealthy politician who had served as elected sheriff of Wade County, member of the House and Senate of the General Council, Supreme Court judge from 1885 to 1889, and circuit judge of the Apukshunnubbee District from 1889 to 1895. He worked as national auditor from 1895 to 1897 and had been the interpreter for the Senate in 1889. Later, in 1900, Dukes was elected chief of the Choctaws with the support of the Progressive McCurtain family, mainly because, like the McCurtains, he was an advocate of allotment and statehood.[27]

Perhaps another intended target was Crawford J. Anderson, the educated, mixed-blood son of the Choctaw Confederate leader John Anderson and Elizabeth Perry, a white woman. Anderson stayed impressively active in Choctaw affairs, most notably as journalist of the Choctaw General Council and district court clerk, county clerk of Wade County, and district court clerk of Pushmataha District. He also found time to serve as a member of the Council Finance Committee, as a district school trustee for six counties, and as deputy court clerk for three two-year terms. Anderson, however, is the only person to state that he was a target. His testimony in 1937, forty-five years after the incident, does not match the story told by Indian Agent Bennett and the newspapers. Like other testimonies from elderly "pioneers," his lengthy story appears to be overdramatized.[28]

What is known for certain is that Simeon Wade and his men proceeded to kill Progressives Elam Colbert, Frank Frazier, and Robinson Nelson. Silan Lewis and his group rode to the home of Joe Hukolutubbee, the full-blood former sheriff of Gaines County, who lived six miles from where the Nationalists plotted the murders. Hukolutubbee was a former lighthorseman and the representative of the chief of the Choctaw Nation and was evidently likable. According to one man who knew him, "He was a low heavyset fellow; he was dark with black hair and he had a gruff appearance, though he was really a good fellow and friendly when you came to know him."[29]

As the Nationalists approached Hukolutubbee's property a few of Lewis's party rode ahead to make certain Hukolutubbee was home before the remainder of the group arrived. In the warm and humid

morning, the men left their horses a short distance from Hukolutubbee's home and in the cover of darkness snuck close to the front
of his home where he lay asleep on the front porch. One version is
that Lewis's men called Hukolutubbee's name to make certain it
was him. Dazed from sleep, the man stood and cautiously walked
to the end of his porch to look around the corner of his house. One
of the Nationalist men hiding by the house then grabbed Hukolutubbee's hand to keep him from running as his colleagues shot him
at least five times.[30] It is doubtful, however, that he was shot that
many times since one of Lewis's men stood next to him. Another
more cinematic version states that Hukolutubbee stood as Lewis and
his men rode onto the property on horses and the former sheriff
quickly succumbed to the bullets from sixteen Winchester rifles.[31]

James Culberson, who worked at a dry goods store in LeFlore at
the time of the killings, claimed that he too was the object of the
wrath of the "Last League of the Choctaws," as he would later label
them. He gave two different recollections about events. In one version,
he states that his name appeared on the list to be killed and that he
"lived in constant terror."[32] But in another statement, he recalls that
one afternoon a large man entered the store with the intention of
giving him a "good sound licking" instead of killing him because
he was deemed too young to shoot. Culberson stated in his memoirs
that he held the man off for an interminable two hours by convincing
him that he supported the Nationalist cause. The man left, but Culberson remained on the "to kill" list. At the time of the murders, Culberson worked as attorney and county clerk of Sugar Loaf County,
and in that capacity he not only witnessed the prosecution of Silan
Lewis, he transcribed the now-missing court files. His recollections
are apparently the only record of the details of the Nationalists' attack
on the Progressives, and these were textualized forty-one years after
the events.[33] It is interesting that Culberson was deemed old enough
to hold the responsibility of court clerk, yet according to him, was
not killed because the Nationalist who cornered him thought him
"too young." Considering that the Nationalists were in a hurry to
complete their jobs, it also is unlikely that any of them would spend
two hours bickering with Culberson.

After Hukolutubbee was killed, Lewis's group returned to their horses. The men decided to split into two groups to avoid attention. One group of fourteen men rode five miles south with the intention of targeting the wealthy full-blood rancher Abner Pusley, a member of the large and Progressive Pusley family. Some of the Nationalists felt concerned that they had taken too long to dispose of Hukolu-tubbee and believed that if Pusley had any idea they were coming he would fight back. Once again, they sent a scout ahead to assess the situation. This time the man they sent, William Taylor, had been a childhood friend of Pusley. The latter invited Taylor inside, but instead of agreeing to enter the home and chat, Taylor told Pusley of the plot to kill him and tried to convince Pusley that his life would be spared if he joined the League's fight to defend their Nation. Pusley refused, telling Taylor that he believed the Nationalists' behavior was wrong. Taylor replied that he would take his time talking to his colleagues in order to give Pusley enough time to escape through the back door. Since Pusley did not have a horse, he seemed out of luck until by chance his neighbors drove by his house in their hack. Pusley then borrowed the wagon and took his wife to Hartshorne. Meanwhile, Taylor returned to his colleagues and told them that Pusley was heavily armed and it would be dangerous to pursue him. Everyone agreed they should retreat.[34] Apparently, Taylor warned more Progressives than just Pusley, but it is unknown who else he informed.

The second, and larger, group led by Simeon Wade focused on killing the sheriff of Gaines County and Silan Lewis's rival for that position, J. W. Perry; but, he lived too far from Hukolutubbee's place. By eight o'clock in the morning the men found themselves eight miles west of Wilburton and realized they had taken too long to arrive at their destination. Out of convenience they killed another Choctaw Progressive named Robertson Nelson who was at work butchering hogs. Unfortunately, Nelson had enlisted the assistance of two young Choctaws in his killing of the hogs that morning. After shooting Nelson, the killers chased them into the barn where the young men hid in the horse stalls. The Nationalists stuck their rifle barrels through the holes in the wooden walls of the stalls and shot both boys.[35]

Numerous Indian Territory storytellers created tales about the activities of the Last League of the Choctaws. One account is that one member of the League, the Chickasaw freedman Tom (Peymus), had a crippled leg and his horse threw him in the excitement of the gunfight. Despite the hard fall, he sat up and proceeded to point his Winchester toward a house, firing until he killed three Progressive men. Who the men were and who owned the house, however, is not known.[36] Yet another storyteller (who, according to all other documentation, had nothing to do with the episode but merely wished he had) states that other targets included Campbell Frazier, who was killed in a Hartshorne blacksmith shop, and a Samboy man named Drake. The riders intended to kill Progressive James Brown, but he was warned by his Nationalist brother Newt Brown to be prepared for the worst. Six men—Charley Austin, Milton Brown, Aphriam Collins, Bill Hawkins, Ross McGlish, and Lorden McGlish—reportedly guarded Brown's house from the Nationalist' intrusions. This information, however, comes from a tenth-grade (undated) paper with no notes other than the statement at the end: "Information from Ross McClish." The paper also claims that the two leaders were "Silla" Lewis and Simeon Wade, both of whom were taken into custody and held for six months by James Brown. Lewis and Wade constructed their own coffins, and in this fabricated version Lewis died of pneumonia after four months, while Wade rode to his execution with Brown.[37]

Entertaining, yet unlikely, stories aside, it is probable that the group decided to rejoin their colleagues without murdering Sheriff Perry. Luckily for the Moshulatubbee district judge, Noel J. Holson, and his brother, county judge S. F. Holson, they had been warned about the attack by one of their relatives, Mac LeFlore, and were able to elude the killers. News of the attacks continued to spread throughout the Nation. Chief Wilson Jones barricaded himself inside his Caddo home and called for the Choctaw militia to look for the assassins. Meanwhile, the Nationalists led by Lewis and Wade had already returned to the heavily timbered areas of Gaines County and Bushy Creek where they decided to separate to avoid capture.[38]

Lewis and Wade had not yet discovered that other Nationalists who were supposed to kill specific targets had been thwarted after William Taylor leaked their plan to Progressives. The intended victims either fled their homes to hide, or, like Chief Jones, they armed and barricaded themselves in their houses. Lewis's group located Wade and most of his men, and then that large party rode west throughout the night toward McAlester with the intention of killing more Progressives.[39] Along the way they collected more supporters, so by the time they reached the outskirts of McAlester they numbered almost fifty men. According to Indian Agent Bennett (and it is unknown how he had access to this information) Lewis expressed the Nationalists' plans to kill one of their own, presumably William Taylor or Mac LeFlore, the men who snitched to the Progressives about the Nationalists' plot.[40]

Upon hearing the news of the murders, the residents of the Choctaw Nation understandably became alarmed, especially the intermarried white men. According to one W. L. Austin, a white businessman who had lived with the Choctaws most of his life,

The white men intermarried with Choctaws, are uneasy—you know under Choctaw law and Treaty, a white man who marries a Choctaw woman is the same as a Choctaw Indian, these white fellows, talkes [sic] too much, on both sides, and the political campaign was very bitter, and the newspapers were bitter, and the Indian got *mad*, and now, things are very lively. I hope the war will end without further trouble, but I don't think it will because the [Jacob] Jackson men would not have started in to kill unless the whole party had made up their minds to fight it out until they got their rights.[41]

Unbeknownst to Lewis and Wade, Chief Jones had also sent a message by telegram to the Agent Bennett, stationed in Muskogee, Creek (Muscogee) Nation. Thus began an exhausting series of events beginning on Sunday morning, September 12, when Bennett received a telegram from Jones asking him to come to McAlester along with the Indian police via train in order to "suppress lawlessness committed by bodies of armed men." He wanted these policemen to stay at least until the General Council convened in October at Tuskahoma.[42] Bennett could not honor that request, but he did order the captain of the tribal police to proceed to McAlester. The latter informed Bennett about the urgency of the situation and pleaded with Bennett to come deal with the highly emotional and dangerous state of affairs himself. Bennett relented, acknowledging later in his annual report that the citizens of the Nation indeed lived in "constant dread that an assassin will take their lives."[43]

Bennett learned that the Nationalists camped two miles west of McAlester and sprung into action. The next morning, September 13, he traveled one hundred miles on the Missouri, Kansas, and Texas Railroad to South McAlester, where he encountered fifty heavily armed Nationalists inside the courthouse. He then proceeded the hundred miles to Caddo to meet with Jones and discuss their course of action. The next day, Jones left for South McAlester in the company of thirty men, while Bennett went back to McAlester to meet with leaders of both factions. Two days later, on September 16, the weary Bennett sent a telegram notifying the War Department that the crowd at McAlester had grown to at least three hundred armed Choctaws, but that they reasonably agreed to a conference. Bennett received an answer on the same day, with the message that the Commissioner of Indian Affairs advised the War Department that troops should be made readily available.[44] Physically and mentally exhausted, Agent Bennett forged ahead and met the two factions on a white horse, waving a U.S. flag asking for a truce so they could come to an agreement. Otherwise, asserted Bennett, he had the authority to "abolish the tribal governments."[45] In the meantime, Bennett received yet another telegram informing him that another thirty Nationalists had surrounded the home of Gaines County Sheriff Perry (Lewis's rival for that position in the election), twelve miles east of Hartshorne. Bennett then hastily sent runners to inform the Nationalists not to shoot because an agreement would be formed at McAlester.[46]

After four days of discussion, Agent Bennett, along with Chief Jones, Charles LeFlore (captain of the U.S. Indian police), Napoleon B. Ainsworth, E. N. Wright, and Ward W. Hampton, representing the

Progressive Party, and Joe Gardner, Andle Anderson, and Daniel Bell as representatives of the Nationalist Party, signed a six-part agreement. The agreement stated that all those Choctaws who took part in the assassinations of Elam Colbert, Frank Frazier, Joe Hukolutubbee, and Robinson Nelson were to surrender to a Nationalist sheriff and that all the armed bodies within the Choctaw Nation must disband. Bennett was required to attend the upcoming session of the Choctaw General Council with the Indian police and U.S. soldiers to prevent further violence. In addition, a statement had to be written acknowledging that the intoxication of many of the Choctaws, in combination with the illegal carrying of arms and the policemen's neglect of the laws, contributed to the tribe's difficulties. Finally, it was agreed that many of the problems between the Progressives and the Nationalists were fueled by the "inflammatory utterances by irresponsible men, not Choctaw Indians."[47] Although the editors of the *Citizen* accused other editors of publishing defamatory commentary, the *Citizen* editors had done the same thing.

On September 21, 1892, the Nationalists held a convention at Antlers in an effort to settle the controversy. Ironically, the Nationalists advocated tribal sovereignty, yet the situation within the tribe had become so serious they saw only one way to solve their current dilemma: request assistance from the federal government. Jacob B. Jackson therefore made the following written statement to Chief Jones:

> Believing that no decision of our council, however just it may be, will be satisfactory to all our people and restore confidence in our Government, I very respectfully submit to you the following proposition: Under an arrangement entered into at McAlester, September 13, 1892, United States Indian Agent, Dr. Leo E. Bennett, is to be present at council during the counting of votes with a detachment of United States troops. This agreement, as I understand it, is for the preservation of peace, and could not possibly settle any misunderstanding regarding the legality of any votes or precincts. Realizing the fact that the United States Indian agent of the Union Agency was a United States officer, placed here by the United States Government for our interest and protection, and having the utmost confidence in the honesty and integrity of Dr. Leo E. Bennett,

our present agent, I propose to you that all disputes and misunderstandings that may arise during the counting of the votes shall be referred to him for settlement.[48]

Although Bennett felt somewhat relieved that the Nationalists were amenable to peaceably solving the issue, he remained apprehensive that violence could recur. After all, dozens of Choctaws had armed themselves with Winchester rifles and Colt revolvers and "both parties believe they are right in the matter" and "are willing to fight and die" for their beliefs. Bennett agreed to try and keep order during the recount, but not without military assistance. Self-proclaimed Chief Jones, however, stated on September 22 that he refused to agree to any participation by the federal government until the General Council convened on October 3.[49]

Within twenty-four hours, thirteen Nationalist men turned themselves in and four more surrendered after they heard about the agreement made by the Nationalist leaders. Further, they agreed to disband and not to try and settle their differences without the assistance of the tribal courts. Subsequently, the remaining Nationalists—Silan Lewis among them—scattered back to their homes. To the Progressives' surprise, they soon realized that the men who had been turned in as the murderers were not the ones who killed Colbert, Frazier, Hukolutubbee, Nelson, and the two boys.[50]

An angry Wilson Jones brought his own men to South McAlester to combine forces with the men already there, totaling almost two hundred men, many of whom were incensed enough with the Nationalists to start a battle at the first opportunity. Those Nationalists who had surrendered were taken into custody and placed in a guarded camp west of McAlester. Bennett told these men that they and all the Nationalists must uphold the agreement made to deliver the guilty parties. They requested yet another conference, but all the other Nationalist men had scattered, making it a challenge to get word to them. It was therefore not possible to meet until the representatives of the Nationalists could be summoned by wire.[51]

Forty irritated and impatient Progressives then rode to McAlester where the Nationalist prisoners were held. On arrival, one of the guards informed them that no one could enter the camp without Bennett's permission. The forty men acted aggressively enough for the camp guards to prepare for a gun fight. Fortunately, the forty Nationalists realized they could not reach the prisoners, so they departed.[52]

Still, the Progressive riders continued to fume. Bennett knew that something needed to be done lest a fight break out, so Bennett, McCurtain, and Jones went to McAlester to meet again with as many Nationalists as they could find. Clearly, the Progressives meant to take hold of the Nationalist prisoners for "mob justice," and Bennett realized that he had to call for military protection. Bennett told his twenty Indian officers that they would give up the prisoners "over our dead bodies" and as a precautionary move sent out scouts to check for hostile behaviors. Bennett knew, but the Choctaws did not, that an 1888 act of Congress stated that an Indian could not interfere with an agent or policeman while performing his duty.[53] Both the Progressives and Nationalists were unpredictable, and he considered removing the prisoners by train to a secret locale to keep them safe. The Progressives remained determined to keep the Nationalists prisoners; but, they opted to cooperate after hearing the warning that they would be hung if they did not stop interfering. Bennett must have been sarcastic when he stated that a "friendly conference" ensued.[54]

Bennett then went to South McAlester and asked Chief Jones to allow Perry, the Gaines County sheriff, to come and take the Nationalists back to Gaines County where the murders took place. Over a hundred Progressives had gathered at the camp to watch the sixteen prisoners leave with Sheriff Perry to travel back to the Gaines County jail. Prymus Brown, however, had high hopes of not being tried in the Choctaw Nation because he had previously served as a posse man for a U.S. marshal. He wanted to be tried at Fort Smith where he thought he would receive a fairer hearing than in a biased Choctaw Court. Deputy sheriffs hustled Brown off to Fort Smith, but because Brown was an enrolled freedman who had killed Indians, Judge Isaac Parker ordered him to return to the Nation via train where another Choctaw deputy sheriff retrieved him. As one story goes, at the Red Oak depot the deputy ran his rope through Brown's handcuffs and supposedly forced him to "run" the twelve miles to the courthouse.[55] Meanwhile, the prisoners had left, and the armed forces had dissipated.[56] But the anger of both parties had not. Many citizens hoped that the news emanating from Antlers about armed men gathering together were rumors, but at least 125 Nationalists had indeed banded together and so had several other smaller groups scattered throughout the Nation.

Despite the reality that Lewis and other Nationalists had killed numerous prominent Choctaws, Wilson Jones stated plainly that the killers were not to be shot; rather, they were to be taken alive and tried in court. Lewis, in the meantime, was reportedly arrested by lighthorsemen after he surrendered to Edmund Lewis in a dusty South McAlester blacksmith's shop while his horse was being shod. The remaining Nationalists turned themselves in by the end of September.[57]

Great trepidation spread throughout the Choctaw Nation over the murders. Most Choctaws feared that the killings would hasten the dissolution of the "existing Indian management" of the Choctaw Nation.[58] They were justified in feeling nervous. The *Purcell Register*, a Chickasaw newspaper, proclaimed that "the Choctaw troubles are only another argument in favor of the entire abolition of the petty Indian governments and the substitution of a staple form of state government therefore. Events of the last week, while to be deeply deplored, hasten the inevitable end that awaits the present system of regulating Indians affairs." In defense of the Choctaw Nation as a whole, the editor of the *Indian Citizen* replied, "Why not as well say that the U.S. Government be abolished because a riot occurred some where or a mob killed a man or men?"[59]

While many in the Choctaw Nation remained agitated, the arrested men were taken to Hartshorne and put under guard. Lewis and other Nationalists were to be tried in December in Judge Holson's court at the Gaines County Courthouse with the lighthorsemen on guard to ensure that all proceedings went peacefully.[60] Although the Nationalist ringleaders of the Progressive killings were set for trial, rumors of more impending murders continued to circulate. Ever the champion of the Nationalists, the *Indian Citizen*, claimed that the Progressives had long before started the murder threats against the Nationalists and that the Progressives "were not afraid to see blood run." The editors rationalized the killings by claiming that the Nationalist men who committed murder acted in a "spontaneous outburst of an indignant and outraged people," believing that slaying the Progressives was the only way to save themselves from the same fate. Besides, the *Citizen* editors continued, killing "has always been the method of Indian warfare among themselves."[61]

Conversely, the Progressives continued to claim that the Nationalists had planned premeditated murder and pointed to the Nationalist Convention held at Atoka on August 29 as the site of the murder plot. The Nationalists, however, countered that accusation by stating that the Atoka convention was held in order to elect a committee to count votes.[62]

Verbal sniping continued throughout September, and on October 2, the day before the General Council was to meet to count ballots, forty-eight armed Nationalists organized themselves into groups to march to the capitol. Once again an informer told of their plans; Chief Jones sent out a party of lighthorsemen to arrest the Nationalists and then had them locked up in the top floor of the capitol building.[63] As word spread of the arrests, Nationalists and Progressives saddled their horses and readied their wagons. On October 3, before the start of the council meeting, Tuskahoma quickly flooded with people from across the Choctaw Nation. Everyone appeared to understand the seriousness of the situation and they behaved, no doubt in part because Agent Bennett had arrived with the U.S. Cavalry just as he had promised and those in attendance might be taken into custody. Bennett's September 22 letter had stated that in a joint conference between Chief Jones and leaders of the Nationalists, all noncitizens would be barred from attending the General Council session at Tuskahoma on October 3, warning that he had "sufficient military force at hand and otherwise available," and was "determined to uphold the laws."[64]

Instead of immediately dealing with the crucial matter of counting votes, the first order of business for the General Council was to elect officers in the Senate. They elected C. S. Vinson the president of the Senate and Wesley Anderson the Speaker of the House. It was not until the end of the first day that Progressive and Nationalist leaders met with Agent Bennett to discuss Jackson's request for a recount. Chief Jones agreed to the recount, but he was concerned about losing control of the situation and refused to concede that any questions over the recount would be given to Bennett to decide.[65]

On October 4, in anticipation of the recount and with the Nationalists still imprisoned in the capitol, the overwhelmingly Progressive Senate and House (although Nationalist Jacob Jackson was the national secretary) passed a bill stating that only members and officers of the General Council would be allowed to be present during the recount. It also authorized the principal chief to request of the U.S. Indian agent that U.S. soldiers work in conjunction with the national lighthorsemen in guarding both entrances to the capitol yard.[66]

On October 5, the official recount results were revealed: Jones received 1,705 votes and Jackson received 1,697—a difference of only eight votes. The Nationalists believed that there had been vote tampering and that a poll book or two were missing, but perhaps out of sheer fatigue they acquiesced. Bennett expressed concern that another fight might ensue, so he stayed at the capitol until October 12 while the troops lingered in the Choctaw Nation for another two weeks.[67]

Jones's inaugural speech clearly revealed that he was not in a peace-making mood. Even though Jones won by a miniscule margin and almost half the Choctaw voters preferred Jackson, he asserted that the citizens of the Choctaw Nation had indeed elected him and those who had not voted for him were attempting to destroy the Nation. He remained wary of his opposition and asked that the General Council be prepared to create new laws to keep them in check:

> After a period of thirty years of quietude and unusual prosperity of the people, it is with grave apprehensions for your prosperity and welfare as a nation that it is necessary that the convening for the legitimate exercise of your official functions as legislators should be under supervision of United States troops. . . . Suffice it to say an armed mob unduly excited over supposed wrongs and wrought to madness by the

inflammatory speeches and printed articles of leaders who are not friendly to our institutions, wantonly and willfully assassinated four of our citizens and openly proclaimed, if necessary to carry out their nefarious designs, to murder all from the Chief down.[68]

The General Council evidently agreed with him because it passed a bill that overturned the earlier law of November 28, 1888, which suspended militia law. The bill thereby declared the militia to be "in full force and effect" and appropriated eight thousand dollars for its maintainance.[69]

As the narrow election results revealed, many citizens still did not support Jones nor like those who did. The *Citizen* continued its commentary on the Progressives by focusing on two Progressive lighthorsemen, Peter Consaw [*sic*] and Tecumseh Moore, by calling them "light heads" instead of "light horse" after they arrested an innocent man for drinking and shooting (even though he had done neither) and then accusing them of stealing money from another Nationalist. The newspaper asked once again why it was that "all but one of the votes thrown out" happened to be votes for Jackson and that the precinct in which the poll book disappeared happened to be a strong Jackson precinct. The *Citizen* editors proceeded to accuse the Progressives of "running blind tiger" over the outnumbered Nationalists in the October 3 council meeting in which the Progressives claimed a win for Jones.[70] Agent Bennett still felt uneasy and commented on October 26, 1892, that while the Nation seemed quiet, he did not rule out the possibility that violence might flare once the inevitable indictments against Lewis and other Nationalists took place. Still, he felt confident that the Choctaws would not need him again and that the tribe could handle any difficulties.[71] In the meantime, the murdered Progressives Elias Colbert, Robinson Nelson, and Frank Frazier were buried, their graves costing $3.33 each to dig.[72]

Chief Jones's desire for a militia turned out to be a wise request, for animosities reared up again in December 1892. One reason was that at the "special term" of the Moshulatubbee District court held on December 16, the grand jury indicted Silan Lewis for the murder

of Joe Hokolotubbee.[73] Also that month, Chief Jones received a request
from the circuit judge of the Mosholatubbee District to arrest one of
Lewis's supporters, Willis Jones (no relation to Wilson N. Jones),
who had been indicted at a special term of the Moshulatubbee District
but had managed to elude arrest.[74] And on December 14, Nationalist
Bill Anderson, the Nationalist nominee for Gaines County judge in
1892, killed Progressive Abe Smith outside of McAlester by shooting
him three times and then cutting his throat.[75]

Chief Jones once again emerged from his barricaded home and
directed the lighthorsemen to arrest Willis Jones, and they did so in
late February 1893. But that arrest only ignited the power keg once
again. An armed group of Nationalists, including a man named
Albert Jackson, subsequently rescued Willis at gunpoint from the
lighthorsemen. They took him to the home of the affluent Victor M.
Locke, a white merchant living in Antlers.[76]

The Nationalists implicitly trusted "Uncle Dick" Locke, an intermarried white man (his wife Susan Priscilla McKinney was daughter
of Thompson McKinney) who staunchly supported the Nationalists.
Before moving to Indian Territory, Locke supported the Confederacy
during the Civil War and had been imprisoned for a short time. Some
recall that the once poor Locke wore "rags and tatters" before he
recovered to serve as clerk of the circuit court of Towson County
and as superintendent of public schools. He then opened a mercantile
business in 1879. When he moved to Antlers in 1887, his business
grew into one of the largest stores in the Choctaw Nation.[77] Ironically,
Nationalists normally did not trust or like wealthy white men, but
they felt comfortable around Locke. Their reliance on Locke illustrates
the somewhat contradictory behaviors of the Choctaws during this
period: it appeared that almost everyone, regardless of socioeconomic stature or cultural adherence, was willing to side with any
person who could help one's cause.

On March 11, 1893, Chief Jones realized that a violent confrontation might occur so he issued an order for the tribe's militia under
the command of Gilbert Thompson to apprehend Willis Jones again,
as well as Albert Jackson and anyone else interfering with Willis's
arrest. In response, a group of at least one hundred Nationalists

Victor M. Locke, the white man whose Antlers' home served as the siege point during the "Wilson-Locke War" between the Progressives and the Nationalists after the controversial election of 1892. Courtesy Research Division of the Oklahoma Historical Society.

converged on Locke's home with the intent of protecting Willis Jones and Albert Jackson. The problem then grew worse as the number of Nationalists increased. Not surprising, on March 27, Agent Bennett received a telegram from Paris, Texas, stating that a "bloody feud" had begun at Antlers. He also read press dispatches from McAlester that twenty-five people had been killed and many wounded. The Choctaw Nation, however, had not yet officially reported any problems.[78] Perhaps this lack of a public statement was intended to keep the U.S. government from once again thinking the tribe could not handle its own problems. The military presence did not upset every citizen, however, because some men and women profited from the militia, who bought their milk, butter, and eggs and paid for the use of their water wells.[79]

On March 31, Agent Bennett received a telegraph asking him to make haste to Antlers because Nationalists and Progressives were camped only four miles apart and both factions were preparing for confrontation. Bennett needed to assess the problem and decide what could be done by the U.S. forces. Bennett sent a telegram to the commissioner from Muscogee to make it clear that he needed military aid. The Commissioner cited Bennett's messages in his own message to the War Department in which he requested assistance for Bennett.[80]

To make matters more explosive, Thompson's militia became intoxicated and engaged in a drunken shooting spree throughout Antlers. Some of the riders had become so drunk they could barely sit upright on their horses. Despite barricading themselves in their homes, some citizens were nevertheless wounded by bullets penetrating the walls and windows. The Masonic Hall, churches, the railroad station, and the home of the local Methodist minister all sustained considerable damage. A local physician, Dr. Charles Lynch, later commented that "the church was shot to thunder." The latter remained in his house at the time along with his wife and children, none of whom were permitted by the militia to leave before the shooting began. Heavily armed Nationalists took cover in Locke's home and mounted a defense as the rowdy Progressive men arrived at Locke's home ready for battle. After a furious gun fight several men on each side were injured, while Solomon Battiste, the sheriff of Kiamitia County, was killed. Before the fatigued Agent Bennett arrived to arrange another truce, the barrage of bullets almost destroyed Locke's house.[81] Progressives shot Locke and although he healed, he carried a bullet in his body until he died; the same happened to a Progressive named Will Everidge, the son of Progressive leader (and Robert Benton colleague) Joe Everidge.[82]

According to militia Captain Gilbert Thompson, as his fifty men approached the house they heard a shot. He claimed that he had tried to keep his force from firing, but to no avail. This statement is in line with the assertion that many members of the militia were drunk, although in Thompson's version, not surprising, there is no mention of the militia being intoxicated. He does recall, probably accurately, that the firing was fast and furious, so much so that "the house was shot all to pieces. I do not think that there was any place in that house that didn't have a hole through it and the men we wanted were not there." Thompson also recalls that Locke had only seven men with him to fight his fifty. One of Thompson's men and at least one horse were killed, while several other men were slightly wounded. Along with the Nationalists, one of Locke's daughters, Dollie, was inside and a bullet nearly killed her; instead, it cut off a portion of her bangs. Thompson also was lucky as a bullet sheared off some of the hair on the back of his head.[83]

Crawford J. Anderson, who claims to have been part of the "light-horse militia" (it was actually the militia, not the lighthorsemen) under Captain Gilbert W. Thompson, has a different story to tell. He claims that his Choctaw militia camped at the Davenport homestead, about three miles from Locke's home. In contrast to Agent Bennett's story, Anderson asserts that as the "lighthorsemen" approached the house the Nationalists opened fire. After a significant exchange of gunfire, a truce was made between Captain Thompson and Dick Locke. In Anderson's version, the Nationalists were all arrested and put in jail in Paris, Texas.[84]

On April 3, 1893, Bennett sent a telegram to the commissioner of Indian Affairs, giving a realistic commentary on the situation: "Temporary truce arranged yesterday. Armed forces disbanding; situation yet serious, seemingly uncompromising under present Choctaw government. . . . While great relief experienced at disbanding armed forces, feeling one of dread uncertainty."[85] Bennett was right to feel uneasy. After the skirmish, Thompson relates that his frustrated men met at Goodland to plan how they would arrest the Nationalists that Jones wanted in jail.[86] Agent Bennett told Thompson he thought it best that the Choctaw militia disband, but Thompson wanted to stay until he completed the job. Bennett continued to have serious concerns with this latest incident and blamed the Nation's militia as the instigators of the carnage at Locke's home. He believed that citizens of the Choctaw Nation remained fearful and anxious that more violence would result; therefore, the best course of action would be to put the Nation under martial law.[87]

Crawford Anderson, the man who served under Thompson, later recalled in his 1937 interview that the militia members were told to return to their homes and that some of the men had to walk since they did not have enough money to pay for the train fare. Anderson asserts that he was so fearful of being ambushed by a Nationalist on his walk from the train station to his home that he ventured from the road and instead walked through the woods to avoid being shot. He refers to the Nationalists as "conspirators," "stealthy Snakes," and "assassins" with "murderous designs" who were "openly defying the Tribal authorities." Clearly he already felt some paranoia. Though it is not substantiated elsewhere, he also claims that after their release, some Nationalists were overheard by a young white boy (who just happened to speak fluent Choctaw) plotting to kill more Progressives, including Crawford Anderson. The unnamed boy notified another alleged target, Gilbert W. Dukes, at which point all those targeted met at Dukes's home. Why they stayed all night at Dukes's home is unclear, but Anderson also asserts that the next morning they discovered "tracks freshly made which told in unmistakable language that the boy's warning had been timely, well-founded, and the means of foiling the purposes of the conspirators." Much of Anderson's story is apparently either fabricated or imagined since the incident at Locke's house occurred months after the murders of the Progressives were committed.[88]

Bennett believed that Chief Jones was to blame for the incident at Locke's. He stated that rallying the militia was "unnecessary and unlawful" and that Jones's action was not in harmony with the established laws and Constitution of the Choctaw tribe. Further, he asserted that the militia was indeed intoxicated: "The conflict precipitated by them was the act of a drunken, irresponsible, and uncontrollable mob, who were banded together as militia for the evident purpose of murdering men, women and children, thereby removing their political opponents, and so intimidating others that the powers of the present party in authority may be perpetuated." In his report to the commissioner he stated that the militia acted like "wild beasts" and that "I know that the present Choctaw government will never bring these attempted murderers to trial, but will uphold them in their unlawful acts." Bennett continued with his damning report by stating that Chief Jones violated his pledges and that it would be "judicial murder" to permit the militia to continue to make arrests in the Choctaw Nation because the Nationalist prisoners have been "robbed of their liberties and deprived of their rights."[89]

Following Choctaw law, the militia's attack on Locke's home was a serious offense. Although the militia men had the right to carry weapons, Choctaw law stated that anyone under the influence of intoxicating liquor who disturbed "any religious meeting, social gathering, school or family by whooping, shooting fire arms" could be fined and/or dealt one-hundred lashes on the bare back.[90] None of the drunken militia men, however, were punished for their behavior.

The *Purcell Register* reported that on April 10, the militia heard Bennett's report and they were "nonplused." Chief Jones and some of "his advisors" arrived at Paris, Texas, with the intention of talking with attorneys about the Locke situation. Jones's only comment to reporters was that he had a letter from Locke dated February 1893 in which Locke allegedly stated that he "would under no circumstances submit to the Jones government." Others were not allowed to read the letter, and its whereabouts remains unknown. Jones also stated that the militia sought Locke not because he harbored fugitives from the law but because he had not paid his royalty on timber sales. The *Purcell Register* pointed out the inconsistency in that claim, saying that Jones had disallowed Locke the right to even have a permit.[91]

After contemplating Bennett's report, the commissioner sent the message to the secretary of war, who then dispatched Captain Guthrie and forty-one men to the Choctaw Nation; they arrived on April 11, 1893. Special Agent Faison was in charge, with both Bennett and Guthrie under his command. In late June, Captain Guthrie issued orders for the federal troops to leave, but Judge Holson strenuously objected, believing that without the U.S. militia the unrest in the Choctaw Nation would reignite.[92] His protests must have worked, because although the Nationalists and Progressives once again signed a truce agreement in May, the U.S. militia stayed in the Choctaw Nation until October.[93]

After a brisk investigation of the events, Faison stated that Chief Jones's militia acted in a "perfectly regular and lawful proceeding," and he exonerated the men from any charge of drunkenness. Next, he arrested Willis Jones and Albert Jackson when they went to Antlers to buy supplies. They were placed in the Hartshorne jail until it suited him to turn them over to the Choctaw courts. This action especially upset the Nationalists, because, as they argued, martial law had not been declared and, further, they believed that Jackson and Willis had been handed to their enemies and might even be executed. Locke's men went as far as to say they believed Faison acted as he did in retaliation for Locke saying earlier that Faison was incompetent and "generally unfit."[94] That the Choctaw light-horsemen had no compunctions against firing at their fellow tribesmen who were defending Choctaw sovereignty should not be surprising. Morris Wardell makes a good point in *A Political History of Cherokees: 1838–1907* (1938), where he states that, among the Cherokees, "the men constituting the police were adventurous and enthusiastic over the idea of forcing the minority to submit." Wardell wrote about the infighting between the Treaty and Ross parties, factions with strong opinions about the tribe's removal.[95] A parallel can be made with the Choctaws here since the lighthorsemen were appointed by the Progressive leader Wilson Jones to apprehend their adversaries, the Nationalists. Both Nationalists and Progressives were willing to fight and kill for their ideologies. And, just like the Cherokees, some Choctaws enjoyed their positions of authority.

Unfortunately for all the Choctaws, the Nation unfavorably impressed the U.S. government. Clearly, the government was looking for additional rationales to disband the tribal governments, and the violence among the Choctaws proved a good reason to highlight. Members of both political parties of the Choctaw Nation remained on edge because the remaining men charged with the murders of the Progressives had not yet been tried, and they were aware that the U.S. government was paying close attention to how those events would unfold. It did not help the Choctaws' reputations when the Nationalists' attorneys, Gardner and McClure, sent affidavits to the commissioner's office on February 24, 1893, complaining that the men were being unnecessarily held and denied a fair trial.[96]

The law creating the Dawes Commission was passed on March 3, 1893. Understandably concerned about the impression the tribe had made on the government, the General Council sent Joe Everidge, Green McCurtain, C. S. Vinson, and Dr. E. N. Wright as "delegates or commissioners" to explain what happened at Antlers. They also sent J. W. Ownby as counsel and paid him $2,500.[97] Judge A. R. Durant, a Progressive and prominent Choctaw lawyer and good friend of Governor Jones, expounded on what he believed to be the solution to the violence within the Choctaw Nation:

> I think it [the trials] will result in making of a state of the Indian Territory . . . and it will be the best thing that ever happened for the Indian. He ought to be placed on equal footing with the white people of the United States and will be placed on his own resources. It sill stop so much lawlessness and murder and robbery in the Indian country, and will stop one faction banding together for the extermination of another.[98]

While the tribe considered the violent events that had unfolded and what those actions looked like to the federal government, the Nationalists finally got their first of several trials, *Choctaw Nation v. Sam Jefferson, et al.* But the trial was hardly fair.

CHAPTER 4

THE NATIONALIST TRIALS

Surely no one can find a shred of blame for these children of nature, to love this place of contentment with all their hearts and souls, and be willing to die for it.

—James Culberson, court clerk of the Nationalist trials

The Choctaws anxiously awaited the trials of the Nationalist men accused of murdering the Progressives. Both sides were well aware of the political game being played, and the stakes were very high. Progressives believed that the killings were motivated by intense frustration on the part of the Nationalists, who in turn were convinced that the Progressives were working primarily for themselves and against tribal sovereignty. Nationalists knew the Progressives wanted revenge, and the trials would prove that they were willing to punish the Nationalists by both subtle and obvious means.

The Nationalists learned that the deck was stacked against them as soon as they learned the name of the trial judge—Noel J. Holson. Even though Holson was on the Nationalists' "hit list" and was a Progressive and supporter of Chief Wilson N. Jones, he remained the judge of the proceedings that began in June 1893. This despite article 10, section 6 of the Choctaw Constitution, which states that "no Judge shall preside on the trial of any cause in the event of which he may be interested, or where either of the parties shall be connected with him by affirmaty or consanguinity."[1] Holson serving as judge on this case was clearly illegal and offensive to the Nationalists, but their objections did not prevent him from serving. The prosecuting attorney, S. E. Lewis, also was a Progressive, but there was no law against him practicing in these cases.

The first set of accused murderers to go to trial—Sam Jefferson, Joshua Calvin, Simeon Wade, and Primus (Thomas) Brown—worried that the men chosen as their jurors were the same men who had guarded them while they were in jail. Not only that, but the jurors also were the Nationalists' confirmed political enemies. The court grudgingly acquiesced to the defense attorneys' argument that the jury was prejudiced and provided twelve new jurors; but, even after the new jury was selected, at least eight of the twelve new jurors— John Bascom, William Blue, Adam Cooper, Morris Garland, Simeon Hampton, Sweeney Hampton, William Hendrickson, Thomas Hickman, Ben Hoteyubbee, John Naile, Simon Nelson, and Dennis Wade— were Progressives.[2]

According to James Culberson, the county clerk, at least one hundred guards and special deputies gathered at the courthouse to stand watch during the proceedings. The accused and their supporters were fearful of the jury, and the Progressives were convinced that the Nationalists would try to swoop in and rescue the accused men.[3] Tensions ran so high that the trial had to be suspended briefly.

Despite the intermittent testimonies, defense and prosecuting statements (which have disappeared from the record), and the alleged attempts of the attorneys to gather sympathetic jurors, the twelve men found the defendants guilty of murder on June 17, 1893. Judge Holson subsequently decreed that the men be shot to death on July 7, 1893. Naturally, the Nationalists again pleaded for a new trial, but Holson overruled the motion.[4]

Interestingly, at about the same time as this trial, on June 12, William Anderson, the Nationalist who shot and cut the throat of Abe Smith, was quickly found not guilty by the almost all-Progressive jury. Why they did not convict him of the violent crime may at first seem odd, but considering that the Progressives were eager to punish the Nationalists, it may have been nothing more than a political move to allow at least one of them to go free and instead focus on Silan Lewis and on the trials featuring more than one defendant.[5]

Next came the trial known as *Choctaw Nation v. Price Tallipoose, et al.*, a case with conflicting documentation.[6] The "et al." were ten men, five of whom attended the trial: Silan Lewis, Moses Williams, Thomas McGee, Robert Carter, and Kingsberry Harkins. The other men, Houston Perry, Eli Loman, Robert Miller, Nolis Carney, and James Walker were returned to jail. For unknown reasons (the court files are nonextant), the name Tallipoose is not mentioned in the court records other than in the case name. The men pleaded not guilty, and, once again, their attorneys pleaded for a new jury consisting of men who had not served as jailors of the accused. That motion was overruled, and the men were judged by jurors Adam James, Dennis Wade, Thomas Luce, Robert Pearson, Morris Carney, Joseph Jones, John Naile, Johnson McFarlan, R. P. Jennings, Norris Cooper, Adam Cooper, and Eastman Pusley.[7] Adam Cooper and John Naile had already sat in judgment of Nationalists in the case *Choctaw Nation v. Sam Jefferson, et al.*

As in the previous case, the jury for the *Choctaw Nation v. Price Tallipoose, et al.* trial was overwhelmingly Progressive.[8] Thomas Luce was an especially notable juror, with a variety of criminal activities attributed to him that are found in the court documents including rape, disturbing the peace, and violating the pistol law. But like other men with political connections, Luce later found himself in authoritative positions such as serving as national officer from the Iron Bridge Precinct of San Bois County in 1893.[9] With this jury then, it was not unexpected that on June 26, 1893, the twelve men found Lewis, Williams, McGee, Carter, and Harkins, guilty of murder and sentenced them to be shot on July 14.[10]

The decision did not go over well with Nationalists. One annoyed writer to the *Indian Citizen* known as "P" stated that the same jurors who sat in judgment of the first set of men also passed judgment on the second. Further, "P" noted, Eastman Pusley and Ben Hatubbee [*sic*][11] had assisted in arresting the alleged culprits and had guarded them for months. During that time they had repeatedly expressed their opinions as to what should be done to the Nationalists. "P" also asserted that "their prejudices [were] aroused and kept alive by repeated detailed accounts of their crime; the men who were strict partisans could hardly constitute a fair and impartial jury."[12]

Not only did "P" feel upset with the "farcical trial" and murder sentence, he expressed concern that the Nationalists continued their stay in the "hot little dungeon." He commented that the prisoners had turned themselves in with a guarantee of protection, but they were instead violated in "justice, right and humanity." In addition, some Nationalists thought that the arrest of Albert Jackson (the man who helped free Willis Jones from the lighthorsemen) in the Second District was unwarranted, that Jackson had nothing to do with the murders and that he had, in fact, been arrested six months after the murders took place. But he still suffered in the uncomfortable cell with the other prisoners in the First District. The frustrated writer perceived "much political jugglery going on by a political faction [Progressives] in order to oppress their adversaries."[13] Colonel Faison also witnessed much in the courtroom that alarmed him, because shortly after the trial Faison asked Chief Jones to stay the executions. The Department of the Interior was also sent the "translated evidence" in hopes that Secretary Hoke Smith would intervene and halt the executions.[14] That evidence is now missing; not only did the Gaines County Courthouse burn in 1895 along with all the court files, but Hoke Smith's correspondence, which probably included the court transcripts, burned in the 1920s. Letters regarding the issue, however, are available and shed light on the opinions and concerns of both the Choctaw administration and the U.S. government.[15]

In response to reading that evidence, Assistant Attorney General Hall of the Department of the Interior sent a message to Governor Jones, asking if it were possible to overturn a murder conviction according the Choctaw law. According to the *Purcell Register*, this was the first time the federal government had made the move to interfere with those sentenced to die under Choctaw law.[16]

In addition, Colonel Faison sent a report to Washington in which he stated that the men condemned to die were not literal criminals "in the ordinary acceptation of the term." He conceded that they were leaders of the rampage, but they did not deserve to be executed. He also made it clear that Chief Jones remained determined to have the Nationalist men shot because Jones possessed a strong sense of revenge. Faison warned that if the men were executed there could be even more bloodshed because of the bad feelings between the two factions. Other "prominent men" from the Choctaw Nation also sent letters of outrage to Washington, stating that they believed the executions would be murder. There were apparently so many letters streaming in to Secretary Hoke Smith that he became alarmed and wrote to Chief Jones with the order to stay the executions; if Jones did not comply, Smith would dispatch troops.[17]

Faison also pointed out to Secretary Smith that Chief Jones could not have captured the Nationalist culprits without the aid of the U.S. troops. Faison and Smith reasoned that if the United States assisted Jones in making the arrests, then perhaps the federal government could also interfere with what Secretary Smith viewed as a political execution. Smith's initial preference, however, was to make a strong suggestion to Jones that a stay of execution would go a long way toward healing the intertribal strife. He stated that Jones should also consider the reality that as chief, he would be able to take credit for making peace. But, if Jones refused, then he might be humiliated if the federal government marched into the Choctaw Nation and declared martial law. Further, if Jones could not find the legal means to stop the executions, then it would appear to the federal government that the tribe was not capable of functioning in a civilized manner, and interference by the federal government would be inevitable—and certainly welcome by those who wanted to hasten the advent of allotment. Jones's reign as chief would more than likely be over.[18]

Faison speculated that the Jones administration was resentful over the report that he presented to Smith. The feeling among some Choctaws was that Faison was biased against the tribe and that he may have given Secretary Smith embellished information. Nationalists were, therefore, suspicious of anything the federal government might do regarding the trials. In fact, some Choctaws were angry that Faison had been sent to Indian Territory in the first place. They argued that Faison had never seen an Indian before and that he was completely unfamiliar with how they conducted their business. Many Choctaws believed that the executions of the men would be a terrible political mistake. Others were not as concerned with a resurgence of bloodshed between the Choctaws; they seemed to be more preoccupied with the United States intruding into their affairs.[19]

Wilson Jones did respond to Judge Holson, stating that he had received a letter from Secretary Hoke Smith asking him to order a stay of execution. Jones claimed that it was "not within my power or within the power of the Council to interfere with the order of the court." Nevertheless, he told Holson to postpone the execution of Jefferson, Calvin, Wade, and Brown Wade from July 7 to August 4, 1893; he also told the judge to postpone the executions of Lewis, Carter, Williams, Harkins, and McGee from July 14 until August 4 as well.[20] Nevertheless, Jones asserted that the men had been "regularly tried and defended" without political prejudice in a fair and impartial trial, and he made clear his belief that the federal government had no right to interfere with or to even order an investigation into the Choctaws' legal affairs.[21]

The men were returned to jail, but someone continued to pay attention to the conditions the twenty-eight Nationalist prisoners faced in their jail at Wilburton. The *Indian Citizen* reported that Captain J. B. Guthrie was appalled that they had only two "filthy rooms," each being nine foot square without any chairs, blankets, or bedding. All were chained together and forced to sit on the hardwood floor. None were allowed outside, nor could they speak with their attorneys. The *Indian Citizen* claimed that it had heard the same complaints from other informers for weeks.[22] That the Nationalists were chained together can also be substantiated by the statement submitted by Uriah Cook to the treasurer on October 17, 1892, in which he lists "shackeling [*sic*] 16 prisoners" at a rate of $6.20; in another statement on October 15, he notes the charge of one dollar for "hauling prisoners two trips from the jail to Blacksmith shop to be shackled."[23]

The Nationalists' uncomfortable accommodations compounded their misery. Until the 1870s, Choctaws carried out justice quickly. Because Choctaws did not punish by prison sentence there were not many jails in the Nation. And although the Choctaws began building jails after the Civil War they were built slowly. Prisoners who were arrested far from one of the few jails had to bide their time in homes of Choctaw residents, usually a sheriff (there is, unfortunately, no information that informs us how the sheriffs' wives felt about this). Prisoners were either chained to trees or front porches, but sometimes they had the run of the small home. Although many Choctaw transgressors were often allowed to wait out the time prior to their executions outside of jails, sheriffs were responsible for the prisoners, which meant they had to pay attention to their charges' whereabouts.[24]

In 1886, the General Council passed an act requiring that the district jails be constructed of rock, but because only unsuitable rock could be procured in Pushmataha and Apukshunnubbee districts, builders used wood and brick. An example of the design is the jail at Mayhew (in Pushmataha District), which was fifteen feet square with a steel cell in the center. It included two small windows and one door; the windows and door were crossed with strips of one-quarter-inch steel one-half inches wide, so tightly bound that only a few fingers might fit through.[25]

The letter writing continued while the Nationalists languished in prison. On July 1, 1893, Assistant Attorney General Hall wrote to Wilson Jones asking if he had the power to commute the sentence of death of anyone convicted under tribal law. Hall, of course, was trying to find out if there was a way to halt the execution of the Nationalists who were set to die on July 9.[26] But the determination of the Progressives to simultaneously punish the convicted men and keep the federal government out of tribal business was unrelenting. In a July 5, 1893 letter to Secretary of the Interior Hoke Smith, W. N. Jones stated repeatedly that he had no authority to grant a reprieve to the condemned Choctaws and that the men had been fairly tried by a jury of impartial citizens of the Choctaw Nation. But, according to Jones, if the men had not been fairly tried, then the U.S. government would have power to protect the men from execution. Chief Jones told Secretary Smith that there existed no laws in the Choctaw Nation allowing him to grant a stay of execution. Though the trials were clearly unfair, Jones tried to explain to Smith that "under our simple system of the administration of justice there can arise no possibility of a conviction being had through more political prejudice or political causes." Further, Jones reasoned, "The United States had for three times in succession and without just cause, we think, interfered with and thereby obstructed the due and proper administration and execution of the law, and this without there existing any 'domestic strife' to authorize and excuse such interference on the part of the United States." The trials had certainly created "domestic strife" in the Nation, but this was something Jones was not prepared to admit; he fully understood the ramifications of a U.S. intrusion into Choctaw affairs.[27]

Meanwhile, Hoke Smith sent a letter to Paul Faison telling him that it would be in Chief Jones's interest to postpone the executions until at least September 8. That letter made its way to Jones, who wrote to Judge Holson and stated that he would abide by the request. To the probable frustration of the judge, he issued a writ of habeas corpus to prevent the sheriff of Wilburton from executing the men.[28]

At the time of the trial, James Brazell was a U.S. deputy marshal working in the Damon Prairie Courthouse office, located approximately ten miles south of Wilburton. In 1940, Brazell told an interesting but unsubstantiated story. He stated that he was present with Judge Stuart when the telegram from President Cleveland (not Hoke Smith, as the records show) arrived, giving Lewis a stay of execution. At 10 A.M., Brazell saddled a horse and made it to the first of the stagecoach relay stations at Baird's Station. He changed horses, and then galloped to Riddle Station where he mounted a fresh horse to run to the Gaines County Courthouse. Exhausted from the forty-mile ride, Brazell says he climbed the stairs to the courthouse and when he entered, the only person present was Judge Holson, the Choctaw Judge whom Brazell claimed could not speak or read English. Brazell then went back outside to see if anyone else was present who could interpret the letter to Holson. A Choctaw attorney (and future chief), Gilbert Dukes, was sitting in the shade of some brush awaiting Lewis's execution when Holson called to him to read the letter. While all this transpired Silan Lewis sat on his coffin outside. He already had an x marked over his heart and the executioner was standing thirty feet from Lewis waiting for the order to shoot him. After Holson heard the contents of the letter, he ordered Lewis to be released. Lewis wasted no time in mounting his horse and riding the fifty miles back home. A representative from the Choctaw government later traveled to Lewis's home to deliver the message that he must return on November 5 for his execution. This vignette, however, may be a fanciful story since no place else in the written record is there mention of more than one preparation for Lewis's execution with all the players present, and Brazell has the dates incorrect.[29]

On July 26, 1893, a large number of Choctaws and Chickasaws met at Atoka to discuss allotment. According to the *Purcell Register*, many of those present agreed with Chief Jones that the lands should be partitioned. Also discussed were the impending executions of the Nationalists. Despite the Progressives' hatred toward the Nationalists, it was generally agreed that the fate of the condemned men must be carefully considered because if they were executed against the wishes of the federal government, then it was conceivable that the tribe's autonomy would be challenged.[30]

In the 1893 election for tribal officers, the entire Nationalist ticket won, with Willie Wilson as treasurer; C. E. Nelson as attorney; Thomas E. Oakes as auditor; and Wilson N. Jones's nemesis, Jacob Jackson, as secretary. Obviously, the Nationalists either must have rallied or some Progressives changed political allegiances. Or, as the *Indian Citizen* editors observed, it could have been that because the Nationalists were supporters of the intermarried whites receiving per capita payments, the white citizens of the Choctaw Nation were more interested in getting their claims money than in politics.[31]

It is interesting that in 1890 there are forty precinct poll books (one is unidentified) available to study, while forty-four are on hand for the 1893 election. However, ten of those available for 1892 are not present for 1893, and twelve precincts that do not have poll books available for the 1892 do exist for the 1893 election. If vote tampering did not take place, then it might be assumed that all the poll books should have ended up in the same place for historic posterity. On the other hand, it could be that as with the court files, some of the poll books could have ended up being taken home with court clerks.[32]

There were other methods used to deal with political enemies. In August 1893, Judge Nelson of Cedar County—an overwhelmingly Nationalist county of almost two hundred full-bloods—was murdered. Nelson had been elected to his post a year prior, but Chief Jones attempted to remove him from his position in order to replace him with a Progressive judge.[33] During the April 1892 term, the Supreme Court had issued an opinion about an 1887 law dealing with the removal of officers, perhaps concerned that it had happened to Silan Lewis and might happen again: "The court is of the opinion that the Principal Chief has not the right to remove an officer with out first preparing charges against said officer as the law passed and approved November 8th, 1887, is very plain."[34] Nelson refused to relinquish his position because, as happened to Silan Lewis, no formal charges of wrongdoing were ever brought against him. As many Choctaws believed, Nelson refused to step aside, so he was murdered by an unknown assailant.[35]

Chief Jones realized the dangerous situation, so on September 4, 1893, seven of the nine condemned men were released on their own recognizance for a new trial. Only Simeon Wade and Lewis were held for execution.[36] The men's counsel asked that the charges be changed to manslaughter and one hundred lashes, arguing that the lesser charge would alleviate the tension between the Nationalists and the Progressives within the Choctaw Nation. Judge Holson and the prosecuting attorney did not agree.[37]

Lashing, however, would have only been a mildly "lesser" punishment. Whipping remained a brutal reprimand among all the Five Tribes. Those convicted of murder, treason, and rape a second time could be executed by firing squad. The first offense for a man raping or "forcibly ravishing" a female carried a penalty of one hundred lashes "laid on his bare back."[38] In the late 1850s, travelers observed Choctaws using whipping, fines, and executions as forms of punishment. A problem was that there were no jails to imprison criminals so justice had to be meted out quickly lest they escape.[39]

The Choctaws had learned lashing from Euroamericans and applied some of their own methods. The accused's hands were tied to a tree limb above his head, his legs were tied together, and a log was placed above that rope. A man sat on either end of the log, thus rendering the prisoner immobile for the lashing, which was carried out with a hickory stick that had been run through a fire to make it more flexible.[40] In 1822 at Six Towns, Chief Aboha Kullo Humma stated that his "company of faithful warriors" punished thieves and those committing infanticide by tying them to a tree and doling out lashes. Those who were accused of stealing received fifty lashes for the first offense and one hundred lashes for the second; those committing a third offense were shot dead. Men and women who decided to "run off" with others' spouses received thirty-nine lashes.[41] The "bare back" stipulation was occasionally ignored, probably because lashing quickly shredded a shirt anyway. In 1885, it was noted that a man who was tried and convicted of larceny could receive his lashes with a shirt on. One man even wore six shirts to his punishment in the hope that no one would notice the extra padding; but they did, and he was stripped of all but one shirt.[42]

Those who committed murder were punished with a "quick death" from one rifle bullet, hopefully through the heart. The "three strikes and you're out" rule seems to have been the norm among the Five Tribes. Those men sentenced to be shot had the option of being blindfolded, but some did not like the idea. Hillie Jackson, a Creek man sentenced to be executed after already being whipped twice for thievery, made a strange face at the man who was to shoot him, causing the shooter to miss twice. According to this storyteller, only two shots were allowed to kill a Creek criminal; because the second shot flew wide, Jackson was set free. Like many other criminals in the other tribes, Jackson later was appointed a Creek lighthorseman.[43]

Seminole lashing was reportedly often brutal. Some victims became unconscious after fifty lashes because after the first twenty-five the lighthorseman administering the lashes would hand the whip to another man to ensure that the lashes remained strong. Occasionally the lashing was so severe that the victim's skin split and his intestines spilled out, or he bled to death after the whip lacerated his blood vessels. One man who had witnessed numerous floggings commented that the Indians rarely grunted as the whip tore their skin and, in fact, someone stood to the side and "grunted for him."

"Negroes," however, were extremely loud, and one could hear them "screaming for four miles."[44] In 1850, Congress abolished the use of flogging as punishment in the U.S. Navy and did the same for the Army in 1861.[45] Choctaws, however, continued to use whipping until statehood, with the rationale being that it was preferable to the more demoralizing imprisonment. Although in the case of the Nationalists, the Choctaws in power clearly had no compunctions against their adversaries suffering in an inadequate jail, nor did they balk at condemning them to be shot.

If a person was deemed guilty and sentenced to death, then usually that person was killed. Indian Territory newspapers were replete with stories about murderers and executions. One compelling story is about Reuben Lucas, a "boy-faced" thirty-three-year-old Choctaw who was shot in 1882 for murdering his "friend" Thompson McKinney. As the papers report, on the afternoon of Saturday, December 17, 1881, after Lucas and McKinney had left McCurtain's store, they proceeded to drink whiskey for the next twelve miles down the road until Lucas lured McKinney off the beaten path and then shot him twice and robbed him. The body was discovered sometime the next day. Lucas decided to surrender instead of waiting for McKinney's friends and family to hunt him down.[46]

Lucas was tried, convicted, and sentenced to be shot to death. In early summer 1882, Lucas dressed in a calico shirt and blue jeans tucked into his brogan boots and was taken to the San Bois Courthouse. That morning the Reverend Willis Folsom preached to the assembly of almost three hundred people the Twenty-third Psalm in Choctaw. Lucas's brother then offered a prayer. After more singing, Lucas spoke to the assembly for five minutes in Choctaw. In an interesting display of remorse and hindsight, Lucas talked about the evils of whiskey and how it had led to his downfall. He urged his friends and family to stop crying for him and to have faith in Jesus because he felt confident that he would be delivered to heaven. Then he took his hands from his pockets and locked his fingers behind his head. Edward McCurtain then told the crowd that after Lucas was dead they must consider the matter over and forget his transgression. The entire congregation, men and women, both Choctaw and white, lined up to shake Lucas's hand as he held the Bible in his left. After shaking hands, he was taken to a room to view the coffin that the he had selected, and then he changed into his burial clothes: white shirt, black pants, jacket, and fur hat. Sheriff W. W. Carney read Lucas his death warrant and instructed him to pin a piece of white paper over his heart. Deputy Sheriff Thompson Cooper and P. H. Roony led Lucas to a blanket where he proceeded to sit and raise his arms toward heaven. Sheriff Carney knelt from a distance of four feet away and shot Lucas through the chest with his 14 caliber Colt revolver. After eight minutes, Lucas stopped moaning and his mother knelt next to him and sobbed. His body was taken away by his brothers to be buried at his home.[47]

In Indian Territory, tribespeople had differing views on shooting as a form of execution. Choctaw Joe Bird was executed by gunshot for committing murder on July 6, 1893, and the *Purcell Register* took the opportunity of Bird's execution to focus on the various forms of the death penalty and concluded that execution by a gun shot was barbaric. In the Bird case, although he was sentenced to death by a judge, the actual execution was the responsibility of one man. The *Purcell Register* pointed out that in military executions the condemned person faced at least a half dozen men armed with rifles, some loaded with real ammunition and others with blank cartridges to keep the actual killer's identity secret. The paper also asserted that hanging was the most civilized form of execution. The story continued with its assessment of the "gory deed" of beheading the condemned in "the Orient," the "fatal knife" of the guillotine in France, the "horrible" electric chair in the United States, and the "horror-inspiring" garrote in Spain. Bird's fate was to be shot to death by one person. He knelt down in front of Sheriff John Perry with his arms held out to his side by two men, with a piece of white paper pinned over his heart. Perry was expected to keep a steady hand and to shoot through the paper. The *Register* believed it took a "strange human make up to bring about the successful accomplishment." The editors argued that for one man to act as the shooter was too similar to the "Oriental barbarity," and that it was not acceptable for "one man to legally shoot another to death single-handedly and conscious that his finger alone sent the missile of death on its unerring way."[48]

Considering Jones's hatred of the Nationalists, it is doubtful that anyone short of Hoke Smith could halt their executions. On September 5, 1893, Hoke Smith sent a telegram to Paul Faison with his opinion about the case. He believed that Lewis and Wade were no more guilty than the other Nationalists who carried out the murders, and, further, he did not see that "sufficient grounds" existed for only those two men to be shot. He believed that either all the Nationalists should be punished, or else the General Council should revisit the entire situation.[49]

The reasons why Lewis eventually stood as the lone condemned man are not clear, but it can be deduced that the Choctaws wanted the U.S. government to know it could handle its own problems—therefore, someone had to face punishment. Indeed, the popular sheriff Joe Hukolutubbee had many angry friends and five children, and the district judge and his brother were among the intended targets.

The situation became even more convoluted when Chief Jones sent a letter to Judge Holson on September 6, with orders to stay the executions. He also said that, "while it is painfull [sic] for me to do so," all should be retried separately, or they should be tried in a U.S. court. He then ordered any action on Lewis and Wade to be suspended until November when the Choctaw Supreme Court could discuss the matter.[50] Holson then sent a message to John Taylor, the circuit clerk of the First District, telling him that he had complied with that order and issued an order to Sheriff John W. Perry of Gaines County to stay the executions of Lewis and Wade.[51]

Even Chickasaws tried to suggest rationales for Jones to stop the executions. In September 1893, the Chickasaw legislature met at Tishomingo to discuss tribal business, including how to counteract the impending allotment and tribal dissolution. The attorney for the Chickasaws, Halbert E. Paine, stated that one way to convince the federal government of the Choctaws' ability to peacefully govern themselves was to convince Jones to halt the executions.[52] Eventually, after more political maneuvering, Simeon Wade was released, which left only Silan Lewis to face the executioner. The other eight were forced to leave the Choctaw Nation for the Chickasaw Nation, although it is unknown what happened to them after they got there.[53]

The General Council met on October 6, 1893, and discussed, among other things, a bill introduced by Senator Harris that would exonerate the condemned Choctaws:

> Be it enacted by the general council of the Choctaw nation assembled, that a general amnesty is hereby granted and extended to all persons, charged with political crimes in the late trouble from August 1, 1892 up to October 1, 1893, against the Choctaw nation, that all persons that are indicted or that are subject to indictment in this political trouble from August 1, 1892 to August 1, 1893, shall have the benefit of said amnesty and stand as though they had never committed any crime against the Choctaw Nation; that this act take effect from and after its passage.[54]

The General Council killed the amnesty bill, perhaps because they feared that the U.S. government—which was still keenly observing the council's decision making—would believe that amnesty was not a proper way to deal with transgressors. Some also believed that the council was fearful of the condemned Nationalists.[55] After all, some of the Progressive men on the council had participated in prosecuting the Nationalists. Setting the Nationalist leaders free to possibly retaliate would be a huge chance they did not want to take.

Not everyone worried about the consequences of an execution. Judge A. R. Durant, a Progressive Choctaw lawyer and good friend of Chief Jones illustrated the anger many Progressives felt toward the Nationalist prisoners: "There is no doubt that the nine murderers at Wilburton will be executed," he stated confidently. "If I had been governor of the Choctaw Nation I would have summoned all the militia in the territory to enforce the sentence of the court upon those condemned men or kill every man who interfered. . . . the United States Government overstepped the provisions of the treaty when it interfered."[56]

Nevertheless, J. F. Wisdom, who was son and chief clerk of Indian Agent Wisdom, convinced Chief Gardner to order Judge Holson to stay the execution for thirty days. So many appeals were made on behalf of Silan Lewis that the *Citizen* commented, "It is very doubtful if he will ever be shot."[57]

The newspaper editors voiced their anger at both Green McCurtain and Wilson N. Jones, the latter of whom the *Caddo Banner* referred to as having "about as much brains as a half grown gourd." Evidently, amid the debates over the outcome of the trials, Jones had also commented publicly that the editor of the *Banner*, John S. Hancock, was an intruder in the Nation.[58] He was, technically, because he had not paid his ten dollars. But that editor also pointed out that Jones's "despotic form of government" had not bothered to challenge the many intruders who had not paid for their permits. Chief Jones had focused on the editor in retaliation because he had reported Jones's "Pet"—Green McCurtain—as being the one responsible for a significant shortage of money in the tribe's coffers. In addition, the *Banner* also stated that the editor notified the public that Jones allowed a whopping $38,000 to be paid to his "pet militia" for making a "cowardly attack" on Locke's home without allowing Locke's family to leave before the fighting started or without first making a warrant for Locke's arrest. As for McCurtain, the *Banner* also claimed that he was at least $70,000 short in his accountings of expenditures; when questioned by the finance committee, the *Banner* claimed that McCurtain replied, "Me don't know anything 'bout this book keeping. Me spent it for the nation. Me kept none of it back." The *Banner* expressed outrage that the administration did not require McCurtain's bondsmen to replace any of the lost funds.[59] The *Purcell Register* estimated that the shortage was as great as half a million dollars.[60]

To make McCurtain look even worse, the *Banner* reported an occasion when McCurtain got as drunk as a "biled owl" while meeting in Tuskahoma. He allegedly became so drunk that he had to be assisted to his hotel and in the process waved his pistol around and threatened to shoot anyone who accused him of taking funds. The *Banner* also reported that McCurtain's friends on the finance committee refused to analyze his Leased District account. Moreover, the paper expressed dismay that a House resolution that would have given the chief the authority to create a separate committee to scrutinize the books was defeated, presumably to protect McCurtain.[61]

While tension continued to swirl about the upcoming executions and the behavior of tribal officials, other issues brewed in the Nation. By September 1893, the number of "boomers" (prospective white settlers) had increased dramatically.[62] Not only were the intruders steadily encroaching onto Indian lands throughout Indian Territory, the number of murders escalated. Every issue of the *Indian Citizen* featured stories about men and women being shot, hacked, beaten, and knifed. The well-known Nationalist Ben Foreman, for example, was shot one evening while changing into his sleeping clothes. His killer—who remains unknown—walked into his room, and a family member overheard Foreman say, "Get out of here you son of a bitch," before he was shot five times.[63] That same month the captains of rival *ishtaboli* (stickball) teams shot and killed each other in San Bois County. At first it was thought that Green McCurtain did some of the shooting, but it turned out that McCurtain had attempted to stop the gunplay and had his horse shot out from under him. In another incident, Dr. M. A. Baldwin was shot and killed by another man named Baldwin. A few days later the Progressive John Carney shot the Nationalist lawyer Handy LeFlore in the back of the head. A clock merchant was shot five times with a Winchester and three times with a pistol, which literally blew his head off, as he tried to collect monies owed by one Jim Owens. And Chickasaw citizen L. D. Powell was robbed and murdered after being shot in the back of the head.[64]

Meanwhile, on November 13, 1893, Sam Jefferson, Joshua Calvin, Prymus Brown, and Simeon Wade requested, but did not receive, a new trial.[65] The court, however, agreed to hear the case of *Choctaw Nation v. Price Tallipoose et al.*, except the only man tried out of that group was Silan Lewis. This time, the Nationalist was up against the jury of Israel Cooper, "Filmuchubee" (Fleema Chubbee, who also testified in the Jack Crow murder case), Simeon Hampton, Jacob LeFlore, Josiah Willis (the bailiff), J. J. Schropshire, Abel Harris, Lysander Trahern, John Jones, Sam Wilson, William Amos, and David Folsom.[66]

As in the previous trial, Lewis faced a jury made almost entirely of Progressives. On April 19, 1894, they found Lewis guilty of murder yet again.[67] Lewis did not escape conviction, and it was not until 1898 that Price Tallipoose and the others were finally exonerated, when the case against them was dismissed.[68] The *Indian Citizen* also again complained that one juror who had convicted Silan Lewis in 1893 also sat on the jury for his trial in 1894. On the contrary, Simeon Hampton had not judged Lewis the first time, but he had sat in the jury that convicted Lewis's colleagues.[69]

Wasting no time, Judge N. J. Holson handed down his sentence on April 20, condemning Lewis to die on May 4, 1894:

> The Grand Jury duly sworn, tried and empanelled at the December Special Term 1892, of the Mosholatubbee Circuit Court, Choctaw Nation, did return an Indictment against you on the 16th day of December 1892, in Gaines County, Choctaw Nation and within the Jurisdiction of the Court; and on the 19th day of April 1894, after a fair and impartial trial by a Jury of twelve good and Lawful Citizens of your Country, you have been found guilty as charged in the indictment. It now becomes my solemn duty as Judge of this Court, to carry out the Law in pronouncing the sentence of death upon you and I now admonish you to prepare to meet your God in peace; you need not expect delay in the execution of this sentence by appeal or otherwise.
>
> The sentences of the Court is that you be taken to the most convenient Jail in this District or other suitable place and there securely kept and confined by the Sheriff of Gaines County, Choctaw nation until Friday the 4th day of May 1894, at which time you shall be conveyed to the Circuit Court of Misholatubbee District., Choctaw Nation and then and there between the Hours of Ten o'clock A.M. and Four o'clock P.M. on the said 4th day of May 1894, you shall be shot until you are dead by the sheriff of Gaines County or his Deputies and may God have mercy on your soul.[70]

Lewis's attorney immediately appealed the decision and asked that the Choctaw Supreme Court intervene. The Court did, but the news was not good for Lewis. The solidly Progressive Court stated that it "had in the case fail[ed] to find sufficient cause for a reversal of said proceedings in said case. Hence the decision of the lower court is hereby affirmed and the decrees of the lower court is hereby ordered to be carried out."[71] Judge Holson then issued his resentencing of Silan Lewis:

> No longer delude yourself with false hopes of a new trial, or commuta-
> tion, but make peace with your God. It is the sentence of this Court that
> you be taken into custody of the Sheriff of Gaines County, and securely
> kept in some jail or other suitable place in this District until the 5th day
> of November 1894, when you shall be conveyed to the Moshulatubbee
> District Court grounds, where between the hours of 10 o'clock A.M. and
> 2 o'clock P.M. you shall be shot until you are dead, by the Sheriff of
> Gaines County, and may God have mercy on your Soul.[72]

There are conflicting statements as to what Lewis said to the judge in response. The county clerk claims that he heard Lewis say, "I will be there on that day." Another version is that Holson said to Lewis, "I sentence you to be shot until you are dead, dead, dead."[73] Despite the drama of that oft-used scenario, at no time did Holson say "dead" three times. The more romantic interpretation of that sentencing was created by Glenn Shirley, the western writer with a penchant for embellishment:

> "Silan Lewis." The Judge repeated the defendant's name slowly. "You
> have been granted a fair and impartial trial by the high tribunal of our
> nation. It therefore becomes my duty as judge, clothed by the great power
> of Our Father, and I do hereby sentence you to be executed by rifle shot
> at twelve o'clock, high noon, on the fifth day of November 1894. It is
> the command of this court that you appear at this council house at that
> time and on that date, prepared to pay the penalty. Shee-ah!"[74]

One of life's passages that Lewis dealt with after his trial was his marriage to his wife, Martha. Among the court dockets of the Moshulatubbee District is mentioned a case (barely legible), *Silan Lewis v. Martha Lewis*. It is customary to list the plaintiff first, which in this case would mean that Lewis felt he had good cause to divorce Martha, but there is no file available to be sure. The court sided with Lewis the plaintiff. Possibly, Martha left him after she learned that he would be executed. Another factor is that a white man who worked on Lewis's property had a young daughter named Sally, and he no doubt knew what Sally stood to inherit if Lewis married her. The *Indian Citizen* described Sally as a "beautiful young white woman not over 18," which might explain why Lewis became interested in her.[75]

To complicate the mystery, Silan had married the teenager Sally Halloway on June 4, 1894, immediately after he made bail.[76] It is conceivable that the plaintiff was actually Martha (and the plaintiff and defendant were written incorrectly on the court records) and that she wanted a divorce since Silan may have been seeing Sally. Since Sally and Silan married on June 4 and the court case for divorce was June 8, one could appreciate that Martha probably would have filed charges of adultery against him. But adultery is not listed in the case heading. Nevertheless, Martha, the mother of Silan's eight deceased children, disappeared from the picture.

After being sentenced, Lewis was allowed to go home to put his affairs in order. Considering the animosities between the political parties and the furor over the Nationalists' trials, it was indeed an extraordinary move to allow Lewis his freedom and to trust that he would voluntarily return for his execution. Given the extreme stress that permeated the Choctaw Nation, if Silan Lewis had decided to leave the Choctaw Nation it is probable that no Choctaw would have tried to find him, including Chief Jones. Not having to deal with Lewis would probably have been a relief.

Other than marrying Sally, not much else is known about Lewis's life from the time of his release to his execution. There are testimonies of numerous people who claim to have known Lewis or have a vested interest in keeping the romance of his story alive; but, many of these stories contradict each other. It is obvious that some individuals who have told the story of Lewis's execution have embellished the events leading up to his death and the events of the execution itself. It has indeed been fascinating to discover that some descendants of those men who were involved in the politics of Lewis's day and who committed serious transgressions are happy to talk about

Lewis the killer but neglect to mention the crimes of their own ancestors. Notable among those who changed the historical record was Progressive Lyman Pusley the executioner who, as an aged man, told quite a tall tale.

Of what is available in the historical record it can be fairly well ascertained that Lewis and Sally remained busy managing their farm, which included over one hundred horses. Some said they owned cattle and hogs.[77] According to court records, however, there is no mention of the livestock, merely that that Lewis's homestead consisted of a house of four or five rooms, a few out buildings, a well, and thirty acres of farmland.[78] They made short trips to nearby McAlester for supplies, and they made at least one trip to Hartshorne, where they had their photograph made by Illinois native Frank Raymond, an apprentice to Arkansas photographer H. F. Doughton. The men had traveled in September 1894 to Indian Territory via the Choctaw, Oklahoma, and Gulf Railroad from Fort Smith in search of "danger and adventure." After Doughton decided to move to Texas, Raymond stayed in Hartshorne to set up his business in a tent.[79]

Silan Lewis was reportedly between fifty and sixty years old but looked young enough that Raymond assumed him to be about forty years old. He also recalls that Lewis "couldn't talk much English, so his wife did most of the talking. She was friendly and intelligent, and she told me before they left that her husband was going to be executed before long." The photograph he took is the only one of Silan and Sally.[80]

We can only surmise the anxiety Lewis felt. According to a 1957 interview with Sally, which is the only formal statement she has made about her husband's death, during these months they made no future plans beyond the date of his death and rarely discussed his upcoming execution. Sally claimed that her family pleaded with Silan to leave Indian Territory, as did numerous sympathetic law enforcement individuals. She asserts, however, that he stated he intended to die in November, that he must "face the music."[81]

In September, officials sent Lewis notice to appear at the sheriff's office in Hartshorne. According to one legend, instead of pondering an escape Lewis saddled his favorite horse. As Lewis cinched the

Silan Lewis and his young white wife Sally, days before he was executed in November 1894. Courtesy Research Division of the Oklahoma Historical Society.

saddle, Sally's father urged his son-in-law one last time to leave the Territory, telling Lewis that if he went to Hartshorne, "you will never come back." Lewis gave him the same response that he had heard repeatedly: "White man will never understand, but I have got to go."[82] Perhaps Lewis adhered to the long-gone custom of clan/blood revenge and was altering it a bit to fit his notions of Choctaw traditionalism. Maybe Lewis's sense of honor is what gave him the courage to face his execution.

After a week, Sally received a letter from her husband asking her to join him at a home where he was held on the outskirts of Hartshorne. Sally traveled to see Silan and stayed with him for a week— under the watchful eyes of guards—when he asked her to return home. According to Sally, Lewis felt sad to see her go, but seemed satisfied that she appeared to be holding up under the growing stress.[83]

Deputies transferred Lewis to yet another home for another week, and at the end of that time Lewis once again asked his wife to join him at the home of Sheriff Frank Battles, who lived outside of Hartshorne. From there, the couple made the final leg of the journey to the Choctaw courthouse on Brown's Prairie, outside of Wilburton. But when Sally arrived, pressure had been put on Sheriff Battles by Progressives to more carefully sequester Lewis, so he assigned twelve men to surround Lewis's wagon during the trip, and neither she nor Lewis's in-laws were permitted to talk with him.[84] Chief Jones did not take any chances on a protest against Lewis's execution, so he appointed a "Private Militia" to guard the execution proceedings. Not surprisingly, most of the militia men were Progressives.[85]

According to interviews, though, the guards capitulated and allowed Silan and Sally to travel together on November 4, 1894, to the courthouse in their wagon laden with camping gear and food.[86] Although Lewis arrived by wagon, that did not stop Lyman Pulsey, the man who would execute Lewis, from claiming that Lewis rode to the site of the execution on his favorite horse, dismounted, then led the horse to where Sheriff Moore stood and said, "Pony go long way." Because several witnesses have stated that Lewis's English was not good, this quote probably is not stereotypical, provided that he actually said it. Lewis then stated to Moore that "he wanted his [Moore's] eldest son to have the pony when he was gone." Lewis "gave the pony a gentle pat, and tied it to a tree."[87]

But before the alleged events with the horse, Sally claims that she and Silan stopped at Jim Blaylock's store on the outskirts of Hartshorne for lunch and to have the notary public Blaylock notarize Silan's last will and testament that left all his possessions and property to Sally. According to the *Indian Citizen*, up until this point Silan's will left all his possessions to his brother.[88] In reality, Lewis had already written one will leaving everything to another person (who was not his brother, as reported by the paper) only two days before changing it to give everything to Sally. This last-minute will writing and changing turned into a highly contested issue shortly after Lewis's death.

After thinking they had legalized the document, Silan, Sally, and their group (which may have consisted of Sally's parents) continued their trip, but instead of stopping at the small, dingy gray-colored courthouse they set up camp next to a small creek close to the building. Although he remained guarded, for five days Lewis was allowed to walk around the area. He ate meals at the camp he and Sally had made, and he slept the best he could knowing his fate.[89] On the other hand, their anxiety may not have been as great as some reports state, because the *Indian Citizen* commented on November 8 that Sally felt confident that Lewis's friends would rescue him. The *Citizen* also reports that Sally's mother attended the execution, but there is no documentation as to how she arrived there except perhaps in the wagon with Silan and Sally.[90]

On November 5, Lewis, dressed in a blue serge suit, ate breakfast with his family. Afterward, Silan and Sally looked at the pinewood coffins that sat under a shelter next to the courthouse. As a condemned prisoner, Lewis had the opportunity to choose from three coffins. Unimpressed with the workmanship of the pine boxes, Lewis allegedly commented to Sally, "I don't want to be buried in one of those things. Take me home and place the body beside my two children." Sally agreed and the officers acquiesced.[91] This story differs from what the *Indian Citizen* reported, that Lewis was placed in a coffin of "rough pine with no dressing or trimmings."[92]

The frosty November morning took on a new meaning for Silan Lewis. By 10:00 A.M., approximately three hundred people—representatives of both the Progressives and the Nationalists—gathered around the courthouse or around the log fire to keep warm. Maybe forty lighthorsemen armed with Winchester rifles walked among the crowd to keep peace. Frank Raymond, the man who had taken Lewis and Sally's photo in Hartshorne, mentioned that of the hundreds of people only a "small percent" were white and that he mainly heard Choctaw being spoken.[93] Raymond also later stated that he was afraid of the Choctaws because he "had seen lots of Indians before, but never so many at once." Eager to record the proceedings, he asked if he could take pictures of them: "About all I got in answer to my questions were grunts, but the Indians all seemed to understand when I asked if I could take pictures; they always shook their heads and looked angry."[94]

The noon hour and the execution grew closer. The crowd remained quiet and pensive until a rider bolted into the camp from the north at a "stretching run." Everyone stood up and strained to hear him speak. Raymond recalled the rider appeared to be "part Indian" and acted eager to tell the crowd his news. Although Raymond could not understand Choctaw, some of the whites standing around him did. They interpreted for Raymond that the rider told Sheriff Holson not to proceed with the execution because a large group of Indians in the woods north of the courthouse planned to free Lewis.[95]

The *Citizen*, however, reported that a note was sent to the sheriff stating that when the first shot fired, four hundred of Lewis's supporters would rush to the site and kill everyone, and that the hated Lyman Pusley would be the first to die.[96] In order to hasten the execution before anyone could intervene, Judge Holson quickly called Lewis to the site to read him his death sentence. One version has Lewis suddenly appearing out of the woods (when in fact he was already on the site with his wife), leading his "pony," then saying, "Pony tired. I ride long way."[97]

Another version more realistically has Lewis simply saying *"Ula lishke"* (I am here).[98] Sally stated that concerns about a rescue by Silan's Nationalist friends continued to circulate throughout the crowd. She recalled that Sheriff Tecumseh Moore commented that "if they come, we will give him up without a fight," before he ordered Silan Lewis to be taken to one side of a small hill.[99] This comment by Moore is quite opposite to the one made by an unknown person who claimed that Moore handed a relative of the murdered Joe Hukolutubbee a Winchester, and said, "If Silan [*sic*] runs, kill him."[100]

The execution commenced. Frank Raymond wondered at the time why the lighthorsemen lined up on the north side of the courthouse instead of taking cover behind the numerous ricks of piled wood that would have afforded them protection in case of an attack by Silan's would-be rescuers. He did not wonder long; he took his photography equipment up a small hill about fifty yards from the courthouse in case of shooting. After a while he realized no one was coming to save Lewis, so he went back down to get a closer look at the proceedings.[101]

Some Choctaw men emerged from a brushy area southwest of the courthouse carrying a coffin that they set down at the corner of the building. Two others disappeared downhill into the brush toward the southwest, and twenty minutes later they reappeared with Silan Lewis between them. As they took Silan to the south side of the courthouse, Raymond noticed the coffin again and realized that it was lined with black cloth. Someone then threw a white sheet over it.[102]

According to one account, Lewis said a short prayer before deputies spread a blanket on the ground and told him to sit on it, facing north. He removed his blue serge suit coat, vest, and shoes, and a Choctaw official reached from behind him and unbuttoned his white shirt. The location of Lewis's heart then became a matter of debate. One report states that Lewis told the officials that his heart was located within the right side of his chest, not the left. A local physician listened for Silan's heartbeat and, strangely enough, concluded that Lewis had an abnormal anatomy, that his heart was indeed on the right side. Numerous officials debated the matter, but after listening to Lewis's heartbeat (whether the physician possessed a stethoscope is unknown), they agreed with the physician. That official used white powder (Raymond thought it was flour) taken from a small tin to draw a circle on the right side of Silan's chest—over the site where the physician believed his heart to be. One version states his eyes were covered with a red bandanna.[103]

Lewis then made a short speech in which he stated that he did not think it fair for him to die when everyone else involved in the killings of the Progressives had been allowed to go free. As Lewis sat waiting to die, the crowed remained silent, while a dog in the next valley howled and a turkey gobbled.[104]

Two men, Amos Williams and Houston Johnson, held Lewis's arms out to the sides. According to custom, the sheriff, Tecumseh Moore, was to shoot Lewis, but Moore refused and the task was appointed to Deputy Sheriff Lyman Pusley. The myth of Silan Lewis being friends with Tecumseh Moore and Lyman Pusley was started by Pusley himself. In his 1935 interview he gave the impression that Lewis had even requested that Lyman kill him, with Silan Lewis uttering this string of "Tarzan-speak": "Time is up. Sheriff going read death. Choctaw law say must be shot. Want Pusley do it."[105] It continues in tear-jerking fashion in Thomas Smith's novel, A Choctaw's Honor: "Deputy Pusley replied, straight faced, 'Yeah, I'll shoot him.' His voice trailed off in bereavement to a whisper. For he, too, was a friend of the honor man, Silan. Silan agreed, 'I want him, Lyman, to do it,' pointing in the direction of the deputy sheriff."[106] Glenn Shirley parrots the melodrama in his book by calling Pusley "one of Lewis's close friends."[107] Sally Lewis, however, was there and she never mentions any friendship, nor does Raymond recall any such dialogue (at least, not in English).

Though not guaranteed by Choctaw law, choosing one's executioner was not unheard of. In a 1937 interview, Mary Long Darneal, daughter-in-law of the son of half-blood Choctaw Sheriff James Darneal, stated that during the course of her marriage she observed much about how Choctaw laws were maintained and carried out and that it was her understanding that the accused prisoner often had the opportunity to choose his executioner. Obviously, because the executioner was allowed only one rifle shot, the doomed individual picked the man he deemed the best shooter so he would not suffer. Because Sheriff Darneal had garnered the reputation of having a steady hand, he was requested repeatedly. After a career of executions,

Mary recalled that her father-in-law suffered from insomnia and nightmares featuring the faces of the men he had killed.[108] Although it is not recorded anywhere that the condemned could request an executioner (nor is their a "custom" requiring the Sheriff to perform the deed), it is possible that Silan Lewis had requested that Sheriff Moore kill him.

In an unlikely dialogue created by Smith in his fictitious account of Lewis's life, Pusley readies himself to shoot: "The executioner stood twenty-three feet to Silan's front, rifle dangling in this right hand, waiting. Deputy Pusley looked down, with sadness in his heart, at the spot on his friend's chest. "Friends don't shoot friends," he thought. "But Choctaw code demands it. Silan understands."[109]

That Lyman Pusley executed Lewis is ironic indeed, and not because Lyman was related to Abner Pusley, one of the men that Lewis and Wade had on their list to kill. Lewis and Pusley could not have been more morally different. Lewis did indeed kill, but out of frustration over what he considered a threat to his culture. Lyman Pusley was a repeat criminal and a liar. In 1883, Lyman was found guilty of not working on the road from Arbuckle to McAlester.[110] Two years later, he was tried and found guilty of grand larceny. The next year he was guilty of adultery. Also in 1886, Pusley was sued by Mary Ann Pusly [sic] for a "bill for dinner." Strangely, he apparently had recently married her and the courts decreed that in regard to that "bill for dinner" the bonds of matrimony "heretofore existing between Plantiff and deft. be found annulled and dissolved."[111] Following that episode, he pled guilty to murdering his cousin George Pusley after an argument and he was tried and convicted to be executed.[112] For reasons not documented, but certainly speculated, Judge Garland of the Choctaw Supreme Court at Tuskahoma overturned the verdict and Pusley was a free man.[113] As if that was not enough bad behavior, in 1888 Lyman was found guilty of violating the Choctaw liquor law. Despite his criminal record, by 1891 Lyman Pusley had been appointed "Special Deputy" and Bailiff of a Grand Jury in 1892 under Judge N. J. Holson.[114]

It is inconceivable that Lewis would have requested that the staunchly Progressive Pusley—the man who had been found guilty

of murder, adultery, grand larceny, and violating the liquor law—
be the one to kill him. The claim that these men—who were so
completely different in their political beliefs, worldviews, and value
systems—were "friends" is equally implausible.

Regardless of what Lewis may have thought about the executioner and exonerated criminal Pusley, the latter took up his .44
Winchester and fired from less than twenty feet away. He hit Lewis
in the circle, the powder and blood flying as the bullet passed through
his body, along with a "large stream" of blood.[115] Frank Raymond
saw the bullet strike the ground behind Lewis and later attempted
to find it, but the bullet had buried itself deep in the dirt amid
thick roots.[116]

Sadly, because the deputy put the circle on the right side of Silan's
chest instead of over his heart (that was, of course, situated within
the left side of his chest), Lewis did not die. Because bloody froth
emanated from his nose and mouth, he probably suffered a lung
shot. The *Indian Citizen* contradicts the stories of Lewis's heart being
situated in the wrong side of his chest. The paper reported that Pusley
was Lewis's "enemy" and shot him through the lung in hopes that
Lewis would suffer and die "as hard as possible." Considering Pusley's
past behaviors and political standing, this supposition is not improb-
able.[117] According to Raymond, Lewis was unconscious, shaking
and fighting for breath. Because Lewis did not die immediately,
many of the witnesses had seen enough and turned away. Lyman
Pusley, however, leaned against a thin oak tree, one hip cocked, as
he casually watched Lewis suffer.

Houston Nelson squatted as he held Lewis's right arm with one
hand and put his other hand on Lewis's chest. The other man tightly
held Lewis's left arm straight out to the side, while another held his
feet. During this ordeal, Frank Raymond had set up his camera and
was intent on taking a sensational photograph or two that would
"sell readily and make me some money."[118] He reported that after
fifteen minutes Lewis still tried to speak through the froth and
blood in his mouth and it was clear that he had no intention of
dying if he could help it.[119] The *Eagle-Gazette* claims that he lived for
thirty minutes after being shot.[120] This was supposed to be a quick

and painless execution, but it instead turned into a horrific display of suffering, with Lewis uttering "a number of loud and pitiful groans."[121] One source claims that the man holding Lewis's right hand had enough of watching Lewis's ordeal and placed a handkerchief over Lewis's mouth and nose until he suffocated.[122] Another version says the edge of the blanket was used to smother him, while the *Eagle-Gazette* writes that Sheriff Moore pinched Lewis's nose until he died.[123] Ely Wade, who claimed to have attended the execution, asserted in 1937 that it was not a Choctaw, but rather a white man named John Gross, who "choked" Lewis.[124]

Yet another individual who believed Lewis had killed "some of the crooked Progressives" and was "a good Indian," says he helped dig Lewis's grave (but could not have, since Lewis's body was taken back to his home) and asserts that "Silen" never admitted having killed anyone; that a "mock court" had hurriedly convicted Lewis because they believed Chief McCurtain would "send in his militia to stop them"; that Tecumseh Moore did not shoot Lewis because he did not believe the execution to be a "just death"; and finally, that "they stuffed a handkerchief in his mouth and let him bleed to death inwardly."[125] Another "eyewitness" claims that Lewis was "a great worker in the National Party," and asserts that the mark over Lewis's right side of his chest was instigated by one Indian only and that Lewis sat on his coffin when Pusley took aim.[126]

Executioner Pusley had a different tale to tell about the shooting. He claimed that the crowd wanted to hurry up and kill Lewis, so he shot hurriedly without making certain that the mark was on the correct side of Lewis's chest. He also stated that two deputies stuffed the handkerchief into Lewis's mouth "to keep the blood from spurting on them."[127] Regardless of the sad and gruesome events of his death, all witnesses agree that Lewis's body jerked and then finally stilled. There was a quiet moment before the crowd began talking. Many were sickened by the ordeal. Even those who had arrived to watch Lewis die became angry. Lewis had been sentenced to die by one bullet from a rifle, not to be suffocated. Since the shot failed to kill him, some began claiming that his death by suffocation had been nothing short of murder.

The execution of Silan Lewis at the Wilburton Courthouse. Executioner Lyman Pusley is leaning against the tree in the foreground. Courtesy Research Division of the Oklahoma Historical Society.

Frank Raymond, in the meantime, had focused his camera, snapped a picture, and then "ran to my pony and mounted him and got away from there." As he rode away, he heard a woman's high-pitched scream.[128] Sally had been taken to the other side of the hill and did not witness her husband's death. It appears that she heard the gunshot but waited for the news that her husband had expired to show any emotion. Lewis's body was placed in the wagon and she and her parents started for home. They intended to stop in Hartshorne at a funeral home to have his body prepared for burial, but darkness closed in before they arrived, so they camped for the night. Sally recalls that a wolf pack came close to their camp searching for the source of the blood smell. Despite the large bonfire that Sally's father built to keep the predators away, the wolves stayed close all night, their eyes shining in the glare of the fire. It was indeed a grievous night for Lewis's family. Sally could barely compose herself;

the frightened horses threatened to run from the persistent wolves, and the November cold made sleeping difficult.[129]

The next morning the wolves had departed and the family resumed their trip to Hartshorne, where Lewis was placed in a casket, one nicer than those he had viewed at the courthouse. When they arrived back at the Lewis farm, Silan was buried, per his wishes, next to his children.[130] The names and ages of these children, as well as their mother (it is unknown if Martha was the mother of them all), remain a mystery.

Several weeks later, according to the *Eagle-Gazette*, seven of the men who rode with Lewis and Wade were to have appeared for trial. Only Daniel Bon arrived. The paper stated that most people believed the men had gone to the Chickasaw Nation to avoid sentencing.[131] Frank Raymond returned to Hartshorne where he developed his one photograph of Lewis's execution and "sold quite a few copies." He also created his version of events in a painting, "an accurate enlargement, true to scale."[132]

For his role as executioner, Lyman Pulsey received the sum of five dollars. And he would later punish other criminals: he gave Simon Johnson one hundred lashes for manslaughter, and on another occasion he doled out one hundred lashes each for John Peters and Bill Hanson for stealing cattle.[133]

Years after his execution almost everyone who was interviewed about Silan Lewis had sympathetic feelings toward him. The exceptions, of course, were those Progressives and their supporters. Some simply ignored the reasons why Lewis and other Nationalists attempted to destroy the Progressives. Lyman Pusley made up his own rationale: that Lewis ran for "an office in the Indian Government," and when he was not elected he took his frustrations out on Progressives by killing them. That Pusley did not recount the real reasons why Lewis was angry is understandable. Pusley's family was prominent in the Choctaw Nation and was clearly aware of every move the Nationalists and Progressives made during the 1890s. Considering the extreme hardship placed on the tribe in the 1880s through statehood, at least, Pusley would hardly want to admit that the Nationalists may have been correct in their arguments about the Progressives. But decades later, perhaps in an effort to identify with those Nationalists, Pusley made the questionable claim that he and Lewis shared a "hearty breakfast" together prior to Pusley killing him, rather than Lewis sharing those last few minutes of his life with his wife, suggesting that Pusley and Lewis somehow shared the same sentiments.[134]

After Lewis's execution his family, friends, and supporters retuned to their homes to mourn him and what he stood for. For a while, at least, all was quiet in the Nation. The *Indian Citizen* commented on the climate of the Nation after the execution: "The war clouds which have been hanging like a funeral pall over the Choctaw Nation for the past week have been dispersed, and the white angel of peace again reigns over the fair country."[135] Two years after Lewis died, James Culberson, the court clerk who recorded the trial proceedings of Silan Lewis and other Nationalists, certified the marriage of Charles Wilson's daughter Ida, who my aunt claims had been completely spoiled by her daddy.[136]

Unlike Lewis, Pusley, the man who killed his cousin, had the luxury of living a long life. He once dined with Frank and Jesse James and met Tom and Belle Starr. He also had a penchant for waxing poetically about the need for the return of Choctaw laws: "People Oklahoma be better off if they had old laws Choctaw nation with whipping post. . . . People more wild now than Indian days. Indian used have may be $100 in pocket. Get drunk; have Indian law and whipping post be better off than have jails and penitentiary."[137] He did not, of course, ever publicly discuss his past crimes, but he did continue to tell tales about the Lewis execution, even telling his children that he had kept Lewis as a prisoner in his home, "hand-cuffed to the bed at night."[138]

In 1896, two years after his execution, Silan Lewis's wife Sally remarried, this time to George W. Beams, Silan's former Deputy Sheriff.[139] Although Silan's last will, signed on November 3, left his property to Sally, he had actually written another will just two days before, leaving everything to one John King. Why Lewis would will his property to John King is more than a bit puzzling. The *Indian Citizen* stated that Lewis had left his property to "his brother," but a study of the demographic information does not reveal King as being related to Lewis.[140] Further, it is not possible to ascertain King's political stance. In 1892, King voted in the Red Oak Precinct of Atoka County in which Wilson Jones received ten votes to Jacob Jackson's five, but that poll book does not stipulate the individual voter's choices. In 1893, King voted in the Medicine Spring Precinct of the same county in which Jackson was elected National Secretary by a vote of 26 to 0 over the Progressive challenger Hunter.[141] But political adherence is only one part of the equation.

A subsequent fight ensued over Silan's property; the first recorded case had Sally Lewis contest the first will her husband had written on November 1, which left King all of Silan's property. In the sketchy details (the actual wills are missing) of case no. 45, *Sally Lewis v. John King* (March 1895), King the defendant produced witnesses who testified on his behalf. The witnesses included the Progressives Tecumseh Moore, Jackson Nelson, Aaron Holmes, and, of all people, Lyman Pusley.[142]

What makes that group peculiar is that Moore and Pusley were confirmed Progressives, with Pusley, at least, being particularly hostile to Lewis. On the other hand, Aaron Holmes was apparently a Nationalist.[143] To make the case even more convoluted, there are only two John Kings on the final Dawes Roll. One might think that the elder one, white man John King who was forty-four at the time Silan's will was written, would be the King in question.[144] Considering that Lyman Pusley served as his witness, one might also consider that Lewis had been manipulated to leave his land to King, who surely had no familial relation to Lewis.

But a look at the other John King reveals something just as intriguing. This John King was ten years old at the time the will was written. The census card information reveals that this King's parents were the deceased James King and Lizzie King, both from Gaines County. James King (John's father) sat on the jury that allowed Robert Benton and his accomplices go free in 1886, which reveals a bit about his political affiliation. But what is most curious is that at the bottom of that enrollment card is the statement about person number 6 on the roll, a "Philastine King," who is marked off the list because "no. 6 is duplicate of Willie Pusley #2 on Choctaw card

#3329." A perusal of that latter card and of the questions posed by a representative commissioner to the Five Tribes reveals a complex situation. On card no. 4734, Philastine is listed as being five years old. On card no. 3329, Willie Pusley is listed as being nine years old. The oral testimony of John King's uncle, Jackson King, is that Philastine King was sometimes known as Willie Pusley. John King, however, states that he did not, nor had he ever heard of a Willie King. But he did know a Philistine Pusley, child of the infamous Lyman Pusley. Lyman apparently fathered the child when James King and Lizza King were separated.[145]

According to the attorneys for Sally Lewis in her case against John King, Silan Lewis had "revoked" the will of November 1 (naming King as his executor) on November 3. Lewis evidently wrote a letter stating just that, but Aaron Arpelar, the county and probate judge, postponed the case until the April 1895 term.[146] The case was not mentioned in that term, but it came up again in July 1896 as the case titled *John King v. Sally Lewis*. This time King's petition was granted, and the judge ordered that "Silan Lewis's Place" be delivered to King within ninety days, unless Sally Lewis paid King seven hundred dollars in cash. But the case appeared again in March 1897, and that time defendant Sally Lewis did not appeal the decision. Therefore the Silan Lewis place was given to King.[147] In the September term of 1897, the case once again came forward and the court ruled that "the sheriff take possession of property as asked for by S. E. Lewis," who was the attorney for King.[148] Sally took her complaint to the Supreme Court, but in October 1897, the court sent the case back to the lower court.[149] There is no further mention of whether Sally managed to stay on the Silan Lewis place. One interview states that Sally and her husband raised their eight children on a Blanco farm for twenty years, but it is not clear if the farm had belonged to Lewis.[150] What is known is that Sally later moved to McAlester, where her husband died in 1933 and where she lived until her death.

Without a doubt, Silan Lewis was a complex individual. He championed Choctaw rights and customs, yet he married a white woman with white parents who lived with them. He also wrote a will giving all his property to a man with strong connections to

Lyman Pusley. One also might question why Lewis and his Choctaw wife divorced and he married a white woman. It is likely that Lewis had been coerced to change his will by either Sally or her father. It is also important to remember that Silan and Sally were married on June 4, only five months before he was to be executed. Sally and her parents knew perfectly well that Sally would be a widow in only a few short months.

No one will know what was going through Lewis's mind prior to his execution. Considering the pressure he felt to even consider murdering the men that he did and then enduring years of trials and blame and the loss of eight children along the way, one could surmise that Lewis was emotionally charged, to say the least. In addition, he divorced a Choctaw wife in favor of an attractive white woman almost forty years his junior when he was about to die; so one might figure that when he dictated his wills he was in a state of mind perhaps not entirely rational.

Lewis was a seemingly honest and earnest man who behaved uncharacteristically when he killed. Before being executed for his actions, Lewis was given a year to live freely and to arrange his affairs; but instead of running, as many people might have done, Silan Lewis lived as normally as he could before arriving at the exact time and place he was ordered by the judge to be executed. Like the other stories dealing with violence and murder in this book, Lewis's account has inspired a number of individuals to create their own whimsical interpretations about him. Some men claim to have been witness to the execution and give entirely different testimonies from those who actually did attend. Glenn Shirley gives Lewis a backhanded compliment in his anthology of tales, *Toughest of Them All* (1953), when he talks about the individuals profiled: "Cattlemen, lawmen, renegades, lawyers, judges, and gun-slingers. Some were good, some were bad. All were tough in their own hard way." By process of elimination, Lewis was probably the "renegade."[151]

Lewis even figures as the model of a few romance novels in which the hero nobly strides in to accept his date with the executioner after being sentenced to death for murder. More accurately, in the romance novel *Warrior's Honor*, by Georgina Gentry, the hero

"Nightwalker" says as he returns to be killed: "My father, I have returned to take my punishment as I gave my word I would." Then as all the romantic Indian fathers say, "The Nashoba's hand shook as he reached out and touched his favorite in a blessing. 'I knew you would come, my son. I never doubted how much you valued our family honor and your own.'" In this story, the father is "an honored old warrior," the lighthorsemen in charge of the execution is named "Raven," and instead of being blindfolded, Nightwalker shakes his head, as all noble, principled Indians do, and says, "I would see the sun as I go up to meet the Great Spirit in the sky."[152]

Besides the aforementioned *A Choctaw's Honor*, in which the real story of Lewis is embellished to make him more honorable, Lewis is also the main character in the novel *The Choctaw Code* (1961), in which Lewis is portrayed as Jim Moshulatubbee, a wise, "traditional," very tall Choctaw with "white, even teeth" who speaks perfect, articulate English and wears buckskin. Jim befriends a young white boy and teaches him to hunt and fish before having to return to his execution for murdering a man. The theme about honor permeates the story.[153] It is fairly obvious why this novel focuses on the young white Tom Baxter: it is appealing to those white readers with a yen for a wise old Indian friend.

Rilla Askew's *Strange Business* is surely that. In the opening chapter, "The Killing Blanket," she thoroughly fictionalizes Lewis's story, yet uses real names. Not only are the events out of order, she even adds that a "yellow panther" jumped on the back of one of the Nationalists as the group rode to Joe Hukolutubbee's house, effectively slowing down their plans. Most of the details are wrong, but there is just enough correct information and embellished action to make the story movie worthy.[154]

The saga of Silan Lewis is what novelist James N. Frey might call the "germinal idea," the makings of a very interesting novel. In his book *The Key: How to Write Damn Good Fiction Using the Power of Myth*, Frey discusses the characteristics of a hero: the hero has courage and a special talent; is clever and resourceful; is an "outlaw," living by his or her own rules; is good at what he or she does for a living; is a protagonist (takes the lead in a cause or action); has been wounded or is wounded (that is, maimed, disgraced, grieving, etc.); is motivated by idealism; and is sexually potent.[155] If one considers the traits of a hero (even if only for fiction), Lewis pretty much possessed those same traits.

Lewis had courage enough to risk his life to try to save tribal sovereignty. His special talents could have been his abilities to track and shoot, and he was good at farming, which was how he made his living. Lewis was clever and resourceful enough to formulate a plan and to evade the law at least for a short time. He was certainly considered to be an "outlaw" in purely legal terms, but he also could be considered an outlaw because of his political stance, which was opposed to that of the tribal leadership in power. He was concerned about Choctaw tradition—which is not exactly living by "his" rules, but at the same he did not accept the rules of the status quo. He is a protagonist to those who also believed in his cause. He had been wounded by the deaths of his children and by the change in his tribe's culture. Obviously, he was driven by the Nationalist ideology and that he returned for his execution is the ultimate proof of his adherence to traditional tribal law. Finally, that he married an eighteen-year-old could be proof of his desirability, although some have considered that she seduced him for the land she would inherit after his death.

Lewis's execution affected people in other ways. Minnie Anderson, a woman who knew Silan and Sally Lewis, was strongly influenced throughout her life by the shootings that took place in 1892 and the punishment Lewis received. In 1957 she declared that "I have never voted in my life, and I never expect to." And to expound the obvious, she said, "The shooting was because of politics."[156]

Lewis impressed many people with his behavior. Not the fact that he killed several men, but that after he was tried, convicted, and sentenced to die, instead of running away he returned for his execution. But Lewis was not the only Indian Territory Native to return for punishment. All the Five Tribes had incidences in which a convicted murderer bravely faced his execution.

One vignette tells of a Choctaw who was picking cotton on the land of Hugh McGee in Telephone, Texas, when he stopped picking one afternoon and asked to have his cotton weighed. His concern was that the river was rising and he said he had to be at Mayhew the next day in order to be executed according to Choctaw law.[157] In another episode, a Creek man bravely stood by his coffin, took a red handkerchief from his pocket, folded it, and then asked the captain of the lighthorsemen to tie it around his eyes. The captain pinned a white piece of paper over the condemned's heart prior to the execution squad of five lighthorsemen firing three bullets into the criminal's chest.[158] Still another Creek man bravely met the same fate, and after he was shot, the executioners stuck corks in his spurting wounds before they quickly buried him.[159] Another *Indian and Pioneer* interviewee says that "I recall a man who was convicted of murder and sentenced to die. He was turned loose and told when to come back to be shot. Some of the men tried to get him to ride horseback into Texas and escape. 'No,' he said, 'me come back.' And he did. They had him sit under a tree and put a cross over his heart and a Mr. Posey shot him."[160]

Silan Lewis is not easy to seriously evaluate. Where do we place Silan Lewis amid these lists of American heroes, martyrs, and villains? Do we judge him harshly because he murdered another human? Or do we honor him because, by all reports, he also was an honest man, one concerned with the frightening prospect of losing tribal autonomy and having to capitulate to the laws of the emerging state of Oklahoma, in addition to losing even more land and connections to Choctaw culture? Clearly it depends on the evaluator's point of view. Historians (both non-Native and those Natives willing to capitulate to the status quo) who are concerned with portraying white Americans as justified in their steamrolling over tribal Nations in their quest to spread Christianity and democracy will situate Lewis as a villain. Those looking for heroes and those people who resisted the onslaught of colonization might evaluate Lewis with a different perspective. Whether Silan Lewis's drastic course of action was morally and ethically appropriate will remain a matter of opinion. But his intentions, to fight back against invaders who stole his land and who were prepared to keep the Choctaws subsumed, will never be in doubt.

Decades after Lewis's execution, Oklahomans commented that he was "a good Indian" who "killed some of the crooked Progressives,"[161] "a great worker for the National Party,"[162] and "a very honorable and industrious, good Indian citizen,"[163] and that "Silan Lewis might have been a fanatic as he appeared to be, but what greater sacrifice can any one make for his belief?" As to the other Nationalists, the court clerk Culberson said "they were honest and sincere men and were honest in their convictions."[164]

After the execution of Silan Lewis in 1894, which marked the last legal Choctaw execution before statehood, the violence continued, as did debates over allotment and statehood. But tribal members continued to resist the inevitable chipping away at their culture and sovereignty. Regardless of the internal strife between the Nationalist and Progressive entities within the Choctaw Nation, the tribe still faced collective adversity from the intruders who desired their lands.

CHAPTER 5

Continued Resistance
to Statehood

Our people have always had their own laws and their own government and had everything to suit themselves. That is the best way for
the Indians and they like it best.

—Jacob Jackson, Nationalist, ca. 1906

The Progressives executed Silan Lewis, but the Nationalist ideology
of resistance remained alive. Jacob Jackson had cultivated thousands
of followers and new conservative Choctaw leaders emerged in the
forms of Willis Tobly and Daniel Bell. Even though Nationalists and
Progressives disagreed on many issues, some of the old guard Progressives began protesting against allotment. A growing awareness of
severalty and statehood emerged among the Choctaw citizenry,
and while many idly complained, others become proactive by writing
letters, voicing their concerns to the leadership, voting, and attending
General Council meetings.

Severalty and violent crimes that occurred in almost every county
in the Choctaw Nation continued to be major concerns, as were the
overwhelming numbers of non-Indians who swarmed throughout
Indian Territory.[1] According to the 1890 census, the Choctaw Nation
consisted of approximately 10,017 Choctaws, 4,406 "Negroes"
(including those who were bona fide citizens and those who just
claimed to be), 28,345 whites, and 1,040 Indians of other tribes. While

this census was perhaps inaccurate—it often was hard to differentiate between whites and mixed-bloods—the identifiable Choctaws made up only 25 percent of the population.[2]

White squatters had firmly ensconced themselves on tribal land and refused to leave. The tribe worried about all the invaders, many of whom were by themselves (men, usually) or with their nuclear families. But sometimes the whites brought with them their entire extended family. For example, former chief Edmund McCurtain spoke out against the Tuckers, a group of people numbering close to five hundred claiming to be Choctaw, but whose claims were rejected by the General Council and by the Department of the Interior. The Tuckers, however, were not easily dissuaded, and they continued to plead their case to the government. McCurtain understandably feared that the Tuckers would therefore be qualified to inhabit thousands of acres of Choctaw land. Because the General Council saw the threat posed by the Tucker family and from another large group, the Glen family, in 1891 it approved an act appropriating five thousand dollars to resist their citizenship by employing able counsel.[3]

Chief Wilson N. Jones fretted about the growing "difficulties that our forefathers did not conceive of." He felt increasing pressure because of the number of intruders flooding into the Nation. He also told the General Council that he had received many complaints about lumber being wasted when those leasing the timberlands tried to float the wood down impassable waterways. Jones also wanted a change in the legal system because he thought the Nation spent too much money dealing with "petty offenses" and that the county courts should complete cases instead of transferring them to other counties. He also felt that traders should have to pay royalties on their goods because many of them carried large amounts of merchandise.[4]

Despite Jones's complaints, the *Purcell Register* held a different view of the state of the Choctaw Nation. "The danger to the Indians," the editors wrote, "did they but realize it, comes from within in greater force than from without." They believed that it was not the outsiders who were the land grabbers, but rather, the wealthy Choctaws who created "the greatest land monopoly ever known." Those men were, according to the paper, "crying the loudest" against change. The paper alleged that the wealthy Progressives postured as the full-bloods' "only true friend" while robbing them at the same time.[5] Indeed, in 1894, the *Caddo Banner* stated that Jones was one of those wealthy Choctaws who owned vast acreage, including a pasture with a thirty-two mile circumference. A logical assumption was that Jones's anxiety stemmed not so much out of concern for his fellow Choctaws, but that "some poor homeless Indians will get good homes within his enclosures."[6]

The same could be said about Green McCurtain, whom the *Caddo Banner* claimed owned "twenty times as much land as he could hold should there be an equal division."[7] Like other Progressive Choctaw politicians, Green McCurtain had a history of serving in various capacities. A substantial, balding man who reportedly stood six feet two inches tall, McCurtain had been elected sheriff of Skullyville County in 1872; several years later he was a representative on the General Council and then was elected Speaker of the House. He also served as school trustee and national treasurer.[8] McCurtain initially did not favor allotment, one reason being that he did not want to lose his vast acreage.[9]

By February 1894, Choctaws still argued among themselves about allotment, monies, per capita payments, and who should lead them. In hopes of making a good impression on the U.S. government, Chief Jones stated in his message to the General Council that the Choctaw Nation had never been in a better financial situation and that the schools were prospering. Reporters from the *Caddo Banner*, however, claimed the opposite. The paper stated that there were no funds available for any expenditures, the schools were unable to continue longer than six more months, and Green McCurtain had neglected to turn over almost $120,000 of Leased District money in addition to other monies. Months later, papers stated that amount had increased to $200,000. The *Banner* asserted that Chief Jones had purposely misled the General Council into believing that the tribe was in "splendid financial condition" and that McCurtain would no doubt be "white washed" by his personal and political friends on the General Council. The newspaper tried to portray Jones and McCurtain as robbers, as men who had used funds to their personal

Principal Chief Green McCurtain (1896–1900; 1902–1910). The wealthy Progressive McCurtain at first resisted the idea of allotment, but then changed his mind and became a staunch advocate of the tribe negotiating with the federal government before "Congress will likely do some rash act which will be unjust to us as a people." Nationalists argued that McCurtain advocated allotment since he had found a way to financially benefit from its policies. Courtesy Research Division of the Oklahoma Historical Society.

benefit. McCurtain's biographer, however, ignores the serious accusations of impropriety with tribal funds on McCurtain's part and asserts that as treasurer, he "seems to have been very good."[10]

That year, Green McCurtain and another wealthy and influential Progressive Choctaw citizen, Napoleon Ainsworth (recall that as chief commissioner for freedmen's registration, Ainsworth testified in 1885 that Jackson Crow had registered as a freedman, when in fact, Crow does not appear on any roll), co-authored a formal protest to the Dawes Commission. The bottom line, they argued, was that "we believe . . . that the Indian, unable to cope with the white man in the barter and trade of his possessions, would soon be defrauded of that which they now own in common—that they would become impoverished, separated from each other, crowded from their present quarters and finally annihilated. . . . Land in severalty will be the sword that will cut the Gordian knot—holding our land in common. When the white man touches a part he touches the whole."[11]

But in July 1894, McCurtain did a turnaround and stated that he supported severalty. His change of heart evidently came about after he considered that the federal government was going to act in a way detrimental to the tribe unless the Choctaws decided to negotiate. In his July public speech he railed against the General Council, which he referred to as "so corrupt that an appeal for right and justice has no weight" and whose members have "made the capitalist our god." And, not to leave out anyone in his diatribe, McCurtain blasted other prominent Choctaws by saying that "most of our public men, with few exceptions, are so corrupt . . . that an appeal for right and justice and mercy is treated with contempt."[12]

McCurtain believed that "unless we take some measures of arriving at an amicable solution of the question involved, between us and the Dawes Commission, Congress will likely do some rash act which will be unjust to us as a people." He felt that the tribe had to act quickly because the U.S. government was "striking us below the belt." He also voiced his concern about the vast numbers of white intruders marching into the Choctaw Nation, stating that this "tide of emigration" would be so overwhelming that "our country will be literally overrun with them." He vowed that these noncitizens living in the Choctaw Nation would never be paid for the improvements they had made while living there.[13] Instead, he called for all noncitizens to be removed from Choctaw lands and their property seized and sold to the highest bidder. McCurtain also suggested that the U.S. government settle all unfinished monetary business with the Choctaws and Chickasaws.[14]

The *South McAlester Capital* called McCurtain "wishy-washy" for delivering the July speech, in which he came forward strongly for severalty, and then, when he realized how many Choctaws advocated against allotment, he backtracked a bit by stating he was against statehood and would only treat with the commission if they honored the demands about the noncitizens and unpaid monies.[15] McCurtain then claimed that he had previously been misquoted about his views on allotment and stated, "I am not entirely opposed to allotment, and yet am not in favor of its being done altogether by the United States." He wanted the Choctaws to be the ones to "suggest terms of allotment."[16]

Not surprising, however, McCurtain then stated in a letter to the *Fort Smith Elevator* that the powerful (and white) J. J. McAlester had earned his wealth by hard work, and, even though he had indeed fenced in an enormous amount of land, he had not violated any Choctaw law. To further rationalize McAlester's honored position as a white man among Indians, McCurtain then added that "he has only exercised his privileges" and that the Choctaws who were not allied with McAlester were actually opposed to the other white men who were not citizens. While McCurtain was correct in maintaining that McAlester was a citizen by marriage and therefore was entitled to "privileges," it can be argued that McCurtain knew perfectly well, and yet chose to ignore, the reality that McAlester also was a master opportunist.[17]

For his part, the former chief Wilson N. Jones avoided the problem of allotment for himself by arranging to buy land in Texas and eventually move there. In the late summer of 1894, Jones and Chickasaw Judge Overton Love bought land in Sherman and proceeded to establish well-appointed estates that would later provide their families havens from severalty.[18]

Choctaws continued to argue with each other about the issue of allotment, and it was no small issue in the election of 1894 when Jefferson Gardner defeated persistent Nationalist challenger Jacob

Jackson. Gardner was the son of mixed-blood parents. His father had been educated at the Choctaw Academy and served as interpreter for missionaries. Jefferson attended Norfolk School and Spencer Academy, then married the first of his three wives, Lucy James. She died at Wheelock in 1862, and two years later he married Lucy Christy. When she passed he married her sister Julia. Like other chiefs before him, Jefferson Gardner had farmed, ranched, and run a mercantile store successfully. He served as postmaster at Eagletown, operated a cotton gin, and was appointed treasurer of the Choctaw Nation in 1884 and circuit judge of the Second District in 1894.[19]

In his message to the General Council on October 5, 1894, Chief Gardner gave his opinion on allotment:

> As has been expressed by an almost unanimous vote or expression of the people, we do not desire any change in the tenure of our lands or any change in our tribal government. Therefore let me impress upon you that it is your duty that you act in accordance with the wishes and desires of the people whom you represent in which was fully shown in the protest against any change whatever. I suggest that you carefully consider this matter as it is of grave importance to our people. Knowing that at this time a change of any kind would be detrimental to our people, I earnestly ask that if a change must come, let us stand firm and plead for that which our people have elected us to do. Plead for a continuance of our present government on which depends the happiness of our people. Therefore with all candor and courtesy to the Dawes Commission, I am opposed to a change, knowing that our people are not prepared for it and that a consent will never be given, I beg that this embarrassing proposition be withdrawn and that you make haste in business.[20]

He also cited the promises made by the U.S. government in the 1855 treaty (that was approved in 1880) and the 1866 treaty, which guaranteed that the Choctaws would hold their lands in common, that the tribe was allowed the unrestricted right to self-government and jurisdiction over all persons and property within the boundaries of their land, and that the U.S. government would not in any way interfere with the rights, privileges, or customs of the Choctaws.[21]

Principal Chief Jefferson Gardner (1894–1896). The educated, anti-allotment Gardner was apparently so frustrated with impending severalty that he refused to respond to requests to attend meetings and discuss the issue. His lack of action was one reason he lost to Green McCurtain in the 1896 election for chief. Courtesy Research Division of the Oklahoma Historical Society.

Green McCurtain and his colleague N. B. Ainsworth, however, had a different view. They wanted to treat with the Dawes Commission and proceeded to make a proposal. Although they stood against a territorial form of government, because they believed the whites would outnumber the Choctaws in voting power and that it would be "impolitic" to change the Choctaw form of government, they did believe that the Choctaws should individualize their lands but that the land should remain the property of the Choctaw Nation for twenty-five years. After that time, the owners would receive a title to the land. In addition, they argued for a large school for one thousand Choctaws, financed and maintained by the U.S. government. They also wanted towns to be established, and everyone who lived within those boundaries would pay a fee. At the end of twenty-five years the excess lots could be sold to the highest bidder. McCurtain fervently believed that "the United States Government does not desire to wrong us, nor to see us wronged. Rather, the damage to the Choctaws would come from the white intruders whose flow into the Nation continued unabated."[22]

Some local newspapers did not agree with McCurtain's and Ainsworth's call for a treaty with the Dawes Commission. The editors of the *Minco Minstrel* considered the idea "absurd and impossible."[23] The *Purcell Register* stated that McCurtain left a few things out of his report, namely that all the Five Tribes, except the Seminoles, had large debts. And, the editors pointed out, some former chiefs of those tribes had somehow been able to amass a great deal of wealth, even though they had worked as tribal leaders for relatively small pay. Those editors claimed that the twenty-five years mentioned by McCurtain were for his benefit. As a "boodler," McCurtain could continue to loot the public for decades.[24]

As for Chief Gardner, despite his intense anti-allotment feelings, instead of dealing with the issue head-on he ignored the messages sent to him by federal officials. He refused to attend Dawes Commission meetings and did not call any General Council sessions to deal with the numerous issues associated with allotment, including tribal dissolution. His lack of action did not go over well with many of his supporters who demanded that Gardner take an active role in the dispute. Gardner's refusal to act resulted in a split in the party.

Though Gardner purposely declined to address the severalty threat, he decisively dealt with other issues, such as the ongoing Choctaw factionalism. According to the *Davis Advertiser*, around the first of April, 1895, some "full blooded aborigines took to the war path and have been killing and burning ever since." Subsequently, armed men representing the Nationalist faction (also known by this time as the Locke Faction, named after its leader Victor Locke) and others representing the Progressives (also known as the Jones Faction) were still in the field making the citizens nervous. A third faction representing Chief Gardner also took to the roads in order to try and preserve peace in the Choctaw Nation.[25]

What the *Davis Advertiser* referred to was the incident in which two Nationalists, William Sylvester and John Cooper, shot Progressive

Arnold Islitich in the head and left him for dead in front of his home. A few days later, Solomon and Simpson Lonaker and others ambushed the Coopers and a few others a few miles north of Eagletown. All the men were armed with rifles. The Lonakers fired from behind piles of brushwood as the Coopers headed toward their field to start planting. The groups then fought hand to hand before the Lonaker group left the area, losing Simpson Lonaker and Tom Forbes, a companion, in the fight. One of the Coopers, Cornelius, was killed instantly. William Cooper had been shot at least twelve times but was able to give a description of his assailants before dying. Now both the Jones and Locke factions were aware of how well armed their adversaries were. According to the paper, with the death of the Cooper brothers, "the Nationalists were once again ready to fight."[26] Citizens of the Nation became alarmed after hearing this news, because even though Silan Lewis had been executed less than year before, some of the Nationalists still awaited their day in court. Many believed that the violent feud between the Nationalists and Progressives would escalate with the start of the trials.

Meanwhile, in 1895 Joseph P. Folsom went so far as to propose a bill in the Senate that was designed to severely punish any Choctaw citizen who tried to take over the Choctaw government or its system of landholding or anyone who would "betray said land and Choctaw country into the hands of a foreign power," that, of course, being the United States. Anyone guilty of this treason would be punished by jail time plus a fine for the first offense and would be put to death for a second offense. The bill failed to pass a vote in the House, although it did pass in the Senate. Not surprising, the only dissenter was Joe Everidge, a one-eighth-blood Progressive who had served as a national lighthorseman and sheriff of Kiamichi County (1882) and was a member of the Indian police. Along with Robert Benton, he voted for the right of way for the St. Louis and San Francisco Railway through the Choctaw Nation and he served as part of the commission that traveled to Washington, D.C., to explain the violence after the election of 1892. And, his son had been wounded in the fight at Locke's place. Under Progressive McCurtain, Everidge served as a member of the House of Representatives, member of the

Senate, district collector of the Third District, and superintendent of public instruction. Everidge, like other wealthy Progressives, held a large estate of 640 acres.[27]

Four years after Silan Lewis's execution some of the men who committed murder along with Lewis once again faced a jury trial, this time with jurors William Aipelar, Charles Billy (spelled Billie on the voting records), Nicholas Brown, Jack Burns, James Darneal, Hally Gage, Abel Harris, Ennis James (that reads Ellis in the poll book), Isham James, Silas Pusley, John Williams, and John Jones.[28] For a change, men on this jury held different political views. At least six of the men were Progressives,[29] and two were Nationalists; the affiliations of the others are unknown.[30]

Although this jury represented both parties, all agreed that given the state of Choctaw-U.S. relations, it might not be prudent to convict them. So the prisoners were discharged on May 21, 1896, with the intention of continuing the trial at a later date. The Gaines County Courthouse burned in 1895, and the belief among Choctaws was that the friends of the Nationalists had set the building on fire in the hope that the written testimonies and other evidence would be destroyed. But the court clerk at that time, James Culberson, later commented that "everywhere we went we took the evidence with us."[31] It remains unknown if Culberson kept the documentation of this case through the years or if someone else had it and never brought it forward.

In another memoir written by Culberson, he clearly expresses sympathy with what the Nationalists were attempting to do when they killed the Progressives.[32] What is known is that ultimately in January 1898, Sam Jefferson and Simeon Wade were pleased when the presiding judge, N. J. Holson, dismissed their case citing "there being no indictment among the papers."[33] The reality was that there were no papers. Nationalist Joshua Calvin had died in 1896, but there were still other Nationalists who rode with Silan Lewis and Simeon Wade who needed to be dealt with. All the men had fortunate outcomes: Price Tallipoose was also dismissed, as were Charles McCoy, William Taylor, William Anderson (alias Bill Anderson), and Johnson Parker.[34]

The cases dealing with the 1892 murders had finally closed. But the tribe still had a variety of crises to worry about. While the tribe simmered over the issue of allotment and the continued violence, prior to the election of 1896 part of the Nationalist Party that continued to rally behind Gardner named itself the Independent Party and nominated him for reelection. The other faction of the Nationalist Party nominated the national secretary Jacob Jackson, a man who remained vehemently opposed to allotment and was willing to consider any form of action against it. Just the year before, Jackson had supported the idea of allowing Absentee Wyandottes to settle in the Nation because, to his way of thinking, if the Choctaw Nation was full of Indians, then there would be no room for whites.[35] The third party, the Progressive, or Hawk, Party favored allotment. They nominated Gilbert W. Dukes, but numerous members of the party did not care for Dukes, so in May 1896 the anti-Duke faction split off to form the Tuskahoma Party and chose Green McCurtain as their candidate.

McCurtain did not think much of the other candidates for chief in 1896 and was especially frustrated with Gardner: "Gardner will do nothing, absolutely nothing. No matter how urgent the demand, how imminent the danger, he will remain in his hermit like seclusion among the hills of Eagle County and let the country wag as it may." He let Jacob Jackson off a bit more easily, saying that "he is one of those men who has self-assurance enough to try to do something. He may accidentally stumble on the right thing."[36] McCurtain prevailed with strong support among intermarried whites, winning 1,405 votes to Jackson's 1,195, Dukes's 613, and Gardner's 596. Gardner's showing was no doubt a result of his refusal to directly address the issue of allotment. He was also criticized for asking that the General Council convene in late August for the purpose of organizing the procedures for the next census of the Choctaw Nation. The *Indian Citizen* argued that the Choctaw treasury was almost empty and a council meeting was an additional and unnecessary expense.[37]

But a few weeks later, the *Citizen* clarified that criticism of Gardner a bit by stating that he may have been planning to convince the General Council to disfranchise the freedmen and intermarried whites. In fact, he was planning to make plans to create a roll of the intermarried citizens because there was at that time no complete roll of them and their families.[38]

After becoming chief, McCurtain quickly removed Jacob Jackson as national secretary and replaced him with another Progressive, Solomon J. Homer, under the accusation that as National Secretary, Jackson neglected to publish official notices, failed to provide officials with copies of laws, and did not properly care for the tribal archives.[39] The U.S. Indian Agent, Dew Wisdom, used the recent election as an opportunity to proclaim that "beyond doubt, . . . the Indian mind has undergone a change on this question."[40]

In October 1896, the General Council passed a bill authorizing the chief to appoint commissioners to treat with the Dawes Commission, and one month later McCurtain called together representatives of the Five Tribes to gather at South McAlester for a conference.[41] The usual Progressives were there representing the Choctaws: McCurtain, Wesley Anderson, Napoleon B. Ainsworth, D. C. Garland, Ben Hampton, Amos Henry, J. S. Standley, A. S. Williams, and E. N. Wright.[42] While the Progressives were busy expressing their desire to treat with the federal government, an allied group of Nationalists and old-guard Progressives met at Antlers to pass resolutions against any dealings with the Dawes Commission. They remained steadfastly against any change in their government.[43]

Two months later, the Commission to the Five Civilized Tribes met with a coalition of conservative full-bloods. One of the men was Nationalist Jacob Jackson who vocalized the opposition many Choctaws had to the Dawes Severalty Act of 1887 and the Curtis Act of 1898, which abolished tribal governments and created civil governments. Jackson asserted that "fully three-fourths" of the tribe were adamantly opposed to allotment and read the Dawes Commission their letter claiming that the Choctaw administration in power represented only "negroes and intermarried whites." He also informed the Commission that they had organized an anti-allotment organization called the "Choctaw and Chickasaw Union Party," comprising members of both those tribes who did not "represent any white people, negroes, or intermarried people, but merely the sentiments of the citizens by blood" and who preferred that the tribal constitution and government continue. To sum up their beliefs and arguments, the new Union Party stated that the law is "without warrant of the Constitution" and "a mass of incongruities and conflicting propositions" and that "the passage of the same was procured by intrigue, corruption open and notorious bargain and sale of legislative votes."[44]

The Dawes Commission embarked on an intense question-and-answer dialogue with Jackson in which it attempted to ascertain why, if McCurtain won the election based on his pro-allotment platform, the General Council would not have the right to pass such a law? Jackson responded that indeed, after negotiations with the Dawes Commission were completed, it would be presented to the U.S. Congress for ratification, then to the General Council, and then to the people. Jackson could not at the moment, however, prove the bribery accusation. The Commission tried to reason with one of Jackson's cohorts, S. L. Bacon, to convince him that with severalty he would get much more land—up to "700 acres"—than just the 25 acres he owned at present, but Bacon would have none of it. Reflecting the sentiment of those who were more concerned with keeping their tribal structure and tribal identity intact than personal wealth, Bacon simply stated, "The Choctaw people own the land and do not want a change in their government."[45]

In response, Judge Montgomery lectured the men, saying, "I am not going to fall out with you about politics. . . . The time has come when you should lift yourself above playing politics, and look at the matter as intelligent men and meet the existing conditions, so as to save whatever you can of your government and protect the interest of the people. . . . If you read the President['s] message—he is the best friend you ever had." Then, he proceeded to say the most insulting thing he possibly could have to the Nationalist full-bloods: "You are the worst enemies the fullbloods every [sic] had."[46] One can only imagine the conversations among the Choctaw men on their long journey home.

Indeed, one rationale the federal government continued to use in order to justify severalty was that the Choctaws—as well as other tribes—could not manage their own affairs. The government had

Chief Wilson N. Jones's elaborate home. Courtesy Research Division of the Oklahoma
Historical Society.

observed the violence that pervaded Indian Territory and had paid
close attention to the Nationalist trials. The Choctaws consistently
argued that they could take care of their business and took great pains
to present a united front to outsiders, even when internal arguments were sometimes almost unmanageable.

Wilson N. Jones remained opposed to allotment. In an interview
in April, Jones stated that those who opposed severalty—G. W. Dukes,
Jacob Jackson, and Jefferson Gardner—did so because what they
really wanted was an office within the Choctaw government, and if
the lands were allotted they would not get that opportunity.[47] He
accused McCurtain and Ainsworth, at least, of negotiating and signing
the agreement for selfish reasons. "It smacks of fraud," Jones claimed,
because those men had a direct interest of twenty-five percent of
the Leased District claim.[48] This is a notable accusation.

Like Wilson Jones, Green McCurtain may have been trying to
protect the interests of the tribe, but he also intended to protect his

own. He advocated an appraisal of Choctaw lands so citizens could select a parcel of land equal to a certain monetary value. He also pushed for payment for the remainder of the Leased District and all other monies as treaty agreements, for compensation for the surrender of Choctaw citizenship, and for the lands to be declared nontaxable and inalienable. In addition, he was concerned about mineral rights to the land, the preservation of the Choctaw government beyond statehood, and the retention of the Choctaws' right to determine citizenship.[49]

Congress was also on the move and on June 10, 1896, it approved an act declaring that all persons claiming tribal citizenship had to make a written application to the Dawes Commission at Vinita by September 10, 1896. This resulted in an impressive influx of whites into Indian Territory who had the goal of acquiring tribal citizenship and all the rights and benefits that being member of a tribe might bring.[50]

A group of about six hundred Choctaws led by Jacob Jackson were not about to stand still and allow themselves to be victimized. They met at Smithville to formally create their dissenting group. Jackson was elected chief, and S. E. Coe, J. C. Folsom, and Willis Jones (the individual whose arrest in part precipitated the Wilson-Locke War) were elected as his council. This group formulated a radical idea: Jackson and some two thousand other Choctaws proposed to sell their allotments in Indian Territory and use the earnings to buy new land in Mexico and begin a new Choctaw Nation there. Upset after their meeting with the commission in the winter of 1896–97, Jackson and some of his council traveled to Mexico where they met with Mexican authorities about transplanting the large group of Choctaws from Indian Territory to Mexico. The Mexicans agreed that they would allow the Choctaws to govern themselves and would see to it that non-Indians would not be allowed to enter into the "new" Choctaw Nation.[51]

In 1901 the *Chelsea Reporter* expressed concern about a group of Choctaws called Snakes, and their leader "Wilson Jones," also known as "Crazy Snake." His name actually was Willis, not Wilson, and he allied himself with Jacob Jackson, who was the leader of the group. But no one in that group referred to himself as "Crazy Snake."[52]

There was another group, however, that called itself the Choctaw Snakes. They were similar to Jacob Jackson's group and to the Creek Snakes in that they were anti-allotment, anti-statehood, and wanted the noncitizens out of their Nation. The Choctaws of this smaller group were led by Willis Tobly, a full-blood Methodist minister from San Bois County.[53]

While the Choctaw Snakes continued to organize, Green McCurtain gathered a group of his men, including E. N. Wright, A. R. Durant, Wilson N. Jones, Peter J. Hudson, Wesley Anderson, and Solomon Hotema, at Tuskahoma in January 1896. McCurtain recommended that the General Council enter formal negotiations with the Dawes Commission. The Choctaw delegation and representatives from the Chickasaw tribe met with the Dawes Commission at Atoka and signed the Atoka Agreement on April 23, 1897. The Choctaw signatories were McCurtain and delegates N. B. Ainsworth, Wesley Anderson, D. C. Garland, Amos Ben Hampton, Henry, J. S. Standley, A. S. Williams, and E. N. Wright. The agreement stipulated that, among other things, the tribal laws and courts would be abolished and that all tribal members would become U.S. citizens. Although the tribal courts were to be liquidated, they were to continue until 1906 "in order to carry out the requirements of this agreement."[54] Knowing that the tribal courts would soon be eliminated caused extreme stress, resentment, and frustration among those Choctaws who vehemently disagreed with what the Choctaw signers had done. Many of these disgruntled Choctaws would try to take action.

In 1896, Charles F. Meserve conducted an investigation of conditions in Indian Territory for the Indian Rights Association and summed up the major problem faced by the tribes in Indian Territory:

> This property all belongs to the Indian, but it is the white men who are cutting and shipping the hay, white men who are felling, manufacturing, and shipping his timber, white men who are hauling his stone and asphaltum, white men who are harvesting the corn and cotton from his rich acres, white men who are pasturing his beautiful waving prairies, and shipping the fat herds to his stock yards of Kansas City and Chicago. It is the white man who is omnipresent. The common Indian is well-nigh an alien in the land of his fathers.[55]

He also stated in 1896 that he had proof of at least one hundred murders committed in the Choctaw Nation in a single year. While Meserve was correct in his observation about who was taking over Indian Territory, his assertions about violence in the Choctaw Nation was greater than it probably was. A study of the court dockets and newspapers reveal that although there was indeed much violence and crime, in no year did that many murders occur. He also stated in the same report that "one judge who has been here fifteen years"—who could only be Isaac Parker at Fort Smith—has sentenced "something like 1000 men to be hanged," when in reality Judge Smith had sentenced 174 convicted people to be hung, and only eighty-eight of those actually were.[56]

No doubt Meserve was impressed with the variety of violent crimes in the Nation. Following are examples of such crimes that occurred within just a few months of each other in 1895. While in Jesse Wilson's barber shop, Lon Gardner wanted a drinking partner and when Clint Terry refused to drink whiskey with him Gardner shot him. The bullet passed through Terry's arm, entered his chest between his ninth and tenth rib, and then traveled to his pelvis. In a flourish of detail, the *Citizen* reported that his "innards" had been punctured too many times to treat. That same month the well-known Bob Christian and his band of "Oklahoma desperados" were violently captured by police outside of Wilburton as they "were lying about the camp." The deaths did not stop there; full-blood William Amos was shot in front of his wife by an unknown assassin who watched him drop dead at her feet, and in South McAlester a black man shot the intermarried white man Frank Messick for "cheating him." In late August 1896, a man named Bill Hale was killed at Sweet Town and his mangled body was found one morning nearly eaten by hogs. Two of the three accused killers, Jesse Miller and Dave Quinton, were apprehended, but Nelson Benge escaped.[57] This sort of brutality no doubt left a great impression upon Meserve.

While Meserve overcalculated the number of murders, those that did occur were often vicious. The experiences of the Hudson and Amos families are good examples of what life was like through several generations for some in Indian Territory. In 1897, Wash Hudson, the son of a white missionary (James Hudson) and a Choctaw woman (Ahobatema), and his brother-in-law, Thomas Amos, were killed while traveling from Ultima Thule, Arkansas, to his home by Foston Fobb and Jones James. Sarah Amos Winship, the ex-wife of Simon Winship, was living with her cousin Emos Tonihka while teaching Native children at Kulli Chito. The man she considered her "sweetheart," Nelson Christy, shot her and then killed himself. Unbeknownst to Sarah, Christy had killed his previous wife (and Sarah's cousin), Dora Hudson. The tragedy continued after Virginia Winship Everett, the daughter of Sarah Amos Winship and Simon Winship, lost her first husband, Abner Clay, who was murdered by Henry Stiff. She then married Willie Everett, but she divorced him in 1911. A few weeks later, Willie snuck to the home of Aaron Dyer, where his ex-wife was visiting family members. He peeked through the windows until he saw where Virginia was sleeping on a bed and then shot her through the heart. In the process, the bullet passed through her body and into her daughter's head. Fortunately, the child survived and lived until 1926.[58] Another of the Amos siblings, Sam, died in 1896, a few years after suffering a heart attack and falling into the living room fireplace and burning himself severely. Although he lived a few years afterward, he remained a pain-wracked cripple. Daniel Hudson had served as a lighthorseman who once managed to catch cattle thieves in the Kiamichis without the help of his fellow lighthorsemen who reportedly lagged behind to avoid the confrontation. Hudson stated that he believed the lighthorsemen to be cowards and refused to work with them again.[59] Willie Hudson fought in World War I but soon after returning home was killed by a man who had had an affair with his wife while he was overseas. Still another Hudson—Calvin—the son of Roe and Alice Hudson graduated from Jones Academy and high school in Broken Bow. One evening he unsuccessfully tried suicide, telling his horrified parents that he was tired of living.[60]

As the tribe wrestled with the continued and depressing carnage, it also had to face the reality that extraordinary change was upon them. The *Citizen* continued to badger various tribal leaders about their wealth, including Wilson N. Jones, whose financial condition, the paper persisted in pointing out, was very different than "that of thousands of his own people." The editors of the *Citizen* also claimed that he made all that money from "manipulating the common property of the tribe." Still, his behavior was "perfectly legitimate" because the tribe allowed him to do it. But the point that the editors Butler S. and Norma E. Smiser were making was that Jones was only opposing allotment because he feared losing all his property.[61]

The *Citizen* makes an intriguing and important argument. Jones did state that severalty would be to the detriment of the Choctaws because, as he said condescendingly, they were unable to "cope with the superior intelligence of the white man." But as mentioned earlier, Jones had purchased property in Texas and by the end of 1897 had moved himself and his family to Sherman where he owned a mansion, a saloon, and a wholesale dry goods shop; he also maintained ownership of his property in the Choctaw Nation, which he leased to noncitizens for two thousand dollars per year. "What is sauce for the goose should be sauce for the gander," the editors wrote. Pointing out the obvious, Wilson N. Jones managed to escape the tragedy of allotment and tribal dissolution because he could afford to. "We conclude," the editors wrote, "that the whole thing is bosh and used as a subterfuge to enable such men to hold on [to] the common property." As of June 1898, the Smisers claimed that Jones "has more money today than all the Choctaw put together."[62]

The Nationalists did not nominate a candidate for principal chief in 1898. The Tuskahoma Party, however, nominated Green McCurtain and the Union Party nominated Texas resident Wilson N. Jones. That year, the paper added the sarcastic statement that Jones "is a man of much means and invests his money in Texas property, which, of course, is greatly to the benefit of the Choctaw Nation."[63] At least some of the Choctaws must have either agreed with the paper's assessment of Jones, or they wanted allotment, because Green McCurtain won.

By 1900, the Nationalist Party had revitalized itself largely because of the activities and enthusiasm of the Snakes, and they nominated Jacob Jackson. Because a chief could only serve two consecutive terms, in 1900 the Tuskahoma Party nominated the mixed-blood

Progressive Gilbert W. Dukes to succeed Green McCurtain. Dukes was elected rather handily, but that would be the last time he held Choctaw office. Dukes had previously served as sheriff of Wade County, as a member of the House and Senate of the General Council, as a judge of the Supreme Court (1885–89) and as circuit judge for Second (Apukshunnubbee) District (1889–95). He then was elected national auditor and participated in the Atoka Convention.[64] Dukes postured himself as an unwavering proponent of allotment, believing that the allotment process should proceed because the tribe as a political entity was about to disband. He also stated in 1901 that

> there are many moving considerations in favor of closing the rolls at an early date; the one of primary importance is an early allotment of lands and a division of all our common property. There is a growing anxiety among the Choctaw people to divide this property that each one may know what is his own; that they may build their homes and make other lasting improvements on their lands; that they may get their property in shape to be protected by the property rights laws; that they may be able to give their children something more substantial, something more profitable than an undivided interest in a doubtful estate. This argument is not without reason.[65]

While the candidates prepared for the election, many Choctaws and intermarried whites worried about the Snakes. Others turned their attention to Jacob Jackson and his plans to move to Mexico. Choctaws did not necessarily think badly of Jackson and his followers for wanting to move, but they did place blame on the "Mexican Land Syndicate," an organization out of Kansas City that evidently had one of its representatives make the land deal with Jackson. The *Citizen* argued that men like Green McCurtain were the full-bloods' protectors, while the real estate agents were willing to take the "dimes and dollars" from Jackson and his followers and then "ship the poor fullbloods off to Mexico to starve and die like sheep on a desert waste."[66]

Indeed, many Choctaw citizens sang the praises of McCurtain. "Governor McCurtain is one of the greatest men in our Nation,"

Principal Chief Gilbert W. Dukes (1900–1902). The 1902 election was as fraught with controversy as many of the others, and Dukes even had the poll books locked up so no one could have access to them. The militia was called in to keep peace during the ballot count. Like McCurtain, Progressive Chief Dukes changed his mind about allotment, but he ultimately opposed it. His political enemies argued that he was concerned about losing his land and wealth. Courtesy Research Division of the Oklahoma Historical Society.

wrote the Progressive H. C. Ward to the *Citizen* (that had by now adopted a Progressive stance rather than supporting the Nationalists) in response to the *Antlers American*'s inclusion of a letter from V. M. Locke blasting McCurtain's support of allotment. "I am ready to agree with Mr. Locke that every inch and every foot of this land belongs to the Indians," Ward proclaimed. But he also illustrated the contradictory arguments that many of the pro-allotment Choctaw citizens used to explain their choice by adding, "No one denies that fact, but sometimes a man's estate gets in a condition that he has to change his manner of conducting his affairs and Governor McCurtain saw this was our condition and advocated a change."[67]

Ward admitted that he knew basically nothing about the Dawes Commission except what he had been told by McCurtain and his administration. Considering McCurtain's support of allotment it seems logical that Ward would also say, "I am credibly informed that they give the fullblood preference over everyone else." Since that was the case as far as Ward knew, he urged the full-bloods to use a "common sense view of the matter," and if they would only relent would then become "the happiest, most contented people on earth."[68]

Dukes, like every other Nationalist and Progressive leader, became alarmed at the numbers of white intruders into the Choctaw Nation. In 1900, he referred to the influx of whites as a "grave danger," acknowledging that the "hordes of adventurers without a drop of Indian blood" were taking advantage of the 1896 act of Congress. He also took issue with the federal government seizing control of the tribal schools. And, in violation of the Atoka Agreement, the school fund was not being used to educate the children who were Choctaw by blood. He claimed that at least one-third of Choctaw children were not in school because schools were too few and far between the settlements.[69]

Despite the obvious problems the tribe faced that could have been prevented by the federal government, Dukes naively asserted that "I believe the United States government desires to protect the interests of the Indians."[70] Dukes continued to push for the closing of the rolls and to hasten the allotment process. His rationale was that the Choctaws needed to hurry and change the fence lines and to improve their properties so as to be "fully prepared for citizenship when the time comes that their tribal government is dissolved."[71] Citizens also had to tolerate the rationales of anonymous newspaper letter writers, such as "N," who stated that the Choctaws should gratefully accept their allotments and stop harping on the treaties that gave them land and the right to govern themselves, because "no one who is a U.S. citizen can get over 160 acres of land without buying it."[72]

On the one hand, Dukes recognized the Choctaws' situation for what it was: "Our present condition is one of sore suspense." But on the other, from his perspective, the only resolutions were to close the rolls, allot the tribal lands, and invest individual title. He was convinced that allotment meant "the end of our political existence;

it means a disruption of all government tribal; it means the breaking of concert and political unity in our action." Dukes saw only one way to survive: "safe tribal extinction."[73]

Many full-bloods did not agree with Dukes, and in January 1901, about two hundred of them gathered in Gaines County to clandestinely pass a resolution that deposed Dukes as chief. They elected the sixty-year-old full-blood Daniel Bell to replace him and then ousted the officers from Gaines County and named new ones. They sent their message to the surprised Dukes, who then immediately requested that Fort Smith send police to protect him. The full-bloods had no legal authority to vote out the chief and replace him, of course, but their actions reveal the deep animosities members of the tribe still had for one another.[74] The Choctaw Snakes wanted to take the First (Moshulatubbee) District for themselves and to create their own laws and government. Bell appointed forty of his supporters to serve as lighthorsemen and ordered them to notify the residents of that district of the new government.[75]

The Choctaw and U.S. administrations wanted to get to the bottom of what Bell had planned, so in late January 1901 U.S. Marshal Jasper P. Grady and a captain named Jack traveled to Bell's home at the mouth of Little Wild Horse River, twelve miles west of South McAlester. Bell's property consisted of a small farm with a few log cabins. The anxious men arrived before noon to confront the "insurgent chief," and who they found was an old man doing nothing more than sharpening his cross-cut saw so he could hew a tree. And Bell did not seem surprised to see them, either. They were invited to sit at his table for dinner of "Tom Fuller" and corn bread.[76]

According to Grady, Bell unabashedly told him that the Snakes had organized in every county in the Choctaw Nation. According to Bell, he was indeed the new Choctaw chief and he would be inaugurated within the month; after that time he would take control of Choctaw affairs and then would build a new capital in "the mountains." None of the Snakes, he claimed, wanted to stay in Oklahoma because they believed it "too corrupt and full of evil influences." Bell unwaveringly stood by the terms of the 1832 treaty that guaranteed the tribe the right to make their own laws and to manage their

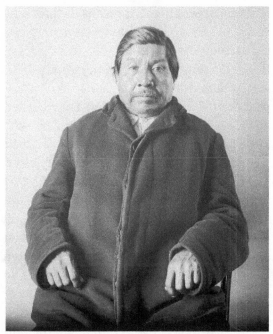

Daniel Bell was leader of the full-blood, conservative Choctaws who were anti-allotment and anti-statehood and who voted Bell as their "chief" in 1901. National Anthropological Archives, Smithsonian Museum.

own affairs. Bell's new government even passed a law stating that any Choctaw who rented or leased land to a white man would be whipped. Anyone who sold land would be shot. Bell felt confident that he could accomplish his plans because he had received a letter from President McKinley promising him that he would enforce the terms of that treaty. But other Choctaws believed that letter to have been written by someone else besides McKinley, a person "desiring to create a disturbance among the fullbloods."[77]

"What will happen to us?" Grady asked Bell. Bell explained confidently that since there would be no federal court in the new Choctaw Nation, there would be no need for marshals. Consequently, Grady would be required to leave the area as would any Choctaw who took the oath of allegiance to the United States. "And what about allotment?" Grady then asked. "No allotment will take place," Bell answered. Apparently, Bell operated under the assumption that somehow the loyalist Choctaws would return to their old ways of living. Because all the houses and buildings within the Nation were made of Choctaw stone, timber, and brick, he declared that all of the structures belonged to the tribe. He did not say how he expected all of this to happen, but he did tell Grady that it would be a "peaceful revolution" and that whites had nothing to fear.[78]

Grady did come away with more than just Bell's plans for a new Choctaw Nation. He also had observed that

> the Indians are literally starving. They don't know how to work; they used to have plenty of hogs, cattle and ponies and could kill game and live pretty well, but they now have nothing to live on and are absolutely destitute. Since the passage of the Curtis Bill they have been so hemmed in by rules and regulations, preventing them from selling anything. . . . A little Tom Fuller, which is nothing by cracked corn, and corn pone, is all the majority of them have to eat, and if the government, instead of sending soldiers to kill them, would send them something to eat and some clothes to keep them warm there would be no trouble.[79]

At the end of January 1901, apparently concerned about what Bell had said to Grady and in response to rumors of a violent "Snake Uprising" that had spread throughout the Choctaw Nation, a Judge Gill ordered U.S. Commissioner Sanson from Muskogee and U.S. Marshal Bennett to "the scene of the uprising," Bell's home. The authorities were so panicked that they set up a temporary court at the troops' headquarters so the leaders of the supposed insurrection would be given a preliminary hearing immediately after their arrest. Marshal Bennett and his five deputies did indeed travel to the home of Bell, the leader of the "uprising," but found only three men on the property. In less than twenty minutes, however, fifty armed lighthorsemen appointed by Bell, arrived. Clearly, Bell knew the marshal was coming and had ordered the lighthorsemen to confront the Marshal so he could leave the area. There clearly was no imminent revolt, so Bennett and his men departed. The *Citizen* commented in the same issue that even if an uprising had taken place, Bell and his Snakes were outnumbered and any fighting would be over in a few hours.[80]

A supplement that the *Citizen* published that week included another story that defended Chief Dukes, whom many Choctaws claimed had fled to Fort Smith because he feared Bell and the Snakes. In reality, Dukes was at Fort Smith serving as defense attorney for one Winchester Towne, a full-blood on trial for murdering Milt Miller near Talihina in 1900. "The newspapers which print this stuff show their total ignorance of Governor Dukes," the *Citizen*'s editors explained. "He is nerve and backbone through and through and will stand his ground in the thickest of the fight." No fight occurred, but the editors added anyway, "Besides, he as all the others informed, know[s] this little handful of dissatisfied Indians can be scattered like a bunch of quail."[81]

The paper may have been a bit optimistic, because in February at least fifteen hundred displeased Choctaw Snakes met sixteen miles south of South McAlester. The Snakes said they did not plan anything unlawful but instead planned to petition the government—that is, Congress and the "Great White Father"—so they could "go back to their old customs and [. . .] govern themselves under old treaties."[82]

Whether Dukes could stand his ground in a fight will never be known, but he apparently had no problems in dispatching his political enemies when possible. In August 1901, he removed Jeff Ward, the Skullyville County judge. Ward refused to comply and was arrested and jailed along with his court clerk. Attorneys for Ward successfully argued for their client and had him reinstated, but not until he had languished in jail for two weeks. Then in January 1902, Dukes removed Ben Grubbs as sheriff of Tobucksy County and replaced him with Solomon Mackey. Grubbs applied for a restraining order to protect himself from being removed, but when Mackey and Grubbs met face to face, the former demanded the latter's weapons and when Grubbs refused, the two men fought. Grubbs then charged Mackey with assault. Green McCurtain chastised Dukes for removing an elected officer, and, after a bit of sniping, the attorney for Mackey reminded the people that McCurtain had done the same thing in addition to other transgressions while chief, thus rendering his administration "honey combed" with corruption.[83]

The tribe's concerns were not limited to politics. The railroads created considerable havoc for tribal citizens. Full-bloods continued to complain that the trains stuck and killed their cattle, horses, and hogs. In Ardmore, a Santa Fe passenger train struck a horse-drawn carriage and killed the young driver. At South McAlester, a Missouri, Kansas, and Texas Railroad train and a Choctaw, Oklahoma, and Gulf train collided, telescoping a few cars, and in the process crashed into the depot platform, throwing a young boy and a conductor under the wheels; the two lost both of their legs. Train mishaps were quite common; a review through the papers reveals a startling number of people of all ages throughout the Choctaw Nation and indeed, Indian Territory, who lost their legs by being run over after somehow falling onto the tracks. Hundreds of coal miners also died each year, often dozens at once from "windy shots," a high-pressured explosion in a mine caused by the build up of gases.[84]

The tribe still faced the whiskey scourge and the loss of control over their cases that involved tribal members. Tribal members continued to drink, which directly led to the death and injury of some, including one man who fell in a ditch after an evening of imbibing and lay there throughout night as the snow and sleet covered him. He was found the next day, frozen into the ice and had to be chopped free. He then lost both hands and all his toes to frostbite.[85] Choctaw law enforcement also struggled to rein in liquor sellers. Simpson Colbert, the deputy sheriff of Eagle County tried to arrest one Sim James for selling liquor, but when the young James spurred his horse to get away, the horse ran into a tree, killing its rider. After Colbert was charged with murder and tried in federal court at Goodwater, the tribe passed a bill that would allow the tribe to pay for his defense. Luckily for Colbert, he was released.[86] In another alcohol-related case, San Bois County Sheriff Jeff D. Surratt was shot to death by his drunken deputy, Nicholas Wooldridge, for unknown reasons; the inebriated deputy did not know he had killed the sheriff until he was told the next morning.[87]

The list of strange and terrible things that happened throughout the Nation is extensive. One of the oddest incidents occurred in 1899 when the Progressive, educated, and affluent full-blood Solomon Hotema, one of Green McCurtain's followers who had attended the Tuskahoma conference and was also an ordained Presbyterian minister, killed three people whom he believed were witches. Hotema was intoxicated at the time and had expressed his concern that the three he deemed witches were responsible for deaths in the Choctaw Nation. Although the killings all took place on the same day, Hotema was subjected to three separate trials in federal court in East Texas. He was found not guilty for the first two on the basis of insanity; but he was found guilty on the third killing and subsequently sentenced to be executed. The U.S. Supreme Court intervened, however, and declared that Hotema may have had a "diseased brain" and was therefore insane. But the Supreme Court decided to leave the decision to the president. Based on the advice of U.S. Attorney General Knox—who advocated that Hotema was insane—Theodore Roosevelt commuted the sentence to life in prison.[88] And in another incident in January 1902, 142 prisoners at the South McAlester jail attempted to escape by cutting through a wall. They were subdued after attacking the guards and beating an elderly trustee who they believed told administrators of their plans.[89]

In addition to these issues, judging from the number of contemporary newspaper ads offering cures for health problems, tribal citizens were suffering from an array of physical ailments. A smallpox outbreak killed hundreds in 1901 (and some blamed the "Negroes" for being the carriers), but for many who survived that disease, they suffered from a vast array of other illnesses: piles, bowel problems, weak and fretful children, catarrh, painful menstruation, liver complaint, appendicitis, dizziness of the head, sour stomach, nervous prostration, indigestion, colic, cholera, wind on the stomach, biliousness of the blood, and a host of other familiar and bizarre problems.[90] As with many current tribal peoples, the adoption of a colonization diet—that is, white flour, coffee, sugar, processed foods, and milk (wheat, cows, and goats were not indigenous to this hemisphere)— in addition to lack of knowledge about proper sanitation, as opposed to a diet of fruits, vegetables, and plenty of exercise, resulted in dramatic health problems.[91]

In 1895, Special Agent John W. Lane commented on the dearth of old people in the Choctaw Nation. Indeed, many Choctaws were not well educated and did not have access to physicians or a variety of foods; but a lot of them did. Lane observed that many Choctaws grew an "abundance" of vegetables, although most decayed quickly, except sweet potatoes. In 1890 the tribe suffered a severe drought, but tribal members had numerous hogs "well fitted for slaughter" since those animals found their own foods rooting about in the forests.[92] Compared to what many tribes faced on reservations (poor food and shelter, depression, etc.) the Choctaws may have fared well. Still, it is easy to understand why it was that during the last decade of the nineteenth century and the first decade of the twentieth the population of Indians in the United States dropped to less than 250,000.[93]

Anger and frustration still dominated Choctaw politics. Like many other Choctaw tribal elections, the 1902 election arrived replete with personal animosities. Anger once again surfaced and continued for the next two years. Politics became so volatile that the Nationalist Party chose not to participate in that year's election. Gilbert W. Dukes, however, believed that he should have been nominated by the Tuskahoma Party so he could serve a second term, but his party instead supported Green McCurtain. Stung by their rejection, Dukes then threw his support to the Progressive Party and their nominee Thomas W. Hunter.

As in the past, voting was held on the third Wednesday in August. But when the poll books arrived in Tuskahoma, Dukes, the scorned chief, had them locked in a shed and refused to allow them to be counted. In a display of illegal favoritism, Dukes declared Hunter the new principal chief and even called the General Council into an early session to have him confirmed. Reportedly, McCurtain and Hunter, along with their supporters, were at Tuskahoma and both sides were convinced that they had won. Because of the potential for violence, Marshal Hackett, along with Agent Shoenfelt, mounted police, and seventy police deputies and deputy marshals also attended. Armed lighthorsemen guarded the entrances to the capitol, which angered citizens who felt they should have access to the building. Despite Shoenfelt's attempts to keep the crowd calm, a group of 150 men stormed the doors. Shoenfelt finally convinced the group to back away, and Chief Dukes agreed to allow five men to enter and attend the council meeting.[94]

The next day proved even worse when more men appeared and demanded to be admitted into the capitol. The crowd quieted upon hearing that Green McCurtain of the Tuskahoma Party had requested that U.S. Army troops from Fort Reno come to Tuskahoma to supervise in the vote counting. In a letter to J. George Wright, commissioner to the five civilized tribes, McCurtain stated that Dukes ordered the lighthorsemen to take the poll books away from Judge Wesley Anderson. McCurtain believed that "this kind of conduct is calculated to cause trouble if pursued, and I have every reason to believe that it will be pursued even to more desperate ends." He also alleged that Dukes was "under the influence of whiskey, patent medicine and other intoxicating liquors, which is no difficult task, until he has almost reached the state of irresponsibility."[95] Not only did he take the poll books from Anderson, Dukes also served notice on Anderson a few days before the election and told him that he intended to remove him from office for incompetence. Luckily for Anderson, Supreme Court Justice Garland issued an injunction that effectively kept Dukes from removing him.[96] The tension remained high, however, even when the two companies of federal soldiers under the command of Major Starr arrived. Already, Hackett's deputies and the U.S. police remained inside and the lighthorsemen guarded the entrance. McCurtain's supporters grew to at least two hundred men, who mingled quietly as they waited. Starr then announced that everyone, including the Choctaw law enforcement officers, lay down their arms. Those who wanted to enter the building could, provided they carried no weapon.[97]

The *Twin Territories* newspaper commented rather dramatically on the atmosphere, describing "the very air heavy with lurking trouble" and "keen anxiety, of so great promise for real trouble and bloodshed, or of tragedy barely averted" between men who would have "fought like very devils" without the law present. The paper poetically described the "evil atmosphere" among the "grim full bloods" and "wiry half bloods" that had developed over the ballot counting as similar to a dark cloud "that portends of thunder, lightning and drenching down-pour." Whether McCurtain would have had to "wade through blood" to the capitol if the military had not arrived can only be imagined. The votes were finally counted (the last time until 1971 that the tribe would elect a chief), and Green McCurtain had defeated Hunter, 1,645 votes to 956.[98]

The trouble surrounding Dukes did not stop there. The October 1902 council meeting had all the ingredients of a Keystone Cops plot. After Chief Justice Garland swore in the members, the results for the representatives of two counties, Towson and Kiamitia, were contested by McCurtain supporters, who argued that Washington, Joe Everidge, and Choate, representing Towson, Kiamitia, and Tobucksy counties, respectively, be admitted as the representatives. In response, Dukes argued that the election in Tobucksy County was not valid because the proceedings had been under the direction of Sheriff Solomon Mackey. But, Mackey had been prohibited from serving as sheriff by order of the General Council, and Dukes was shrewd enough to realize that he would be guilty of contempt of court if he recognized Mackey as sheriff. He then appointed Dr. Wright as the Tobucksy representative, even though this was in violation of the Constitution, which stated that any representative had to be resident of that county for at least one month prior to the election. After someone discovered that detail, Wright found himself replaced by Green LeFlore. Then, Robert Benton (who killed Charles Wilson in 1884) objected, saying that he was entitled to represent Sugar Loaf County and that the current person was not the proper representative. Not surprising, Benton's claims were unfounded, but McCurtain's supporters remained furious and threatened violence, so Dukes acquiesced at the urging of Indian Agent Shoenfelt and Marshal Hackett.[99]

To complicate the already tense situation, James Bowers had been elected president of the Senate before the new representatives had taken their seats. Shoenfelt and Hackett loudly interjected and attempted to halt the proceedings. Bowers agreed to suspend his duties, but he refused to rescind his new position. When Shoenfelt and Hackett went to find the four representatives—Benton, Choate, Everidge, and Washington—the men refused to enter the building. A short while later, three of them returned to the building and elected a speaker, another McCurtain man, R. J. Ward. In clear violation of all laws, a coalition of McCurtain men met again to conduct business, even though the General Council had adjourned for the day. When Dukes heard of these goings-on he immediately sent in tribal police to clear the building.[100]

No more about those particular shenanigans are mentioned in the records. But in March, federal commissioners signed an agreement with the representatives of the Choctaws and Chickasaws stipulating that a special election would be held to decide the ratification of an act approved by Congress on July 1, 1902, that would assign allotments to tribal members. Voters did go to the polls on Wednesday, October 1, at Atoka, and the final count was 2,140 for and 704 against ratification.[101] This number is intriguing, for if the population of Choctaws by blood in 1904 was 15,898, and half of those were women and children who were not allowed to vote, then obviously, many Choctaws did not vote. As with the other tribes, many tribal members refused allotments and declined to participate in the process. It stands to reason that many Choctaws would not take part in an election. And, it is not clear in the above report if this number is Choctaws only, or if Chickasaw males are included in that final vote. The number of Chickasaws by blood was 4,956.[102]

Events surrounding the elections of 1890, 1892, and 1902 were indeed memorable and the 1904 election would prove to be the same. Alarms sounded about almost all the candidates for the various positions, especially those who ran for the most powerful offices. One report stated that even though Dukes was no longer chief, when he was in that position he had ordered the national auditor to write national warrants for his friends and partners. The editors of the Indian Citizen believed that Dukes pursued the national treasurer position so he could cash the warrants.[103]

The election of 1904 produced numerous points of contention. For one thing, many voters received compensation for their votes.[104] For another, the voting was reportedly manipulated. In a letter to George W. Scott, the national treasurer, F. P. Semple wrote, "The most shameful and outrageous election that I have ever saw held in the history of the Choctaw people was held here yesterday." According to Semple, "Intoxicated voters were not allowed to vote their true sentiments, but were voted by the Protective Party [opposition to the Tuskahoma Party] regardless of all that we could do." Just like previous elections, Semple stated that feelings were so intense that fighting broke out between voters and those overseeing the voting tables. He believed that Hunter was "backed by a lot of non-citizens of this town. People who used their influence and spent their money on him." Frustrated, Semple said that "if all had been sober, I know more votes would have gone for Green McCurtain. Men who had McCurtain tickets made out were forced to change them."[105]

After the results, another McCurtain man, H. L. Sanguin, had more to complain about. He wrote to his "friend George" a few days later and told him that they had lost the county, "but we done our best." He said that he had seen Hunter on the way home and that "he were sick and mad to [*sic*]. He said the first time one of his men said anything about McCurtain steling [*sic*] he were going [to] hit him in the face. He has it in for several of his men, esp. Dukes." Apparently, Hunter had been assured by his supporters that he would win by a majority by two hundred votes.[106]

Hunter was willing to bounce back even if that meant siding with his former opponent. In a letter to Scott, William H. Harrison commented that Hunter had been in Hugo after the election and was "very much down in the mouth." Although Hunter reportedly felt unhappy about losing, he was heard saying that "from now on he is a McCurtain man and will do everything he can to keep him." Harrison was dubious: "Talk is cheap. But I suppose he wishes to get into the band wagon again."[107]

While all these political struggles transpired, the Choctaw Snakes had not slowed one bit in their quest to make their newly organized council and government functional. Talk of their hopes for a new Choctaw Nation stayed alive in the face of continued advertising in the papers for millions of acres of rich bottom and prairie Choctaw lands for lease to whites. In February 1902, for example, an advertisement appeared in the *Citizen* for half a million acres of such land east of Atoka "which has heretofore been overlooked." The ad stated the unconfirmed claim that "the Indians have expressed a desire to lease their lands to farmers who want to put in a farm, and allow them to keep it for a number of years." But even more brazenly, the ad also claimed that "there are many Choctaw orphan children who want white people to improve a farm for them."[108]

The instigators of that ad, the Atoka Commercial Club, were challenged over the truthfulness of their assertions, and in response they stated that they did indeed have at least thirty Indians on a list willing to lease their lands. The spokesman for the club rationalized that "you will hear some say, 'Oh, the Indian can't risk this, he will get cheated.'" He apparently did agree with that statement, because the next thing he said was, "Don't businessmen of all classes get cheated at sometime in life? One Indian out of ten may get cheated, but the good to the other nine is a great and good thing." Then, to let the world know just who the Choctaws would be dealing with, the ad continues, "He has got to cope with the white man in less than five years, and now is a good time to begin to learn how."[109]

Purportedly, the Snakes tried to intimidate other Choctaws from accepting allotments. In June 1903, Chief Green McCurtain expressed his concern in a letter to Tams Bixby, the acting chairman of the Dawes Commission, about Willis Tobly and his threats that he allegedly made to other full-bloods. He wanted Tobly "put down"—that is, put under arrest—to stop his "intermeddling." McCurtain, a staunch supporter of allotment, stated that "I have known Tobly a long time and have never known anything good of him."[110] McCurtain enclosed a letter written to him from L. W. Cobb, in which Tobly is claiming to be chief of the Snakes and that if Choctaws went to the land office with the intent of getting their allotments, then they would be murdered.[111]

Bixby wrote back with a reiteration of section 2111 of the Revised Statutes, which states that "every person who sends any talk, speech, message, or letter to any Indian Nation, tribe, chief, or individual, with an intent to produce a contravention or infraction of any treaty or law of the United States, or to disturb the peace and tranquility of the United States, is liable to a penalty of two thousand dollars." To that end, Bixby also said that because the letter from Cobb was written in Choctaw, he was unable to ascertain exactly what was said by Tobly; therefore, he suggested that Cobb be summoned as a witness.[112]

In the meantime, R. S. Frazier, sheriff of Cedar County sent in two (undated) reports in which he identifies some of the Snakes who kept the other full-bloods from taking their allotments by threatening them.[113] McCurtain followed with another letter a few months later to J. Blair Shoenfelt to express his concerns about the Choctaw Snakes, who he labels dangerous, yet "poor deluded creatures" because they believed that the secretary of the interior promised them that all the stipulations provided by the 1830 Treaty of Dancing Rabbit Creek would be in effect, including a provision that the government would remove all noncitizens of the Choctaw Nation by January 1, 1904, and that twenty thousand soldiers would help accomplish the job. The Choctaw Snakes asserted that the Dawes Commission was without authority and they had armed themselves in protest. Chief McCurtain grew intolerant of the Snakes, however, and wanted them arrested.[114] Not much happened besides the Choctaw Snakes refusing to accept allotments, so the Dawes Commission made selections for them.[115] Tobly eventually took his 150 acres of land where he lived out his life and held meetings among the Snakes from the Creek, Seminole, and Cherokee tribes.[116] Tobly's idea for a new Choctaw Nation had failed, and the *Citizen* expressed sympathy for the man by describing him as a "poor, defenseless Crazy Snake (of an Indian) and a bug bear."[117]

Around the same time, the overwhelming problem of white intruders was once again addressed by Chief Green McCurtain. In a letter to the Choctaw Nation's auditor, Peter J. Hudson, Chief McCurtain instructed him to draw a national warrant for four hundred dollars for Alf McCay to remove intruders and their property, including cattle, from the Choctaw Nation.[118]

Lewis, Jackson, Tobly, Bell, and other Nationalists were hardly the only Natives to stringently resist colonization. Forms of indigenous resistance against federal policies were alive among the Five Tribes. A Cherokee man named Ned Christie maintained his stance of opposing allotment and the railroads, and he strongly advocated for tribal sovereignty. While Lewis actually did kill some men, the respected Cherokee politician Ned Christie was accused, but never convicted of, killing a white U.S. deputy marshal in 1887 and he had to endure the rumor of being a cold-blooded murderer for the remainder of his life. He avoided capture for five years until the day his well-fortified home was blown up and he was shot dead as he fled—almost exactly two years before the execution of Silan Lewis. Christie's body was then displayed in Fort Smith. What is interesting about Christie is not that he was falsely accused of a crime and hounded relentlessly until he died, but that so many people were willing to put the blame on Christie and his followers for the many violent crimes committed in Indian Territory. The man's legend as a psychopath outlaw seemed to grow by the hour.[119]

The disgruntled Choctaw men were also similar to other Keetoo-wahs of the Cherokee tribe led by Red Bird Smith and to the Muscogee (Creek) Crazy Snakes who were led by Chitto Harjo, a full-blood who organized a government with its own council and laws, one of which forbade Creeks to take allotments, to rent their lands to non-Creeks, or to use whites as laborers. Ironically, Chitto Harjo's English name was Wilson Jones.[120]

Harjo, who was born around 1854, had fought with Isparhecker, the leader of the federal element among the Creeks during the Civil War. In 1892, when Congress created the Dawes Commission, the formally uneducated but intelligent Harjo stepped forward as leader of approximately five thousand disgruntled Creeks who stood firmly against the breaking up of the communal system of land ownership. Like Silan Lewis, Chitto Harjo feared that by placing his tribal members on allotments they would be in direct competition with whites who knew better how to manage farms and businesses. After the Indians' lands were taken, then so would their culture and identity. Harjo also chastised his more progressive tribespeople (usually, but not always, the educated mixed-bloods) for becoming too much like the whites, for accepting their ways of life, and being too amenable to the will of the land grabbers.[121] Like other strong personalities in Indian Territory, Chitto Harjo is also the subject of exaggeration and differing opinions. While one writer, Mace Davis, asserted that blacks were welcome to join the Crazy Snakes, W. W. Bray commented that "the real uprising in the Snake Uprising was because of some of the darkies who fell in with the Snake Indians just for what they got to eat; they caused all the trouble and had to be whipped, arrested and sent to jail. It was a sorry affair—it put a blot on the Indians for something that was not their fault."[122]

Although Silan Lewis was gone and his followers did not mount another protest like they had in 1892, many Nationalists followed Tobly and Bell. In 1901, the conservative Muscogee Chitto Harjo was declared hereditary chief of the Muscogees, just as some Choctaws had declared Bell their new chief. Harjo also proclaimed Hickory Ground the Creek capital and organized a national council of the House of Kings and the House of Warriors. The council reestablished the ancient laws and courts that had been recognized in the 1825 treaty with the United States and passed a series of laws that included punishments of fines and lashings to anyone who used white labor or leased their lands to whites. Although Harjo was not violent and did not indiscriminately punish transgressors, rumors spread rapidly that hundreds of angry, violent Creeks were planning to attack Bristow. In response, the government sent in troops who arrested Harjo and a handful of his followers; they were subsequently tried and convicted but later released. Their ordeal did not deter the Snakes; they did not accept allotments and continued to meet to discuss strategies of resistance.[123]

Harjo was known throughout Indian Territory. The whiskey problem in the Choctaw Nation had indeed grown to the point where it permeated all the tribal Nations. As Harjo sat in jail, the editors of the *Citizen* made a comparison between him and liquor: "The U.S. jail has the Chitto Harjo, or the most harmless specimen," wrote the editors. "But the real Crazy Snakes are in the drug store. May be that is where Chitto Harjo got his stock to begin on." The insulting comparison did not stop there: "Such an evil eating unceasingly at such vital and fundamental principles and institutions should indeed be crushed."[124]

Although Oklahoma became a state in 1907, Harjo and his followers established a village of sorts at Hickory Ground. Mixed Muscogees and Africans were allowed to live there and soon they outnumbered the Natives. They, along with some of the other mixed-bloods—but not Harjo—engaged in raids and other escapades including the theft of at least one thousand pounds of smoked bacon from Morey Springs in east-central Oklahoma. Another version is that a posse stole a wagon full of bacon from Harjo's smokehouse, while yet another version states that after a dog chased a rabbit under a smokehouse, the outbuilding collapsed. Regardless, the name of the conflicts became the "Smoked Meat Rebellion." In the process of arresting some blacks, a fight broke out, resulting in the deaths of some officers. Almost immediately, rumors circulated that armed savages were on the loose and that Oklahomans needed protection from the Crazy Snakes, but there never was any armed resistance.[125] Still, Chitto Harjo became a wanted man. While taking refuge in his home in McIntosh County he was shot in the hip while his lieutenant, Charles Coker, was shot in the chest. Both Snakes escaped to travel through the Choctaw Nation with the assistance of Harjo's Choctaw friend, Daniel Bob. Harjo lived with Bob for the remainder of his life, which ended on April 11, 1911. Some say he died from complications from his leg wound.[126]

The Cherokees also created organized groups to resist allotment and to express the traditionalists' sentiments. Evan and John Jones organized the Keetoowah Society after the Civil War in order to resist the Union Army's attempts at land grabbing. That particular phase of the Keetoowah Society faded somewhat in the 1870s and 1880s. But the threat to the Cherokees' land and sovereignty resurged anew in the 1890s in the form of the Dawes Severalty Act, of the growing number of aggressive white intruders who were poised to overtake the Indian Territory, and the Curtis Act in 1898. Traditionalist Cherokees then rallied behind Red Bird Smith (1850–1918). Under Smith's leadership, the Keetoowahs tirelessly hired attorneys, lobbied Congress, and continued to fight against the overwhelming tide of whites determined to take their Cherokee lands. The Keetoowahs also became known as the Nighthawk Keetoowahs because they met in secret at night. Smith was arrested in 1902 for refusing to enroll, and the government enrolled him by force. But he became chief of the Cherokees in 1908 and created the traditionalist Four Mothers Society in 1912, which was made of like minds from the other four tribes. Smith continued to strive for the preservation of Cherokee traditions until he died in 1918.[127]

The idea of moving to Mexico was still represented among many of the Choctaw full-bloods, led by Jacob Jackson, J. C. Folsom, S. E. Coe, Saul Folsom, and Willis Jones. In 1906, Jacob Jackson was sixty-two years old and served as the spokesman for the dissenting Choctaws during the Senate's Select Committee interviews. Jackson testified earnestly, talking plainly and honestly about the Choctaw full-bloods' opposition to what they believed was an oppressive policy of allotment. "The allotment of lands and the distribution of tribal funds and the acceptance of a complete United States citizenship meant the extinction of the Choctaw race as a people, the loss of identity as a nation—the end of the Indian as an Indian," Jackson read from a written statement. "With the Indian people, the air we breathed, the water we drank, and the land we lived upon were held in common, and each man had all he used. With the white man, the land is not held in common, the water is shut off from our cattle and we are left with only the air we breathe."[128]

During his testimony, Jackson said, "Now here we are, in it, and in trouble. You have no idea of the extent of that trouble." The committee chairman expressed no sympathy for Jackson and his followers. "The allotment matter is settled," he answered. "And your trouble has come, as you say." He and the committee were willing to listen to what Jackson had to say, but one can only imagine the adverse conditions under which Jackson had to speak.[129]

"It is a ticklish business," Jackson explained. And in brackets after his comment there is the word "laughter," indicating that the white audience was amused. He went on to explain that regardless of whether the restrictions (to be able to sell the land after twenty-five years) are removed or not, the trouble would remain the same for the tribe. In brackets again is "laughter." Jackson advocated that as a solution for the government to honor the Atoka Treaty, the surplus land, but never the tribes' main lands, could be sold. Jackson astutely understood the problem with allowing the tribal members to sell their lands: once they sold it, it would probably never be recovered unless they could afford to buy it back.[130]

Contrary to his argument about the importance of retaining tribal lands, Jackson then proceeded to state his plans to move to Mexico—

and perhaps even South America. As the "father of the movement" he represented over two thousand Choctaws and stated that they protested the forcing of the allotments on them and that he and his tribespeople wanted a return to "the community form of government." Jackson then asked Congress to remove the restrictions on selling their lands so they could have enough money to leave the country.[131]

As the committee had tried to convince S. L. Bacon of the merits of allotment, they also tried to talk Jackson out of his idea of moving to Mexico:

> Senator Long: You could not very well get out of it. If we remove your restrictions you would have to go? [Laughter]
> Mr. Jackson: Yes.
> Senator Teller: You would change your mind.
> Mr. Jackson: I have not changed it since 1889.[132]

The government said no; Jackson and the other Choctaws would keep their allotments. Defeated, Jackson accepted his allotment of 160 acres near Hochatown, where he lived as a farmer until his death in 1909.[133]

Oklahoma became a state in 1907. Tribal law had ceased to exist, and authority rested with elected officials. Wilson P. Jones had died in 1901, leaving behind a large estate in Sherman, Texas. Jones had made sure his grandson Nat was taken care of, but he bequeathed the majority of his property to be used to create a hospital for citizens in north Texas and southern Oklahoma. The family objected, and for the next 28 years they challenged the will. Finally, in 1929, the Sherman Hospital was bought as per Jones's wishes and it was named the Wilson N. Jones Memorial Hospital. In 1916, Nat Wilson, Wilson P. Jones's grandson and the son of the deceased Willie Jones, killed himself after jumping off a ten-story building in Oklahoma City.[134]

That last execution of the Choctaw Nation was Silan Lewis's in 1894. In the Seminole Nation, the last tribal execution took place on 1896 in Wewoka. The prisoner was blindfolded and a white piece of paper in the shape of a heart was pinned over his heart. Timmie Jack, an Euchee, was the last man to be executed under Creek law.

Jack had killed Jimmie Brown, a store clerk and interpreter. Jack was given thirty days to prepare for his death; he returned as promised to the Creek Council House in Okmulgee. Ten lighthorsemen under the command of Captain Dube Berryhill marched ten paces away from the condemned man and fired. Only five of the rifles were loaded; five held blanks. Jack was buried near the courthouse.[135] The last Choctaw to be whipped at the New Mayhew Courthouse grounds was around 1905. The recipient was "a little scrawny full blood" named Douglas McClure, who was convicted of stealing hogs from Sam Harris.[136]

According to Section 28 of the Curtis Act, the Choctaw tribal court was to cease on October 1898.[137] But the courts continued to operate and passed numerous laws until 1904, and the government met into 1906. Chief Hunter commissioned E. P. Pitchlynn as a national light-horseman for the Second District on November 10, 1902, merely days before McCurtain took office. Political sniping continued, as evidenced by this sarcastic, anonymous letter sent to the *Citizen* a year later:

> July 23, 1903
> Green McCurtain,
> Please let me have office. I will help vote for your party. Tom Hunter he make out he chief, give this comishun me light horse. Look a like he aint worth dam. Cant draw money on dis big paper. Look like he got no power. When take out my trunk and look at this big comishun chus make me feel bad and make right sorry man. Cant draw money make eye water run and make me kich bad cold and I want you take it dis Tom Hunter comishun and give me one got power and lots stout. I want light horse in this Wade Co. shame for hiself fool me, good man like dis. Look like he got no think for hiself. Your friend, E. P. Pitchlynn.[138]

At that time, the U.S. Congress put all probate cases under federal jurisdiction. In 1907, the courts were completely abolished by the Indian Appropriation Act and every civil and criminal case of then transferred to federal courts.[139]

In typical patriotic fashion, in 1935 W. B. Morrison wrote about Wilson N. Jones as being "remarkable" and "one of the most notable

men in later Choctaw history, if not the entire Indian Territory."
While the events surrounding the election of 1892 are mentioned in
Morrison's essay, nary a word is said about his removing men from
office because they were his political enemies, nor does he mention
Wilson's complete lack of initiative to retain Choctaw culture, traditions, or language. As opposed to the Nationalists, whom Morrison
presents as merely "the full-blood or conservative element in the
nation" with no apparent moral stance, Jones is heralded as "one of
the ablest and most successful of the Choctaw chiefs."[140]

Green McCurtain also has been immortalized. His fellow tribespeople remarked that he was "truly a remarkable man and his continued
successes prove that abundantly" and that "the glories of Oklahoma,
whatever they may be and as long as they shall endure, rest in part,
upon the name of Green McCurtain." Even while he was alive, McCurtain was called "the greatest living Indian." While those comments
are clearly patriotic—especially the ditty, "The Choctaws loved
Governor McCurtain sincerely and with a passion akin to that of
a love for one's kinsman"—it is also obvious that these types of
comments were made by those without a true understanding of
Choctaw history, in which tribespeople verbally and physically fought
each other for decades.[141] Even the historian Angie Debo (who knew
that the policy of allotment was highly disagreeable with most Choctaws), in *The Rise and Fall of the Choctaw Republic*, makes this odd
statement about McCurtain: "So great was his ability and patriotism
that his countrymen upon the whole were glad to trust his judgment, and follow his leadership."[142] To the contrary, Silan Lewis,
the Nationalists, and the Choctaw Snakes would never have followed
Green McCurtain, nor any of the other Progressive chiefs, for that
matter. That McCurtain was not willing to resist is what angered the
Nationalists. On the other hand, if allotment was indeed inevitable,
what else might McCurtain have done?

In no record does Gilbert Dukes mention making an attempt to
resist severalty. Still, he also has been heralded as belonging to the
"public spirited, useful and helpful types of men who[se] ambitions
and desires are centered and directed in those channels through
which flow the greatest and most permanent good to the greatest

number." Not only that, he is also viewed as a "genius" and one of those men whose character was exemplified in "probity and benevolence, kindly virtues and integrity in the affairs of life."[143] Of course, Jones, McCurtain, and Dukes were held in high esteem by the white writers who immortalized them because they were pro-allotment, which was exactly what the whites wanted.

Two men commented many years after Jacob Jackson's death that he "went to his grave with a broken heart when his hopes that, by some means, the Treaty of 1866, in which it was provided that tribal existence be brought to an end, might be at least modified, were met with disappointment."[144] Another Choctaw also mused twenty-seven years after statehood about Jacob Jackson and his hopes:

> One is led to wonder if after all, Jacob Jackson and his tribal pride would not have served the best interests of the tribe. Many who espoused the cause of his opponents now realize the truth of the statements which he made at that time as to the ultimate results of the ending of tribal existence and many who then scoffed at his ideas now are eager to acclaim him a martyr for his people.[145]

And what about Silan Lewis? How do we assess his life? Do we judge him harshly because he murdered another human? Or do we honor him because, by all reports, he also was an honest man, one concerned with the frightening prospect of losing tribal autonomy, land, and culture, and having to capitulate to the laws of the emerging state of Oklahoma?

If we consider the violence within Indian Territory, after the Civil War especially, and the stark situations the tribes found themselves in, violence was, in a sense, a way of life. In times of war, however, killing usually is excusable except when innocent people die. But declaring who is innocent in wartime depends on who is doing the categorization: winners, losers, pacifists, or hawks. One might also argue that the influence of growing up in a violent environment is not an excuse to murder.

Whom do Americans value as heroes? Faces carved into the venerated Mount Rushmore tell us much about those whom many living in this country revere. However, presidents Washington and Jefferson owned slaves. In the first of the Lincoln-Douglas debates, known as the "House Divided Speech" (August 21, 1858), Lincoln stated that he did not believe in equality between the races. Lincoln also did not pardon thirty-eight Dakotas sentenced to be hung in the wake of the U.S.-Dakota War of 1862, a war precipitated by white settlers encroaching onto Dakota lands. President Theodore Roosevelt wrote in his *Winning of the West* that Indians were "faithless," "filthy," and "treacherous," and led lives that were "but a few degrees less meaningless, squalid and ferocious than that of the wild beasts with whom they held joint ownership."

Other admired individuals offer more clues. Americans still celebrate Christopher Columbus as a hero for "discovering America," despite his goal to exploit indigenous peoples for his own gain. President Andrew Jackson essentially sentenced thousands of Natives to death when he ordered their removal from their homelands to Indian Territory so white settlers could take their lands. George Armstrong Custer massacred Cheyennes at the Washita and strived to defeat more of them on the northern plains in an effort to win the presidency. Despite his attitude and behavior toward Natives, Custer is held up as a martyr and has reenactments dedicated to him, and patriotic Americans have objected to the erection of a monument dedicated to the Natives who fell at Little Big Horn defending their lands. Pioneers, mountain men, ranchers, and farmers all are viewed as intrepid pathbreakers who valiantly overcame the "uncivilized" obstacles on their way to spreading white civilization from coast to coast.

Many of the aforementioned "heroes" made statements or exhibited behaviors that are conveniently ignored, shrugged off by patriots as being typical "of that time period" and therefore excusable, or that the Natives had it coming because they were too unintelligent and not Christians. Those same patriots take advantage of (but refuse to acknowledge) their privileged positions when they say, "Well, it wasn't me—I didn't take the land or kill any Indians." Ironically, the list of Natives many Americans considered—and still consider—to be "savages" is as long as the list of those who perpetrated violence against them. Geronimo, Crazy Horse, Sitting Bull, Manuelito, Quanah Parker, Black Kettle, Little Crow, Red Cloud, Cochise, Dull Knife, Gall, Captain Jack, Satanta, and Osceola are only a few of the indigenous peoples who have been stereotyped as uncivilized and vicious—all because they were defending their homes and ways of life.

Violence, racism, treaty abrogation, stereotypes, sports mascots, cultural and image appropriation, theft of skeletal remains and sacred cultural objects, intolerance of indigenous intellectuals who speak out to confront a host of purposeful transgressions in the scholarly arena are all part of this country's legacy. Even President George W. Bush cannot coherently discuss sovereignty.[146] It appears that ignorance about Natives and the desire to take advantage of them are indeed part of all American time periods.

So where do we place Silan Lewis amid these lists of American heroes, martyrs, and villains? Clearly it depends on the evaluator's point of view. Historians who are concerned with portraying white Americans as justified in their steamrolling over tribal nations in their quest to spread Christianity and democracy will situate Lewis as a villain. Those looking for indigenous heroes—those people who resisted the onslaught of colonization—might evaluate Lewis with a different perspective. I shared the concept with numerous Natives, all of whom made similar comments: "we need heroes," "I would have done the same thing," "what choice did he have?" and so forth. One way to think about Lewis is to ask ourselves what we would do if placed in the same situation he faced. If we lived during that time, and if it was indeed true that colonization was inevitable, would we try and find ways to retain our culture in the midst of almost overwhelming odds? Would we accept the "superiority" of white society, become imitation white people, and then perhaps live in shame and guilt? Or, in the worst case scenario, would we come to truly believe that because white society had taken over the New World it is inherently better? Whether Silan Lewis's drastic course of action was morally and ethically appropriate will remain a matter of opinion. But his intentions, to fight back against invaders who stole his land, who committed genocide against his people, and who were prepared to keep the Choctaws subsumed, will never be in doubt.

Lewis had ample opportunity to escape. He had married a young woman who apparently loved him, owned many horses and cattle, and could have lived a long life. Instead, he gave up everything for what he thought was right, for what he thought was the best for his Nation. Whether his life would have been satisfying had he not committed his crime will never be known. But one thing is certain, unlike many of his contemporaries who did nothing to combat the rising tide of colonization and racism, Lewis acted. If a hero is considered to be someone who stands up for what is right with the cost being everything they hold dear, then perhaps Silan Lewis can be put into that category. Descendents of those he dispatched might disagree with the assessment of Lewis as a hero, but Lewis's basic goal, which was to save his people and his culture, is something that anyone who lives in a state of colonization can understand.

AFTERWORD

The Oklahoma Choctaw Nation Tribal Complex is located at 16th and Locust in the southwestern Oklahoma city of Durant. The magnolia capital of Oklahoma, Durant sponsors the annual magnolia festival, features a statue honoring the world's largest peanut, and is ten miles from Lake Texoma, one of the largest lakes in Oklahoma and a mecca for scuba divers, skiers, and sport fishermen.

The Choctaw Nation comprises ten and one-half counties, surrounded by Arkansas, the Red River, the South Canadian River and a line west of Durant that runs north to the South Canadian. Governing the Choctaw Nation is the tribe's Constitution, ratified in 1983, and providing for three bodies of government, just like the U.S. system of governance. The Executive Branch is composed of the chief who is elected every four years; the Legislative Branch, consisting of twelve elected Tribal Council members who represent each of the districts, is responsible for listening to the citizens in their respective districts and for maintaining and strengthening the tribe's economy. The chief and the Tribal Council members must be at least one-quarter Choctaw blood. The Judicial Branch consists of three judges—two of whom may be nonlawyers—who are appointed by the chief and approved by the council.

The tribe is highly successful in its economic endeavors and features an array of programs available to its members who live within the boundaries of the Nation: Children (preventive health, day care, WIC); Economic Development (travel plazas, casinos, restaurants, archiving); Education (scholarships, adult education, Upward Bound, Choctaw language); Elders (eyeglasses, dentures, hearing aid program); Health (diabetes wellness center, recovery center, hospital and clinic); Heritage (annual Labor Day and Memorial Day festivals and Commemorative Trail of Tears Walk, museum, veterans' services); Housing (home buyer education, rental assistance, home finance); Property (appraisals, land titles, forestry, firefighters); Social Services (food distribution, relocation, emergency, burial assistance); in addition to youth sports camps, the *BISHINIK* newspaper, genealogical assistance, and a host of other services. The government today works with millions of dollars, is sophisticated in its ability to function in the competitive world, and is the official governing body of over 182,000 tribal members who range from full-bloods who speak the language and who are knowledgeable about Choctaw culture, to those who look white, know nothing about Indians, and who have never even seen the tribal Council House.

With statehood, the Choctaw tribal government was dissolved and their lands were allotted. As hard as many white Americans tried to take the Choctaws' resources and to make Choctaws turn away from their culture, the tribe once again bounced back and is now a thriving entity. Stories about what happened to the Choctaws socially and politically between statehood and the tribe's political resurgence, however, are for others to tell.[1]

A Note on Methodology

The majority of the documents used in this project were authored by Choctaws. Not only did they write many editorials in the newspapers, they also authored letters to each other and to newspaper editors, gave (textualized) speeches, offered opinions about the events, left behind records as to whom they voted for in elections, and served as transcribers and recorders for the court cases and tribal council meetings. But, there are important drawbacks to choosing Wilson and Lewis to write about. The Nationalists case files of the men tried in the 1890s, including Silan Lewis, are lost. And, while the case file for the Jackson Crow murder trial is available, it has to be pieced together from both the Fort Worth Federal Records Center and the Fort Smith National Historic Site archives. The witness testimonies reflect the interrogation methods of the day; that is, many questions were not asked by the attorneys and therefore remain answered. Based on the lawyers' inadequate questions to witnesses and the logic behind asking them in the Crow case, as well as other cases, I can say that I feel great sympathy for those innocent people on trial in the 1800s.

Without attorneys' questions and witness testimonies, it was challenging indeed to piece together details of the Wilson and Lewis cases. This investigation required not only an assessment of the many oral testimonies with conflicting versions of names and dates, but also of the court records, the political adherences of the players involved, and the political climate of the Choctaw Nation at the time of the event. While I was able to write a commentary on Silan Lewis for the *American Indian Quarterly* in 2005, that was primarily an opinion piece based on his political beliefs. For a more serious study of Lewis, I needed much more information.

Unfortunately, the court records of the Silan Lewis trial that contained the witnesses' testimonies were burned in 1895 when the Gaines County Courthouse—where Lewis and other Nationalists were tried—was destroyed. So was another courthouse in Moshulatubbee District in 1893. Nor are the detailed court transcripts of other Choctaw trials found in other logical sites such as the Oklahoma Historical Society, the Western History Collections, the University of Tulsa, the National Archives in Washington, D.C., or Fort Worth (Southwest Branch), the Gilcrease Institute, among the Annual Reports of the Commissioner of Indian Affairs, the courthouse at McAlester, the present-day Gaines County Courthouse, and the Five Civilized Tribes Museum in Muskogee, Oklahoma.

Silan Lewis's court records were sent to Hoke Smith at the Department of the Interior in 1894, and I had high hopes that a copy of the proceedings would be available someplace in the National Archive system. Sadly, Smith's records also burned in the 1920s. A second round of investigation turned up nothing regarding Silan Lewis or the other Nationalists at the Richard B. Russell Library for Political Research and Studies at the University of Georgia, nor at the Old Military and Civil Records National Archives and Records Administration. I even resorted to sending personal letters to individuals in the Wilburton area and to the Choctaw Nation newspaper, *BISHINIK* (with over 183,400 readers) asking if anyone was by chance related to the court clerk who served during Lewis's trials and had their ancestor's old papers? I had visions of the court files packed away in a trunk in someone's attic. I received no replies.

Without the court records, I thought of abandoning the project. Then I gave serious thought as to what I might have to say without use of the court transcripts, but with a thorough investigation into other available records. Could the focus on Lewis be salvaged? I thought about it for a year and during that time proceeded with the Wilson case. Then I revisited Lewis to see how far I could take the investigation. What I have learned in the course of this project is that it is possible to reasonably reconstruct motives and events without the full court record. But even with court transcripts, many questions remain. Indeed, even the lengthy Fort Smith court file on Jackson Crow is what one might deem merely the outline of a complicated case.

After reading hundreds of documents, I wonder if any Choctaw case tried in the Choctaw Nation prior to statehood can be discussed thoroughly since there are few complete court files available. All that remain of the hundreds, perhaps thousands, of trials conducted in the Choctaw Nation are the court dockets, newspaper commentaries about selected cases, listings of juries, letters to the condemned men, and an occasional letter found in an archive file. This lack of primary data is not a recent problem. In 1890, John W. Lane, the special agent in charge of conducting the Choctaw census, commented about the Choctaws' careless record keeping. Along with noting the lack of detail in the school financial records, he stated that other files and papers containing political, legal, and financial data had been nearly destroyed by insects. He also asserted what modern scholars of Choctaw legal cases have unfortunately discovered: that if the files were not eaten by insects, they simply did not exist in 1890, and therefore do not exist today in Choctaw libraries.[1]

As stated previously, some records pertaining to Gaines County were destroyed by fire or insects. But that does not account for the hundreds of other cases in the seventeen counties of the three districts. As per an 1883 act that defined the duties of the court clerks, the clerks were required to "record the judgments, decrees and orders of the court, and deliver over to his successor in office all records, minutes, books, papers, presses and whatever belong to said officer of Clerk." The clerk was supposed to "take in his care and safe keeping all such record[s], books, papers, presses, stationery." He was then required to "take charge of all books, papers, and record[s] of cases, civil and criminal, that have been disposed of in any of the Circuit

Courts aforesaid . . . and shall file away and preserve the same in his office in the order in which they were decided."[2] Were these files taken home by the clerks? Time may tell.

For information on the trial of the men accused of killing Wilson and for information on the case of Silan Lewis, I researched several topics simultaneously while reading the tribal records. One had to look into the personalities of these cases—that is, the jurors, the witnesses, the men who lived in the vicinity of Wilson, who rode with Lewis, the Choctaw elite, the less affluent, and the political leaders. Even though at some points I felt I was drowning in minutia, the challenge remained of forming a meaningful understanding of the players' behavior.

One way to do that is to understand the politics of those involved. For example, scrutinizing the precinct voting poll books of the various counties can help in understanding an individual's political allegiances. Poll books also can reveal where a person lived, even if only for the time period surrounding an election. Some precinct poll books conveniently tell us for whom a person voted; but, by 1890, the poll books are for the most part only summaries of how the entire precinct voted and do not record the votes of individuals. Still, if voters of a particular precinct had an overwhelming preference (i.e., in 1884, the voters of the Luk Fataha Precinct of Bok Tuklo County in Apukshunnubbee District soundly preferred J. P. Folsom for chief to Edmund McCurtain by a margin of 29 votes to 1 vote), then it is fairly obvious where the citizens of that precinct stood as a whole, politically speaking, especially if one double-checks to see if those voters voted in several elections with similar results.

Some poll books are missing from the Choctaw record, but a look through old newspapers can sometimes reveal that precinct's tallies. Newspapers—although often biased—become important sources because in some elections the results were aggressively contested and the poll books were allegedly taken by political rivals. Such was the case in the 1884 Sugar Loaf County elections for sheriff, ranger, representative, and judge, and the 1892 election for chief in which the Gaines County Precinct poll books (among others) are apparently gone, but the results are shown in the *Indian Citizen*.

Newspapers such as the *Indian Citizen* contain a wealth of information, especially about the intrigues surrounding the 1892 election and the disdain the Progressives and Nationalists felt for each other. But, as with other documents, one cannot take every item in the paper at face value. Letter writers often were biased, and the newspaper editors were prejudiced toward one candidate or the other. But if one can decipher the personal drama and political maneuverings, then the newspapers can serve as informative and entertaining sources of data.

To make research more challenging, much of the handwriting in the records is messy and in some cases illegible. Names are often misspelled, thus requiring cross-checking of census records and the Dawes Rolls, although this only works occasionally because many of the people mentioned in this book died prior to enrollment. While it seems easy enough to say, "Just look at the previous rolls," the problem that can emerge is that some of the men moved around. This means, of course, that if you are looking for one person in particular, you must look through every roll, every county census, and every precinct poll book to see where that person lived at a particular point in time.

Census records are usually straightforward—that is, the names are easy to recognize. But, with few exceptions, it was not until the 1890s that women and children were listed by name. An 1885 census, for example, only lists the male head-of-household with a check to indicate if he was Indian or white, and numbers (1, 2, 3, etc.) tell us how many males, females, children, hogs, horses, and so on lived on his property. Looking for Choctaw males is infinitely easier than finding the women. For example, women were not allowed to vote and therefore do not appear in any of the precinct poll books.

If you want to locate a female prior to the Dawes Rolls and if she is not the spouse of someone prominent (and even then, she may be only known as "Mrs. So-and-So" with no mention of her name), occasionally the court dockets dealing with divorce, adultery, or murder cases might list her name if she was killed by someone charged with the crime. But sometimes murderers and rapists are in the record, but their victims' names are not. Even many who murdered, robbed, or assaulted women are not mentioned for the simple reason that some killers, thieves, and attackers were never punished.

The handwritten documents used here become even more difficult to use when the court clerk, letter writer, or Senate recorder decided to write in Choctaw. While some of the writing is not particularly challenging to translate, it becomes dicey to decipher when the writer was as messy writing in Choctaw as in English. Words can be misspelled in any language, and it is almost impossible to figure out some of the abbreviations.

The *Indian and Pioneer Histories*, a series of interviews of residents of Oklahoma conducted by Works Progress Administration (WPA) workers in the 1930s, contain useful information; but any astute student of Indian Territory, however, can quickly ascertain that while some of the *Indian and Pioneer Histories* stories are certainly fascinating, many "reminisces" of Indian Territory also are embellished and fabricated.

Similar sentiments could be held about the authors of some of the older essays in the *Chronicles of Oklahoma*. While many of the articles are well researched and accurate, others are not and oftentimes reflect the biased views of the authors. Many of the white players mentioned in this book are often idolized in the *Chronicles* because they were self-styled entrepreneurs; that is, they became wealthy after purposely marrying Indian women in order to become a citizen of her tribe and then could proceed to exploit that tribal nation for all they could. Even the indigenous individuals profiled in the *Chronicles* are sometimes glorified because of their similarities to the wealthy white men of Indian Territory and Oklahoma and/or because they were proponents of what the colonizers were after: allotment. Basically, if that indigenous leader was Christian, educated, and pro-allotment, then that leader was a hero according to the early writers in the *Chronicles*.

Many of these Choctaws interviewed in the 1930s are reminiscent of the Cherokees interviewed during the same time period in that they prefer to think of their tribe as always having been without strife or disagreements among the members. There are many records to show that the opposite was true.[3] Some interviewees with claimed knowledge or memories of the 1880s through the time of statehood have revealed their lack of knowledge about Choctaw politics and they have not contributed many ideas as to why people behaved the way they did. Very few of the Indians, pioneers, or authors in the *Chronicles* can insightfully discuss motivations or cause and effect.

One also needs to use books about Fort Smith, "gunfighters" of the west, and Web sites that feature "outlaws" with caution because many of the writers (and Web masters) merely copy one another's works without doing any original research on their own. Scholars can glean much from these sources, although they must use these interviews and writings in conjunction with other documentation.

Letters Regarding Silan Lewis

1. W. N. Jones to N. J. Holson, July 4, 1893
Source: CTN 49, vol. 339, pp. 427–28

July 4th, 1893

Hon. N. J. Holson
Circuit Judge
1st Judicial Dist., C.N.

Hon. Sir,

I write you this letter to inform you that matters have assumed this shape.

I received a letter of inquiry to day [*sic*] from Washington asking that a stay of execution be granted those prisoners who are under sentence of death, if it were within my power or within the power of the Council.

I replied that it was not within my power or within the power of Council for us to interfere with the order of the court. However, I received a letter to day [*sic*] asking that in any event I would grant a stay of execution for thirty days until they had examined the evidence that was given before the court.

After assembling the principal officers and considering the matter and as it is a just conclusion of an officer of the United

States, they will bear the censure for any trouble should any occur in the matter; Therefore you will take notice by the letter that we have a greed [*sic*] that it is proper to grant the request of a stay of execution for thirty days.

And also that you will postpone the execution of the sentence of death on Sam Jefferson, Columbus Brown, Joshua Calvin and Simeon Wade from the 7th day of July 1893, and order them to be executed on the 4th day of August, 1893.

And also in addition you will postpone the execution of the sentence of death on Silan Lewis, Robert Carter, Moses Williams, Kingsbury Harkin and Thomas McGee who are to be executed on the 14th day of July 1893, and order them to be executed on the 4th day of August 1893.

Therefore you will go to Wilburton at once and order all of these men to be executed in the 4th day of August 1893. And also you will inform your Clerk why you have granted a stay of execution and he will enter the same on the records of the court.

Very respectfully,
W. N. Jones
P.C.-C.N.

I hereby certify that the above and fore going [*sic*] is a true and correct copy of the stay of execution the original of which—on file in my office.

                                          John Taylor
                                          Circuit Court
This is the 8th day of July 1893   By James Culberson

2. W. N. Jones to Hoke Smith, July 5, 1893

Source: Wilson N. Jones Collection, box 1, folder 11, Western History Collections, University of Oklahoma

(Received by Hoke Smith on July 15, 1893)

Executive Office, C.N.
Tushkahoma, Ind. Terr.
July 5, 1893

To Hon. Hoke Smith, Secretary of the Interior
Dear Sir:

July 3, 1893, message from Hon. J.I. Hall of your department was received at Tushkahomma by me while at said place at the special session of the Choctaw nations general council, desiring to know if I had as governor the power to commute the sentence of any one convicted of murder and sentenced to death under the laws of this nation.

To this message answer was returned in the negative. There is no law or constitutional provision authorizing the principal chief to commute or stay the sentence of any one convicted of murder and sentenced to the death penalty under the laws of the Choctaw nation. No power whatsoever by our constitution and laws is conferred upon the executive to grant retrieve, commutation of sentence or pardon in any case.

Thereafter on the 4th day of July, 1893, Col. Faison, United States Indian inspector, called on me at said place and presented your letter of the 30th ultimo, with a request that your wishes be complied with and that at least a suspension of the execution for thirty days be ordered, claiming we had power under the treaty of 1856 in the interest of domestic peace. Col. Faison was advised that there was no law or constitutional provision authorizing any such course.

However, after fully discussing the matter with Col. Faison, a conference was had with hon. W. W. Wilson, national auditor, Hon. Green McCurtain, national treasurer, Hon. J. B. Jackson, national secretary, in regard to the matter so suddenly presented, it being almost upon the evening of the time fixed for executing the death penalty upon the parties sentenced to death as aforesaid. As a result of said

conference I have arrived at the conclusion that it would be advisable and politic to have the execution of the aforesaid parties stayed
by the judge of the court in which said parties were tried until
August 4th, 1893, if at my request he saw fit to do so, and I have
requested the judge to stay the executions until aforesaid date.

There is no law authorizing any such action on my part or on the
part of the aforesaid judge, but I am satisfied the judge will accede
to my request and grant the stay of execution desired. The council
being in session, steps will be taken before it authorizing such action
on the part of Judge Holson, but even this course will leave a very
grave question open, and afford the aforesaid parties an opportunity
to escape merited punishment meted out to them by the courts of
this nation, and if so it will be the result of the request made by you
through Inspector Faison.

Be this how it may, in justice to the people of the Choctaw nation
and myself as principal chief of said nation, I desire to inform you
of the motives and reasons that prompted such action on my part,
because it must not be for a moment thought we concede and admit
the right of your department to obstruct and impede the administration of justice and the enforcement of our laws.

Under the treaties with the United States the Choctaw nation is
secured in the unrestricted right of self government and full jurisdiction over persons and property within its limits, in so far as may
be compatible with the constitution of the United States and laws
made in pursuance thereof regulating trade and intercourse with
the Indian tribes. Under this guarantee laws were passed for the
punishment of crimes, including that of murder, and for the indictment
by a fair and impartial grand jury of persons charged with murder
and other crimes, and for trial after indictment of persons charged
with crime by jury of twelve men fairly and impartially selected from
the body of the district. I suppose statements or complaints must
have been made to your department. Without the attention of the
authorities of the Choctaw nation having been called to such statements or complaints, so that an opportunity might be afforded them
to refute such calumny, for such they are, in time to avoid the present
complications, an intimation amounting practically to a command

is conveyed, desiring a stay of sentence of said parties pending an investigation of such baseless statements or complaints by your department, this almost on the verge of the execution of said sentence.

Under our simple system of the administration of justice there can arise no possibility of a conviction being had through more political prejudice or political causes. The commission of the crime must be proven and established the same as in all your states and territories and under the same rules of evidence which prevail in the courts of the white man, and parties accused of crime in the courts of the Choctaw nation, like those in the states and territories, are tried by a jury of twelve men selected as prescribed by law and given the benefit of a reasonable doubt. All these parties were regularly and duly indicted by the grand jury, tried by a pettit [sic] jury of twelve men, ably represented and defended council and convicted in accordance with the law. All proceedings against these parties have been held strictly as provided by law and the assurance given your department that said parties should be fairly and impartially tried in strict conformity to the law has been faithfully carried out and complied with.

Nonwithstanding that the right of self-government has been guaranteed us by a treaty, and that our laws are being fairly and impartially enforced, the United States had for three times in succession and without just cause, we think, interfered with and thereby obstructed the due and proper administration and execution of the law, and this without there existing any "domestic strife" to authorize and excuse such interference on the part of the United States.

However, being anxious and desirous of fostering amicable and friendly relations with the United States throughout our department, and to ascertain where the line will be drawn when the United States, through the departments, will cease from interfering with the execution and administration of our laws so that we could govern ourselves intelligibly, I concluded as herein advised, to request the judge aforesaid to stay the execution of the sentence until Aug. 4, 1893, so that the fullest investigation could be made by you, and the evidence and proceedings had in our courts in the trials of the parties aforesaid could be forwarded to you, assuring you that we court and challenge investigation without fear and favor. This course was further deemed advisable in justice to my people and myself, feeling certain you will be fully and amply convinced that in these cases justice has been dealt out to the parties fairly and impartially by our courts and that they had meted to them a merited and deserved sentence.

Kindly permit me to call your attention to the fact that if these parties have been convicted without authority of law or without due process, of law, the courts of the United States have ample power to protect them. Globe.

Very Respectfully,
W. N. Jones
Principal Chief,
Choctaw Nation

3. Hoke Smith to Paul Faison, July 7, 1893
Source: CTN 49, vol. 339, p. 428

True Copy

Department of the Interior
Washington July 7th 1893

Mr. Paul Faison
Indian Inspector
Antlers, Indian Territory

Sir,

Your telegram amending? The suspension of the execution of the nine Choctaws —will be shot till August—was duly received.— will be absent until about the first of August and——during the interim. You will therefore call——Gov. Wilson Jones and advise him that—desirable that?——further postponement until at least September 8th be had. You will——the importance of taking this action and the keen interest the Government has in securing such an adjustment of the present troubles as will—the best interests of the Choctaw people. Advise me of the result of your efforts.

Very respectfully,
Hoki Smith
Secretary

5055 Ind. Div.—

4. W. N. Jones to N. J. Holson, July 14, 1893
CTN 49, vol. 339, pp. 428–29

Executive Office
Choctaw Nation
Caddo I.T. July 14, 1893

Hon. N.J. Holson
Circuit Judge First Judicial Dist. Choctaw Nation.

Dear Sir,

Col. Paul Faison, Indian Inspector called on me today bringing with him a letter from Hon. Hoke Smith Secretary of the Interior, a copy of which letter is hereto attached and which will explain to you my report. I recognize the fact that such procedure is irregular and not found in our Laws, but I deem it our duty to set for the best interests of your government acting under the authority given us implications.

I hope that you will not consider it unreasonable – me to request that you further extend the time from Aug. 4, 1893 and set Sept. 8, 1893 as the day for the Execution of the nine prisoners now under sentence of Death in your District. This request is made by Secretary Smith through Col. Faisom Inspector, and I hope the courtesy due will be extended. Please attend to this matter at once and notify Col. Paul Faison Indian Inspector at Fort Smith Ark, of your action immediately. Also report to me.

Very respectfully,
W.N. Jones
P.C., C.N.

5. N. J. HOLSON TO JOHN TAYLOR, JULY 18, 1893
CTN 49, vol. 339, p. 429

Hon. John Taylor Clerk   LeFlore, Indian Territory
    Bokosha?, I.T.   July 18, 1893

    Dear Friend,
    As I enclosed for which you will find that a letter from Hon.
Hoki Smith Sec. of the Interior to Col. Paul Faison Indian Inspector
attached to Gov. W.N. Jones letter which I promptly acted on it and
attended the matter as their request. I further extended the time
from Aug. 4, 1893 and set Sept. 8, 1893 as the day for the execution
of the nine prisoners now under sentence of death by shot, and
now recorded this letter in your office.

                              Your friend,
                              N.J. Holson
                              Circuit Judge of the 1st Judicial District
                              Choctaw Nation

I hereby certify that the above and foregoing letters and stay of execution is a true and correct copy the original of which is now on file in
my office. This the 22d day of July 1893.

                              John Taylor
                              Circuit Clerk

6. Paul Faison to N. J. Holson, August 28, 1893
CTN 49, vol. 339

> Department of the Interior
> Indian Inspection Service
> Caddo, I.T. Aug. 28, 1893

Hon. N.J. Holson
Circuit Judge 1st Judicial Dist.
Choctaw Nation
Caddo I.T.

Dear Sir,

Yours of this date as a result of the interview held with Gov. Jones and yourself relative to the execution of the nine condemned Choctaws redc., the government contained therein is satisfactory, and your suggestion that there will be no further interference by the Dept. of the Interior with the execution of Silan Lewis and Simeon Wade will be complied with.

> Yours truly,
> Paul F. Faison
> U.S. Ind Inspt.

7. HOKE SMITH TO PAUL FAISON, SEPTEMBER 5, 1893

CTN 49, vol. 339, p. 430

Copy of the Telegram

Record 6:55 P.M. Sept. 5, 1893
Washington D.C. 5
To Inspector Paul F. Faison,

Muskogee, I.T.

A careful examination of the Record fails to Show that Lewis and Wade were the active leaders of the parties as the testimony indicate that they were no more guilty than the other seven and that the instigation of the Murders have not been tried in view of the fact that the testimony does not Sustain the Statement contained in the letters of Judge Holson to yourself. It is the opinion of this department that no sufficient grounds exist for the selection of the two to be shot, but that the death penalty should be remitted as to all or else the entire question should be refered [sic] to the Council of the Nation. You will communicate immediately with Gov. Jones and wire me at once his Decission [sic].

Hoki [sic] Smith
Secty

8. W. N. JONES TO N. J. HOLSON, SEPTEMBER 6, 1893
CTN 49, vol. 339, p. 431

Executive Office, Choctaw Nation
Indian Tr., Sept. 6th, 1893
To the Hon.N.J. Holson

Dist. Judge for 1st Dist. Choctaw Nation,

The bearer of this J.R. Lawrence I send with on over to stay the execution of one Lewis and Wade who are 2 of the nine that were tried and condemned by your court, upon this proposition which I have this day made to Col. Faison who comes to me with a Telegram from the Department, while it is painfull [sic] for me to do, the Government seems to hold all in their hands, the condition are such that I have agreed to extend this matter on which Col. Faison will send to the Department, Gov. Jones proposes that the agreement of the 28th be annulled, that all be retried separately letting the evidence show who were leaders, or let them all if can be legally done be tried by U.S. District Court. Instructions have been sent by messenger to Judge and Sheriff to suspend execution on Lewis and Wade till next Nov. court. The Council will convene in the mean time and can take action. Now you are hereby notified to issue an order to the Sheriff to stay the execution until further orders or action of the Department so that Justice and Peace may prevail. Herein fail not.

I am most Respectfully yours

W.N. Jones
Principal Chief
Choctaw Nation

9. N. J. Holson to John Taylor, September 8, 1893
CTN 49, vol. 339, p. 431

Leflore Ind. Ter. Sept 8th 1893

Hon John Taylor
Circuit Clerk of the 1st District CN

Dear Sir,
1st I herewith send you Col Paul Faisons [*sic*] letter to me.
2nd A copy of Telegram of Hoki Smith to Inspector Paul F. Faison;
Gov. Jones letter to me which I take an action on it for his request,
and I issued an order to Hon John W. Perry Sheriff of Gaines
County, Choctaw Nation to stay the execution of Silan Lewis and
Simeon Wade until further order. And now Recorded in your office
for the same.

Yours truly
N.J. Holson
Circuit Judge of the 1st Judicial
District Choctaw Nation

I hereby certify that the communications on this and the preceding
page is a true and correct copy of the originals now on file in my
office. This is the 16th day of September 1893.

John Taylor
Circuit Clerk

10. SAM JEFFERSON, JOSHUA CALVIN, PRYMUS BROWN, AND SIMEON
WADE TO P.J. HOLSON, NOVEMBER 13, 1893
CTN 49, vol. 339, p. 432–33

Choctaw Nation
Mosholatubbee District

To the Hon N.J. Holson Circuit Judge of the 1st Judicial District,
C.N. In vacation.

We the undersigned defendants in case No. 55, would most
respectfully pray your Honor to grant us a new trial for the following reasons, to wit:

1st, that one of the jurors who tried our case was one of our guards
at the time.

2d that at the time of the trial party strife and the causes as we
believe prevented us from obtaining a fair and impartial trial. But
now we believe that the prejudice which existed against us at the
time of the trial has to a certain extent subsided and that if we are
granted a new trial we can obtain a fair and impartial trial at the
next term of this Court.

> Sam Jefferson
> Joshua Calvin
> Prymus Brown and
> Simeon Wade

Sworn to and subscribed before me this the 13th day of
November 1893.

SEAL

> John Taylor
> Circuit Clerk

The motion is granted.

> N.J. Holson
> Circuit Judge
> 1st Judicial Dist. C.N.

I hereby certify that the above motion and granting of the new trial is a true and correct copy of the original now on file in my office.

This the 13th day of November 1893.

John Taylor
Circuit Clerk

11. Joseph Garland, memorandum, October 1894
CTN 53, vol. 396, 94

Silan Lewis

v.

Choctaw Nation

In Supreme Court

October Term 1894

The above entitled cause having been brought to this court upon a write of certiorari from the circuit court of the First District CN for a final hearing and adjudication and after a careful investigation of the proceedings had in the case fail to find sufficient cause for a reversal of said proceedings in said case.

Hence the decision of the lower court is hereby affirmed and the decrees of the lower court is hereby ordered to be carried out.

Joseph Garland, Chief Justice

C. B. Wade

Attest

T. D. Hibben

Clerk Supreme Court, C.N.

12. N. J. Holson to Silan Lewis, October 16, 1894
CTN 49, vol. 339, p. 493

LEWIS RE-SENTENCED

Musholotubbee District
Choctaw Nation
To Silon Lewis:

At the special term of Moshulatubbee District Court, held in December 1892, you were indicted by the Grand Jury on the 16th day of December 1892, for the awful crime of murder in killing of Joe Hukolotubbee on, or about the 10th day of September 1892. On the 19th day of April 1894, after a fair and impartial trial by a Jury of twelve good and lawful Citizens of your Country you were found guilty of the terrible crime and sentenced to be shot.

You took an appeal from the judgment of this Court to the Supreme Court of the Choctaw Nation, where, on the 2nd day of October 1894, the judgment of this court was reaffirmed.

It now becomes my imperative and solemn duty to re-sentence you for this awful crime, and I appeal to you to make preparations to meet your maker. No longer delude yourself with false hopes of a new trial, or commutation, but make peace with your God. It is the sentence of this Court that you be taken into custody of the Sheriff of Gaines County, and securely kept in some jail or other suitable place in this District until the 5th day of November 1894, when you shall be conveyed to the Moshulatubbee District Court grounds, where between the hours of 10 o'clock A.M. and 2 o'clock P.M. you shall be shot until you are dead, by the Sheriff of Gaines County, and may God have mercy on your Soul.

N.J. Holson
Circuit Judge, 1st Judicial District, C.N.

I hereby certify the foregoing to be true and correct copy of the original sentence of Silan Lewis, now on file in my office. This October 16 1894.

Wallace Bond, Clerk

Choctaw District Judge N. J. Holson to Silon Lewis, Judge Sentence of the Court in Choctaw Nation Mosholatubbee District, October 16, 1894.

Notes

INTRODUCTION

1. In an interview with Crawford J. Anderson (November 15, 1937, *IPH*, 2:330–43), Anderson used the term "Snakehead" in reference to the Nationalists of the early 1890s. It is possible that Anderson adopted the "Snake" reference for the Choctaw Nationalists after observing the Muscogee (Creek) Chitto Harjo and his followers who also opposed allotment.

2. *Indian Citizen*, January 31, 1901.

3. Anonymous quote in Lane, "Choctaw Nation," 60.

4. Pickens also was a tribal commissioner who assisted in negotiating a treaty at Washington in 1852. He signed the agreement with the Choctaws at Doaksville in 1854 and helped negotiate the separation of the Chickasaws and the Choctaws. He served as a member of the Chickasaw Senate, signed the treaty of alliance

with the Confederate States in 1861, and assisted in the negotiation of the Treaty with the Choctaws and Chickasaws, April 28, 1866 (Treaty of 1866; 14 Stat. 769, 773).

PROLOGUE

1. Robert L. Owen to CIA, August 21, 1885, in *ARCIA* (1885): 103.

2. Morrison, *Seven Constitutions*.

3. See sections 2–4, 8, and 20 of the Choctaw Constitution of 1860, in *CLAIT*, 11:5–25; *CLAIT*, 19:134–36; Testimony of Robert J. Wood, June 4, 1885, and testimony of Napoleon B. Ainsworth, May 26, 1885, both *Report of the Committee on Indian Affairs*, 396–7, 224. The results of some of these elections are contained in CTN 63, CTN 64, CTN 65, CTN 66, and CTN 67.

4. Article 4, sections 5–7 of the Constitution of 1860, in Morrison, *Seven Constitutions*.

5. Article 4, sections 10, 11, and 16 of the Constitution of 1860, in Morrison, *Seven Constitutions*. See also, "Testimony of Sam Six Killer," May 26, 1885, in 45th Congress, 1st sess., 2 Senate, report no. 1278, in *Report of the Committee on Indian Affairs*, part 2, p. 224.

6. Champagne, *Social Order and Political Change*; Cushman, *History of the Choctaw, Chickasaw and Natchez Indians*; Eggan, "Historical Changes in the Choctaw Kinship System"; Spoehr, "Changing Kinship Systems"; O'Brien, *Choctaws in a Revolutionary Age*; O'Brien, *Pre-Removal Choctaw History*; Swanton, *Source Material*.

Other notable works on the Choctaws include Adair, *History of the American Indians*; Akers, *Living in the Land of Death*; Anderson and Zachary, *A Choctaw Anthology*; Baird, *Peter Pitchlynn*; Bonnifield, "The Choctaw on the Eve of the Civil War"; Carson, *Searching for the Bright Path*; De Rosier, *Removal of the Choctaw Indians*; Debo, *Rise and Fall of the Choctaw Republic*; Faiman-Silva, *Choctaws at the Crossroads*; Karr, "'Now We Have Forgotten the Old Indian Law'"; Kidwell, *Choctaws and Missionaries in Mississippi* and *The Choctaws in Oklahoma*; Lewis, *Chief Pushmataha, American Patriot*; Miner, *The Corporation and the Indian*; Morrison, *Social History of the Choctaw Nation* and "Problems in the Industrial Progress and Development of the Choctaw Nation"; Pesantubbee, *Choctaw Women in a Chaotic World*; Tate, *Edmund Pickens (Okchantubby)*; White, *Roots of Dependency*; Washburn, *Assault on Indian Tribalism*.

Many of the aforementioned books and essays explore acculturation and events that spurred cultural change. Carson, for example, discusses four cultural aspects that lasted long after contact: the chiefdom organization, matrilineal descent, a male/female division of labor, and specific cosmological beliefs, including beings that many Choctaws use in storytelling today.

7. For information on the early history of the Choctaws, see Cushman, *History of the Choctaw, Chickasaw and Natchez Indians*; Claiborne, *Mississippi as a Province*; Swanton, *Source Material*, especially 76–77 for variations in the names.

8. Constitution of the Choctaw Nation, 1857, in *CLAIT*, 16:5–24. For information on the town of Skullyville, see Morrison, "Saga of Skullyville." Within Apukshunnubbee District were the counties of Bok Humma (Red River); Bok Tuklo (Two Creeks, although the English version is not seen in the documents), Chuahla (Cedar), Nashoba (Wolf), Osi (Eagle), Tausin (Towson; named after Colonel Nathan Towson), and Wet (Wade). Chickasaw District: counties of Kvlolachi (Caddo); Pali (Perry); Ponola (Cotton); Wichita (same in English). Within Moshulatubbee District: counties of Kenis (Gaines), Iskvlli (Skullyville; combination of "small piece of money" and "-ville"), Nvnih Chufvk (Sugar Loaf), and Sambai (San Bois). Pushmataha District: counties of Chak Fak (Jacks Fork), Kiamichi (from the French word "kamichi" meaning "horned screamer"), Koi Kulih (Panther Spring), and Shappaway (no English version). In 1854, Koi Kulih was changed to Okchamali (Blue) County and Shappaway County was changed to Atoka County, after a Choctaw captain and signer of the 1830 Treaty of Dancing Rabbit Creek. For a summary of the assignment of Choctaw counties, see Wright, "Organization of Counties in the Choctaw and Chickasaw Nations." The origins/meanings of the names can be found in numerous places, including Shirk, *Oklahoma Place Names*.

9. O. L. Blanch, June 9, 1937, *IPH*, 15:318.

10. Testimonies of freedmen in the 1880s reveal that some slaves of the Choctaws continued to be held in servitude after the war was over. This is discussed briefly in the next chapter. Article 38 of the 1866 treaty reads, "Every white person who, having married a Choctaw or Chickasaw, resides in the said Choctaw or Chickasaw Nation, or who has been adopted by the legislative authorities, is to be deemed a member of said nation, and shall be subject to the laws of the Choctaw and Chickasaw Nations according to his domicile, and to prosecution and trial before their tribunals, and to punishment according to their laws in all respects as though he was a native Choctaw or Chickasaw." See Treaty of 1866, in *CLAIT*, 11:57.

11. Article 5 of the Treaty with the Choctaw and Chickasaw, 1855, states: "The members of either the Choctaw or the Chickasaw tribe, shall have the right, freely, to settle within the jurisdiction of the other, and shall thereupon be entitled to all the rights, privileges, and immunities of citizens thereof; but no member of either tribe shall be entitled to participate in the funds belonging to the other tribe. Citizens of both tribes shall have the right to institute and prosecute suits in the courts of either, under such regulations as may, from time to time, be prescribed by their respective legislatures." Kappler, *IA:LT*, 2:708.

12. Article 8, section 8 of the 1866 treaty states that the tribes "also agree that a court or courts may be established in said Territory with such jurisdiction and organization as Congress may prescribe: Provided, That the same shall not interfere with the local judiciary of either of said nations" (Kappler, *IA:LT*, 2:922). See also article 6 of the 1855 treaty, which states, "Any person duly charged with a criminal offence against the laws of either the Choctaw or the Chickasaw tribe,

and escaping into the jurisdiction of the other, shall be promptly surrendered, upon the demand of the proper authorities of the tribe, within whose jurisdiction the offence shall be alleged to have been committed" (Kappler, *IA:LT*, 2:708). Article 15 of the 1855 treaty states, "The Choctaws and Chickasaws shall promptly apprehend and deliver up all persons accused of any crime or offence against the laws of the United States, or of any State thereof, who may be found within their limits, on demand of any proper officer of a State, or of the United States" (Kappler, *IA:LT*, 2:710). Article 42 of the 1866 treaty states, "The Choctaw and Chickasaw Nations shall deliver up persons accused of crimes against the United States who may be found within their respective limits on the requisition of the governor of any State for a crime committed against the laws of said State, and upon the requisition of the judge of the district court of the United States for the district within which the crime was committed" (Kappler, *IA:LT*, 2:929).

    13. Session III, section 16, in *CLAIT*, 13:16.

    14. Session IV, section 7, in *CLAIT*, 13:26.

    15. "An Act Compelling White Men Living with an Indian Woman to Marry Her Lawfully," approved October 1849, in *CLAIT*, 11:106.

    16. Lane, "Choctaw Nation," 61.

    17. CTN 4.

CHAPTER 1: THE MURDER OF CHARLES WILSON AND THE EXECUTION OF JACKSON CROW

    Epigraph: Interview with Jesse J. Robbs, "The Murder of Charles W. Wilson, A Choctaw," March 18, 1938, *IPH*, 113:514–15. Robbs incorrectly refers to Wilson's middle initial as "W."

    1. Wright, "Notes and Documents," 202–3. Shirk, *Oklahoma Place Names*, 135; *South McAlester Capital*, July 12, 1894; Interview with Elijah Conger, *IPH*, 2:196–97.

    2. His name has also been spelled as Filmuchubbe, Fehekatubbee, Filiktubbee, Felehmachubbee, and Frelay machubbee. This lack of consistency is affirmed by personal correspondence with his descendant, J. Myles Felihkatubbe. I opt to use the spelling seen in the court records in testimony of Fleema Chubbee, October 25, 1887, in *United States v. Jack Crow*, at the Fort Smith National Historic Site Archives, Fort Smith, Ark. He has a record of serving as election judge and juror for a variety of trials in the 1870s and 1880s. CTN 42, vol. 225; "Fiscal Year Commencing 1 August 1878 and Ending the 31st July 1879" in CTN 90, vol. 41.

    3. CTN 87, document no. 22526; "Judge Isaac Charles Parker, 'Hanging Judge' of Ft. Smith, Arkansas Fame," freepages.genealogy.rootsweb.com/~rkinfolks/deputies.html; "Oklahoma United States Marshals, Deputy United States Marshals and Possemen," www.okolha.net/dusm_usm_A.htm; "U.S. Deputy Marshal in the Federal District Court for the Western District of Arkansas, Indian Territory at Fort Smith, Arkansas, circa 1872–1896," Living the Legacy Curriculum Materials,

section 4, National Park Service, Fort Smith National Historic Site, www.nps.gov/fosm/forteachers/upload/legacy%20part%204.pdf; "Violent Deaths of U.S. Marshals," www.silverstarcollectables.com/killed.htm; Martin, "Unsung Heroes," 25. "Wilson, Charles B.: Deputy United States Marshal," in Owens, *Oklahoma Heroes*. No picture of Wilson exists, so I will claim author creativity and envision him as actor Sam Elliott.

4. Testimony of Fleema Chubbee, October 25, 1887, in *United States v. Jack Crow*, 58–60.

5. Testimonies of Jasper Baker, C. C. Mathies, Adam Morris, Abel Harris, and Sam Parker, October 25, 1887, in *United States v. Jack Crow*, 1–2, 4, 8, 18–23. According to my family stories, the tattered coat was given to the Oklahoma Historical Society decades ago, but there exists no record of it. Another less likely version of events is from J. J. Robbs, who in an interview said that Morris saw a bridled, saddled, and riderless horse trot past his home. Morris commented, "Here comes Charlie Wilson's horse." Knowing what had happened at the debate the night before, he added, "I guess Charlie got drunk and fell off him." Then a boy came running up from behind the horse and excitedly told the men that Charles Wilson was lying dead in the road and that he also saw "Benton and a Negro" not far from Wilson's body. See interview with Jesse J. Robbs, "The Murder of Charles W. Wilson, a Choctaw," March 18, 1938, *IPH*, 113:514–15. Robbs incorrectly refers to Wilson's middle initial as "W."

6. Treaty of Dancing Rabbit Creek, September 27 1830, U.S.-Choctaw, 7 Stat. 333, Proclamation, February 24, 1831; "Death of the Choctaw Merchant," *Indian Champion*, August 16, 1884; CTN 42, vols. 225 and 227; "Census of Atoka County, Choctaw Nation, Filed March 4, 1868," in CTN 2.

7. Choctaw Nation Enrollment Card no. 2320 (Edmund Pickens, son of Mary Wilson Pickens), Enrollment Cards for the Five Civilized Tribes, 1898–1914, Choctaws by Blood, M1186, National Archives, Southwest Region; Meserve, "Chief Wilson Nathaniel Jones," 433. See also information on the Pickens Genealogy Information Group at freepages.family.rootsweb.com/~pickensarchive/bg/okhist.html.

8. Interview with William Dellwood Fields, June 16, 1937, *IPH*, 64:2–4.

9. Interview with George W. Sorrels, November 12, 1937, *IPH*, 59:436.

10. See also "U.S. Marshals: Charles B. Wilson, Deputy U.S. Marshal," www.oklemem.com/W.htm; *Indian Champion*, August 16, 1884; and "The Marshals: Violent Deaths of U.S. Marshals," www.silverstarcollectables.com/killed.htm.

11. Baird, *Peter Pitchlynn*; Foreman, "Notes of Interest Concerning Peter P. Pitchlynn," 172–74. "Lighthorsemen" is spelled several ways in the court records, Choctaw laws and in other historical documents, such as lighthorsemen, light-horsemen or light-horse-men. I prefer the former.

12. Robert L. Owen, Union Agency to CIA, September 1, 1887, *ARCIA* (1887): 1 House, serial 2542, p. 100.

13. It is mentioned in only one source that the lighthorsemen could make decisions about executing an accused murderer. See Cushman, *History of the Choctaw, Chickasaw and Natchez Indians*, 158.

14. "An Act Giving Power to Judges to Direct Light-Horse-Men to Force Criminals to Attend Court, and Also for Securing the Attendance of Witnesses at Court, Approved October 12, 1839," in *CLAIT*, 14:30; "An Act Empowering the Chief to Offer Rewards for the Apprehension of Outlawed Murderers," approved October 1859, in *CLAIT*, 15:72.

15. "An Act Making It the Duty of the Light-Horse-Men to Apprehend Murderers and Criminals," approved October 1840, in *CLAIT*, 15:31. See also "An Act Murderers to Be Arrested by Order of the Chief or Judge," approved October 1840, in *CLAIT*, 15:27; "An Act Relating to All Strays and the Duty of Those That Take up, Judge, District Clerk and Light-Horse-Men, with Respect thereto; and Also the Pay of District Clerk, and the One That Takes up," approved October, 1843, in *CLAIT*, 14:46–48; "An Act Provided for the Pay of Jurymen," approved October, 1843, in *CLAIT*, 14:49.

16. Riggs, "Bits of Interesting History," 149.

17. Information about foods, their uses and preparations can be found in Swanton, *Source Material* and Romans, *Concise Natural History*.

18. John Payne to John Watterston, December 2, 1840, quoted in Foreman, *Advancing the Frontier*, 326.

19. Pitchlynn to his father, August 17, 1860, box 3, folder 66, and Pitchlynn to his father, December 31, 1858, in box 3, folder 37, in Peter Pitchlynn Collection, WHC.

20. Session II, section 1, approved October 8, 1835; session III, section 3, approved October 4, 1836, in *CLAIT*, 13:16.

21. "An Act One Light-Horse from Each District to Attend the General Council by Order of the Chiefs," approved October, 12, 1848, in *CLAIT*, 15:59.

22. "An Act Attendance of Light-Horse-Men at the Schools," sec. 2, approved November 1842, in *CLAIT*, 15:33.

23. "An Act in Relation to Salt Works," approved October 1838, in *CLAIT*, 15:25.

24. "An Act Improvement How Near," approved October 11, 1839, in *CLAIT*, 15:25–26.

25. Article 5, section 21, Constitution of the Choctaw Nation, 1857, in *CLAIT*, 16:19; article 5, section 14 of the Constitution of 1860. The elected sheriff had ten days from the election to take the oath of office and to submit bond, otherwise, the election would be declared void by the county judge and another sheriff would be appointed by the principal chief. Neither the sheriff nor the deputies were allowed to perform any duties until they had taken their oaths of office. Sheriffs could appoint additional "special deputy sheriffs" to assist them during the circuit courts, and who could receive two dollars a day each day they attended the court. Both sheriffs and deputies were responsible for their actions; if they

did not execute their orders, then not only could his securities be liable, but so could his heirs, "executors and administrators." Section 8 of the Constitution of 1860, in *CLAIT*, 19:132. Sheriffs had the same responsibilities as the lighthorsemen, in addition to numerous others. A sheriff was supposed to "keep the peace within his county" and to require anyone accused of a crime to enter into bond with securities before appearing in court to answer to charges leveled against him or her. In cases of murder, however, the county court or circuit judge would set the bail. Sheriffs were to suppress all unlawful assemblies and jail anyone charged with treason, felony, and other serious crimes. Sheriffs were required to execute all orders presented to them by the principal chief or the U.S. Indian agent including the arrest and detainment of those charged with crimes.

26. Interview with Dillard Duncan, March 28, 1938, *IPH*, 101:363.

27. Interview with Lemuel Jackson, June 24, 1937, *IPH*, 31:34.

28. Section 7, p. 165, in *CLAIT*, 11:165.

29. Pitchlynn to his father, June 17, 1860, box 3, folder 66, Peter Pitchlynn Collection, WHC.

30. For the activities of Benton, see the various records of the House of Representatives in CTN 10 and CTN 11. For Benton's voting regarding the railway, see CTN 11, vol. 316, p. 304; CTN 42, vol. 225, p. 188, in Scrip Book (some of the first pages of the ledger book are partially torn away, but one can see Benton's name, position as judge, and date on some of the page remnants); CTN 42, vol. 226; "Abstract of the Returns of the first Judicial Circuit of County Officers," in CTN 63; CTN12, vol. 305.

31. CTN 42, vols. 225, 226, and 230.

32. See for example, discussions in Minor, *The Corporation and the Indian*.

33. Article 18 of the 1855 treaty stipulated that the United States "or any incorporated company," had the right of way to build railroads through the Choctaw and Chickasaw lands. Kappler, *IA:LT*, 2:706–14, 918–31, also in *Chickasaws and Choctaws: A Pamphlet of Information Concerning Their History, Treaties, Government, Country, Laws, Politics and Affairs*, in *CLAIT*, 11:3–19; Treaty of 1866, in Kappler, *IA:LT*, 2:918–31.

34. Johnson, "Brief History of the Missouri-Kansas-Texas Railroad Lines."

35. Information about the McCurtain family is found in Meserve, "The McCurtains." "An Act Granting a Charter to the Poteau Slack Water Navigation Company," bill no. 38, approved October 26, 1883, in *CLAIT*, 18:25–27. The company had the responsibility of building the dams and locks and was privileged to use all the timber, stone, and miscellaneous building materials from the public domain.

36. *Indian Citizen*, November 7, 1895; *ARCIA* (1895): 67.

37. *ARCIA* (1860): 354.

38. Testimony of Edmund Pickens, October 25, 1887, *United States v. Jack Crow*, 38; interview with Mrs. Sarah C. Griffith, April 29, 1937, *IPH*, 3:184. Another testimony is that Wilson ran for the position of sheriff of Sugar Loaf County. See Robbs, "The Murder of Wilson," 510.

39. Robbs, "The Murder of Wilson," 511; interview with Griffith, IPH, 3:184; Testimonies of Abel Harris, Joseph Jackson, and Edmund Pickens, October 25, 1887, *United States v. Jack Crow*, 25, 47, 87.

40. CTN 42, vol. 227, case no. 60.

41. Testimonies of Sam Parker, Adam Morris, October 25, 1887, in *United States v. Jack Crow*, 5–6, 9.

42. "Poll Book, Spring Hill Precinct, Sugar Loaf County, for an Election on the 3rd Day of August, 1884," in CTN 63.

43. Testimonies of Sam Parker, Adam Morris, October 25, 1887, in *United States v. Jack Crow*, 5–6, 9.

44. Interview with Griffith, *IPH*, 3:184.

45. "Death of the Choctaw Merchant." Charles Wilson's first wife was Lizzie Bryant. See Pickens County Records 1864–1893 for Marriage of Charles B. Wilson and Elizabeth Bryant (Chickasaw), in CKN 11; and "Marriages in the Chickasaw Nation-Bride List B–F," www.chickasawhistory.com/b_mar_2.htm. Edmund Pickens, the son of Charles's sister Mary, is listed as one-half Choctaw on the Choctaw rolls, which also clearly identify his mother (Charles's sister Mary) as full-blood Choctaw. Ida Wilson Self and Charles's other children are therefore incorrectly listed as one-quarter Choctaw on the Dawes Rolls. They were one-half Choctaw and one-half Chickasaw.

46. "The Gallows," *Fort Smith Elevator*, October 28, 1887. Testimony of Jasper Baker, October 25, 1887, *United States v. Crow*, 17–18.

47. Peter Conser's name is spelled a variety of ways in the Choctaw and Fort Smith records: Concer, Concor, Coinsaw. I opt for the common spelling used today: Conser. A photograph of the headstone of Willis Wilson is on the Vaughn Cemetery Web site, www.rootsweb.com/~oklefcem/vaughn5.html.

48. Adam Morris testified in 1887 that he had known Crow since "he was a little chunk of a boy" and that Crow belonged to his mother and the Perry family. Morris did not believe that Crow was an Indian: "I always thought he was a negro—never heard nothing else." Nail Perry, however, whose mother also owned Crow, asserted that Crow's father was Creek. Testimonies of Adam Morris, Nail Perry October 25, 1887, in *United States v. Jack Crow*, 9, 68. That Crow was a slave at one time to the Perry family is substantiated by Angela Walton-Raji, Crow's great-great-great-granddaughter. Jackson's wife, Kitty, also had been enslaved by the Perry family. Their daughter Amanda's daughter Sallie was freed at age three (Walton-Raji, personal correspondence, June 20, 2007).

49. Treaty of 1866, Art. 38, 14 Stat. 769, 779. This act passed by the tribe is mentioned in the Indian Appropriation Act of March 3, 1885 (23 Stat. 362, 366). "Freedmen Bill: An Act, Entitled an Act, to Adopt the Freedmen of the Choctaw Nation," approved May 21, 1883, in *CLAIT*, 18:1–4; "Registration Bill," approved May 22, 1883, in *CLAIT*, 18:5–8.

50. "Criminal Defendant Case File for Jack Crow, 1884," murder jacket no. 44, file unit from record group 21: Records of District Courts of the United States, U.S. District Court for the Fort Smith Division of the Western Division of Arkansas, National Archives, Southwest Region, Fort Worth, Tex.

51. *Lucas v. United States*, 163 U.S. 612 (May 25, 1896).

52. There are many writings about the life and times of Parker, many sensational and exaggerated. An even-handed and comprehensive work is Michael J. Broadhead's *Isaac C. Parker: Federal Justice on the Frontier*. See also the National Park Service's Web site on Fort Smith, www.nps.gov/fosm, for information about Parker, as well as information about conviction rulings, the history of the courthouse, and a list of individuals hung there.

53. Testimony of Judge Isaac C. Parker, June 4, 1885, *Report of the Committee on Indian Affairs*, 399.

54. Court cases of Fort Smith are located at the federal Archives in Fort Worth, Texas. The Oklahoma Historical Society in Oklahoma City houses an index of the cases, but they are arranged in alphabetical order by the last names of the deputy marshals who brought the alleged criminals to Fort Smith, not by the criminals' name.

55. Wright to Council, 1866, in Phillips Collection, WHC.

56. Wright to Council, 1869, in ibid.

57. "Criminal Defense Case File for Edmond Folsom, 1881," murder jacket no. 71; and "Criminal Defendant Case File for Jack Crow, 1881," murder jacket no. 44, in National Archives, Southwest Region.

58. Testimony of T. A. Brown, October 25, 1887, *United States v. Jack Crow*, 49.

59. CTN 49, vol. 339, p. 118.

60. "Journal to be Used in the House of Representatives, Tushka Homa, Choctaw Nation, October 6, A.D., 1884," in CTN 12, vol. 305.

61. *CLAIT*, 19:10.

62. "A Resolution Making an Appropriation of a Reward for the Arrest and Delivery of the Murderer of the Late Sheriff of Scullyville County," bill no. 7, approved October 20, 1881, in *CLAIT*, 17:8.

63. CTN 63. Up until this election, Wilson's name is in the precinct poll books from Sugar Loaf County, often close to the top of the voter's list.

64. Ibid.

65. Article 3 of the Choctaw Constitution, approved October 1838, in CLAIT, 8:6–7.

66. "An Act Defining the Time of Holding Elections in the Several Districts," approved October 1843, in *CLAIT*, 14:49.

67. "Elections," in CLAIT, 19:147–51.

68. *Indian Champion*, August 23, 1884. Election results compiled from CTN 63. Some results are given along with the election judges' names, but no county or precinct is mentioned, implying a missing cover page.

Precincts	Edmund McCurtain	J. P. Folsum
Apukshunnubbee District		
Bok Tuklo County		
Tohwali Precinct	10	8
Luk Fataha Precinct	1	29
Luksukla Precinct	16	8
Cedar County		
Black Jack Grove Precinct	2	37
Cold Springs Precinct	20	11
Sulpher Springs Precinct	12	30
Eagle County		
Bohanna Precinct	63	3
Hocher's Precinct	2	24
Robinson Precinct		
Nashoba County		
Battiest Precinct	40	0
Post Oak Grove Precinct	32	1
Taylor Precinct	53	4
Red River County		
Good Water Precinct	44	0
Hampton's Precinct	10	27
Boggy Depot Precinct	14	3
Koai Illi	41	1
Kully/Kullih Tuklo Precinct	7	27
Towson County		
Clear Creek Precinct	33	0
Doaksville Precinct	50	14
Wheelock Precinct	9	12
Wade County		
Anderson Precinct	33	0
High Hill Precinct	32	1
Koutchatowaka Precinct	0	23
Kunchat Owaka Precinct	10	13
Oka Achukma Precinct	21	5
Pushmataha District		
Atoka County		
Atoka Precinct	39	76

Precincts	Edmund McCurtain	J. P. Folsum
Jacks Fork County		
James Colbert Precinct	33	14
Sardis Precinct	35	12
Kiamichi County		
Big Lick Precinct	22	9
Clear Spring Precinct	22	9
Sugar Creek Precinct	63	12
Moshulatubbee District		
Gaines County		
Bailey Precinct	33	9
Pusley Precinct	20	14
Riddle Precinct	31	17
San Bois County		
Little San Bois Precinct	45	41
Okchanak Chito Precinct	34	2
Oklahoma Precinct	27	33
Skullyville County		
Double Springs Precinct	19	12
Green Hill Precinct	11	9
Greenwood Precinct	12	20
Skullyville Precinct	28	56
Sugar Loaf County		
Hochubbee Precinct	83	5
Long Creek Precinct	68	16
Tobucksy County		
Double Springs Precinct	22	3
McAlester Precinct	32	40
Savanna Precinct	39	27
No County Listed		
Long Creek (?) Precinct	24	34
Sugar Creek (?) Precinct	63	12
No district, county, or precinct listed		
--	61	110
--	14	10
--	5	26
--	28	17

69. CTN 48, vol. 336, case no. 209. In that court docket, however, Crow's name is still listed along with Benton, Perry, Allen, and Conser (spelled "Concor" in the docket) as being not guilty.

70. CTN 49, vol. 339, p. 118.

71. Slaughter was a full-blood Choctaw farmer who only went by "Slaughter," at least until 1874 when he added John as his first name. Testimony of John Slaughter, January 11, 1887, criminal defense file for Jack Crow, 1884, and testimony of John Slaughter, October 25, 1887, in *United States v. Jack Crow*, 53–54; CTN 48, vol. 338, p. 46; "1885 Choctaw Nation Census, Sugar Loaf County," in CTN 4, vol. 472.

72. Testimonies of John Slaughter, January 11, 1887, and October 25, 1887, in *United States v. Jack Crow*, 51–57.

73. Joseph Jackson, who rode with Benton, also testified that Benton said "not to tell nothing." Testimony of Joseph Jackson, October 25, 1887, in *United States v. Jack Crow*, 45. The "Carrying Pistols" law, passed November 1, 1883, and October 21, 1884, states, "It shall not be lawful for any person to carry a pistol of any kind within the limits of the Choctaw nation, except the sheriffs and their deputies and the lighthorsemen and militia on duty and officers connected with the reserve service of this nation." *CLAIT*, 15:165–66.

74. The Choctaw General Council passed a bill in October 1883 that reiterated the concern over the number of weapons in the Nation. The bill stated that anyone who wounded another with a firearm, knife, or other sharp-edged weapon would be "deemed guilty of assault with an intent to kill." "An Act Defining the Crime of Assault with Intent to Kill, and Fixing the Penalty," bill no. 32, approved October 25, 1883, in *CLAIT*, 18:20. A month later, the council approved another bill that forbade anyone from carrying a pistol, except for sheriffs, deputies, the lighthorsemen, and the militia. And it was the responsibility of the Sheriffs, their deputies and the lighthorsemen to arrest all violators. "An Act to Prevent the Carrying of Pistols and Fixing the Penalty Thereof," bill no. 45, approved November 1, 1883, in *CLAIT*, 18:34–35.

75. Isham is listed as being sheriff of Sugar Loaf County in CTN 42, vol. 225, Scrip Book.

76. Testimony of John Slaughter, October 25, 1887, in *United States v. Jack Crow*, 51–57.

77. Testimony of Joseph Jackson, October 25, 1887, in *United States v. Jack Crow*, 46.

78. In less than a decade, Benton had become an influential enough Choctaw to be elected captain of the militia. Jurymen Dave Moshumeutubbee (also spelled "Mishumoutubbee" and "Mishiamatabi" in tribal records) and John Pulcher, were appointed by Benton as two of the private militiamen in 1893 after the explosive uprising over the election for principal chief between the Progressive Wilson N. Jones and the Nationalist Jacob Jackson. See Mihesuah, "Choosing America's Heroes and Villains," and CTN 87.

79. See lists of voters and their choices in CTN 63. Pulcher voted for McCurtain in 1884; see "Poll Book for Principal Chief Election Held at Pusley Precinct of Gaines County, Choctaw Nation, this the 6 day of August, A.D., 1884," in CTN 63.

80. Thompson's name appears in the poll book "Sans Bois County, Okchanak Chito Precinct, 1892," in CTN 64.

81. CTN 42, vol. 225, p. 89. His "No. 1 of Cavanal Coal and Mining Cos." was leased for twenty cents per ton of coal acquired.

82. CTN 63. "Unknown district" means that the voters are listed along with their choices, but there is no designation as to the precinct or county. See also CTN 64.

83. CTN 43, vol. 244.

84. Foreman, "Choctaw Academy,"455; case no. 236 in CTN 49, vol. 339; CTN 12 vol. 301; Senate, 1884–1888.

85. CTN 12, vol. 305.

86. CTN 87.

87. Wright, "Historic Places on the Old Stage Line," 815.

88. "Poll Book for Principal Chief Election Held at Pusley Precinct of Gaines County, Choctaw Nation, this is 6th day of August A.D., 1884 in CTN 63, Elections.

Edmund Pusley (the name Pusley is also seen in places as "Pussey," "Purcley," or "Pursley") was a member of the prominent Pusley family with many wealthy members, many of whom also gained notoriety for their criminal and political activities. In 1876, William Pusley, along with Dr. Daniel Morris Hailey (who also joined with J. J. McAlester in sinking the first shaft in the coal veins of the McAlester district—the old No. 5 Krebs mine), discovered coal at Savanna, and subsequently developed for a time the largest mining industry in the Choctaw Nation. Savanna became the largest town in the territory. Hailey and Pusley also operated the mine store at Savanna. See Williams, "Dr. Daniel Morris Hailey," 215, 217.

Edmund was the father of Lyman Pusley, another notable violator of the law who executed the Nationalist Silan Lewis in 1894. The Pusley family had a variety of enterprises: "Pusley Place" or "Pusley's Station," on the Fort Gibson Road (also known as the Texas Road) twenty-five miles north of McAlester, which served as a stage stop on the Butterfield Overland Mail route to California which crossed southeastern Oklahoma from 1858 to 1861. The site was added to the List of Registered Historic Places in 1972 as site no. 72001072; see http://www.nationalregisterofhistoricplaces.com/OK/Latimer/state.html, and Shirk, *Oklahoma Place Names*, 199.

The district blacksmith shop of Moshulatubbee District was located at Captain George Pusley's place until 1850. The Pusley family also operated the "Old Pusley Place" near the Gaines Creek Crossing (with a small branch known as "Pusley Creek"), which was well known as the home of Captain Pusley's three sons, Calvin, Nicholas, and Narras. Nicholas was allowed to build the toll bridge across Gaines Creek in 1875. See Wright, "Historic Places on the Old Stage Line from Fort Smith to Red River," 809; for Nicholas Pusley, see bill no, 9 in CTN 10, vol. 312. Extending permission to citizens to charge tolls was not unusual as prior to the Civil War, the tribe had allowed many individuals the privilege of building toll roads and bridges and that consent increased afterward. In 1858 alone, seven men were granted the right to build toll gates, including A. W. Garey, who was allowed to build a bridge on Little Boggy Creek in 1858 and to charge between one and fifty cents depending on how many wagons, horses, oxen, or people crossed; see "An Act Granting A. W. Garey the Privilege to Erect a Bridge on Little Boggy and Establish a Toll Gate," approved October 21, 1858, in CLAIT, 16: 46–47. See also "An Act Granting William Holloway the Privilege to Turnpike the Narrows and Establish a Tollgate Thereon," approved October 21, 1858, in CLAIT, 16:49–50; "An Act Granting the Heirs of W. R. Guy the Privilege to Erect a Bridge on Clear Boggy and Establish a Tollgate Thereat," approved October 26, 1858, in CLAIT, 16:60–61; "An Act Granting Jos. D. Davis the Privilege to Erect a Bridge on Middle Boggy and Establish a Toll Gate," approved October 26, 1858, in CLAIT, 16:61–62; "An Act Granting Capt. Jno. Riddle the Privilege to Erect a Bridge on Fouchmalien and Establish a Toll Gate Thereat," approved October 26, 1858, in CLAIT, 16:62–63; and "An Act Granting Washington McDaniel and Charles M. James the Privilege to Erect a Bridge and Toll Gate on Bayouzil Creek," approved October 27, 1858, in CLAIT, 16:63–64. Although Choctaw citizens were allowed to cross the toll bridges and roads for free, noncitizens had to pay high tolls. Many of these prominent men made tidy profits from tolls, and the tribe continued to grant more of them permission (Lane, "Choctaw Nation," 57). Another of Lyman's relatives, Osburne Pusley, was charged with murder in 1880 (see Choctaw Nation v. Osburn Pusley, CTN 48 vol. 247, case no. 144). Another relation, Austin Pusley, was found guilty of petit larceny in March 1892 and paid a fine, then was accused again of larceny, but that was dismissed on the motion of the district attorney. That same year he faced a rape accusation. Seven years later he violated the permit law (CTN 48, vol. 369; CTN 49, case nos. 208, 353, 406, and 488; CTN 50, vol. 344). Still other Pusleys also were in trouble with the law. Archy violated the pistol law in 1888 and died before his case came to court (CTN 48, vol. 336, case no. 298). Edward Pusley committed adultery, as did another relative, Simon Pusley, but the former died before the judge heard his case (CTN 50, vol. 344, case nos. 987 and 1017). Another relation, James Pusley, was named a special deputy sheriff in 1892 (CTN 49, vol. 339, p. 364). Dixon Perry (also seen as "Dickson" and "Parry" as some of the records show) was not notable as a political figure. What can be ascertained is that he was a three-quarter-blood Choctaw who worked twenty-two acres of land as a farmer (CTN 4, vol. 472). He had been deemed respectable enough previously to be asked to serve as a grand jury witness for an 1883 larceny case (CTN 48, vol. 369).

89. CTN 49, vol. 339, p. 120.

90. Testimony of Algie Hall, October 25, 1887, p. 63; "The Gallows," *Fort Smith Elevator*, April 27, 1888. For more information about Barnhill, see Owens, *Oklahoma Heroes*, 260.

91. Harmon, *Hell on the Border*, 24–25.

92. Testimony of [Marshal] Thomas Boles, June 4, 1885, *Report of the Committee on Indian Affairs*, 394.

93. Hudson, "Reminiscences," 304; Dawes, *A United States Prison*, 214–15. The allegation that at least one hundred prisoners were held at once in the jails is substantiated by the Cherokee lighthorseman Sam Six Killer in 1885. See "Testimony of Sam Six Killer, May 26, 1885," *Report of the Committee on Indian Affairs*, 223. Six Killer was a captain of the U.S. Indian police and was shot and killed by a Missouri bootlegger named Solomon Copple on December 24, 1886.

94. Dawes, *A United States Prison*, 143.

95. Testimony of William M. Cravens, and comment of Judge Isaac Parker, June 3, 1885, *Report of the Committee on Indian Affairs*, 390.

96. Testimony of Judge Isaac Parker, June 4, 1885, *Report of the Committee on Indian Affairs*, 401.

97. "Criminal Defendant Case File for Jack Crow, 1884."

98. Testimony of Judge Isaac Parker, June 4, 1885, *Report of the Committee on Indian Affairs*, 401.

99. Testimony of Edmund Pickens, October 25, 1887, *United States v. Jack Crow*, 28.

100. Interview with Mary Elizabeth Goodnight, *IPH*, 2:513–18. Goodnight, who was born in 1853, mistakenly refers to Charley Wilson as Charley Barnet, another Sugar Loaf resident. She has the year of Wilson's murder incorrect and is also wrong about how Jackson Crow ultimately was dealt with. There is, however, a note by the interviewer that states: "Mary Elizabeth Goodnight does not have a very good memory like she did two or three years ago."

101. Jackson was a half-blood Choctaw who was thirty-six years old at the time of the murder (CTN 4, vol. 472; testimony of Joseph Jackson, October 25, 1887, *United States v. Jack Crow*, 48). Joe Jackson's testimony does not give clear indication as to who he supported in this incident; nor does his voting record: in 1890 he voted in a precinct that had the Progressive Jones in the majority over the Nationalist Smallwood, yet in the 1892 election he voted in a precinct that heavily favored Jackson over Wilson Jones. See "Poll Book, Spring Hill Precinct, Sugar Loaf County, for an Election on the 3rd day of August, 1884," in CTN 63, and the 1892 poll book "Sans Bois County, Little Sans Bois Precinct," in CTN 64.

102. Benton also admitted that registering Crow was merely incidental to him wanting to meet with Green McCurtain at the Long Creek Precinct. Testimony of Charles Benton, October 25, 1887, pp. 68–69. See also the page titled "U. States v. Jack Crow," with stamp in top left corner reading "Leghorn Abstract from Geo. D. Barnard & Co., St. Louis," in "Criminal Defendant Case File for Jack Crow, 1884."

The Crow surname does not appear in the following volumes of CTN 7: 340, 341, 355, 355a, 361, 373–75, 382, 432, 452, 461, 464, 468, 477, 479, 482.

103. Testimony of Sam Six Killer, May 26, 1885, *Report of the Committee on Indian Affairs*, 217.

104. Lane, "Choctaw Nation," 57; *Indian Citizen*, December 6, 1900; interview with James T. McDaniel, May 5, 1938, *IPH*, 78:435.

105. See motion for a new trial in "Criminal Defendant Case File for Jack Crow, 1884." Cooper Conser's testimony is missing from the file but is summarized in the motion for a new trial.

106. Robert L. Owen to CIA, September 20, 1886, *ARCIA* (1886): 156.

107. Session III, section 2, October 6, 1836, in *CLAIT*, 13:20–21.

108. "An Act: Runaway Negroes," approved October 8, 1840, in *CLAIT*, 15:29.

109. Session 13, section 3, approved October 15, 1846, in CLAIT, 15:45–46.

110. Article 7, section 2, Constitution of 1842, in *CLAIT*, 15:14.

111. J. H. Heard to O. O. Howard, October 24, 1865, and petition of Daniel Looman, October 12, 1865, in Registers and Letters Received by the Commissioner of the Bureau of Refugees, Freedmen and Abandoned Lands, 1865–1872, Record Group 105, Records of the Bureau of Refugees, Freedmen and Abandoned Lands, Roll 21, M752, NA; John B. Sanborn to James Harlan, January 5, 1866, USS. H.exdoc. 147 (39-2) 1284: 284. Other works discuss this topic in more detail. See, for example, Saunt, *Black, White and Indian*.

112. See testimony of Napoleon B. Ainsworth, May 26, 1885, *Report of the Committee on Indian Affairs*, 227; *Branding Iron*, March 1, 1884.

113. Testimony of Napoleon B. Ainsworth, May 26, 1885, *Report of the Committee on Indian Affairs*, 237. The Cherokees established the Colored High School, also known as the Negro High School.

114. Testimony of G. W. Harkins, May 26, 1885, *Report of the Committee on Indian Affairs*, 277.

115. Proposed bills dated October 4 and October 15, 1875, in CTN 10, vol. 312, pp. 133–34.

116. Testimonies of Casar Gilbert, Henry Nail, Charles Fields, and Roland Butler, all May 26, 1885, *Report of the Committee on Indian Affairs*, 295–99.

117. Testimony of Lem Reynolds, May 26, 1885, *Report of the Committee on Indian Affairs*, 301.

118. Interview with Mrs. Allie Mae Statham, no. 84.028, March 8, 1984, Living Legends Collection, Oklahoma Historical Society, Archives and Manuscripts Division, Oklahoma City.

119. From the 1917 manuscript of Sarah Ann Harlan, obtained August 24, 1937, *IPH*, 28:79.

120. "The Gallows," *Fort Smith Elevator*, April 27, 1888.

121. Ibid; Crow's execution is also listed in "Executions in the U.S. 1608–1987: The Espy File Executions by Name" at www.deathpenaltyinfo.org/ESPYname.pdf,

and in "Arkansas Executions" at users.bestweb.net/~rg/execution/ARKANSAS
.htm; both lists have him as "NA," that is, Native American.

122. "Poll Book, Spring Hill Precinct, Sugar Loaf County, for an Election on
the 3rd Day of August, 1890," in CTN 64, doc. 16649; Scrip Book, in CTN 42, vol.
225, p. 188.

123. See, for example, Bill of Sale dated May 4, 1894, in CTN 42, vol. 230, p.
131. Benton appears in numerous Choctaw documents, including CTN 42, vols.
225 and 226; "Abstract of the Returns of the first Judicial Circuit of County
Officers," in CTN 63; CTN 88; "Fiscal Year Commencing 1 August 1878 and Ending
the 31st July 1879," in CTN 90, vol. 41.

124. CTN 87.

125. CTN 49, vol. 339, p. 868.

126. CTN 4, vol. 472.

127. See also "Bill of Sale to John H. McClure, November 2, 1895," in CTN,
vol. 230, p. 49, regarding Conser's sale of the "top of Rich Mountain."

128. The Peter Conser Home is showcased on numerous Web sites that focus
on Oklahoma tourism; see, for example, www.shareyourstate.com/oklahoma/
ConserHouse.htm.

129. Peck, in *The Proud Heritage of LeFlore County*, devotes a chapter to Conser
(316–24).

130. As with the lighthorsemen, some individuals served in the specific role
of deputy sheriff or sheriff for only one day or a week for a specific occasion,
while others served for years (such as Simon J. Watson, sheriff of Jacks Fork County
from 1882 to 1888). Some changed positions, such as Michael W. LeFlore, who was
elected sheriff of Jackson County in 1898, 1899, and from 1903 to 1905. In 1905 he
was appointed county and probate judge of Jackson County by Chief McCurtain.
Sheriffs were elected, and they in turn appointed men as their deputies. In some
cases, the men were relatives, while others were business partners or political
cronies. There are hundreds of men who served as deputy sheriffs through the
years. Very few men were "career" sheriffs, deputies, or lighthorsemen. Compiled
from CTN 87.

131. "Garfield County Elections," *Enid Eagle*, April 10, 1902.

132. CTN 87.

133. "Poll Book, Spring Hill Precinct, Sugar Loaf County, for an Election on
the 3rd Day of August, 1894," in CTN 64; see payment slip dated August 1894.

134. "The Gallows," *Fort Smith Elevator*, April 27, 1888. Slightly reworded in
Harmon, *Hell on the Border*, 274.

135. "The Gallows," *Fort Smith Elevator*, April 27, 1888.

136. Peck, *The Proud Heritage of LeFlore County*, 41 (Peck incorrectly states Crow's
hanging date as March 9, 1885); "Crow Caged," *Fort Smith Elevator*, January 7, 1887.

137. "Hangman's Day: Execution of Owens D. Hill, George Moss and Jack
Crow," *Fort Smith Elevator*, May 4, 1888.

138. Robbs, "The Murder of Wilson," 514–15.

139. CTN 75, see document dated 1906.

140. Abbott, "'Gentleman' Tom Abbott"; "Five Slain in Battle by Gang to Free Oklahoma Bandit," *New York Times*, June 18, 1933; "Patrolman Tom Abbott New Police Chief; Is Successor of Reed, Killed by Bandits," *McAlester News-Capital*, July 4, 1933; "Turning Back the Clock," *McAlester News-Capital and Democrat*, July 3, 1983, and January 7, 1922; *Pittsburg County, Oklahoma*, 1–2; Clyde Wooldridge, *McAlester, The Capital of Little Dixie*, 35, 48, 63, 65, 204; "Dr. William Elliott Abbott," typed pages in Abbott Collection, Pittsburg County Historical Association, McAlester, Okla.

141. Indian Appropriation Act of March 3, 1885 (23 Stat. 362, 366); also *ARCIA* (1884): 36–37. H. Ex. Doc. No. 1, pt. 5, 48th Cong., 2d Sess., pp. 36–37.

142. "An Act to Establish a United States Court in the Indian Territory, and for Other Purposes," March 1, 1889, 25 Stat., 783, in Kappler, *IA:LT*, vol. 1, chap. 333, p. 39.

143. Leo Bennett to CIA, September 21, 1889, *ARCIA* (1889): 1 House, serial 2725, p. 203.

144. Interview with George Brown, April 12, 1937, *IPH*, 12:358.

145. Leo Bennett to CIA, September 21, 1889, *ARCIA* (1889): 1 House, serial 2725, pp. 202–203. Section 2145, Revised Statutes, provided that "the general laws of the United States as to the punishment of crimes committed within the sole and exclusive jurisdiction of the United States, except the District of Columbia, shall extend to the Indian country." Section 2146 states that "the preceding section shall not be construed to extend to crimes committed by one Indian against the person or property of another Indian." "An Act to Establish a United States Court in the Indian Territory, and for Other Purposes," March 1, 1889, in Kappler, *IA:LT*, vol. 1, chap. 333, p. 39, note a.

146. Leo Bennett to CIA , September 21, 1889, *ARCIA* (1889): 1 House, serial 2725, p. 203.

147. "A Resolution Expressing the Sense of the Choctaw Nation in Reference to the Location of Federal Courts," approved December 20, 1889, in *CLAIT*, 20:43.

148. Robert L. Owen to CIA, September 20, 1886, *ARCIA* (1886): 1 House, serial 2467, p. 156; Leo Bennett to CIA, September 21, 1889, *ARCIA* (1889): 1 House, serial 2725, p. 203.

149. The county name is given as both "Kiamichi" and "Kiamitia" in the records.

150. "An Act Making an Appropriation for the Relief of Thompson Nowahaya and John Bohanan," bill no. 38, approved November 7, 1889, in *CLAIT*, 20:25–26.

151. *United States v. Rogers*, 45 U.S. (4 How.) 567, 572 (1846). This case is thoroughly discussed in Berger, "'Power Over This Unfortunate Race.'"

152. Act of February 6, 1889 (25 Stat. at L. 655); Act of March 3, 1891 (26 Stat. at L. 862).

153. CTN 50, vol. 344, case nos. 175 and 279. Lucas's fees for the trial of the murder of Levy Kemp included fine assessed, $5; district attorney, $5; clerks, $2 (Clerk John Taylor) and $1.25 (Clerk William Bond); sheriff, $4.50; and witnesses, $28.50.

154. "Criminal Defendant Case File for Eli Lucas, 1894," larceny jacket no. 429, file unit from Record Group 21, Records of District Courts of the United States, U.S. District Court for the Fort Smith Division of the Western Division of Arkansas, National Archives, Southwest Region, Fort Worth, Tex. It is of note that this case, along with the subsequent murder trial file, is mostly typed.

155. CTN 49, vol. 339, case no. 142.

156. "Sans Bois County, Okchanak Chito Precinct, 1892," poll book, in CTN 64. Lucas's name is not listed on the Dawes Rolls.

157. *Indian Citizen*, July 13, 1889.

158. "Criminal Defendant Case File for Eli Lucas, 1894," murder jacket nos. 112 and 385; *Lucas v. United States*, 163 U.S. 612 (1896).

159. *Lucas v. United States.*

160. *Ex Parte Mayfield* (May 25, 1891), 141 U.S. 106, 112 , 11 S. Sup. Ct. 939.

161. *Alberty v. United States* (April 20, 1896), 162 U.S. 499, 16 Sup. Ct. 864.

162. *United States v. Rogers*, 45 U.S. (4 How.) 567, 572 (1846).

163. Broadhead, *Isaac C. Parker*, 150–51.

164. Treaty of 1866, in *CLAIT*, 11:16. The tribe considered Belvin's arrest and detention at the U.S. District Court in Paris to be a "disregard for the rights of said Belvin and of the Choctaws." ("An Act to Provide for the Protection of the Rights of the Choctaw Nation and Her Citizens against Increased Encroachments by U.S. Courts," approved November 14, 1889, in *CLAIT*, 20:32–33). In 1885, Belvin was a 35-year-old from Blue County. CTN 2, Census Records and Lists, 1830–1896, Atoka County.

165. "An Act to Provide for the Protection of the Rights of the Choctaw Nation and Her Citizens against Increased Encroachments by U.S. Courts," approved November 14, 1889, in *CLAIT*, 20:32–33.

166. Edmund McCurtain to Leo E. Bennett, August 25, 1890, and Bennett to CIA, September 10, 1890, *ARCIA* (1890): 1 House, serial 2841, p. 103.

Chapter 2: Nationalists and Progressives

Epigraph: Interview with Wesley McCoy, March 21, 1938, *IPH*, 102:86.

1. Testimony of Sampson Cole, May 26, 1885, U.S. Congress, *Report of the Committee on Indian Affairs*, 244–45.

2. Testimony of Napoleon B. Ainsworth, May 26, 1885, *Report of the Committee on Indian Affairs*, 230, 233.

3. Ibid., 236.

4. Ibid.; testimonies of Sampson Cole and E. F. Krebs, both May 26, 1885, *Report of the Committee on Indian Affairs*, 236, 243, 252–53.

5. Testimony of Judge Albert Carney, May 26 and June 4, 1885, *Report of the Committee on Indian Affairs*, 241. In order to accommodate those who desired to become like the whites and/or to be able to compete with them, by 1842, the council had passed an act establishing Spencer Academy, Fort Coffee Academy, Koonsha Female Seminary, Ianubbee Female Seminary, Chuwahla Female Seminary, and Wheelock Female Seminary. Instead of teaching them the Choctaw language or tribal traditions, the boys were instructed in "agriculture and the mechanical arts" and letters, and girls were taught letters, "housewifery, sewing, &c." The children were required to live at the school; any child who ran away was returned by either the child's parents or a lighthorseman. See "An Act Respecting Public Schools, Approved November, 1842," and "An Act Requiring the Return of Runaway Children from the Schools, &c," approved November 1842, both in *CLAIT*, 11:79–81. Forty years later, the tribe still attempted to keep their schools on par with U.S. schools by enacting laws stating that preference would be given to teachers and administrators who were Christians, and that all teachers must be a graduate of a "college of established reputation." Female teachers had to be graduates of either a normal school or "some higher institution of learning" and proficient in two languages besides English (knowing Choctaw was not specified). See "An Act Relating to the School System of the Choctaw Nation," approved October 31, 1890, in *CLAIT*, 21:41–52. For more information on the Choctaw schools, see Debo, "Education in the Choctaw Country after the Civil War."

6. Testimony of Sampson Cole, May 26, 1885, *Report of the Committee on Indian Affairs*, 244–45.

7. Testimonies of Napoleon B. Ainsworth, Sampson Cole, E. F. Krebs, and Dr. Louis C. Tennant, all May 26, 1885, *Report of the Committee on Indian Affairs*, 236, 243, 252–53, 263.

8. Testimony of Dr. Louis C. Tennant, May 26, 1885, *Report of the Committee on Indian Affairs*, 264.

9. James Culberson to Czarina Conlan, September 16, 1940, in Vertical File: Choctaw Executions, OHS, 7.

10. O'Beirne and O'Beirne, *Indian Territory*, 146–47; Meserve, "Chief Benjamin Franklin Smallwood and Chief Jefferson Gardner"; Baird, "Spencer Academy, Choctaw Nation, 1842–1900."

11. Meserve, "Chief Benjamin Franklin Smallwood and Chief Jefferson Gardner"; O'Beirne and O'Beirne, *Indian Territory*, 146; CTN 11, vol. 316, p. 304.

12. Morrison, "Biographical Sketch of Wn. N. Jones," *Daily Oklahoman*, May 12, 1935 (typescript also in the Wilson N. Jones Collection, box no. 1, folder no. 42, WHC); Hudson, "A Story of Choctaw Chiefs"; John Bartlett Meserve, "Chief Wilson Nathaniel Jones."

13. Morrison, "Wn. N. Jones"; Interview with Willie M. Griggs, November 10, 1937, *IPH*, 26:465.

14. *Jones v. Baer, et al.*, 37 L.C.P. 947; 149 U.S. 777 (1899); Morrison, "Wn. N. Jones."

15. Morrison, "Wn. N. Jones"; interview with Mattie Lou Ray Harris, December 3, 1937, *IPH*, 63:444–45.

16. Interview with Mora (Cap) Duncan, n.d., *IPH*, 23:68–69; CTN 52, vol. 368, case no. 154. As noted in CTN 52, vol. 368, p. 153, Belvin was elected sheriff, commissioned, and took his oath of office on August 21, 1889.

17. Morrison, "Wn. N. Jones."

18. CTN 87. Included in the records are separate scraps of paper signed by Belvin and Bench in which they swear to support the Choctaw Constitution and to "discharge to the best of [their] abilities the office of Deputy Sheriff" (regular standing deputy in Bench's case). Also within the records is documentation (no document number) stating that Bench was paid $24 for serving as deputy sheriff at the Third Judicial District's special term in February 1887.

19. CTN 52, vol. 368, case no. 154, pp. 117–18.

20. CTN 52, vol. 368, p.153.

21. Morrison, "Wn. N. Jones."

22. CTN 48, vol. 336.

23. Interview with Mora (Cap) Duncan, *IPH*, 23:64; interview with Dillard Duncan, March 28, 1938, *IPH*, 101:362.

24. Interview with Dillard Duncan, *IPH*, 101:362.

25. Morrison, "Wn. N. Jones"; see also CTN 52, vol. 368, pp. 200, 273, 368. "Tuck" Bench's real name was probably Darnil, as it reads on the court documents. Since the Nationalist Smallwood was chief in February 1890, it is conceivable that he had a hand in keeping Belvin and the Bench brothers from trial, although this cannot be substantiated.

26. Interview with Belly Turley, May 25, 1937, *IPH*, 47:379–80.

27. One person claims to have been on the grand jury that convicted "that Negro," implying that only one man was responsible for the killing. This same person, however, is unsure as to what happened to that alleged killer. Interview with Dillard Duncan, *IPH*, 101:362.

28. "Message of W. N. Jones," *Indian Citizen*, October 18, 1890.

29. Ibid.; Lane, "Choctaw Nation," 59; Testimony of J. D. James, June 3, 1885, *Report of the Committee on Indian Affairs*, 359.

30. Interview with Levi Pickering, July 27, 1927, *IPH*, 40:78–79.

31. "Leasing Lands" and "Limitations to Non-Citizens," in *CLAIT*, 19:191–92, 194.

32. "An Act Prohibiting a Citizen or Citizens to Employ Non-Citizens to Take Charge of Stock of Any Kind as Herdsmen," passed, over veto of principal chief, November 9, 1887, in *CLAIT*, 21:14–15.

33. *Indian Citizen*, July 26, 1890; Robert L. Owen to CIA, August 27, 1888, in *ARCIA* (1888): 127.

34. *Indian Citizen*, October 12, 1889.

35. "Treaty with the Choctaw and Chickasaw," June 22, 1855, 11 Stats., 611, ratified February 21, 1856 and proclaimed March 4, 1856, in Kappler, *IA:LT*, 2: 706–14. The treaty was signed by Choctaw commissioners Peter P. Pitchlynn, Israel Folsom, Samuel Garland, and Dixon W. Lewis, and Chickasaw commissioners Edmund Pickens and Sampson Folsom. The treaty set the following boundaries: "Beginning at a point on the Arkansas River, one hundred paces east of old Fort Smith, where the western boundary-line of the State of Arkansas crosses the said river, and running thence due south to Red River; thence up Red River to the point where the meridian of one hundred degrees west longitude crossed the same; thence north along said meridian to the main Canadian River; thence down said river to its junction with the Arkansas River; thence down said river to the place of beginning."

36. "Treaty with the Choctaw and the Chickasaw, 1866." April 28, 1866, 14 Stats., 769, ratified June 28, 1866, proclaimed July 10, 1866, in Kappler, *IA:LT*, 2: 918–31. See also a summary of the treaties in "Claims of the Choctaw and Chickasaw Indians, May 15, 1930," Senate Report No. 652, 71st Cong., 2nd sess., calendar no. 658, pp. 1–21.

37. Debo, *Rise and Fall of the Choctaw Nation*, 210. The Net Proceeds Commission was created by an act of the Choctaw General Council on January 18, 1889, for the purpose of overseeing the distribution of net proceeds money. See "An Act Suspending an Act Making Distribution of the Net Proceeds Money," bill no. 45, approved October 30, 1889, in *CLAIT*, 11:288.

38. Owen to CIA, in *ARCIA* (1888): 127.

39. *Purcell Register*, August 7, 1891.

40. "Message of W. N. Jones," *Indian Citizen*, October 18, 1890.

41. Bennett to CIA, September 10, 1890, *ARCIA* (1890): 1 House, serial 2841, p. 89.

42. Jno. Q. Tufts to CIA, August 29, 1884, *ARCIA* (1884): 98; Lane, "Choctaw Nation," 59.

43. Lycecum, "Life of Apushmataha."

44. Sec. 7, sess. 3, approved October 8, 1836, in *CLAIT*, 15:22; "An Act Preventing Any Indian, Not a Choctaw, to Settle in the Nation without Permission from the General Council," approved October 1836, *CLAIT*, 15:22–23; sec. 4, sess. 6, approved October 11, 1839, in *CLAIT*, 13:32.

45. Lane, "Choctaw Nation," 60.

46. Testimony of Robert J. Wood to Committee on Indian Affairs, June 4, 1885, *Report of the Committee on Indian Affairs*, 398–99.

47. Interview with William Joshua Ervin, December 14, 1937, *IPH*, 23:494.

48. Interview with D. Morgan, October 16, 1837, *IPH*, 108:399–402.

49. National Archives Microfilm Series M-1301, Chickasaw rolls, card no. 1125; Nebitt, "J.J. McAlester."

50. Testimony of Napoleon B. Ainsworth, May 26, 1885, *Report of the Committee on Indian Affairs*, 235–36.

51. "The Practice of Medicine," approved October 29, 1884, in *CLAIT*, 19: 180–81.

52. "Pioneer McAlester Doctor," *McAlester-News Capital*, March 28, 1966; *McAlester News-Capital*, January 7, 1922; *Pittsburg County, Oklahoma*, 1–2; Wooldridge, *McAlester, The Capital of Little Dixie*, 35, 48, 63, 65, 204; "Dr. William Elliott Abbott," typed pages at the Pittsburg County Historical Association; Abbott, "'Gentleman' Tom Abbott." See also, "Five Slain in Battle by Gang to Free Oklahoma Bandit," *New York Times*, June 18, 1933; "Patrolman Tom Abbott New Police Chief; Is Successor of Reed, Killed by Bandits," *McAlester News-Capital*, July 4, 1933; "Turning Back the Clock," *McAlester News-Capital and Democrat*, July 3, 1983.

53. CTN 44, vol. 250; CTN 45, vol. 258. See how J. J. McAlester demonstrated his knowledge of business in his testimony to the Committee on Indian Affairs by answering all questions about coal mines, fees, worker wages, and so on, with authority and complete confidence in himself as a member of the Choctaw community. Testimony of J. J. McAlester, May 26, 1885, *Report of the Committee on Indian Affairs*, 266–73.

54. CTN 44, vol. 250.

55. CTN 44, vol. 250, p. 268.

56. *Indian Citizen*, January 20, 1898; *Washington Post*, January 12, 1898.

57. Interview with D. Morgan, October 16, 1837, *IPH*, 108:401–2, 404.

58. Interview with Mattie Lou Ray Harris, December 3, 1937, *IPH*, 63:444–45.

59. "Message of W. N. Jones," *Indian Citizen*, October 18, 1890.

60. Interview with John War Edwards and William Welch, April 28, 1938, *IPH*, 105:123.

61. For information on Spencer Academy, see Baird, "Spencer Academy, Choctaw Nation, 1842–1900."

62. Interview with Edwards and Welch, April 28, 1938, *IPH*, 105:124–25.

63. James Culberson, "The Political Side of My Life," August 27, 1937, *IPH*, 65:332.

64. Interview with Elias Parish, July 29, 1937, *IPH*, 39:28–36.

65. CTN 50, vol. 344. The Cook Gang, or "the most desperate and dangerous gang that ever operated in the Indian country," was led by William Tuttle Cook (a.k.a. "Cherokee Bill") that robbed throughout the Cherokee Nation in the mid-1880s to mid-1890s. Harmon, *Hell on the Border*, 642–60.

66. "A Biographic Sketch of Nancy Whistler," n.d., *IPH*, 67:179–80.

67. Interview with Houston Tecumseh, March 1, 1938, *IPH*, 112:83.

68. *Purcell Register*, February 23, 1893; "Claims of the Choctaw and Chickasaw Indians, May 15, 1930," p. 5.

69. "Message of W. N. Jones," October 8, 1891, in Wilson N. Jones Collection, box 1, folder 5, WHC.

70. Treaty with the Choctaw and the Chickasaw, 1866, in Kappler, *IA:LT*, 2:918–31.

71. Ibid.

72. Acceptance letter of Jacob Jackson, *Indian Citizen*, April 28, 1892.

73. *Indian Citizen*, May 19, 1892.

74. See Treaty of 1866 with Cherokee Nation, Articles Pertaining to African Cherokee Citizens and Ending Slavery in the Nation, July 19, 1866, Ratified July 27, 1866, Proclaimed Aug. 11, 1866, in Kappler, *IA:LT*, 2:942–50.

75. See Testimony of Napoleon B. Ainsworth, May 26, 1885, *Report of the Committee on Indian Affairs*, 227. In 1876, Ainsworth served as clerk of the Court of Claims for Moshulatubbee District. "Fiscal Year Commencing 1 August 1878 and Ending the 31st July 1879," in CTN 90, vol. 41.

76. *Indian Citizen*, July 14, 1892.

77. Ibid.

78. "An Act Preventing the Introduction of Whiskey," approved October 1834, in *CLAIT*, 15:17; Morrison, "News for the Choctaws," 213; Senate Report 1278, part 2, 49th Cong., 1st sess., U.S. Senate, Report of the Committee on Indian Affairs, 498; "An Act Citizens Interfering the Light-Horse in the Exercise of His Duties Liable to be fined," approved October 10, 1849, in *CLAIT*, 15:67. If a person was not overly forceful in their protest of having their whiskey destroyed, however, they could be fined five dollars, with the money split among the lighthorsemen. Many peddlers with small whiskey-selling operations had much to lose if they lost their product and made the mistake of resisting. And they defended their property at their own risk because the lighthorsemen were protected by the law. In a month's time, three men were killed in "whiskey encounters," that is, they were involved in drunken fights. Session III, section 10, approved October 10, 1837, in *CLAIT*, 13:27; "Laws of the Choctaw Nation," sec. 2, approved November 8, 1834 (approved a month earlier, but wording changed slightly in the amended version), in *CLAIT*, 13:2–3; "An Act Laying a Fine on Those Who Sell Whiskey, and Also for the Disposal of Said Fine," approved October 5, 1837, *CLAIT*, 15: 23–24.

79. "Laws of the Choctaw Nation," sec. 13, approved November 8, 1834 (approved a month earlier, but wording changed slightly in the amended version), in *CLAIT*, 13:15.

80. Senate Report 1278, part 2, 49th Congress, 1st sess., U.S. Senate, *Report of the Committee on Indian Affairs*, 498; "An Act; Light-Horse to Have the Right to Call upon Any Citizen for Aid," approved October, 12, 1848, *CLAIT*, 15:59–60.

81. "An Act to Raise and Equip a Force of Militia," approved November 1, 1883, *CLAIT*, 18:28–29.

82. "A Biographic Sketch of Nancy Whistler," n.d., *IPH*, 67:181.

83. Interview with James Wilson, August 4, 1937, *IPH*, 67:379–80.

84. Bennett to CIA, September 21, 1889, *ARCIA* (1889): 1 House, serial 2725, p. 210.

85. See Bennett to CIA, September 10, 1890, *ARCIA* (1890): 1 House, serial 2841, p. 92.

86. For pharmacological information on fishberries, see Felter, *Eclectic Materia Medica*, 112–13. For more discussion about Choc Beer, see Sewell's "Choctaw Beer."

87. Bennett to CIA for 1892, *ARCIA* (1891): 1 House, serial 3088, p. 249.

88. Bennett to O. W. Case, April 14, 1890, in Bennett to CIA, September 10, 1890, *ARCIA* (1890): 1 House, serial 2841, p. 92.

89. O. W. Case, to Bennett, May 22, 1890, in Bennett to CIA, September 10, 1890, *ARCIA* (1890): pp. 92–93.

90. *Indian Citizen*, April 21, 1892.

91. *Indian Citizen*, May 5, 1892, and May 12, 1892.

92. *Indian Citizen*, May 19, 1892, and July 14, 1892.

93. Wisdom to CIA, August 28, 1884, in *ARCIA* (1884): p. 143.

94. *Indian Citizen*, January 16, 1892.

95. *Indian Citizen*, May 5, 1892.

96. *Indian Citizen*, April 21, 1892.

97. *Indian Citizen*, June 16, 1892.

98. *Indian Citizen*, June 30, 1892, and October 5, 1893.

99. The writer gives two names as examples of this type of cat: freedmen Pryor Allen and Richard Colbert. *Indian Citizen*, July 28, 1892.

100. *Indian Citizen*, July 14, 1892.

101. "An Act Regulating the Granting of Permits to Trade, Expose Goods, Wares or Merchandise, for Sale within the Choctaw Nation, and to Reside within the Same, and for Other Purposes," approved November 20, 1867, in *CLAIT*, 11: 483–87; article 39 of the Treaty of 1866; "An Act Regulating the Granting of Permits to Trade, Expose Goods, Wares or Merchandise for Sale within [the Choctaw Nation and to reside within] the Same, and for Other Purposes," approved November 12, 1875, and "An Act Regulating the Granting of Permits to Trade, Expose Goods, Wares or Merchandise for Sale within the Choctaw Nation and to Reside within the Same, and for Other Purposes," approved October 30, 1876, in CTN 10, vol. 312, pp. 163–64, 235–41.

102. "An Act to Secure the Choctaw Nation against Misstatements of Royalty and Taxes," approved November 6, 1883, in *CLAIT*, 18:63–64.

103. Interview with Houston Tecumseh, March 1, 1938, *IPH* 112:78–79.

104. Interview with L. F. Baker, *IPH*, 51:69–70.

105. Letter to editor, *Indian Citizen*, August 5, 1892. The Nationalists who signed the letter were (in order): W. P. Ward, T. D. Bell, W. L. Rodgers, K. G. Bell,

W. P. Boyce, Charles Ward, Jas. Colbert, G. W. Secoe, W. W. Kelly, Roy Henderson, Q. W. Bell, Henry Thompson, and George W. Pounds.

106. *Indian Citizen*, September 1, 1892.

107. "A Resolution Asking Pardon for Willie Anderson, of Jackson County, for Assault with Intent to Kill," in *CLAIT*, 21:6–7.

108. Culberson, "Political Side of My Life," *IPH*, 65:329.

109. *Indian Citizen*, April 14, 1892, and May 5, 1892.

110. *Indian Citizen*, May 5, 1892.

111. Edmund McCurtain to Leo E. Bennett, August 25, 1890, in Bennett to CIA, September 10, 1890, *ARCIA* (1890): 1 House, serial 2841, p. 103.

112. "Message of W. N. Jones," *Indian Citizen*, October 18, 1890.

CHAPTER 3: THE ELECTION OF 1892 AND THE LAST LEAGUE OF THE CHOCTAWS

Epigraph: Comment from an anonymous letter written to the *Indian Citizen*, March 31, 1892.

1. "An Act for the Better Securing the Safety of the Election Returns in the Election of Principal Chief and of the National Officers," approved November 13, 1890, in *CLAIT*, 21:31–33.

2. Leo E. Bennett to CIA, n.d., *ARCIA* (1892): 1 House serial 3088, p. 260.

3. The seventeen counties in the Choctaw Nation were Bok Tuklo, Cedar, Eagle, Nashoba, Red River, Towson, and Wade (Apukshunnubbee District); Gaines, San Bois, Skullyville, Sugar Loaf, and Tobucksy (Moshulatubbee District); and Atoka, Blue, Jackson, Kiamichi, and Jacks Fork (Pushmataha District). The results from Oak Hill Precinct are missing. That precinct had been created by "An Act Changing an Election Precinct in San Bois County," act no. 25, approved April 10, 1891, in *CLAIT*, 21:6–7.

4. "Poll Book of an Election Held at High Hill Precinct, Tobucksey County, Choctaw Nation, on the First Wednesday in August 1892," in CTN 64.

5. *Indian Citizen*, September 1, September 15, September 22, 1892.

6. *Indian Citizen*, September 8, 1892. The *Choctaw Herald*'s count is included in the *Indian Citizen* issue.

7. Leo E. Bennett to CIA, September 26, 1892, *ARCIA* (1892): p. 260.

8. See the various methods of tallying in the precinct poll books in CTN 64.

9. *Indian Citizen*, October 13, 1892.

10. See, for example, CTN 87, pay stub no. 838, document no. 22836. John Perry is listed as sheriff in June 1894, which is two years after the August 1892 election but prior to the August 1894 election.

11. Names compiled from various issues of newspapers, court documents, testimonies and letters: issues of *Indian Citizen*, 1892–94; CTN 49, vol. 339, case no. 55; CTN 50, vol. 344, case no. 59; CTN 49, vol. 339, case no. 56; CTN 50, vol. 34,

case nos. 55–60; CTN 87, pay stub 838, document no. 22836; interview, Crawford J. Anderson, November 15, 1937, *IPH*, 2:330–43; Culberson, "Political Side of My Life," *IPH*, 65:329; Culberson to Conlan, September 16, 1940, in Vertical File: Choctaw Executions, OHS; Shirley, *Toughest of Them All*; Smith, *A Choctaw's Honor*; *ARCIA* (various years).

12. In 1872, Lewis was one of five men who voted for Nationalist William Bryant in the election for chief ("Poll Book of Boggy Creek Precinct, August 7, 1872," in CTN 63). In 1890, Lewis voted at the McAlester Precinct of Tobucksy County, in which Smallwood was defeated by Wilson Jones, 72 to 27 ("Poll Book of an Election Held at McAlester Precinct, Tobucksey County, Choctaw Nation, on the 1st Wednesday in August 1890," in CTN 64).

13. CTN 10, vol. 315, p. 147.

14. CTN 11, vol. 316, pp. 316, 365.

15. *Indian Citizen*, January 16, 1892.

16. CTN 44, vol. 250. Lewis's sureties were Audel Anderson and Alfred W. Folsom.

17. CTN 44, vol. 250.

18. "Message of W. N. Jones," *Indian Citizen*, October 18, 1890.

19. "Message of W. N. Jones," October 9, 1890, in Wilson N. Jones Collection, box 1, folder 1, WHC.

20. "An Act Defining the Manner of Trying Impeachment Cases," approved November 8, 1887, in *CLAIT*, 21:12–14.

21. "Message of W. N. Jones," *Indian Citizen*, October 18, 1890.

22. His choices for special deputies included John Simpson, Abel Smith, Edward Williams, Joe Y. Toole, Herbert Quincey, Thomas Lewis, W. S. Folsom, Green Taylor, Allen G. Lee, Johnson Frazier, Geoff Beams, Jackson Byington, W. G. Hollowman, and Charles Ward. His picks for regular deputies were Columbus Kawpalubbee, Aaron Arpela, Joe Anderson, Solomon Mackey, Dickson Nail, and J. S. W. Flinchum. CTN 44, vol. 250.; CTN 45, vol. 258.

23. CTN 44, vol. 250.

24. Culberson to Conlan, p. 8. Culberson wrote the letter to Conlan, who worked for the journal *Chronicles of Oklahoma* and was seeking publication of his reminisces as court clerk in the Moshulatubbee District. He was the clerk during the various Nationalist murder trials.

25. CTN 48, vol. 338, case no. 140, p. 303. Kingsberry (spelled in the poll book as "Kingsbursie") Harkins voted in the High Hill Precinct, Tobucksy County, in 1890 and 1892 ("Poll Book of an Election Held at High Hill Precinct, Tobuckey County, Choctaw Nation, on the First Wednesday in August 1890, for the election of Principal Chief, Officers," CTN 48, vol. 336). Prymus Brown voted in the Boiling Spring Precinct, Gaines County, in 1890 and the Savanna Precinct of Tobucksy County in 1892 ("Poll Book of an Election Held at Savanna Precinct, Tobuckey County, Choctaw Nation, on the First Wednesday in August 1892, for the election

of Principal Chief, Officers"). Eli Loma voted in the Cold Spring Precinct, Chuahla County, in 1884 and the High Hill Precinct, Tobucksy County, in 1892. Robert Miller voted in the High Hill Precinct, Tobucksy County, in 1892. Price Tallipoose voted in the 1892 Savanna Precinct, Tobucksy County, and was forty years of age at the time of the 1885 Gaines County Census, making him forty-seven during the Nationalists' killings. Charles (Charley) was forty-four at the time of the 1885 Gaines County Census. William Taylor voted in the Riddle Precinct, Gaines County, in 1890. Daniel Bon voted in the High Hill Precinct, Tobucksy County, in 1892. William Anderson voted in the McAlester Precinct, Tobucksy County, in 1892, and appears in the 1885 Gaines County Census as thirty-three years of age ("Poll Book of an Election Held at McAlester Precinct, Tobucksy County, Choctaw Nation, on the First Wednesday in August 1892, for the election of Principal Chief, Officers"). Robert Carter voted in the High Hill Precinct, Tobucksy County, 1892 ("Poll Book of an Election Held at High Hill Precinct, Tobucksy County, Choctaw Nation, on the First Wednesday in August 1892, for the election of Principal Chief, Officers"). James Walker was thirteen years old at the time of the 1885 Gaines County Census (CTN 63 and CTN 64; M1186. Roll 1, Index to the Five Civilized Tribes, Final Dawes Roll). Harkins also wrote a letter to the *Indian Citizen*, April 26, 1894.

26. Culberson to Conlan, 1–2.

27. Meserve, "Chief Gilbert Wesley Dukes"; CTN 18.

28. Interview with Crawford J. Anderson, November 15, 1937, *IPH*, 2:330–43.

29. Interview with William Stuart Walker, *IPH*, 103:424. In his sensationalistic *Toughest of Them All*, Glenn Shirley claims that Hukolutubbee was "the leader of the Progressives," probably to lend weight to Lewis's crime and more rationalization for his eventual execution.

30. Culberson to Conlan, 2–3.

31. Smith, "Matter of Honor."

32. Culberson, "Political Side of My Life," *IPH*, 65:329.

33. Culberson to Conlan, 3–4.

34. Ibid.

35. Ibid., 4. That the Nationalists killed these two young men negates Culberson's claim that he was "too young" to be killed.

36. Smith, "Matter of Honor," 58–59. This scenario is also mentioned in Thomas Smith's *A Choctaw's Honor*, 137–38.

37. Duncan, "Political Strife Among the Choctaw Indians," n.d., Okmulgee High School tenth grade paper, in Choctaw Vertical File Folder, "Politics and Government," OHS. According to the "Choctaw Nation Marriages: Groom Index, 1890–1907," Ross McClish was 24 in 1903, which would make him 13 years old when and if he guarded Brown's home in 1892. See www.rootsweb.com/~okgarvin/kinard/chockmmarr.htm.

38. Culberson to Conlan, 3–4.

39. Ibid.

40. Leo E. Bennett to CIA, n.d., *ARCIA* (1892): 1 House serial 3088, p. 261.

41. W. L. Austin, McAlester I. T. to Judge Temaye Cornells, September 13, 1892, handwritten letter found in between the bound pages in CTN 64. Austin was a white businessman, profiled in O'Beirne and O'Beirne, *Indian Territory*, 317, 319, 320. Austin wrote this particular note on stationery from "Allen and Austin Prescription Druggists." O'Beirne and O'Beirne describe Austin as one who "since youth, . . . has been more or less associated with Indian people, preferring the natural life," and as "a gentleman of rare education, though not the less a sportsman . . . devoted passionately to the rod and gun."

42. *ARCIA* (1893): serial 3210, 1 House, pp. 82–83.

43. Leo E. Bennett to CIA, n.d., *ARCIA* (1892): 1 House serial 3088, p. 261.

44. *ARCIA* (1893): serial 3210, 1 House, pp. 82–83.

45. Hudson, "A Story of Choctaw Chiefs," 192. It is not clear how Hudson knew this information because there are no records to indicate that he was present to witness the events.

46. *Indian Citizen*, September 22, 1892, *ARCIA* (1893): serial 3210 1 House, p. 83.

47. *Indian Citizen*, September 22, 1892.

48. Leo E. Bennett to CIA, n.d., *ARCIA* (1892): 1 House serial 3088, p. 263; *Indian Citizen*, September 22, 1892.

49. Ibid.

50. Bennett to CIA, n.d., *ARCIA*, (1892): p. 260.

51. Ibid, 261–62.

52. Ibid, 262.

53. The act, 25 Stat. (1888) 178, c. 382, reads,

Any Indian hereafter committing against the person of any Indian agent or policeman appointed under the laws of the United States, or against any Indian United States deputy marshal, posse comitatus, or guard, while lawfully engaged in the execution of any United States process, or lawfully engaged in any other duty imposed upon such agent, policeman, deputy marshal, posse comitatus, or guard by the laws of the United States, any of the following crimes, namely, murder, manslaughter, or assault with intent to murder, assault, or assault and battery, or who shall in any manner obstruct by threats or violence any person who is engaged in the service of the United States in the discharge of any of his duties as agent, policeman, or other officer aforesaid within the Indian Territory, or who shall hereafter commit either of the crimes aforesaid in said Indian Territory against any person who, at the time of the commission of said crime, or at any time previous thereto, belonged to either of the classes of officials hereinbefore named, shall be subject to the laws of the United States relating to such crimes, and shall be tried by the district court of the United States, exercising criminal jurisdiction where such offense was committed, and shall be subject to the same penalties as are all other persons charged with the commission of said crimes, respectively; and the said courts are hereby given jurisdiction in all such cases.

54. Leo E. Bennett to CIA, n.d., *ARCIA* (1892): p. 262.

55. Culberson to Conlan, 8–9.

56. Leo E. Bennett to CIA, n.d., *ARCIA* (1892): p. 262.

57. Smith, *A Choctaw's Honor*, 140.

58. Quote from L. A. Benton, brother of Robert Benton, who wrote a letter to the editor of the *Indian Citizen*, October 11, 1892.

59. *Indian Citizen*, September 22, 1892, reprinted in the *Purcell Register*, n.d.

60. The lighthorsemen were charged by law to watch court proceedings: "Any person or persons who should come and threaten the life of any person at court, or treat the court with contempt while in session, shall be taken into custody by the light-horse-men and fined not exceeding fifty dollars." "An Act Authorizing Judges to Preserve Order in Time of Court, Session XI-1844, Sec. 1," approved October 1844, in CLAIT, 15:41.

61. *Indian Citizen*, September 22, 1892.

62. The vote-counting committee consisted of G. M. Bond and W. S. Hall from the First (Moshulatubbee) District; J. D. Wilson and J. J. Watkins from the Second (Apukshunnubbee) District; and J. C. Folsom and Tom Oakes from the Third (Pushmataha) District. Joe Gardner served as president and chair; B. S. Smiser as secretary; and J. C. Folsom and Hon. J. B. Jackson as interpreters. The convention determined that Jackson won by 34 votes, then corrected that number to 32 votes. *Indian Citizen*, September 1, 1892.

A group of Nationalists, including J. C. Hampton of Caddo, H. P. Ward of Kiowa, D. N. Robb of Atoka, Charles LeFlore of Stringtown, H. C. Harris of Harris Ferry, John Wilson of Doaksville, William Harrison of Lehigh, G. M. Bond of Savanna, J. J. Watkins of Kully Inla, Martin Charleston of Atoka, and J. Gardner of McAlester also took issue with the *Herald*'s claim that their convention was organized for planning the murders. See *Indian Citizen*, September 22, 1892.

63. *Indian Citizen*, October 6, 1892.

64. *Indian Citizen*, September 22, 1892.

65. *Indian Citizen*, October 6, 1892; Leo E. Bennett to CIA, n.d., *ARCIA* (1892): p. 26.

66. "Bill No. 1," approved October 5, 1892, in *CLAIT*, 22:3.

67. *Indian Citizen*, October 13, 1892; Leo E. Bennett to CIA, n.d., *ARCIA* (1892): p. 26.

68. The October 13, 1892, issue of the *Indian Citizen* contains Jones's message.

69. "An Act Appropriating $8000 for the Relief of the Militia," bill no. 15, approved October 26, 1892, in *CLAIT*, 22:9–10.

70. *Indian Citizen* October 13, 1892. This is in contradiction to another report in the same issue in which the *Citizen* editors claim that Jones won by only eight votes.

71. Telegram from Agent Bennett, September 14, 1892, to War Department, cited in *ARCIA* (1893): serial 3210, 1 House, p. 83.

72. Statement to pay Peter Adamson, Albert Parish, and Edmond Thomas, October 18, 1892. Green McCurtain Collection, box 17, folder 3, WHC.

73. CTN 49, vol. 339, case no. 55.

74. *Indian Citizen*, December 22, 1892.

75. Ibid. It is not clear why Abe Smith was killed except that he was apparently a Progressive, as evidenced by the voting poll book of his precinct. His name can be found in a list of witnesses for a murder case in 1880. CTN 48, vol. 247, p. 117.

76. One version of this rescue has events confused and mistakenly places Albert Jackson in the place of Willis Jones. This storyteller relates that Jackson had killed a Jones supporter and was ordered to Mayhew for trial. He was afraid that he would be executed if taken to Mayhew, so while out on bond the light-horsemen came to arrest him and he resisted. The lighthorsemen opened fire, and he returned that fire. More lighthorsemen arrived and arrested him. While traveling along the Rock Chimney Crossing on the Kiamichi River, his friends overtook the lighthorsemen, who then ran off leaving Jackson standing cuffed in the road. Jackson's friends took him to Victor Locke's for protection. According to this version, Jackson's friends initially intended to accompany Jackson to court and not free him, because they believed that the lighthorsemen would kill Jackson and throw him into the river if they tried to overtake the lighthorsemen by force. Interview with O. L. Blanche, May 21, 1937, *IPH*, 61:360–61, 363. Interview with Wilson Locke, May 20, 1937, *IPH*, 33:344.

77. See *Soper Democrat*, January 10, 1929; "Necrology of Victor M. Locke, Sr."; Interview with Colonel Victor M. Locke, October 25, 1937, *IPH*, 107:329–37. The post office in Antlers was established in August 1887. Antlers reportedly received its name after a hunter killed a large buck and nailed its antlers to a tree as a challenge for other hunters to meet. Other deer hunters also nailed their animals' antlers to trees, so many that the place came to be known as Antlers Springs. Interview with Victor M. Locke, October 25, 1937, *IPH*, 109:331; Shirk, *Oklahoma Place Names*, 10.

78. *ARCIA* (1893): p. 86.

79. Interview with Laura Scott, August 3, 1937, *IPH*, 103:107; Interview with Wilson Locke, May 20, 1937, *IPH*, 33:344.

80. *ARCIA* (1893): serial 3210, 1 House, p. 87.

81. *Indian Citizen*, March 30 and April 6, 1893; "Report of Jennie Selfridge on Mayhew Church and Court Grounds," July 13, 1937, *IPH*, 82:223–24; Interview with Gilbert Thompson, October 19, 1937, *IPH*, 46:444; *ARCIA* (1893): pp. 88–89.

82. *Hugo Husonian*, May 30, 1912.

83. Interview with Gilbert Thompson, October 19, 1937, *IPH*, 46:445; Interview with Wilson Locke, May 20, 1937, *IPH*, 33:341. The latter interview is interesting in that the interviewee is Wilson Locke, son of Dr. B. Frank Locke, yet

this relation of Victor Locke has the story considerably wrong. He claims that it was Victor Locke's son, "Shub," who killed Jim Ashford in Antlers and that it was Shub, not Willis Jones, whom the militia was after. See also "Locke-Jones War Reference," typescript dated September 10, 1936, in Choctaw Vertical File: Wilson Jones Folder, OHS.

84. Interview with Crawford J. Anderson, November 15, 1937, *IPH*, 12:335. The "lighthorsemen" and the "militia" were two separate entities. This is a common error among those interviewed about their life histories. In "The Story of an Adventure in Railroad Building," J. F. Holden claims that he watched events unfold as he sat on top of his house overlooking the South McAlester church that he (incorrectly) asserts had been taken over by the Progressives. Holden states that Agent Bennett raced at full speed toward the house on his horse, waving a white flag to get their attention and then assisted in making the truce (653).

85. *ARCIA* (1893): p. 87.

86. Interview with Gilbert Thompson, October 19, 1937, *IPH*, 46:445. Goodland is located three miles south of Hugo and was the site of the Goodland Orphanage.

87. Bennett to CIA, *ARCIA* (1893): p. 87.

88. Interview with Crawford J. Anderson, November 15, 1937, *IPH*, 12:336–37, 340–43. Anderson, however, not only has the chronology of events confused, he goes on in considerable dramatic and unproven detail about another arrest that he made of a renegade:

> An attack in accordance with their prearranged plans was seemingly not warranted. It is a well-known fact that a Territory-wide slaughter of the leading Progressives in all parts of the Choctaw Nation was to take place on that same night. Fortunately, however, with the exception of the killing of five leaders in what was then Gaines County, the plans of the conspirators were frustrated. On another occasion a group of the Snake Indians had congregated in an isolated place and after they had held their pow-wow, all spread their blankets upon the ground and prepared to spend the night in sleep. One man had been designated to stand guard near the sleeping conspirators. The now watchful Progressive in some way learned of this bivouac, advanced upon it, found the irresponsible guard soundly slumbering, quietly seized him and then noiselessly advanced upon the main body of the group, whom they found lying close to each other all wrapped in their blankets. The Progressives, being equal if not superior in number's surrounded them before they awoke and then each Progressive, with gun cocked and ready for instant firing, commanded the renegade Indian lying closet to him to arise and surrender. In this manner the arrest of a considerable number of those who had proven themselves to be menaces to the lives of those with whom they did not agree upon

Tribal matters was effected without the loss of life. Such wholesale arrests occurring at about the same time aided materially in quelling the uprisings and finally brought peace and tranquility back into the lives of those who for months had lived in constant fear for the safety of themselves and for the safety of their families due to the sneaking way in which the renegades carried their vindictiveness into effect.

In typical Wild West speak, the *IPH* interviewer textualizes Anderson's experiences:

In that group arrest, it is interesting to note the personal experience of Mr. Anderson. The particular Indian, lying closest to him at the time the signal for the awakening of the sleeping Indians was given, was commanded by Mr. Anderson to arise and throw up his hands. He arose from a prone to a sitting posture and then put down his right hand as though in an attempt to seize a gun. At that instant Mr. Anderson commanded him to drop that gun or he would fire. This latter command had the effect of causing the Indian to again reach for the sky with his hands and elicited the information that as he was a cripple and not for a gun as Mr. Anderson had thought. The instantaneous response to the second command of Mr. Anderson is all that stood between the still sleepy Indian and instant death for Mr. Anderson was not at that time in a mood to unnecessarily put himself up as a target for the gun of a renegade Snake Indian.

89. *ARCIA* (1893): serial 3210 1 House, pp. 88–89.

90. "An Act to Prevent Disturbance of Schools, Religious Devotion or Families," bill no. 40, approved October 26, 1883, in CLAIT, 18:27.

91. *Purcell Register*, April 14, 1893.

92. *Indian Citizen*, June 26, 1893.

93. *Indian Citizen*, May 1, May 4, May 18, June 19, June 26, and October 5, 1893.

94. *Indian Citizen*, June 29, 1893. Hartshorne was established in 1890 as a coal mining town and is located in eastern Pittsburg County. It is named after Dr. Charles Hartshorne, a railroad official. Shirk, *Oklahoma Place Names*, 110; Workers of the Writers' Program of the Work Projects Administration, *Oklahoma: Guide to the Sooner State*, 301.

95. Wardell, *Political History of the Cherokee Nation*, 52.

96. *ARCIA* (1893): p. 86.

97. *Indian Citizen*, April 27, July 1, July 3, 1893; "An Act Making Appropriation for V. S. Vinson and Others," approved July 1, 1893, in *CLAIT*, 22:36–37; "An Act for the Relief of J. W. Ownby, Esq.," approved July 3, 1893, in *CLAIT*, 22:38.

98. "Interview with Judge A. R. Durant," Wilson N. Jones Collection, box 1, folder 10, WHC.

CHAPTER 4: THE NATIONALIST TRIALS

Epigraph: James Culberson to Czarina Conlan, September 16, 1940, in Vertical File: Choctaw Executions, OHS, 8.

1. Article 6, section 10 of the Constitution of the Choctaw Nation, in *CLAIT*, 15:11. The Constitution of 1860 authorized the election of prosecuting attorneys and county judges in each district for two-year terms and compensation for all judges of the supreme and county courts for their work. The judges oversaw probate courts and decided on estate matters related to executors and guardians. Judges appointed a clerk to serve as county treasurer. See article 4, sections 9, 12, 15, 19 of the Constitution of 1860.

2. CTN 49, vol. 339, case no. 55, p. 410. Blue and Hoteyubbee voted in pre-cincts that overwhelmingly favored Jones in the 1892 election; in 1890 Cooper voted in a precinct where Jones easily defeated Smallwood; and, also in 1890, Simeon Hampton voted in a precinct where Jackson and Jones tied. Blue's and Hoteyubbee's votes appear in "Poll Book, Blackfork Precinct, Sugar Loaf County for an Election on the 3rd day of August 1892," in CTN 64; Cooper's vote appears in the poll book titled "Sans Bois County, Okchanak Chito Precinct, 1890," in CTN 64; Simeon Hampton's vote appears in "Poll Book of an Election Held at South Canadian Precinct, Tobucksy County, Choctaw Nation, on the First Wednesday in August, 1890 for the Election of National Officers," CTN 64.

Sweeney Hampton and Nelson voted for McCurtain in 1884, and the former, along with Naile, voted for Jones in 1890. Sweeney appears in the Boiling Springs, Gaines County 1884 election poll book as "Swiney"; see CTN 63; Nelson appears in the Cedar County Precinct, Cedar County poll book and served as judge of that County. Naile appears in the "Poll Book of an Election Held at South Canadian Precinct," in CTN 64.

In 1890, Garland voted in a precinct that closely favored Smallwood, so it is not known how he voted. It is also not known how Hendrickson or Hickman voted in any election. San Bois County, Little San Bois Precinct, CTN 64.

Ben Hoteyubbee remained friends with the Progressive Robert Benton, the man exonerated for the murder of Charles Wilson. In 1891 they filed a joint coal claim on Iyahonubbee's old place near Poteau in Sugar Loaf County, CTN 42, vol. 230.

3. Culberson also claims that he served as juryman, but there is no record that he did. Culberson, "Political Side of My Life," *IPH*, 65:330–31.

4. CTN 49, vol. 339, case no. 55, and letter from N. J. Holson, pp. 412–14. James Culberson alleges that Judge Holson sent him to talk to Governor Jones about a new trial, but again, there is no evidence that he did this either. Culber-son, "Political Side of My Life," *IPH*, 65:330–31.

5. CTN 50, vol. 344, case no. 59.

6. Price Tallipoose's name is spelled "Plias Talipoos" in the 1885 Gaines County Census.

7. CTN 49, vol. 339, case no. 56, p. 420.

8. Of what can be located about these Progressive men, nine (Bascom, Carney, Adam Cooper, Norris Cooper, James, Luce, Naile, Pusley, and Wade) voted in precincts in which Jones won decisively over Jackson in 1892. McFarlan and Pearson voted in precincts in which Jones and Jackson tied. Johnson McFarlan's name is in the "Poll Book of Election, Held at Double Springs, County of Skullyville, Choctaw Nation on the 3rd Day of August, A.D. 1892 for the Use of the Principal Chief," in CTN 64.

Adam James's vote is recorded in "Poll Book of Election, Held at Brazil Precinct, County of Skullyville, Choctaw Nation, on the 3rd day of August, A.D. 1892, for the Use of the Principal Chief," in CTN 64; Dennis Wade's and John Bascom's names are in an untitled poll book for Hakshish Precinct, Jackson County; Morris Carney's vote is recorded in "Poll Book, Spring Hill Precinct, Sugar Loaf County, for an Election on the 3rd Day of August 1892," in CTN 64. Robert Pearson's name is in "Poll Book of an Election Held at Folsom Precinct, Tobucksey County, Choctaw Nation, on the First Wednesday in August 1892, for the Election of Principal Chief Officers," in CTN 64.

9. Thomas Luce's vote is in the poll book titled "Sans Bois County, Okchanak Chito Precinct, 1892," in CTN 64; CTN 50, vol. 344, case nos. 106, 107, 108.

10. *Choctaw Nation v. Silan Lewis, et al,* June 26, 1893, CTN 49, vol. 339, case no. 56, p. 420.

11. Also seen spelled as Hoteyubbee, Hoklotubbe.

12. *Indian Citizen,* July 13, 1893.

13. Ibid.

14. Culberson to Conlan, 4.

15. See the appendix for correspondence.

16. *Purcell Register,* July 7, 1893.

17. Ibid.

18. Ibid.

19. Ibid., and *Purcell Register,* July 14, 1893.

20. W. N. Jones to N. J. Holson, July 4, 1893, document no. 1 in the appendix.

21. *Purcell Register,* July 21, 1893.

22. *Indian Citizen,* July 6, 1893.

23. Both statements in Green McCurtain Collection, box 17, folder 3, WHC.

24. Interview with Mary Darneal, October 26, 1937, *IPH,* 21:442, 452; interview with John N. Folsum, May 25, 1937, *IPH,* 51:472.

25. "Report of Jeanne Selfridge on Mayhew Church and Court Grounds," July 13, 1933, *IPH,* 82:222–24.

26. "Editorial on Message of Attorney General Hall to W. N. Jones," Wilson N. Jones Collection, box 1, folder 13, WHC; originally in the *Purcell Register,* July 7, 1893.

27. W. N. Jones to Hoke Smith, July 5, 1893, document no. 2 in the appendix.

28. Hoke Smith to Paul Faison, July 7, 1893; W. N. Jones to N. J. Holson, July 14, 1893; and N. J. Holson to John Taylor, July 22, 1893, document nos. 3, 4, and 5, respectively, in the appendix.

29. "Statement of James Brazell in Regard to the Execution of Silan (Sion) Lewis," October 23, 1940, in Vertical Files: Choctaw Executions, OHS. The statement is typed with several corrections made in handwriting; for example, in the title, "Silan" is struck out and "Silon" is added. Interestingly, Brazell's text states that "his name is given as Silan but it was really Sion." Brazell's claim to have known Lewis for twenty-five years is dubious, at best. One wonders how he would even know if Lewis was indeed "a very honorable and industrious, good Indian citizen" if he did not even know his correct name. Furthermore, there is no other mention of the claim that Holson could not read or speak English. Other versions of the Lewis saga maintain that Holson spoke English and wrote the court orders.

30. *Purcell Register*, July 28, 1893.

31. *Indian Citizen*, August 10, 1893.

32. CTN 64. Results for that election have the Nationalist candidates underlined:

Precinct/County	Jackson/Hunter	Spring/Wilson	Dukes/Oakes	Nelson/Lewis
Apukshunnubbee District				
Alikchi/Nashoba	30/96	79/47	108/18	40/86
Battiest/Nashoba	0/26	23/0	25/1	1/25
Sulphur Springs/Nashoba	1/14	14/1	15/0	2/13
Good Water/Red River	5/14	15/4	19/0	6/13
Doaksville/Towson	103/8	3/112	8/104	100/9
High Hill/Wade	18/11	10/19	15/14	20/9
Pleasant Hill/Wade	15/52	55/12	53/13	53/14
Tushkahoma/Wade	1/19	19/2	20/1	1/19
Pushmataha District				
Atoka/Atoka	54/19	15/58	17/55	54/19
Big Springs/Atoka	4/18	4/18	18/4	2/19
Black Jack Grove/Atoka	31/3	31/2	3/31	30/4
Little Boggy/Atoka	15/0	15/0	0/15	14/1
Medicine Springs/Atoka	26/0	26/0	0/26	0/26
Red Oak/Atoka		No results available		
Round Lake/Atoka		No results available		
Sulphur Spring/Atoka		No results available		
Caddo/Blue		No results available		
Durant/Blue		No results available		
Jones/Blue	14/24	23/15	23/15	24/14
Philadelphia/Blue	4/19	16/7	20/3	17/6
Antlers/Jacks Fork		No results available		
Big Cane/Jacks Fork	2/15	15/2	14/3	2/15
Chickasaw Creek/Jacks Fork	16/6	4/18	5/17	16/6
Nanih Hikia/Jacks Fork	25/18	17/26	18/25	18/25
Sardis/Jacks Fork	0/30	29/1	29/0	2/27

Precinct/County	Jackson/Hunter	Spring/Wilson	Dukes/Oakes	Nelson/Lewis
Many Springs/Jacks Fork		No results available		
Etiakshish/Jackson	7/13	13/7	13/7	8/12
Pigeon Roost/Jackson		No results available		
Fiale Hills/Jackson		No results available		
Good Land/Kiamichi	67/103	120/70	80/99	102/74
Good Water/Kiamichi	19/4	3/21	0/23	20/1
Saw Mill/Kiamichi	8/4	3/9	2/10	8/4
Sugar Creek/Kiamichi	1/11	4/8	4/8	9/3
Moshulatubbee District				
Boiling Springs/Gaines	7/7	7/7	7/7	6/8
Hartshorne/Gaines	1/48	39/10	44/4	6/43
Riddle/Gaines	10/7	2/15	5/10	8/7
Iron Bridge/San Bois	8/20	—	—	3/21
Little San Bois/San Bois	48/1	2/47	1/48	47/2
Okchanak Chito/San Bois		No results available		
Oklahoma/San Bois	13/10	13/10	12/11	12/12
Brazil/Skullyville	13/21	21/14	22/13	12/23
Cache/Skullyville	11/6	6/11	6/11	12/5
Double Springs/Skullyville		No results available		
Greenwood/Skullyville	11/2	2/12	3/11	11/3
Skullyville/Skullyville	38/21	18/40	23/34	33/26
Blackfork/Sugar Loaf	0/19	18/1	18/1	0/19
Easton/Sugar Loaf	15/18	19/14	20/12	15/18
Folsom/Tobucksy		No results available		
High Hill/Tobucksy		No results available		
McAlester/Tobucksy	32/11	9/34	12/31	31/11
Savanna/Tobucksy		No results available		
Unknown/Unknown	0/27	27/0	27/0	0/27
Unknown/Unknown	37/56	57/43	51/43	43/51
Unknown/Unknown	70/2	0/72	0/72	71/0

33. *Indian Citizen*, August 10, 1893.

34. CTN 18, Supreme Court, April 1892 term.

35. *Indian Citizen*, August 10, 1893.

36. *Indian Citizen*, September 7, 1893.

37. *Indian Citizen*, November 15, 1894.

38. Sec. 11, approved October 16, 1846, in *CLAIT*, 15:47–48.

39. Benson, *Life among the Choctaw Indians*, 29.

40. "A. P. Shaw: His Residence with Chief John F. Brown and Life among the Seminoles, March 24, 1937," *IPH*, 69:265; interview with Alec Berryhill, May 21, 1937, *IPH*, 13:475–76; interview with Carrie Cyrus, June 17, 1937, *IPH*, 21:399; interview with Leitka Tiger, September 22, 1937, *IPH*, 46:100–101.

41. Cushman, *History of the Choctaw, Chickasaw and Natchez Indians*, 88–89.

42. Testimony of Napoleon B. Ainsworth, May 26, 1885, in *Report of the Committee on Indian Affairs*, 232.

43. Interview with Simon Jackson, July 21, 1937, *IPH*, 31:72–73.

44. Young, "Live as You Please," 376; interview with Joe M. Grayson, December 17, 1937, *IPH*, 26:378–79.

45. Act of September 28, 1850, Ch. 80, 9 Stat. 513, 515 (U.S. Navy); Act of August 5, 1861, Ch. 54, section 3, 12 Stat. 316, 317 (U.S. Army).

46. Jenkins Boy, "Reuben Lucas Shot for the Murder of Thompson McKinney," *Cherokee Advocate*, June 18, 1882.

47. Ibid.

48. *Purcell Register*, July 7, 1893. Because of the lack of court files, the course of events in the Bird case is unclear. The record for case no. 198 (CTN 48, vol. 348) reveals that he was guilty of violation of the pistol law in 1892. That same year, his wife Alice was granted a divorce from him, and on May 6 he pled guilty to manslaughter and was sentenced to receive one hundred lashes on the bare back; then would be released from custody.

49. Hoke Smith to Paul Faison, September 5, 1893, document no. 7 in the appendix.

50. W. N. Jones to N. J. Holson, September 6, 1893, document no. 8 in the appendix.

51. N. J. Holson to John Taylor, September 8, 1893, document no. 9 in the appendix.

52. "Editorial on Chickasaw Legislature," Wilson N. Jones Collection, box 1, folder 14, WHC.

53. *Indian Citizen*, November 15, 1894.

54. *The Purcell Register*, October 13, 1893.

55. *The Purcell Register*, October 20, 1893.

56. "Interview with Judge A. R. Durant," Wilson N. Jones Collection, box 1, folder 10, WHC.

57. *Indian Citizen*, October 11, 1893.

58. "Necrology of John S. Hancock," 304; *Caddo Banner*, November 24, 1893.

59. *Caddo Banner*, November 24, 1893.

60. *Purcell Register*, October 13 and October 27, 1893.

61. *Caddo Banner*, November 24, 1893.

62. *Indian Citizen*, September 14, 1893.

63. *Indian Citizen*, September 28, 1893.

64. *Indian Citizen*, September 21, October 5, October 19, October 26, 1893.

65. Document #9, Sam Jefferson, et al. to N. J. Holson, November 13, 1893, document no. 10 in the appendix; see also CTN 49, vol. 339.

66. CTN 49, vol. 339, case no. 56, *Choctaw Nation v. Price Tallipoose, et al.*

67. Cooper, Folsum, Jones and Schropshire voted at the Okchanak Chito Precinct of the San Bois County where Jones solidly defeated Jackson 141 votes to 1 in the 1892 election. Wilson and Amos voted in the Spring Hill Precinct of Sugar Loaf County where Jones won 22 votes to Jackson's 7. Simeon Hampton was a

member of the private militia that guarded Lewis in July, 1893 and he also served as member of the 1893 jury that convicted him. Willis hailed from Double Springs Precinct of Skullyville County where Jones and Jackson tied at 9 votes each so it is unknown as to how he voted. Leflore was from Long Creek Precinct in Sugar Loaf County where the two tied at 28 votes each. Harris resided in Caston Precinct of Sugar Loaf County, where Jackson won 27 votes to Jones's 13, but it is unknown how he voted. Fele Muchubbee voted for McCurtain in the 1884 election and was a witness in the Jackson Crow murder trial in Fort Smith. Only Lysander Trahern is unaccounted for, although many Traherns voted for Jones in the 1892 election. It is unknown how Amos and Cooper voted. See poll books in CTN 64.

68. CTN 50, vol. 344, case no. 56.

69. *Indian Citizen*, May 24, 1894; CTN 49, vol. 339, case no. 55.

70. CTN 49, vol. 339, p. 455.

71. CTN 53, vol. 396, p. 94.

72. CTN 49, vol. 396, p. 493.

73. Culberson to Conlan, 5; In *A Choctaw's Honor*, Smith claims that Holson used the "dead, dead, dead" phrase (158). Smith's book is a fictional account of Silan Lewis's life, but it suffers from superficial research. Glenn Shirley, in *Toughest of Them All*, asserts that Lewis said "O-meh" after receiving his sentence (101).

74. Shirley, *Toughest of Them All*, 101.

75. CTN 50, vol. 344; *Indian Citizen*, November 8, 1894.

76. *Tulsa Sunday World*, September 1950; "Man Who Made Picture Tells Story," *Life In Oklahoma* 9, no. 2 (May 1940): 14.

77. CTN 45, vol. 260.

78. *Tulsa Sunday World*, September 1950; "Man Who Made Picture Tells Story," 14.

79. Interview with Frank A. Raymond, February 9, 1938, *IPH*, 41:221–22.

80. Owen Jones, "Wife of Silon Lewis Turns Back Pages of History to Tell of Details Leading up to and Following Indian's Execution," *McAlester News-Capital*, July 1957.

81. Ibid.

82. Ibid.

83. Ibid.

84. Ibid.

85. Private militia of the Moshulatubbee District complied from CTN 87, Archives and Manuscripts Division, OHS. The militiamen included:

Collen, Philian	Guard prisoner, November 2 to November 5, 1894
Belley, Charles [*sic?*]	Guard prisoner, November 2 to November 5, 1894
Belley, Wattson	Guard prisoner, November 2 to November 5, 1894
Benton, John C. [*sic?*]	November 2 to November 5, 1894
Hampton, Ward	Guard prisoner, November 2 to November 5, 1894
Jackson, Joe	November 2 to November 5, 1894

Jefferson, Israel	Guard prisoner, November 2 to November 5, 1894
Jefferson, Joe	Guard prisoner, November 2, 1894
Jefferson, Wallace	Guard prisoner, November 2 to November 5, 1894
Jone, Martson [sic?]	November 3, 1894
Lowman [sic?], Jackson	Guard prisoner, November 2 to November 5, 1894
Lovtubbee [sic?], James	Guard prisoner, November 2 to November 5 1894
McCurtain, Frank	Guard prisoner, November 2 to November 5, 1894
McCurtain, Howerton [sic?]	November 2 to November 5, 1894
McCurtain, Sampson	November 2 to November 5, 1894
McNoel, Eastman	Guard prisoner, November 2, 1894
Perry, Charley	Guard prisoner, November 2 to November 5, 1894
Style, Hanson Halden	Guard prisoner, November 2 to November 5, 1894
Washington, Benson	November 2 to November 5, 1894
White, Campbell	Guard prisoner, November 2, 1894

Joe Jackson was a Progressive who had voted in precincts in which Wilson N. Jones soundly defeated Smallwood in 1890 and 1892. He also had been seen by witnesses riding with Jackson Crow the morning of Charles Wilson's murder. "Criminal Defendant Case File for Jack Crow, 1884," Murder Jacket Number 44.

86. Jones, "Wife of Silon Lewis."

87. "Old Choctaw Law Urged as Cure for Many Evils Today: Aged Executioner Tells of His Customs, How Outlaws Were Handled," *Daily Oklahoman*, January 20, 1935. Much of this "interview," and the writings of Robert Barr Smith, were obviously taken from the November 8, 1894, issue of the *Indian Citizen*.

88. *Indian Citizen*, November 8, 1894.

89. According to another report authored by Wilbur Henry, Sr., in Flossie Chaudoin's *Red Oak Annals*, it is implied that some people speculated that Silan and Sally might have been planning to flee, perhaps to Texas.

90. *Indian Citizen*, November 8, 1894.

91. Jones, "Wife of Silon Lewis."

92. *Indian Citizen*, November 8, 1894.

93. Ibid; interview with Frank A. Raymond, February 9, 1938, *IPH*, 41:223. Raymond lists the following people as being in the photo of Lewis's execution: Jim Brown, Newton Brown, Dennis Carr, Eph Collins, John Denton, Levi Dozier, Charley B. Hulsey, H. C. Hulsey, Houston Nelson (a special deputy sheriff for the occasion), sheriff and executioner Lyman Pulsey, Alfred Sealey, Al Smith, Moss Williams (who appears as "Amos" in the Moshulatubbee records and as a special deputy sheriff for this occasion), and a man with the last name Baldwin.

94. Interview with Frank A. Raymond, February 9, 1938, *IPH*, 41:223–24.

95. Ibid., 224.

96. *Indian Citizen*, November 8, 1894.

97. "Old Choctaw Law Urged as Cure for Many Evils Today."

98. Culberson to Conlan, 5. This may be merely speculation or fabrication since Culberson discusses the events leading up to Lewis's execution but did not attend the event.

99. Jones, "Wife of Silon Lewis."

100. Smith, *A Choctaw's Honor*, 155.

101. Interview with Frank A. Raymond, February 9, 1938, *IPH*, 41:225.

102. Ibid.

103. Ibid. In *A Choctaw's Honor*, Smith writes that "a cork made black by the heat and smoke of a kerosene lamp" was used to mark him (158). The story about the handkerchief seems to be created by Smith to set up the dramatic scene on the following page of his novel: "When Silon's head jerked back, the bandanna moved slightly. He could see. And he saw gawkers, staring at him— just quietly watching. If he had not been in so much pain, Silon would have reacted violently" (159).

104. Smith, *A Choctaw's Honor*, 158. The "Old Choctaw Law Urged as Cure for Many Evils Today" article first mentions the dog and turkey: "A mongrel dog set the woods echoing with a hideous, mournful howl." Glenn Shirley then uses the sentence verbatim in *Toughest of Them All*, 105. Neither Raymond nor Sally Lewis in her interview mention the animals.

105. "Old Choctaw Law Urged as Cure for Many Evils Today."

106. Smith, *A Choctaw's Honor*, 158.

107. Shirley, *Toughest of Them All*, 106.

108. Interview with Mary Darneal, October 25–26, 1937, *IPH*, 21:445–46, 451.

109. Smith, *A Choctaw's Honor*, 158.

110. CTN 43, vol. 244. The General Council had wanted to keep intruders and citizens busy, so in 1854, all free males between the ages of eighteen and fifty years and all U.S. citizens, including licensed mechanics and merchants who lived in the Nation were required to work six days out of every year on the public roads or pay a fine of fifty cents per day, payable to county judges. Students, teachers, farmers, and doctors were exempt. County judges could appoint two competent men out of each county to mark any new road that was necessary. Section 2, of this road law, stated further, "That it shall be the duty of the county judges to notify the people of their respective counties by any light-horse man, at least five days before the time for working on the roads, who, with their axes, hoes and other utensils that may be necessary for the work, shall so work." See "An Act Requiring All Free Males over Eighteen and under Fifty Years Old to Work on the Road," approved November 15, 1854, in *CLAIT*, 11:137–38.

111. CTN 48, vol. 338, p. 28; CTN 48, case no. 218; CTN 49, vol. 339, case no. 78.

112. CTN 49, case no. 318, pp. 203, 221. "In the above case defendant was convicted of murder in the first degree and it is ordered and decreed by this court that for such his offense that on Friday 13th day of December A.D. 1888, at Moshu-latubbee Court Ground that the said Lyman Pusley be taken then and these and

shot until he is dead-dead." Approved by Circuit Court Judge Mitchell Himson [*sic*]. Showing a bit of whimsy, the court reporter made an elaborate "s" in the word "shot" so that the letter s looks like a bull's-eye.

113. "Old Choctaw Law Urged as Cure for Many Evils Today," *Daily Oklahoman*, January 20, 1935. In 1888, the Choctaw Supreme Court overturned the lower court's verdict, stating, "The testimony in this case is not sufficient to warrant a conviction." CTN 53, vol. 395, p. 67; also stated in "October Term 1889, Lyman Pusley vs. Choctaw Nation," CTN 53, vol. 396, p. 46.

114. CTN 48, vol. 338, p. 104; CTN 50, vol. 350, case no. 877.

115. *Indian Citizen*, November 8, 1894.

116. Interview with Frank A. Raymond, February 9, 1938, *IPH*, 41:227.

117. *Indian Citizen*, November 8, 1894.

118. Interview with Frank Raymond, *IPH*, 41:227.

119. Ibid., 228.

120. *Eagle-Gazette*, November 15, 1894.

121. *Indian Citizen*, November 8, 1894.

122. Interview with W. W. Bray, September 13, 1937, *IPH*, 10:435–36; Davis, "Chitto Harjo," 140.

123. "Old Choctaw Law Urged as Cure for Many Evils Today"; *Eagle-Gazette*, November 8, 1894, has the story of the sheriff pinching Lewis's nose until he died.

124. Interview with Ely Wade, March 23, 1937, *IPH*, 11:98.

125. Interview with Samuel L. Davis, November 17, 1937, *IPH*, 22:60.

126. Interview with Stovall Green, July 20, 1937, *IPH*, 54:249.

127. Interview with Lyman Pusley, McAlester, Okla., April 20, 1938, "Execution of Silan Lewis," *IPH*, 93:510.

128. Interview with Frank Raymond, *IPH*, 41:228, 229.

129. Jones, "Wife of Silon Lewis."

130. Ibid.

131. *Eagle-Gazette*, November 8, 1894.

132. Interview with Frank Raymond, *IPH*, 41:229.

133. CTN 87. The check, No. 15 of Choctaw Nation, Mosholatubbee District 22846, reads, "This is to certify that Lyman Pusley is entitled to Five dollars and for services rendered as Sheriff in Execution of Silan Lewis at a Vacation Term of the Circuit Court, held in said District on the 14th day of November 1894," and is signed by "Wallace Bond, Clerk of the First Judicial District, C. N., Jas. Culberson, D. C."

134. Interview with Lyman Pusley, McAlester, Okla., April 20, 1938, *IPH*, 91:509–10.

135. *Indian Citizen*, November 15, 1894.

136. CTN 42, vol. 230, pp. 146–47. Ida Wilson, the daughter of Charles Wilson, was my great-grandmother.

137. "Old Choctaw Law Urged as Cure for Many Evils Today."

138. Samuels and Samuels, *Life and Times of the Choctaw Original Enrollees*, 272.

139. Jones, "Wife of Silon Lewis."

140. *Indian Citizen*, November 8, 1894.

141. "Poll Book for Red Oak Precinct, Atoka County, for an Election Held on the 3rd Day of August, A.D., 1892," and "Poll Book for Medicine Spring Precinct, Atoka County, for an Election Held on the 3rd Day of August, A.D., 1892," in CTN 64.

142. CTN 43, vol. 243, case no. 45, pp. 364–65.

143. Holmes had voted in the High Hill Precinct of Tobucksy County in 1892, where Jackson received 28 votes to Jones's no votes, and he had voted with King in the Medicine Springs Precinct in which Jackson handily received more votes than Hunter in the race for national secretary. Jackson Nelson was from Gaines County and around twenty-six years old at the time of Lewis's execution. See Gaines County Census, 1885; "Poll Book of an Election Held at High Hill Precinct, Tobucksy County, Choctaw Nation, on the First Wednesday in August, 1892, for the Election of Principal Chief, Officers," in CTN 64.

144. Index to the Five Civilized Tribes. Final Dawes Roll, M1186 roll 1; Enrollment Cards for the Five Civilized Tribes, 1898–1914, M186.

145. Ibid.

146. CTN 43, vol. 243, case no. 45, pp. 364–65.

147. CTN 45, vol. 258, case no. 112.

148. CTN 45, vol. 258, case no. 209.

149. CTN 53, vol. 396, case no. 65, p. 115.

150. Jones, "Wife of Silon Lewis"; See Field No. 4675, Choctaw Roll. My great-grandfather, William Elliott Abbott, delivered at least two of their children, Edna May and George W. At the time of the closing of the rolls, Sally Beams was twenty-five years old. Census card number 4675. Final Rolls of Citizens and Freedmen of the Five Civilized Tribes, p. 117.

151. Shirley, *Toughest of Them All*, 101–107.

152. The excerpt from *Warrior's Honor* is available at ebooks.filamentbooks .com/servlet/mw?t=book&bi=29171&si=44.

153. Ashabranner and Davis, *The Choctaw Code*.

154. Askew, *Strange Business*, 1–8.

155. Frey, *The Key*, 43, 45–58. Frey lists other traits: the hero is considered to be sexually appealing; sometimes physically superior; sometimes has a special birth (a parent might be royalty, a god, an Apache warrior, etc.); sometimes has a special destiny (perhaps predicted by a seer); is sometimes branded (mark, scar, hair); is sometimes cynical; and is sometimes "mouthy," perhaps a "wise guy" (59–61).

156. Jones, "Wife of Silon Lewis."

157. Interview with William McCleod Patterson, September 24, 1937, *IPH*, 39:182–83.

158. Interview with A. J. Kennedy, July 27, 1937, *IPH*, 60:193–94.

159. Interview with William J. Luker, April 28, 1938, *IPH*, 78:366–67.

160. Interview with Richard (Dick) Morgan, n.d., *IPH*, 7:301.

161. Interview with Samuel L. Davis, *IPH*, 22:60.

162. Interview with Green Stovall, *IPH*, 54:249.

163. Statement of James Brazell, p. 2 in Vertical File: Choctaw Executions Folder, OHS.

164. Culberson to Conlan, 5, 8.

CHAPTER 5: CONTINUED RESISTANCE TO STATEHOOD

Epigraph: "Statement of Jacob B. Jackson," n.d., U.S. Congress, *Report of the Select Committee*, 958.

1. See for example, CTN 26, Blue County Records; CTN 27, Boktuklo County Records; CTN 28, Cedar County Records; CTN 30, Eagle County Records; CTN 31, Gaines County and Jacks Fork Records; CTN 32 and 33, Jacks Fork Records; CTN 34, Jackson and Kiamichi County Records; CTN 35 Kiamichi and Nashoba County Records (also CTN 36); CTN 37, 38, Red River County Records; CTN 40 San Bois County Records; CTN 41, Skullyville County Records; CTN 42, Sugar Loaf County Records; CTN 43 and 44, Tobucksy County Records. Violent crimes are also mentioned in the district records, but often the county in which the crimes were committed is not mentioned.

2. Extra Census Bulletin, *Five Civilized Tribes in Indian Territory*, 56.

3. Edmund McCurtain to Leo E. Bennett, August 25, 1890, in Bennett to CIA, September 10, 1890, *ARCIA* (1890): 1 House, serial 2841, p. 103; bill no. 18 (no formal title of act), approved April 9, 1891, *CLAIT*, 21:11.

4. "Message of Wilson N. Jones, October 12, 1893," in Wilson N. Jones Collection, box 1, folder 15, WHC.

5. *Purcell Register*, October 13, 1893.

6. *Caddo Banner*, June 22, 1894.

7. *Caddo Banner*, February 23, 1894.

8. Welton, "Life of Green McCurtain," 28.

9. *Caddo Banner*, June 22, 1894.

10. Ibid.; Welton, "Life of Green McCurtain," 28.

11. *Cherokee Advocate*, February 28, 1894.

12. Speech printed in a variety of newspapers, such as the *Chickasaw Enterprise*, July 19, 1894, and the *Tulsa Review*, July 13, 1894.

13. *Chickasaw Enterprise*, July 19, 1894; *Tulsa Review*, July 13, 1894; *Indian Chieftain*, October 18, 1894.

14. This statement also appeared in numerous papers, including the *Talihina News*, July 19, 1894.

15. *South McAlester Capital*, August 2, 1894.

16. *South McAlester Capital*, July 12, 1894.

17. *Talihina News*, July 19, 1894.

18. *Minco Minstrel*, September 28, 1894.

19. Meserve, "Chief Benjamin Franklin Smallwood and Chief Jefferson Gardner"; Hudson, "A Story of Choctaw Chiefs," 192, 208.

20. *Indian Citizen*, October 11, 1894.

21. Ibid.

22. *Indian Chieftan*, October 18, 1894; *Purcell Register*, October 19, 1894.

23. *Minco Minstrel*, October 19, 1894.

24. *Purcell Register*, October 19, 1894.

25. *Davis Advertiser*, April 18, 1895.

26. Ibid.; *Afton News*, April 19, 1895.

27. *Indian Citizen*, November 7, 1895; CTN 11, vol. 316. Everidge voted on the railway bill with Benton on November 9, 1881; "Will Everidge Has Had Much Troubles," *Hugo Husonian*, May 30, 1912; Hudson, "Recollections," 517; "Joe W. Everidge," in Samuels and Samuels, *Life and Times of Choctaw Original Enrollees*, 78–79. In this biography, Everidge is described as being "tall and powerfully built, with a fair complexion." He died in May 1901.

28. CTN 49, vol. 339.

29. Isham James voted in the High Hill Precinct of Wade County, and the mark by his name reveals he voted for Wilson N. Jones in 1892. James Darneal, Jack Burns, Ennis James, Pusley, and John Jones also voted in precincts in which Jones had defeated Jacob Jackson. For Isham James, see "The Choctaw Nation, Apucksunnubbee District, County of Wade, High Hill Election Precinct, August 3, 1892," in CTN 64; for James Darneal and Ennis James, see "Poll Book of Elections, Held at Skullyville Precinct, County of Skullyville, Choctaw Nation, on the 3rd Day of August, A.D. 1892," in CTN 64; for Jack Burns and John Jones, see 1892 poll book for "Sans Bois County, Okchanak Chito Precinct," in CTN 64; Silas Pusley voted in an unnamed precinct book in ibid.

30. Two men, Williams and Billie, had voted for Jackson. Williams voted for Jackson over Gardner in the 1894 election for chief; see "High Hill Precinct of Wade County," in CTN 64. Billie voted for Jackson in 1892; see 1892 poll book for "Sans Bois County, Little Sans Bois Precinct," in CTN 64.

31. Culberson, "Political Side of My Life," *IPH*, 65:332.

32. Culberson to Conlan, in Vertical File: Choctaw Executions, OHS, 2–3.

33. CTN 49, vol. 339.

34. Calvin: CTN 50, vol. 344, case no. 55; Tallipoose: CTN 50, vol. 344, case no. 56 (the case reads *"Price Lallipoose, et al.,"* but does not list any other names; McCoy: CTN 50, vol. 344, case no. 57; Taylor: CTN 50, vol. 344, case no. 58; Anderson: CTN 50, vol. 344, case no. 59; and Parker: CTN 50, vol. 344, case no. 60.

35. *Indian Citizen*, June 18, 1896.

36. *Indian Citizen*, April 23, 1896.

37. *Indian Citizen*, August 27, 1896.

38. *Indian Citizen*, September 3, 1896; *South McAlester Capital*, September 3, 1896.

39. *Indian Citizen*, October 31, 1895.

40. Wisdom to CIA, September 10, 1896, *ARCIA* (1896): p. 154.

41. "An Act Creating a Commission to Negotiate with the Dawes Commission," bill no. 7, approved October 22, 1896, in CTN 14, vol. 321.

42. *Indian Citizen*, November 12 and 19, 1896.

43. *Indian Citizen*, December 3 and 10, 1896.

44. "Delegates of the Antlers' Convention Before the Dawes' Commission," December 9, 1896, in Green McCurtain Collection, box 27, folder 12, pp. 2, 3, 4, WHC.

45. Ibid., pp. 10–12.

46. Ibid., pp. 17–18.

47. *Minco Minstrel*, April 3, 1896.

48. *Indian Citizen*, January 14, 1897.

49. "An Act Creating a Commission to Negotiate with the Dawes Commission," bill no. 7, approved October 22, 1896, in CTN 14, vol. 321, pp. 117–18; Commission to the Five Civilized Tribes, *ARCIA* (1896): 99.

50. Dew M. Wisdom to CIA, September 10, 1896, *ARCIA* (1896): pp. 152–53.

51. *Indian Citizen*, March 17, 1898.

52. *Chelsea Reporter*, January 31, 1901.

53. CTN 4, for San Bois County 1868–96; San Bois County Census, 1885.

54. Kappler, *IA:LT*, 1:179 The Atoka Agreement was added to the Curtis Act of June 28, 1898 (30 Stat. 505), and further modified by the act of July 1, 1902 (32 Stat. 641, 657, c. 1362); *Indian Citizen*, January 30, 1896.

55. Meserve, *Dawes Commission and the Five Civilized tribes of Indian Territory*, 12.

56. Ibid., 21, 42.

57. *David Progress*, September 3, 1896, in Jefferson Gardner Collection, box minor, folder 4, packet 2, WHC; *Indian Citizen*, August 1, August 22, and October 25, 1895.

58. Interview with George Hudson, March 10, 1938, *IPH*, 111:14–19.

59. Ibid.

60. Ibid.

61. *Indian Citizen*, December 2, 1897.

62. Ibid.; *Indian Citizen*, June 23, 1898.

63. *Indian Citizen*, July 14, 1898.

64. Meserve, "Chief Gilbert Wesley Dukes."

65. "Message of G. W. Dukes to the Members of the Senate and House of Representatives in General Council Assembled," ca. 1901, in G. W. Dukes Collection, folder 54, box D-29, OHS.

66. *Indian Citizen*, February 28, 1901.

67. Ibid.

68. Ibid.

69. *Indian Citizen*, October 4, 1900.

70. Ibid.

71. *South McAlester Capital,* January 11, 1901.

72. *Indian Citizen,* May 9, 1901.

73. "Message of G. W. Dukes to the Members of the Senate and House of Representatives in General Council Assembled."

74. *Indian Journal,* January 25, 1901.

75. *Chelsea Reporter,* January 31, 1901. The informers for this story were Willis Wilson, a full-blood Snake, and James Culberson, the circuit clerk of Sugar Loaf County and the man who served as clerk for the Nationalist trials.

76. *South McAlester Capital,* January 29, 1901, as reported in *Indian Citizen,* January 31, 1901. "Tom Fuller" is a casual term for the traditional Choctaw dish of *tamfula,* made from finely ground and sifted corn, water, and wood ash lye that is boiled for several hours. Other items can be added, like beans or hickory nuts.

77. *Indian Citizen,* January 31 and February 28, 1901.

78. *Indian Citizen,* January 31, 1901.

79. Ibid.

80. Ibid.

81. *Indian Citizen Supplement,* January 31, 1901.

82. *Indian Citizen,* February 16, 1901.

83. *South McAlester Capital,* January 16, 1902, and August 21, 1902.

84. *Indian Citizen,* January 2 and January 9, 1902. In my novel *Roads of My Relations,* I include a chapter, "Bad Luck," that describes the results of a windy shot in a Choctaw coal mine at Krebs. The explosion can be so powerful that the force of the blast has been known to toss wagons and to drive a timber through a mule.

85. *Indian Citizen,* February 6, 1902.

86. *Indian Citizen,* January 2, 1902.

87. *Indian Citizen,* December 13, 1900.

88. *Indian Citizen,* April 27, 1899, and April 18, 1901; *Hotema v. United States,* 186 U.S. 413 (1902); "Hotema Will Live," *Arlington Journal,* November 7, 1902; Burchardt, "Spooks," 38.

89. *Indian Citizen,* January 30, 1902.

90. See, for example, any issue of *Indian Citizen* between 1900 and 1903.

91. Current tribespeople suffer from obesity, high blood pressure, diabetes, and all the ailments that go along with those major problems; Choctaws in the 1880s did not have the same quantities and varieties of food available as they do today, but they did have nutritional deficiencies. They also suffered the consequences of not understanding proper sanitation, such as where to place their outhouses, and the benefits of dental care. See Mihesuah, *Recovering Our Ancestors' Gardens.*

92. Lane, "Choctaw Nation," 58.

93. Thornton. *American Indian Holocaust and Survival,* 42.

94. *Indian Citizen,* January 9, 1902; *Twin Territories,* November 1902.

95. Letter from Green McCurtain to Honorable J. George Wright, August 30, 1902, in Welton, "Life of Green McCurtain," 43–44.

96. *South McAlester Capital*, August 21, 1902.

97. *Twin Territories*, November, 1902.

98. Ibid.

99. *South McAlester Capital*, October 16, 1902.

100. Ibid.

101. *Indian Citizen*, October 2, 1902; "An Act to Ratify and Confirm an Agreement with the Choctaw and Chickasaw Tribes of Indians, and for Other Purposes." 239 U.S. 414, 417, 32 Stat. at L.641, chap. 1362, in Kappler, *IA:LT*, 1:771–87.

102. *ARCIA* (1905): p. 141.

103. *Indian Citizen*, July 30, 1903.

104. See the many letters to George Scott, national treasurer, from Choctaw citizens asking to be reimbursed after voting in the "Choctaw Gubernatorial Campaign, 1904" file in "Tribal Letters" box, at the Five Civilized Tribes Museum, Muskogee, Okla.

105. F. P. Semple to George W. Scott, August 4, 1904, in "Choctaw Gubernatorial Campaign, 1904," file in "Tribal Letters" box, at the Five Civilized Tribes Museum, Muskogee, Okla.

106. H. L. Sanguin to George W. Scott, August 7, 1904, in ibid.

107. William H. Harrison to Hon. G. W. Scott, August 8, 1904, in ibid.

108. The advertisement begins, "In a Rich Valley in the Choctaw Nation Which Has Heretofore Been Overlooked." *Indian Citizen*, February 13, 1902.

109. Ibid.

110. Letter to Honorable Tams Bixby, Chairman, Muskogee, Okla., June 19, 1903; and letter from Cobb to McCurtain, June 17, 1903, both in Green McCurtain Collection, box 16, folder 1, WHC.

111. Letter from Cobb to McCurtain, June 17, 1903, in ibid. The Choctaw text reads,

Gov. Green McCurtain, Kinta, Indian Ter.

Aholitopa ma,

Anumpa kanoma/o si fihna kia pil-ohi mahishke okla yakni aiimma illappa iht ayoshoba chinto ahoba hoke anumpa ik a kno/kmo kia anowa kat asha okla Land Office onat yakni shi ka isanali kay anha hoke. Tanapo ak osh tokafa chi achi mia kia osha hoke. Aiahki hok ma nana kano akithano akinli un oak akato pih kanima kia iltanaha kia enohowa hoke.

W. F. Tobley ak osh im ann impoli mia micha kanima moma kat holinio fehimmi ho yammako okla eyein mi hosh yohni mia hoke yohomi kako chimanolili hoke. Okla yakni isha he hik kin otaklami ai ahli vpn? Ahola kak orh? Chimanolili hoke anumpa hat illappak osh oi vhli hoke.

Chittibapishi, L.W. Cobb

112. Bixby to McCurtain, June 24, 1903, in ibid. He referred to section 2111 of the 1878 revised statutes, p. 369.

113. Letter from Frazier in ibid. All of the men listed are full-bloods and range in age from 18 to 48, with the possible exception of Simm Billy, who may be "Simon." See Index to the Five Civilized Tribes, the Final Dawes Roll, M1186, roll 1, Federal Archives, Fort Worth Branch. In the original letter, the names have commas between the first and last names, (i.e., Morris, Tom); but, the surnames actually are second.

One: Choahla Kounti ilappa holatey okohmi aiokali kak oah (sinti Party) mak oki I miko Bob nikka ilapak osh ianiko oki, holissochi; Alfred, Holman, ilopakosl I holisso chi oki. Morris Tom

    1. Simm Billey

    2. Sam Nihka

    3. Clayson Durant

    4. Jessia Tom

    5. Gillum Holman

    6. Noal Nehka

    7. Jones Watkins (ilopva to ilop hoh chiffon I kania)

    8. Louie Houston

    9. Jones William

    10. Silas Bacon micha Turner, Cole, aiena hoke Sinti Party, ibafohkat, Cholili sipokni falamichi bana okla hoh chiffon imissat tahli bana hoke. Inlaka at lawat ai ash apulla hoke. –ohnni kia ai akustini chili etokowe (micha ahli bano ho Reisspir) chim alishke. Chikana, R.S. Frazier, Sheriff of Cedar County, C.N.

Two:

Chauhla County yumma hatak yakahmi aiyokuli kakosh Sinti Party yv mia –miko yut Bob nihka ilapakosh siti-imike miya shik- mik mu iholissa chi yukosh Alfred Holmon

    1. Morris Tom

    2. Simm Billy

    3. Clayson Durant

    4. Nuel Nihka

    5. Jesse Tom

    6. Gillum Hohmon

    7. Jones Watkinds

    8. Levi Houston

    9. Jones William

Silas Bacon micha Turner Cole yakami ayakuli kakosk cholit- sipokni fulumi chi buma hosh hohchiffo holisso fokit maya hokis? Yut hana kukash alane chi.

114. McCurtain to Shoenfelt, October 22, 1903, in Green McCurtain Collection.

115. Commissioner to the Five Civilized Tribes Annual Report, *ARCIA* (1908), p. 210.

116. Interview with Adam Folsom and John W. Ward, September 22, 1937, *IPH*, 91:318–20.

117. *Indian Citizen*, April 25, 1901.

118. McCurtain to Hudson, September 30, 1903, in CTN 13, vol. 307. See also the same proposal (bill no. 23), "An Act Reestablishing the Militia Law," approved October 26, 1892, in CTN 13, vol. 308, p. 324.

119. Nonfiction studies of Christie include Speer, *The Killing of Ned Christie, Cherokee Outlaw*, and Steele, *The Last Cherokee Warriors*. The best-known fictional imagining about Christie is McMurtry and Ossana, *Zeke and Ned: A Novel*, and Robert J. Conley, *Ned Christie's War*.

120. See McIntosh, "Chitto Harjo, the Crazy Snakes and the Birth of Indian Political Activism in the Twentieth Century." The title of this dissertation is somewhat puzzling. While Chitto Harjo may have been one of the first indigenous peoples to be considered an activist in the twentieth century, many other Natives were also active prior to him.

121. Herring, "Crazy Snake and the Creek Struggle for Sovereignty"; Davis, "Chitto Harjo."

122. Interview with W. W. Bray, September, 13, 1937, *IPH*, 16:230–31.

123. Meserve, "The Plea of Crazy Snake (Chitto Harjo)."

124. *Indian Citizen*, February 14, 1901.

125. Interview with W. W. Bray, Weleetka, Okla., September 13, 1937, *IPH*, 16:230–31; Bolster, "Smoked Meat Rebellion."

126. Interview with Bray, *IPH*, 16:230–31.

127. McLoughlin, *Champions of the Cherokees*.

128. "Statement of Jacob B. Jackson," n.d., U.S. Congress, *Report of the Select Committee*, 960–62.

129. "Statement of Jacob B. Jackson," 957.

130. Ibid.

131. Ibid., 960.

132. Ibid.

133. Hochatown was a post office from 1858 to 1863 and is a combination of the Choctaw word *hvcha* (river) and the English word "town." It is now under the Broken Bow Reservoir. Shirk, *Oklahoma Place Names*, 117.

134. Morrison, "Biographical Sketch of Wn. N. Jones." Another report, however, states that the family believed Nat had been pushed over the edge of the roof and that his torn fingernails revealed that he had tried to hang on to the edge of the window. "Wilson N. Jones Will Ignored on Site of Burial," n.d., in Choctaw Vertical Files, Wilson Jones Folder, OHS.

135. "A. P. Shaw: His Residence with Chief John F. Brown and Life Among the Seminoles," March 24, 1937, *IPH*, 8:244–45, 244. See also the testimony of the prosecuting attorney, Samuel J. Haynes, February 18, 1938, *IPH*, 92:340–41. In another interview with Joseph Bruner (July 13, 1937, *IPH*, 17:148–49), Bruner claims that Jack sat on a stump, whereas the recollection of the chief of Tulwa

Thakke and former Creek lighthorseman, Sam J. Haynes (July 26, 1937, *IPH*, 28: 343), is that he was shot while standing.

136. Interview with Mora (Cap) Duncan, n.d., *IPH*, 23:66.

137. "An Act for the Protection of the People of the Indian Territory, and for Other Purposes," chap. 517, June 28, 1898, in Kappler, *IA: LT*, 1:99.

138. *Indian Citizen*, August 6, 1903.

139. *ARCIA* (1904): pp. 521–22; Report Select Committee, vol. 1, pp. 885–89; See the Indian Appropriation Act of 1907 in Kappler, *IA: LT*, 3, p. 278.

140. *Daily Oklahoman*, May 12, 1935.

141. Welton, "The Life of Green McCurtain," 1, 24, 50, 52.

142. Debo, *Rise and Fall of the Choctaw Republic*, 256.

143. Gideon, "Indian Territory" (New York, 1901), 718–20, in G. W. Dukes Collection, box D-29, folder 26, WHC.

144. Interview with John War Edwards and William Welch, April 28, 1938, *IPH*, 105:123.

145. Interview with Houston Tecumseh, March 1, 1938, *IPH*, 112:84.

146. See "Bush on Native American Issues: 'Tribal Sovereignty Means That. It's Sovereign,'" Democracy Now!, www.democracynow.org/2004/8/10/bush _on_native_american_issues_tribal.

Afterword

1. See the recently published books by Lambert, *Choctaw Nation*, and Kidwell, *Choctaw Nation in Oklahoma*. See also Debo, *And Still the Waters Run*, and Faiman-Silva, *Choctaws at the Crossroads*.

Note on Methodology

1. Extra Census Bulletin, *Five Civilized Tribes in Indian Territory*, 57.

2. "An Act Defining the Duties of the Clerks of the Circuit Courts of the Choctaw Nation," bill no. 61, approved November 6, 1883, in *CLAIT*, 17:47–51.

3. Numerous Cherokees interviewed about the Cherokee Female Seminary and those elderly women I interviewed in the 1980s became indignant at the questions about racism at the Seminary based skin color and cultural adherence. Although I had a plethora of written documentation authored by Cherokees from 1850s to 1910 that proved there was indeed a class system based on skin color, wealth, cultural adherence (Cherokee or white), and curriculum chosen by the Cherokee Tribal Council, the interviewees denied it even though some of the letters and newspaper articles were written by their [literal] ancestors. See Mihesuah, *Cultivating the Rosebuds*, and Devon Abbott, "Out of the Graves of the Polluted Debauches," 503–521.

BIBLIOGRAPHY

MANUSCRIPT COLLECTIONS

Five Civilized Tribes Museum, Muskogee, Okla. "Tribal Letters" box.
National Park Service, Fort Smith National Historic Site Archives, Fort Smith, Ark.
Case File, *United States v. Jack Crow.*
National Archives, Federal Records Center, Southwest Region, Fort Worth, Tex.
Index the Five Civilized Tribes. M1186, Roll 1, Final Dawes Roll
Enrollment Cards for the Five Civilized Tribes, 1898–1914, M1186, Choctaws
by Blood, Rolls 1–15
Records of District Courts of the United States, U.S. District Court for the Fort
Smith Division of the Western Division of Arkansas, Record Group 21
Oklahoma Historical Society. Archives and Manuscripts Division, Oklahoma
City, Okla.
Indian and Pioneer Histories, 1861–1936. Edited by Grant Foreman
Living Legends Collection
Vertical Files
Choctaw Indians:
Executions
Lighthorse
Politics and Government
Wilson Jones
Creek Indians:
Crime and Punishment
Lighthorse
Seminole Indians:
Execution Tree
Justice
Lighthorse

Chickasaw Nation (CKN) Records (microfilm):
CKN 11: Pickens County Records, 1864–1893
Choctaw National (CTN) Records (microfilm):
  CTN 2: Census Records and Lists, 1830–1896
    Atoka County
  CTN 3: Census of Choctaws by Blood and Intermarriage.
    Citizens, Kiamitia County, 1868–1896
  CTN 4: Census of Citizens by Blood and by Marriage, 1861(or 1867)–1929.
    Vol. 472: Sugar Loaf County 1868–1896
  CTN 7: Census and Citizenship, Choctaw Freedmen, 1885–1897
    Vol. 340: Freedmen Rolls, First District, 1885
    Vol. 341: Roll of Freedmen Who Elected to Leave the Nation, 1885–1886
    Vol. 343: Choctaw Freedman Census, First District, 1885
    Vol. 355: Roll of Freedmen Who Elected to Leave the Nation, 1885–1886,
      and First District Freedmen Whose Title to Citizenship Is Doubtful,
      Red River County, 1885
    Vol. 355a: Freedmen Who Elected to Leave the Nation, Second District, 1885
    Vol. 361: Freedman Rolls, Second District, 1885
    Vol. 373: Roll of Freedmen Whose Citizenship Is Doubtful, Third District,
      1885
    Vol. 374: Freedmen Who Elected to Leave the Nation, Third Judicial
      District, 1885
    Vol. 375: Freedman Rolls, Third District
    Vol. 382: Freedmen Admitted to Citizenship, Third Judicial District, 1897,
      including Kiamichi, Jackson, Blue, Atoka, and Jacks Forks Counties
    Vol. 432: Minutes of the Citizenship Committee, Choctaw Nation, Freedmen,
      1885
    Vol. 452: 1896 Census of Freedmen, Bok Tuklo County
    Vol. 461: 1896 Census of Freedmen, Jackson County
    Vol. 464: 1896 Census of Freedmen, Kiamichi County, and 1896 Census
      of Freedmen, Red River County
    Vol. 468: 1896 Census of Freedmen, Red River County (also known as
      vol. 77, Census of Choctaw Nation 1896 [Negro] Red River County)
    Vol. 477: 1896 Census of Freedmen, Towson County
    Vol. 479: 1896 Census of Freedmen, Wade County
    Vol. 482: 1896 Census of Freedmen, Skullyville, San Bois and Tobucksy
      Counties
  CTN 10: Records of the General Council, Senate and House of
    Representatives
    Vol. 312: Senate, 1872–1877
    Vol. 315: Journal for the Use of the Senate, 1877–1883

CTN 11: Records of the General Council, Senate and House of Representatives
   Vol. 316: Records, 1877–1883
CTN 12: Records of the General Council, Senate and House of
   Representatives
   Vol. 301: Senate, 1884–1888
   Vol. 305: House of Representatives, 1884–1899
CTN 13: Choctaw, Records of the General Council, Senate, and House of
   Representatives
   Vol. 307: General Council, 1889–1892
   Vol. 308: General Council, 1889–1893
CTN 14: Records of the General Council, Senate and House of
   Representatives
   Vol. 321: General Council, 1893–1901
CTN 18: Letters and Documents Concerning the General Council, Senate
   and House of Representatives, 1888–1893, Choctaw National Council,
   Documents 18367–18415
CTN 26: Blue County Records
CTN 27: Bok Tuklo County Records
CTN 28: Cedar County Records
CTN 30: Eagle County Records
CTN 31: Gaines County and Jacks Fork Records
CTN 32: Jacks Fork County Records
CTN 33: Jacks Fork County Records
CTN 34: Jackson and Kiamichi County Records
CTN 35: Kiamichi and Nashoba County Records
CTN 36: Kiamichi and Nashoba County Records
CTN 37: Red River County Records
CTN 38: Red River County Records
CTN 40: San Bois County Records
CTN 41: Skullyville County Records
CTN 42: Choctaw Sugar Loaf County Records
   Vol. 225: County and Probate Court Records, February 1, 1875–July 1, 1889
   Vol. 227: County and Probate Court Records, January 7, 1878–July 20, 1886
   Vol. 226: County and Probate Court Records, May 20, 1874–March 1, 1886
   Vol. 230: County and Probate Court Records, August 26, 1879–July 27, 1870
CTN 43: Tobucksy County Records:
   Vol. 243: County Probate and Court Records, October Term 1867–
      September 1896
   Vol. 244: County and Probate Court, and Coal Mining Records 1867– 1904
   Vol. 258: County and Probate Court Records, March 1894–August 3, 1904
CTN 44: Tobucksy County Records
   Vol. 250: County and Probate Court, and Coal Mining, Permit and Ranger
      Records, 1876–1907

CTN 45: Tobucksy County Records, County and Probate Court, and Permits and County Treasurer Records, 1891–1906
    Vol. 260: March 1894–August 3, 1904
    Vol. 258: Sept. 1, 1891–March 26, 1897
CTN 48: First (Mosholatubbee) District Records.
    Vol. 247: Circuit Court Records, October 10, 1872–May 21, 1895.
    Vol. 336: Circuit Court Records, May 1883–November 1892, May 13, 1886
    Vol. 338: Circuit Court Records, March 30, 1883–May 1892
    Vol. 369: Circuit Court Records, May 17, 1880–July 20, 1892
CTN 49: First (Moshulatubbee) District Records
    Vol. 339: Circuit Court Records, January 16, 1884–May 6, 1901
    Vol. 369: Circuit Court Records
CTN 50: First (Mosholatubbee) District Records.
    Vol. 344: Circuit Court Records, December 13, 1892–November 24, 1905
    Vol. 350: Circuit Court Records, September 12, 1892–November 24, 1905
CTN 52: Third (Pushmataha) District Records.
    Vol. 368: Choctaw Nation Circuit and Chancery Court Records, February 14, 1883–August 1892.
CTN 53: Records of the Supreme Court 1859–1905
    Vol. 395: October 1, 1883–October 2, 1905
    Vol. 396: October 1884–October, 1905
CTN 63: Choctaw Elections, Documents 16239–16624, August 7, 1861–October 1889
CTN 64: Choctaw Elections, Documents 16625–16955, August 6, 1890–August 1896
CTN 65: Choctaw, Elections, Documents 16956–17185, August 5, 1896–1901
CTN 66: Choctaw, Elections, Documents 17186–17459, 1901–1905
CTN 67, *Elections*, Documents 17460–17508, 1905–1906
CTN 75: Choctaw, Letters Sent and Letters Received and Other Documents. Schools: Jones Academy, 1892 October 12–1905 October 3 and undated
CTN 87: Choctaw, Sheriffs and Rangers, Documents 22522–23088, April 21, 1857–May 29, 1909
CTN 88, Treasurer, Documents 23977–24040, June 22, 1855–July 31, 1890
CTN 90: National Auditor Records
    Vol. 41: National Auditor Records, February 6, 1872–July 31, 1878
Western History Collections, University of Oklahoma, Norman
    G. W. Dukes Collection
    Jefferson Gardner Collection
    Solomon Hotema Collection
    Jacob Battiest Jackson Collection
    Wilson N. Jones Collection
    Green McCurtain Collection

Peter Perkins Pitchlynn Collection
Phillips Collection
Pittsburg County Historical Association, McAlester, Oklahoma
Dr. William Elliott Abbott Papers

GOVERNMENT DOCUMENTS

Constitutions and Laws of the American Indian Tribes. 53 vols. Wilmington, Del.: Scholarly Resources, 1975.

Vol. 8: *The Constitution and Laws of the Choctaw Nation.* Originally published at Park Hill, Cherokee Nation: John Candy, Printer, 1840.

Vol. 11: Folsom, Joseph. *Constitutions and Laws of the Choctaw Nation, Together with Treaties of 1855, 1865 and 1866.* Originally published in New York City: Wm. P. Lyon and Son, 1869.

Vol. 11: *Chickasaws and Choctaws: A Pamphlet of Information Concerning Their History, Treaties, Government, Country, Laws, Politics and Affairs.* Originally published in Ardmore, Indian Territory: Chieftan Print, 1891.

Vol. 13: *The Constitution and Laws of the Choctaw Nation.* Originally published Park Hill, Cherokee Nation: John Candy, Printer, 1840.

Vol. 14: *The Constitution and Laws of the Choctaw Nation.* Originally published at Park Hill, Cherokee Nation: Mission Press, Edwin Archer, Printer, 1847.

Vol. 15: *Constitution, Treaties and Laws of the Choctaw Nation.* Originally published in Sedalia, Mo.: Democrat Steam Print, 1887.

Vol. 16: *Acts and Resolutions of the General Council of the Choctaw Nation at the Called Sessions Thereof, Held in April and June 1858, and the Regular Session Held in October, 1858.* Originally published in Fort Smith, Ark.: Josephus Dotson, Printer for the Nation, 1859.

Vol. 17: *Laws of the Choctaw Nation, Passed at the Choctaw Council at the Regular Session of 1883.* Originally published at Sedalia, Mo: Democrat Steam Printing House and Book Bindery, 1883.

Vol. 18: *The Freedmen and Registration Bills, Passed at a Special Session of the Choctaw Council, Indian Territory, May, 1883.* Originally published by Denison T. Nas: Murray's Stean Printing House, 1883.

Vol. 18: *Laws of the Choctaw Nation, Passed at the Choctaw Council at the Regular Session of 1883.* Originally published at Sedalia, Mo.: Democrat Steam Printing House and Book Bindery, 1883.

Vol. 19: *Constitution, Treaties and Laws of the Choctaw Nation Made and Enacted by the Choctaw Legislature, 1887.* Originally published in Sedalia, Mo: Democrat Steam Print, 1887.

Vol. 20: *Laws of the Choctaw Nation Passed at the Regular Session of the General Council Convened at Tushka Humma, October 7, 1889, and adjourned November 15,*

1889. Originally published at Atoka, Indian Territory: Indian Citizen Publishing Co., 1890.

Vol. 21: *Laws of the Choctaw Nation Passed at the Regular Session of the General Council Convened at Tushka Humma, October 6, 1890, Adjourned November 14, 1890.*

Vol. 22: *Laws of the Choctaw Nation Passed at the Regular Session of the General Council Convened at Tushka Humma, October 3rd, 1892 and Adjourned November 4, 1892.* Originally published at Atoka, Indian Territory: Indian Citizen Publishing Co., 1893.

Vol. 22: *Laws of the Choctaw Nation Passed at the Regular Session of the General Council Convened at Tushka Humma, October 2, 1893 and Adjourned October 27, 1893, and the Special Sessions Convened in February 1892 and Convened in June 1893.* Originally published at Atoka, Indian Territory: Indian Citizen Publishing Co., 1894.

Delegates of the Antlers' Convention Before the Dawes' Commission. Fort Smith, Arkansas: Choctaw Herald Print, December 9, 1896.

Extra Census Bulletin, *The Five Civilized Tribes in Indian Territory: The Cherokee, Chickasaw, Choctaw, Creek and Seminole Nations.* Washington, D.C.: Department of the Interior, U.S. Census Office, 1894.

Kappler, Charles J. *Indian Affairs: Laws and Treaties.* Vols. 1–3. Washington, D.C.: Government Printing Office, 1902.

Lane, John W. "Choctaw Nation," in *The Five Civilized Tribes in Indian Territory: The Cherokee, Chickasaw, Choctaw, Creek and Seminole Nations.* 56–61. Washington, D.C.: Department of the Interior, U.S. Census Printing Office, 1894.

Meserve, Charles F. *The Dawes Commission and the Five Civilized tribes of Indian Territory.* Philadelphia: Office of Indian Rights Association, 1896.

Prucha, Francis Paul, ed. *Documents of United States Indian Policy.* Lincoln: University of Nebraska Press, 1975.

Swanton, John R. *Source Material for the Social and Ceremonial Life of the Choctaw Indians.* Bulletin 103, Bureau of American Ethnology, Smithsonian Institution. Washington: Government Printing Office, 1931.

United States Congress. House Executive Documents:
Annual Report of the Commissioner of Indian Affairs, for the years 1865, 1884, 1885–86, 1886, 1888, 1889–90, 1890–91, 1892, 1893, 1894–95, 1895, 1896, 1905, and 1908.

United States Congress. Senate Executive Documents:
Annual Report of the Commissioner of Indian Affairs: 1860.
Report of the Select Committee to Investigate Matters Connected with Affairs in the Indian Territory with Hearings November 11, 1906–January 9, 1907. Vol. 1 Report Number 5013, 59 Cong., 2 Sess. Senate. Washington D.C.: Government Printing Office, 1907.

Report of the Committee on Indian Affairs: 1886
Registers and Letters Received by the Commissioner of the Bureau of Refugees, Freedmen and Abandoned Lands, 1865–1872, Record Group 105, Records of the Bureau of Refugees, Freedmen and Abandoned Lands, Roll 21, M752,

Report of the Committee on Indian Affairs, United States Senate, on the Condition of the Indians in the Indian Territory, and Other Reservations, etc. In Two Parts, Part 2. Washington, D.C.: U.S. Government Printing Office, 1886.

TREATIES AND ACTS

Treaty of Dancing Rabbit Creek, September 27, 1830, U.S.-Choctaw, 7 Stat. 333
Indian Appropriation Bill, May 17, 1882 (22 Stat. 68, 72)
Indian Appropriation Act of March 3, 1885 (23 Stat. 362, 366)

COURT CASES

Alberty v. United States (April 20, 1896), 162 U.S. 499, 16 Sup. Ct. 864
Ex Parte Mayfield (May 25, 1891), 141 U.S. 106, 112, 11 S. Sup. Ct. 939
Hotema v. United States, 186 U.S. 413 (1902)
Lucas v. United States, 163 U.S. 612 (1896)
United States v. Rogers, 45 U.S. (4 How.) 567, 572 (1846)
1908 OK CR 37, 98 P. 467, 1 Okl.Cr. 452, Case Number: No. 750, Ind. T.; 1908, OK CR 22, 96 P. 597,1 Okl.Cr. 205, Case Number: No. 792, Ind. T.; both Oklahoma Court of Criminal Appeals.

NEWSPAPERS

Afton News
Arlington Journal
BISHINIK
Cherokee Advocate
Daily Oklahoman
Davis Advertiser
Eagle-Gazette
Enid Eagle
Fort Smith Elevator
Hugo Husonian
Indian Champion
Indian Citizen
Indian Territory
McAlester News-Capital
McAlester News-Capital and Democrat
Minco Minstrel
New York Times

Soper Democrat
South McAlester Capital
Talihina News
Twin Territories
Washington Post

Books, Articles, Dissertations, Theses, and Reports

Abbott, Devon I. "'Gentleman' Tom Abbott: Middleweight Champion of the Southwest." *Chronicles of Oklahoma* 68 (Spring 1990): 426–37.

———. "Out of the Graves of the Polluted Debauches: The Boys of the Cherokee Male Seminary." *American Indian Quarterly* 15 (Fall 1991): 503–21.

Adair, James, *The History of the American Indians: Particularly Those Adjoining to the Mississippi, East and West Florida, Georgia, South and North Carolina and Virginia.* New York: Promontory Press, 1973.

Akers, Donna. *Living in the Land of Death: The Choctaw Nation, 1830–1860.* East Lansing: Michigan State University Press, 2004.

Anderson, Jane, and Nina C. Zachary. *A Choctaw Anthology.* Vols. 1–3. Philadelphia, Miss.: Choctaw Heritage Press, 1983–85.

Ashabranner, Brent K., and Russell G. Davis. *The Choctaw Code.* 1961. Reprint, Hamden, Mass.: Linnet Books, 1994.

Askew, Rilla. *Strange Business.* New York: Penguin Books, 1992.

Baird, David W. *Peter Pitchlynn: Chief of the Choctaws.* Norman: University of Oklahoma Press, 1972.

———. "Spencer Academy, Choctaw Nation: 1842–1900." *Chronicles of Oklahoma* 45 (1967): 25–43.

Bearss, Edwin C. "Fort Smith as the Agency for the Western Choctaws." *Arkansas Historical Quarterly* 27 (1968): 40–58.

Benson, Henry C. "Life Among the Choctaws Indians." *Chronicles of Oklahoma* 9 (June 1926): 156–61.

———. *Life Among the Choctaw Indians and Sketches of the Southwest.* New York: Johnson Reprint Corp., 1970.

Berger, Bethany R. "'Power Over This Unfortunate Race': Race, Politics and Indian Law in *United States v. Rogers.*" *William and Mary Law Review* 45, no. 5 (April 2004): 1957–2053.

Bolster, Mel H. "The Smoked Meat Rebellion." *Chronicles of Oklahoma* 31 (September 1953): 37–55.

Bonnifield, Paul. "The Choctaw on the Eve of the Civil War," *Journal of the West* 12 (July 1973): 386–402.

Broadhead, Michael. *Isaac C. Parker: Federal Justice on the Frontier.* Norman: University of Oklahoma Press, 2003.

Bruce, Michael L. "Our Best Men are Leaving Us: The Life and Times of Robert M. Jones." *Chronicles of Oklahoma* 66 (1988): 294–305.

Burchardt, Bill, "Spooks." *Oklahoma Today* 15, no. 4 (Autumn 1965): 37–38.

"Bush on Native American Issues: 'Tribal Sovereignty Means That. It's Sovereign,'" Democracy Now! www.democracynow.org/2004/8/10/bush_on _native_american_issues_tribal, August 10, 2004.

Carson, James Taylor. *Searching for the Bright Path: The Mississippi Choctaws From Prehistory to Removal*. Lincoln: University of Nebraska Press, 1999.

Catlin, George. *Letters and Notes on the Manners, Customs and Condition of the North American Indians*. 2 vols. New York: Dover Press, 1973.

Champagne, Duane, *Social Order and Political Change: Constitutional Governments Among the Cherokee, the Choctaw, the Chickasaw, and the Creek*. Stanford, Calif.: Stanford University Press, 1992.

Chaudoin, Flossie, *Red Oak Annals*. Red Oak, Okla.: Flossie Chaudoin, 1988.

Christian, Emma Ervin. "Memories of My Childhood Days in the Choctaw Nation." *Chronicles of Oklahoma* 9 (June 1931): 155–65; 11 (December 1933): 1034–39.

Claiborne, John Francis Hamtramck. *Mississippi as a Province, Territory and State, with Biographical Notices of Eminent Citizens*. Jackson, Miss.: Power and Barksdale, 1880.

Conley, Robert J. *Ned Christie's War*. New York: St. Martin's, 2002.

Conlan, Czarina C. "David Folsum." *Chronicles of Oklahoma* 4 (December 1926): 340–55.

———. "Peter P. Pitchlynn: Chief of the Choctaws, 1864–66." *Chronicles of Oklahoma* 6 (June 1928): 215–24.

Cushman, H. B. *History of the Choctaw, Chickasaw and Natchez Indians*. Norman: University of Oklahoma Press, 1999.

Davis, Mace. "Chitto Harjo." *Chronicles of Oklahoma* 13 (June 1935): 139–45.

Dawes, Anna. *A United States Prison*. Philadelphia: Indian Rights Association, 1886.

Debo, Angie. *And Still the Waters Run: The Betrayal of the Five Civilized Tribes*. Norman: University of Oklahoma Press, 1989.

———. "Education in the Choctaw Country after the Civil War," *Chronicles of Oklahoma* 10 (September 1932): 383–91.

———. *The Rise and Fall of the Choctaw Republic*. Norman: University of Oklahoma Press, 1986.

DeRosier, Arthur, Jr. *The Removal of the Choctaw Indians*. Knoxville: University of Tennessee Press, 1970.

Dewitz, Paul W. *Notable Men of Indian Territory at the Beginning of the 20th Century, 1904–1905*. Muskogee, Indian Territory: Southwest Historical Company, 1905.

——— ed., *A Pathfinder in the Southwest*. Norman: University of Oklahoma Press, 1941.

Dunkle, W. F. "A Choctaw Indian's Diary." *Chronicles of Oklahoma* 4 (March 1926): 61–69.

Edwards, John. "The Choctaw Indians in the Middle of the Nineteenth Century." *Chronicles of Oklahoma* 10 (September 1932): 392–425.

Eggan, Fred, "The Choctaw and Their Neighbors in the Southeast: Acculturation Under Pressure," in *The American Indian: Perspectives for Study for Social Change*. Chicago: Aldine Publishing Company, 1966.

———. "Historical Changes In the Choctaw Kinship System." *American Anthropologist* 39, no. 1 (January–March 1937): 1–52.

Faiman-Silva, Sandra L. *Choctaws at the Crossroads: The Political Economy of Class and Culture in the Oklahoma Timber Region*. Lincoln: University of Nebraska Press, 2000.

———. "Decolonizing the Choctaw Nation: Choctaw Political Economy in the Twentieth Century." *American Indian Culture and Research Journal* 17 (1993): 43–74.

———. "Tribal Land to Private Land: A Century of Oklahoma Choctaw Timberland Alienation From the 1880s to the 1980s." *Journal of Forest History* 32 (1988): 191–204.

Felter, Harvey Wickes. *The Eclectic Materia Medica, Pharmacology and Therapeutics*. 1922. Reprint, Bisbee, Ariz.: Southwest School of Botanical Medicine, 2001.

Fessler, W. Julian. "The Work of the Early Choctaw Legislature From 1869 to 1873." *Chronicles of Oklahoma* 6 (March 1928): 60–68.

Foreman, Carolyn Thomas. "The Choctaw Academy." *Chronicles of Oklahoma* 9 (1932): 382–411.

———. "The Choctaw Academy." *Chronicles of Oklahoma* 10 (March 1932): 77–114.

———. "The Choctaw Academy." *Chronicles of Oklahoma* 6 (December 1928): 455.

———. "The Lighthorse in Indian Territory," *Chronicles of Oklahoma* 34 (Spring 1956): 17–43.

———. "Notes of Interest Concerning Peter P. Pitchlynn." *Chronicles of Oklahoma* 7 (June 1929): 172–74.

Foreman, Grant. *Advancing the Frontier, 1830–1860*. Norman: University of Oklahoma Press, 1933.

Frey, James N. *The Key: How to Write Damn Good Fiction Using the Power of Myth*. New York: St. Martin's Press, 2000.

Graebner, Laura Baum. "Agriculture Among the Five Civilized Tribes: 1840–1906." *Red River Valley Historical Review* 3 (1978): 45–60.

Hammond, Sue. "Socioeconomic Reconstruction in the Cherokee Nation: 1865–1870." *Chronicles of Oklahoma* (Summer 1978): 158–70.

Harmon, S. W. *Hell on the Border: He Hanged Eighty Eight Men*. Lincoln: University of Nebraska Press, 1992.

Henry, Delaura. "Traditions in the Choctaw Homeland." *Historic Preservation* 26 (January–March 1974): 28–31.

Herring, Sidney L. "Crazy Snake and the Creek Struggle for Sovereignty: The Native American Legal Culture and American Law." *American Journal of Legal History*. 34, no. 4 (October 1990): 365–80.

Holden, J. F. "The Story of an Adventure in Railroad Building." *Chronicles of Oklahoma* 11 (March 1933): 637–66.

Hudson, Peter James. "Recollections of Peter Hudson." *Chronicles of Oklahoma* 10 (December 1932): 501–19.

———. "Reminiscences by Peter J. Hudson." *Chronicles of Oklahoma* 12 (September 1934): 294–304.

———. "A Story of Choctaw Chiefs." *Chronicles of Oklahoma* 17 (June 1939): 192–211.

Huggard, Christopher J. "Culture Mixing Among Choctaws." *Chronicles of Oklahoma* 70 (Winter 1992–93): 432–49.

Johnson, Walter A. "Brief History of the Missouri-Kansas-Texas Railroad Lines." *Chronicles of Oklahoma* 24 (Autumn 1946): 340–58.

Karr, Stephen. "Now We Have Forgotten the Old Indian Law: Choctaw Culture and the Evolution of Corporal Punishment." *American Indian Law Review* 23 (1999): 409–23.

Kensell, Lewis Anthony. "Phases of Reconstruction in the Choctaw Nation, 1865–1870." *Chronicles of Oklahoma* 47 (1969): 138–53.

Kidwell, Clara Sue, *Choctaws and Missionaries in Mississippi, 1818–1918*. Norman: University of Oklahoma Press, 1997.

———. *The Choctaw Nation in Oklahoma: From Tribe to Nation, 1855–1970*. Norman: University of Oklahoma Press, 2007.

Knight, Oliver. "Fifty Years of Choctaw Law." *Chronicles of Oklahoma* 31 (Spring 1953): 76–97.

Lambert, Valerie. *Choctaw Nation: A Story of American Indian Resurgence*. Lincoln: University of Nebraska Press, 2007.

Lane, John W. "Choctaw Nation," in *The Five Civilized Tribes in Indian Territory: The Cherokee, Chickasaw, Choctaw, Creek, and Seminole Nations*. Washington, D.C.: Census Printing Office, 1894.

Lewis, Anna, *Chief Pushmataha, American Patriot: The Story of the Choctaws' Struggle for Survival*. New York: Exposition Press, 1959.

Linton, Ralph. *Acculturation in Seven American Indian Tribes*. New York: D. Appleton-Century, 1940.

Lurie, Nancy O. "Indian Cultural Adjustment to European Civilization," in *Seventeenth-Century America: Essays in Colonial History*. 33–60. Edited by James Morton Smith. 1959. Reprint, Westport, Conn. : Greenwood Press, 1980.

Lycecum, Gideon. "Life of Apushmataha." *Mississippi Historical Society Publications* 9 (1906): 415–85.

Martin, Amelia. "Unsung Heroes: Deputy Marshals of the Federal Court for the Western District of Arkansas, 1875–1896." *Journal of the Forth Smith Historical Society* 3, no.1 (April 1979): 19–26.

McIntosh, Kenneth Waldo. "Chitto Harjo, the Crazy Snakes and the Birth of Indian Political Activism in the Twentieth Century," Ph.D. dissertation, Texas Christian University, 1993.

McKee, Jesse O., and Jon A. Schlenker. *The Choctaws: Cultural Evolution of a Native American Tribe*. Jackson: University Press of Mississippi, 1980.

McLoughlin, William. *Champions of the Cherokees: Evan and John B. Jones*. New Jersey: Princeton University Press, 1990.

McMurtry, Larry, and Diana Ossana, *Zeke and Ned: A Novel*. New York: Simon and Schuster, 1997.

Mihesuah, Devon. "Choosing America's Heroes and Villains: Lessons Learned From the Execution of Silon Lewis." *American Indian Quarterly* 29 (2005): 239–62.

———. *Cultivating the Rosebuds: The Education of Women at the Cherokee Female Seminary, 1851–1909*. Urbana: University of Illinois Press, 1993.

———. *Recovering Our Ancestors' Gardens: Indigenous Recipes and Guide to Diet and Fitness*. Lincoln: University of Nebraska Press, 2005.

———. *Roads of My Relations*. Tuscon: University of Arizona Press, 2000.

Meserve, John Bartlett. "Chief Benjamin Franklin Smallwood and Chief Jefferson Gardner." *Chronicles of Oklahoma* 19 (September 1941): 213–20.

———. "Chief Gilbert Wesley Dukes." *Chronicles of Oklahoma* 18 (March 1940): 53–59.

———. "Chief Wilson Nathaniel Jones." *Chronicles of Oklahoma* 14 (December 1936): 419–33.

———. "The McCurtains." *Chronicles of Oklahoma* 13 (September 1935): 297–312.

———. "The Plea of Crazy Snake (Chitto Harjo)." *Chronicles of Oklahoma* 11 (September 1933): 899–911.

Miner, Craig H. *The Corporation and the Indian: Tribal Sovereignty and Indian Civilization in Indian Territory, 1867–1907*. Columbia: University of Missouri Press, 1976.

Morrison, James D. "Problems in the Industrial Progress and Development of the Choctaw Nation, 1865–1907." *Chronicles of Oklahoma* 32 (1954): 71–91.

———. *Seven Constitutions (Anumpa Vlhpia Untuklo): Government of the Choctaw Republic, 1826–1906*. Durant: Southeastern Oklahoma State University, 1978.

———. *The Social History of the Choctaw Nation: 1865–1907*. Durant, Okla.: Creative Infomatics, 1987.

Morrison, W. B. "News for the Choctaws." *Chronicles of Oklahoma* 27 (Spring 1949): 207–22.

———. "Note on the Abolitionism in the Choctaw Nation." *Chronicles of Oklahoma* 38 (1960): 78–83.

———. "The Saga of Skullyville." *Chronicles of Oklahoma* 16 (June 1938): 234–40.

Nebitt, Paul. "J.J. McAlester." *Chronicles of Oklahoma* 11 (June 1933): 758–64.

"Necrology of Victor M. Locke, Sr. (1844–1929)." *Chronicles of Oklahoma* 11 (December 1933): 1126–29.

O'Beirne, H. F., and E. S. O'Beirne. *The Indian Territory, Its Chiefs, Legislators and Leading Men*. St. Louis: C. B. Woodward Company, 1892.

O'Brien, Greg. *Choctaws in a Revolutionary Age, 1750–1830*. Lincoln: University of Nebraska Press, 2005.

————, ed. *Pre-Removal Choctaw History: Exploring New Paths*. Norman: University of Oklahoma Press, 2008.

Oklahoma Almanac. Oklahoma City: Oklahoma Department of Libraries, 2005–2006.

Owens, Ron. *Oklahoma Heroes: The Oklahoma Peace Officers Memorial*. Nashville, Tenn.: Turner Publishing, 2000.

Pesantubbee, Michelene E. *Choctaw Women in a Chaotic World: The Clash of Cultures in the Colonial Southeast*. Albuquerque: University of New Mexico Press, 2005.

Peck, Henry. *The Proud Heritage of LeFlore County*. Van Buren, Ark.: The Press Argus, 1963.

Pittsburg County, Oklahoma: People and Places. McAlester, Okla.: Pittsburg County Genealogical and Historical Society, n.d.

Prucha, Francis Paul. "Crimes in the Indian Country," in *American Indian Policy in the Formative Years: The Indian Trade and Intercourse Acts, 1790–1834*. Lincoln: University of Nebraska Press, 1962.

Reeves, Carolyn Keller. *The Choctaw Before Removal*. Jackson: University Press of Mississippi, 1985.

Reid, John Philip. *A Law of Blood*. New York: New York University Press, 1970.

Riggs, W. C. "Bits of Interesting History." *Chronicles of Oklahoma* 7 (June 1929): 149.

Romans, Bernard. *A Concise Natural History of East and West Florida*. New York, 1775.

Samuels, Wesley, and Charleen Samuels. *Life and Times of Choctaw Original Enrollees*. Published by Wesley and Charleen Samuels, 1997.

Sanders, J. G. *Who's Who Among Oklahoma Indians*. Oklahoma City: Trave Publishing Co., 1928.

Saunt, Claudio. *Black, White and Indian: Race and the Unmaking of an American Family*. New York: Oxford University Press, 2005.

Sewell, Steven L. "Choctaw Beer: Tonic or Devil's Brew?" *Journal of Cultural Geography* 23 (Spring/Summer 2006): 105–16.

Shirk, George H. *Oklahoma Place Names*. Norman: University of Oklahoma Press, 1974.

Shirley, Glenn. *Laws West of Fort Smith: A History of Frontier Justice in the Indian Territory, 1834–1896*. 1957. Reprint, Lincoln: University of Nebraska Press, 1968.

————. *Toughest of Them All*. Albuquerque: University of New Mexico Press, 1953.

Smith, Allene DeShazo. *Greewood LeFlore and the Choctaw Indians of the Mississippi Valley*. Memphis, Tenn.: A Davis Printing Co., 1951.

Smith, Thomas R. *A Choctaw's Honor*. Ventura, Calif.: Aazunna Publishing, 1981.

Snowden, John Rockwell, Wayne Tyndall, and David Smith. "American Indian Sovereignty and Naturalization: It's a Race Thing." *Nebraska Law Review* 80 (2001): 171–238.

Speer, Bonnie Stahlman. *The Killing of Ned Christie, Cherokee Outlaw*. Norman, Okla.: Reliance Press, 1990.

Spoehr, Alexander. "Changing Kinship Systems: A Study in the Acculturation of the Creeks, Cherokees and Choctaws." *Field Museum of Natural History, Anthropological Series* 33 (January 1947): 153–235.

Steele, Philip. *The Last Cherokee Warriors*. Gretna, La.: Pelican Publishing Co, 1974.

Swanton, John R. *Choctaw Social and Ceremonial Life*. Oklahoma City: Oklahoma Choctaw Council, Inc., 1983.

————. *An Early Account of the Choctaw Indians*. U.S. Bureau of American Ethnology Bulletin 88. New York: AMS, 1976.

Tate, Juanita J. Keel. *Edmund Pickens (Okchuntubby): First Elected Chickasaw Chief, His Life and Times*. Ada, Okla.: Chickasaw Press, 2009.

Thornton, Russell. *American Indian Holocaust and Survival: A Population History Since 1492*. Norman: University of Oklahoma Press, 1987.

Wardell, Morris. *A Political History of the Cherokee Nation: 1838–1907*. Norman: University of Oklahoma Press, 1938.

Washburn, Wilcomb E. *The Assault on Indian Tribalism: The General Allotment Law (Dawes Act) of 1887*. Philadelphia: Lippencott, 1975.

Welton, William Roy. "The Life of Green McCurtain." Masters thesis, Department of History, Oklahoma Agricultural and Mechanical College, 1935.

White, Richard. *The Roots of Dependency: Subsistence, Environment and Social Change Among the Choctaws, Pawnees and Navajos*. Lincoln: University of Nebraska Press, 1988.

Williams, Robert L., "Dr. Daniel Morris Hailey: 1841–1919." *Chronicles of Oklahoma* 18 (September 1940): 217.

Wooldridge, Clyde. *McAlester: The Capital of Little Dixie: A History of McAlester, Krebs and South McAlester*. Rich Hill, Mo.: Bell Books, 2001.

Workers of the Writers' Program of the Work Projects Administration. *Oklahoma: Guide to the Sooner State*. Norman: University of Oklahoma Press, 1941.

Wright, Muriel. "Historic Places on the Old Stage Line from Fort Smith to Red River." *Chronicles of Oklahoma* 11 (June 1933): 798–822.

————. "Notes and Documents: Sugar Loaf Mountain Resort." *Chronicles of Oklahoma* 36 (1960): 202–224.

————. "Organization of Counties in the Choctaw and Chickasaw Nations." *Chronicles of Oklahoma* 8 (September 1930): 315–334.

Young, Rowland L. "Live as you Please, But Die Brave." *American Bar Association Journal* 58 (April 1972): 376–77.

WEB SITES

Arkansas Executions
    users.bestweb.net/~rg/execution/ARKANSAS.htm.
Deputy Barnhill
    http://www.okolha.net/mohler_mynatt_king_names.htm

The Espy File Executions by Name
   www.deathpenaltyinfo.org/ESPYname.pdf
Fort Smith National Historic Site, "U.S. Deputy Marshal in the Federal District
   Court for the Western District of Arkansas and Indian Territory at Fort Smith,
   Arkansas." circa 1872–1896
   www.nps.gov/fosm/forteachers/upload/legacy%20part%204.pdf
Judge Isaac Charles Parker
   freepages.genealogy.rootsweb.com/~rkinfolks/deputies.html
Marriages in the Chickasaw Nation-Bride List B–F
   www.chickasawhistory.com/b_mar_2.htm
National Register of Historic Places, Latimer, Oklahoma
   www.nationalregisterofhistoricplaces.com/OK/Latimer/state.html.
Oklahoma Law Enforcement Memorial, U.S. Marshals: Charles B. Wilson
   www.oklemem.com/W.htm
Oklahoma Outlaws Lawmen History Association (OKOLHA)
   www.okolha.net
Oklahoma United States Marshals, Deputy United States Marshals, and Possemen
   www.okolha.net/oklahoma_united_states_marshals_WI-WY.htm
Peter Conser Home
   www.shareyourstate.com/oklahoma/ConserHouse.htm
Pickens Genealogy Information Group
   freepages.family.rootsweb.com/~pickensarchive/bg/okhist.html
Vaughn Cemetery
   www.rootsweb.com/~oklefcem/vaughn5.html
Violent Deaths of U.S. Marshals
   www.silverstarcollectables.com/killed.htm

INDEX